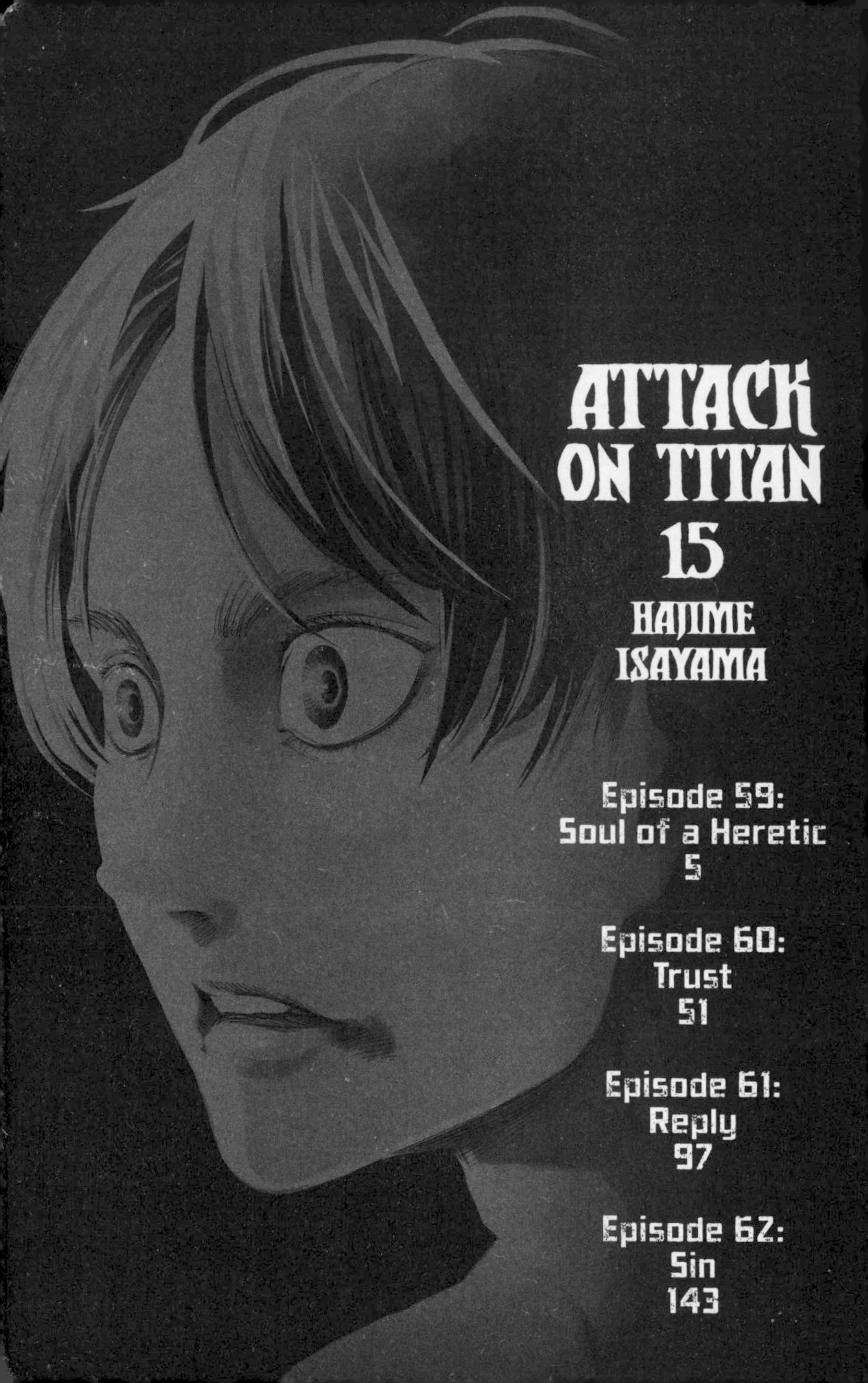

# ATTACK ON TITAN 15

HAJIME ISAYAMA

# "Attack on Titan" Character Introductions

## 104th Corps

uated at op of her ing corps, sa is a y talented er. Her nts were dered re her when she a child. ren saved fe. Since , she has e it her ion to ect him.

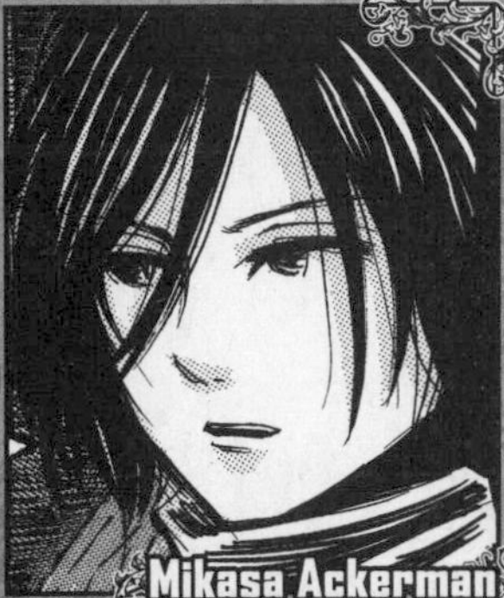

Mikasa Ackerman

Eren joined the Survey Corps out of his longing for the outside world and his hatred of the Titans. He has the power to turn himself into a Titan, but its origins are unknown.

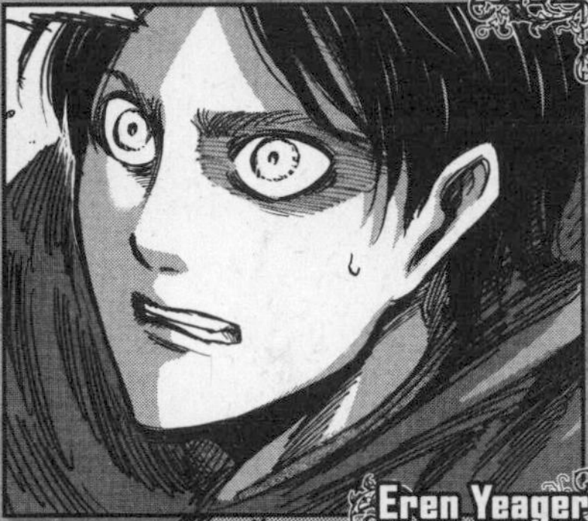

Eren Yeager

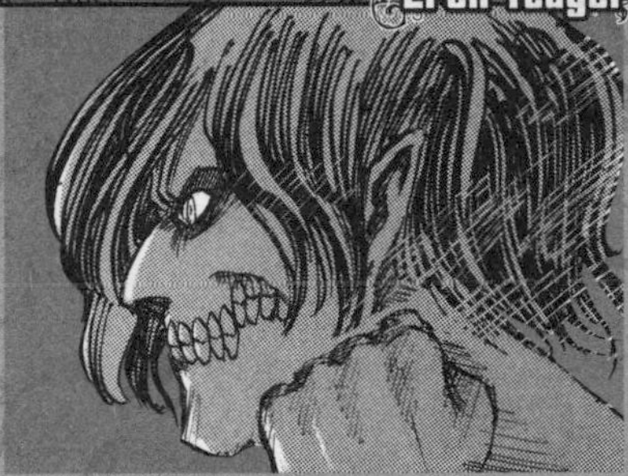

and Mikasa's hood friend. ugh Armin isn't etic in the least, ossesses both p observational ers and keen ht, and he its an raordinary ability evelop ategies.

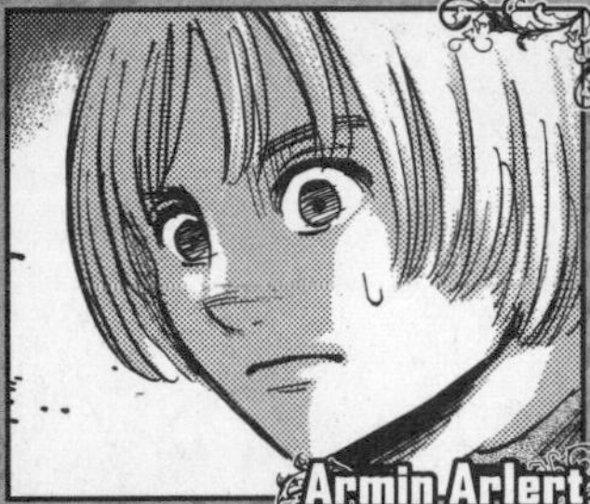

Armin Arlert

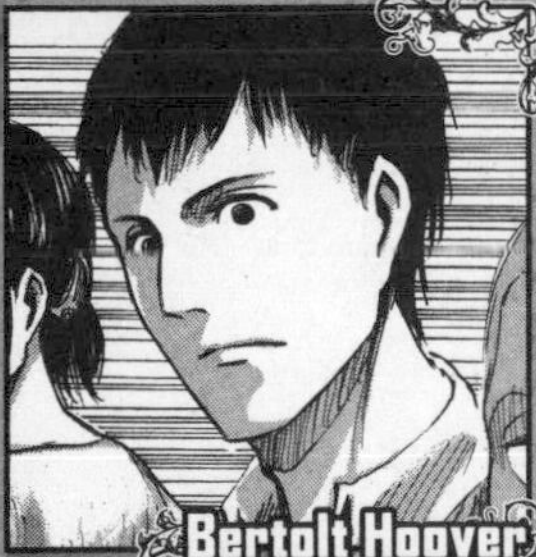

Bertolt Hoover

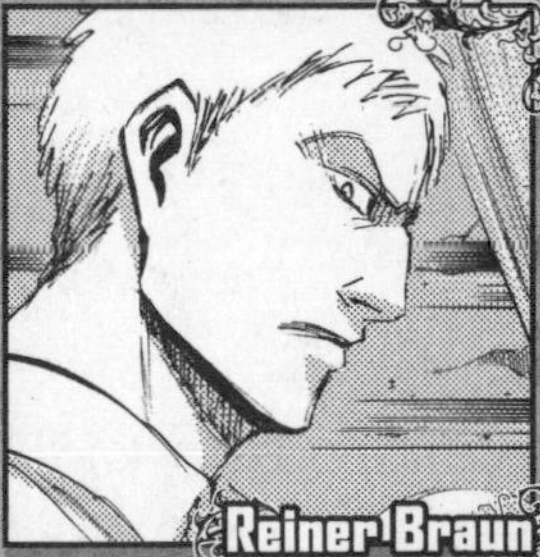

Reiner Braun

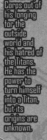

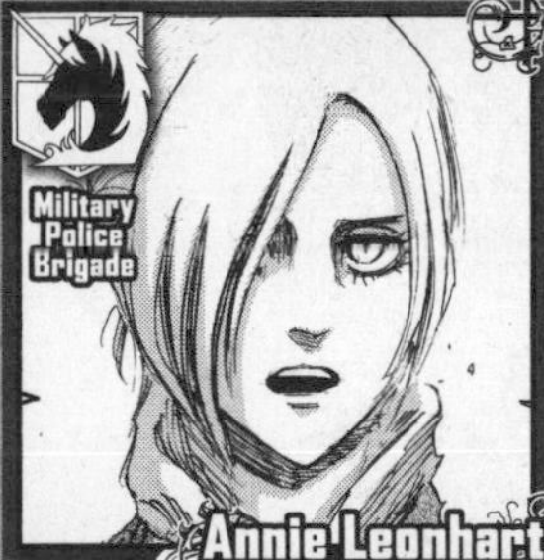
Military Police Brigade

Annie Leonhart

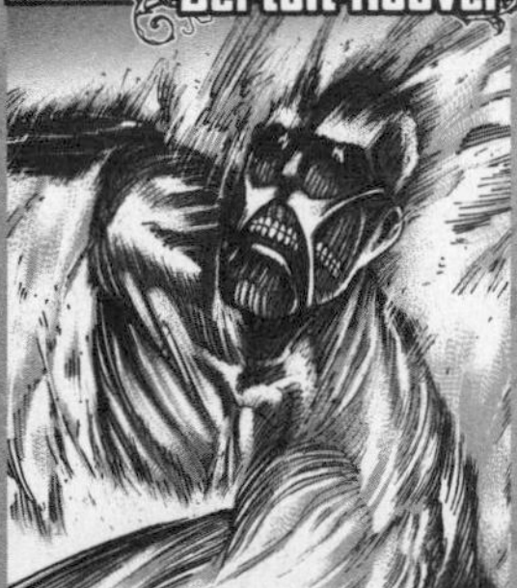

The Colossus Titan

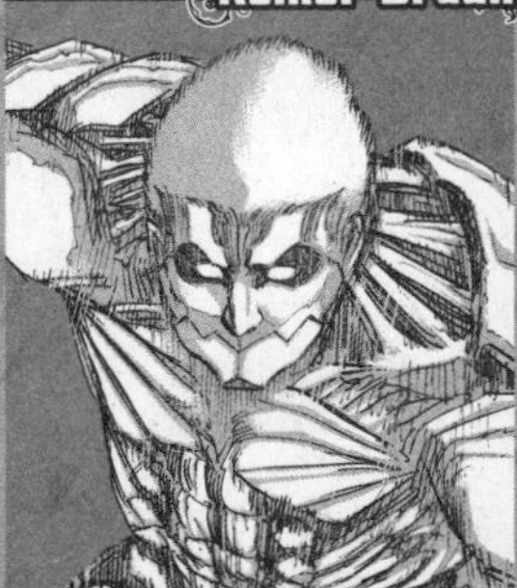

The Armored Titan

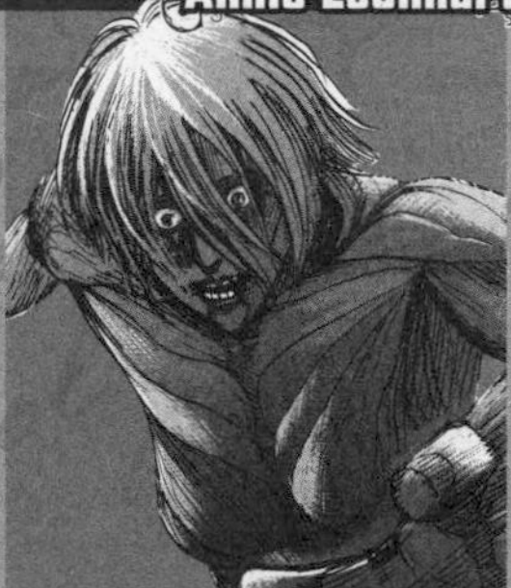

The Female Titan

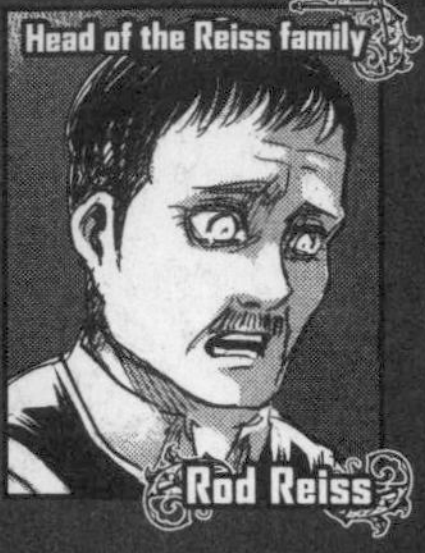
Head of the Reiss family
Rod Reiss

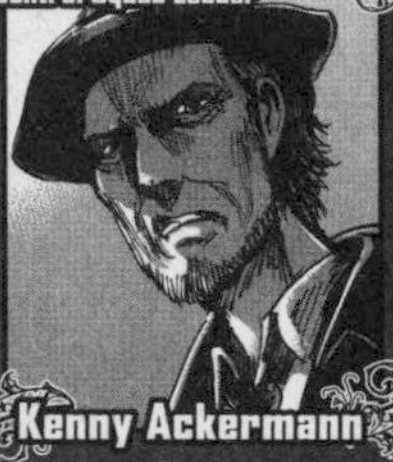
Military Police Anti-Personnel Control Squad Leader
Kenny Ackermann

# Survey Corps

Soldiers who are prepared to sacrifice themselves as they brave the Titan territory outside the walls.

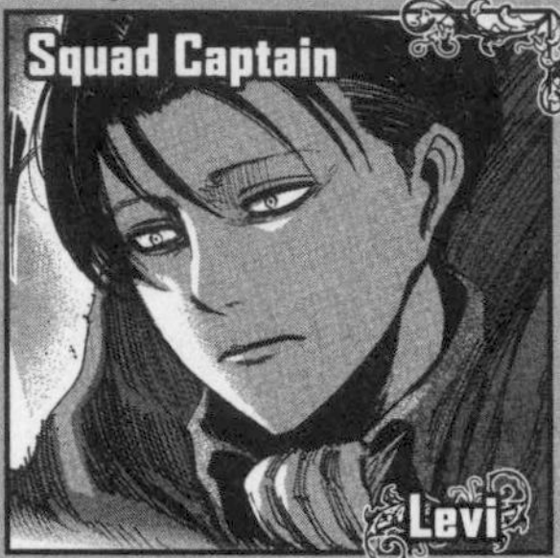
Squad Captain
Levi

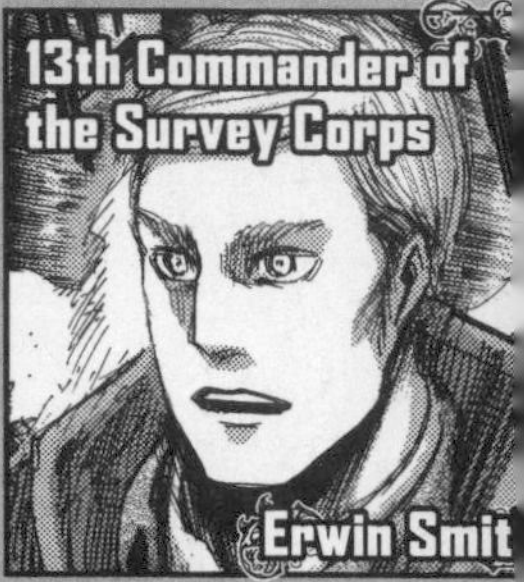
13th Commander of the Survey Corps
Erwin Smit

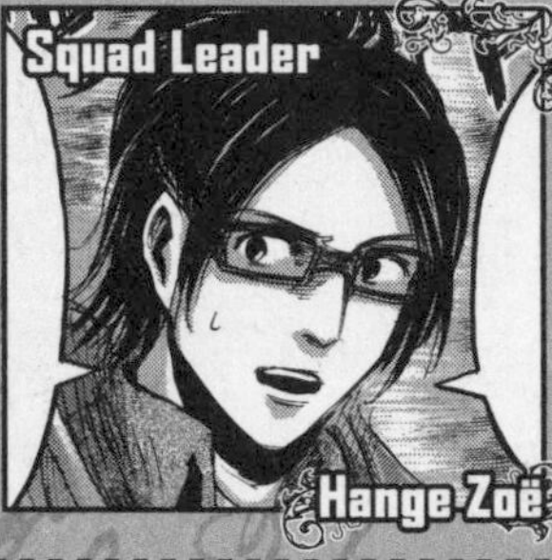
Squad Leader
Hange Zoë

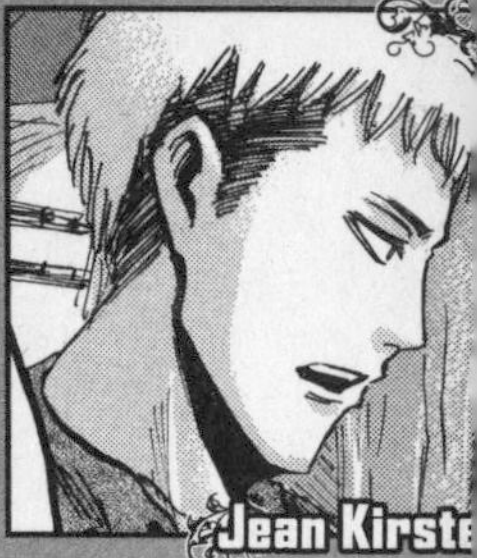
Jean Kirste

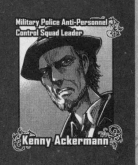

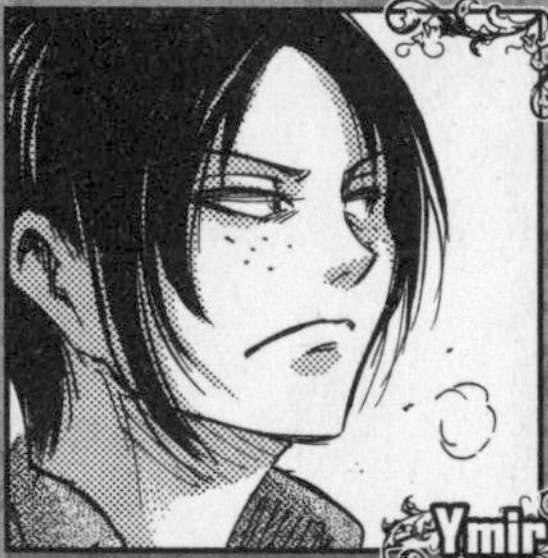
Ymir

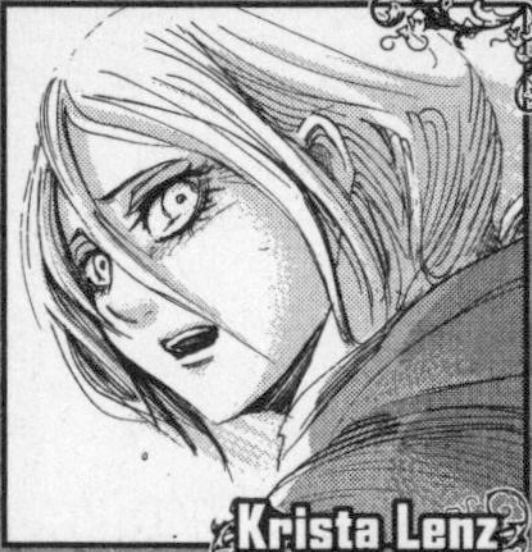
Krista Lenz
(Historia Reiss)

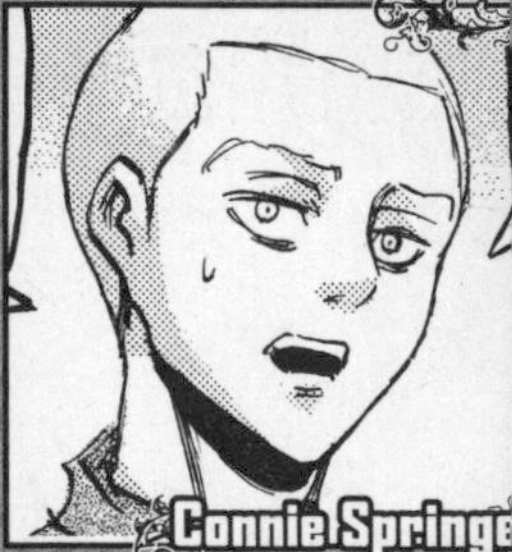
Connie Springe

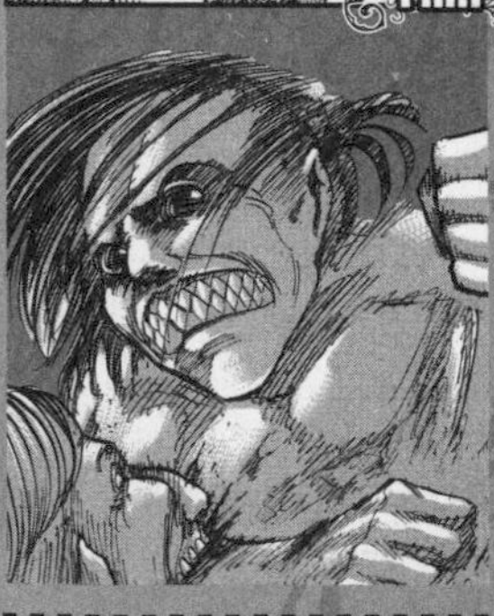

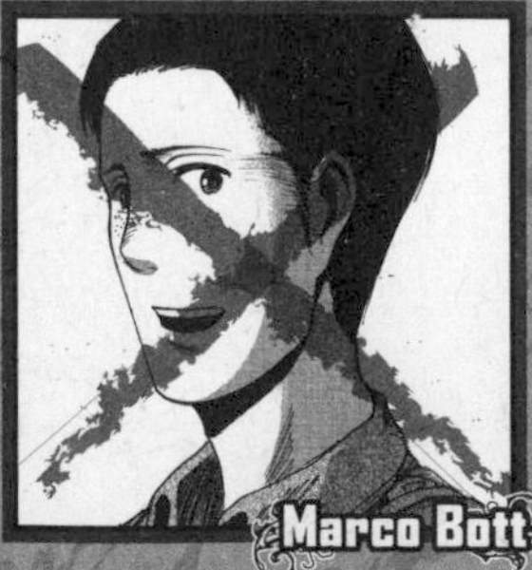
Marco Bott

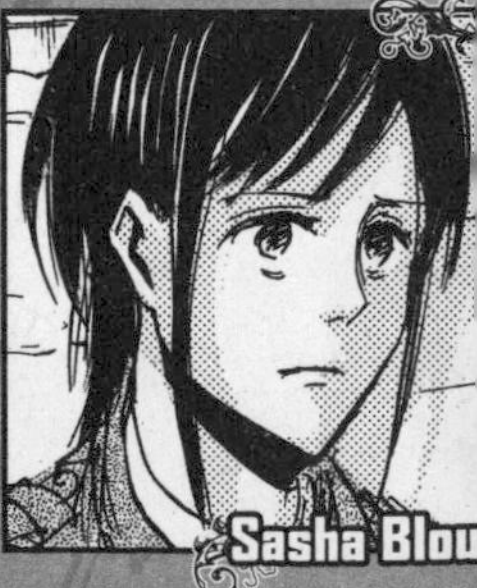
Sasha Blou

# ATTACK on TITAN

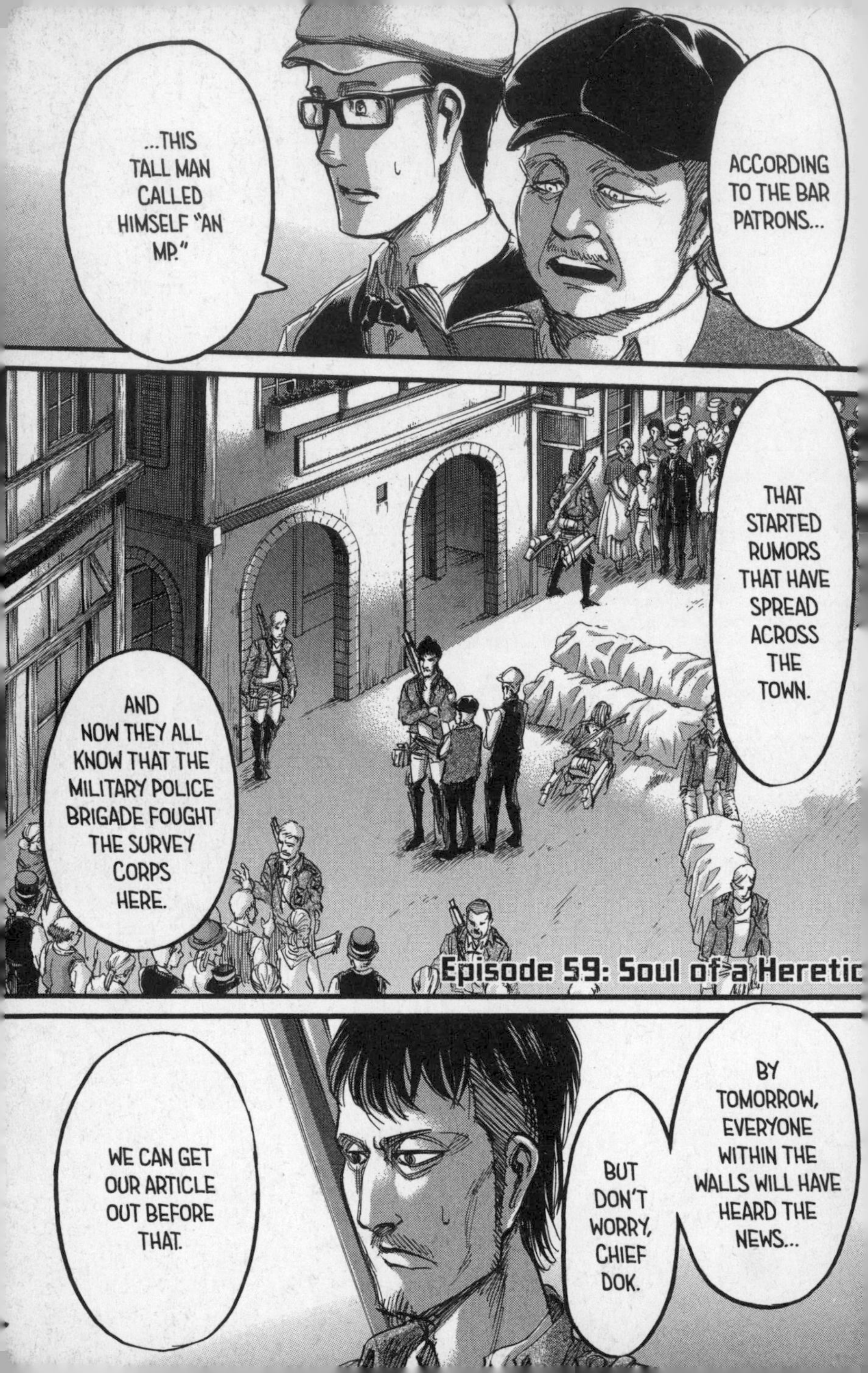
ACCORDING TO THE BAR PATRONS...
...THIS TALL MAN CALLED HIMSELF "AN MP."
THAT STARTED RUMORS THAT HAVE SPREAD ACROSS THE TOWN.
AND NOW THEY ALL KNOW THAT THE MILITARY POLICE BRIGADE FOUGHT THE SURVEY CORPS HERE.
Episode 59: Soul of a Heretic
BY TOMORROW, EVERYONE WITHIN THE WALLS WILL HAVE HEARD THE NEWS...
BUT DON'T WORRY, CHIEF DOK.
WE CAN GET OUR ARTICLE OUT BEFORE THAT.

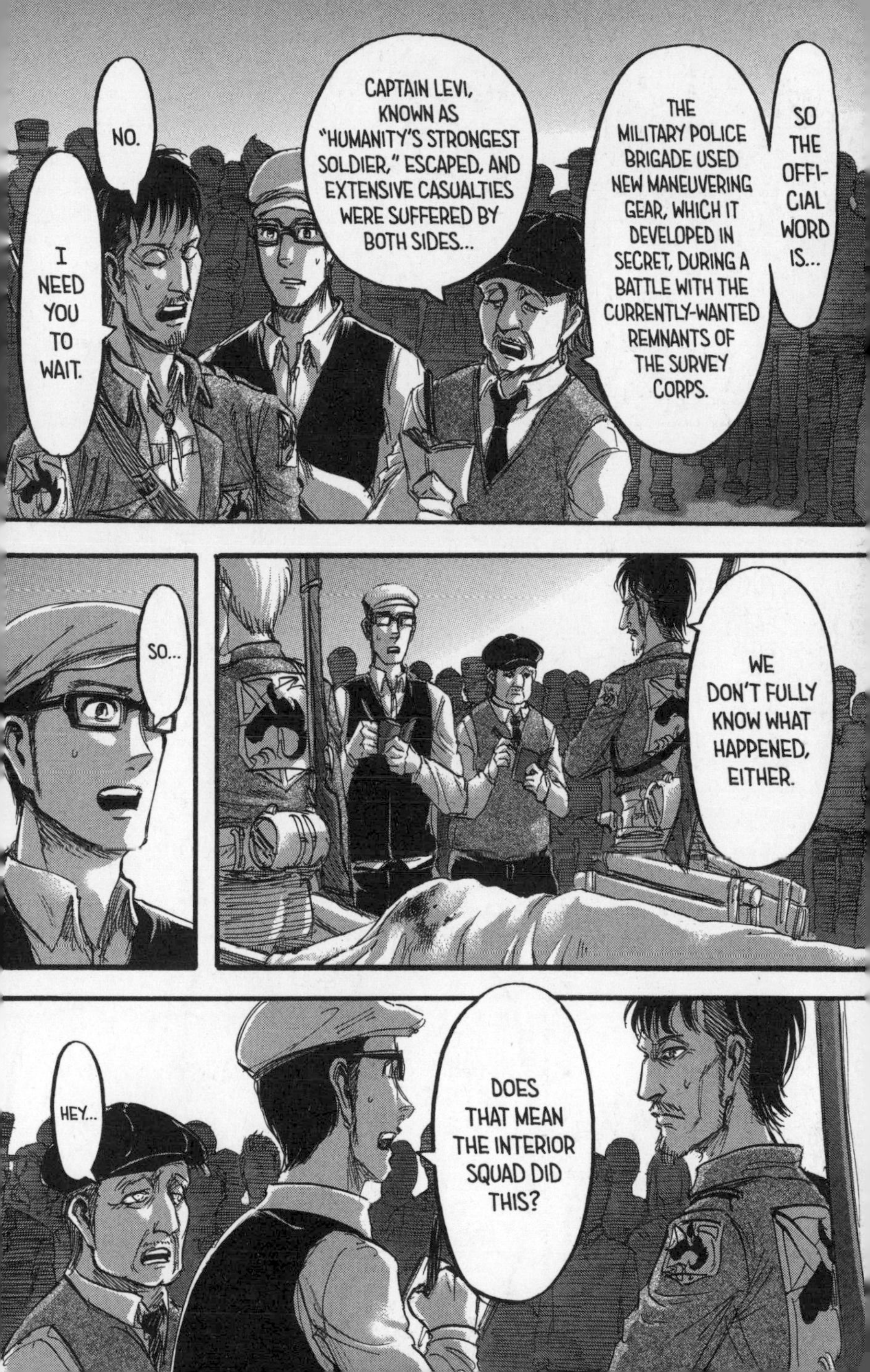
SO THE OFFICIAL WORD IS...
THE MILITARY POLICE BRIGADE USED NEW MANEUVERING GEAR, WHICH IT DEVELOPED IN SECRET, DURING A BATTLE WITH THE CURRENTLY-WANTED REMNANTS OF THE SURVEY CORPS.
CAPTAIN LEVI, KNOWN AS "HUMANITY'S STRONGEST SOLDIER," ESCAPED, AND EXTENSIVE CASUALTIES WERE SUFFERED BY BOTH SIDES...
NO.
I NEED YOU TO WAIT.
WE DON'T FULLY KNOW WHAT HAPPENED, EITHER.
SO...
DOES THAT MEAN THE INTERIOR SQUAD DID THIS?
HEY...

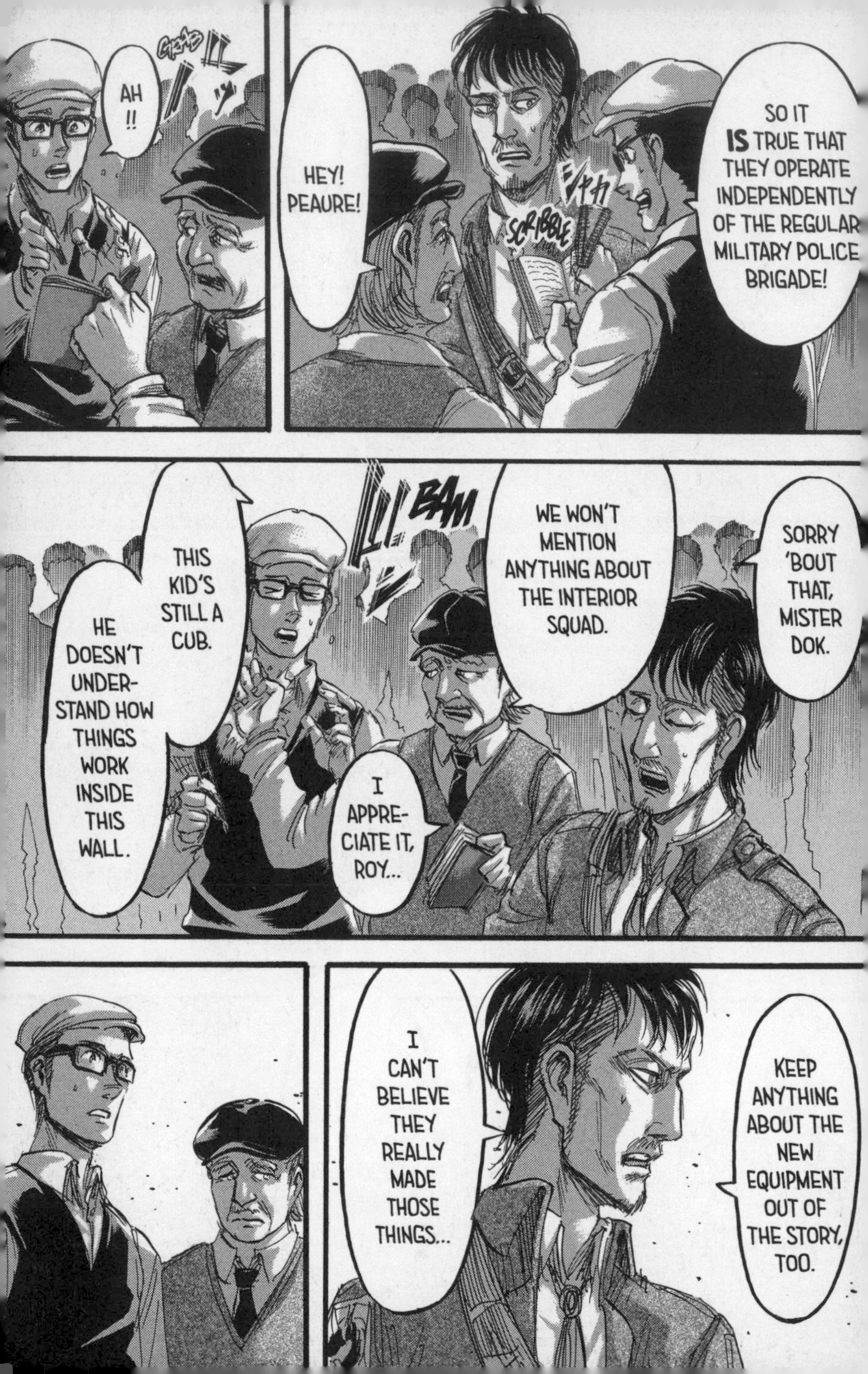
SO IT **IS** TRUE THAT THEY OPERATE INDEPENDENTLY OF THE REGULAR MILITARY POLICE BRIGADE!
SCRIBBLE
HEY! PEAURE!
GRAB
AH !!
SORRY 'BOUT THAT, MISTER DOK.
WE WON'T MENTION ANYTHING ABOUT THE INTERIOR SQUAD.
BAM
THIS KID'S STILL A CUB.
I APPRECIATE IT, ROY...
HE DOESN'T UNDER-STAND HOW THINGS WORK INSIDE THIS WALL.
KEEP ANYTHING ABOUT THE NEW EQUIPMENT OUT OF THE STORY, TOO.
I CAN'T BELIEVE THEY REALLY MADE THOSE THINGS...

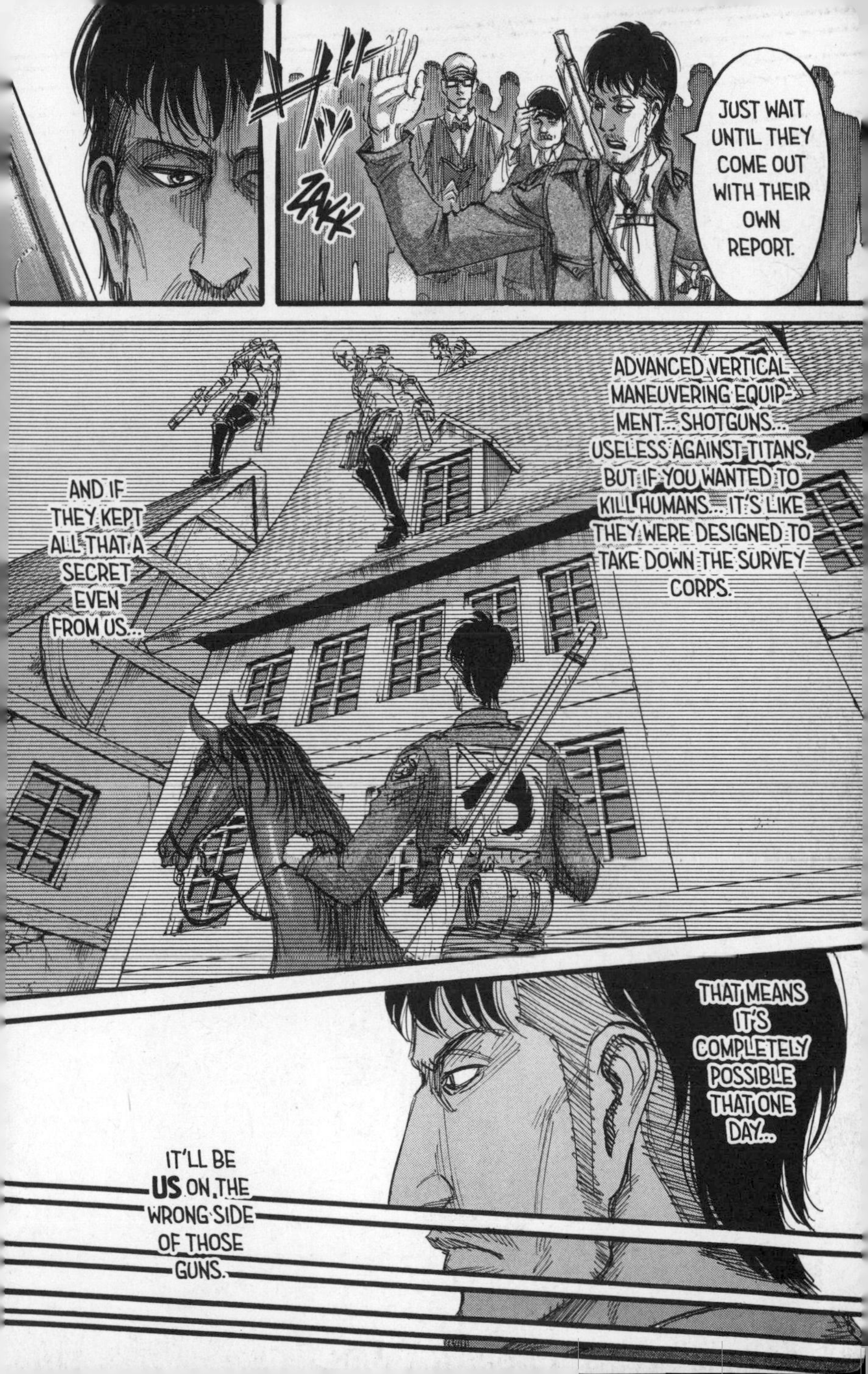
JUST WAIT UNTIL THEY COME OUT WITH THEIR OWN REPORT.
ZAKK
ADVANCED VERTICAL MANEUVERING EQUIP-MENT... SHOTGUNS... USELESS AGAINST TITANS, BUT IF YOU WANTED TO KILL HUMANS... IT'S LIKE THEY WERE DESIGNED TO TAKE DOWN THE SURVEY CORPS.
AND IF THEY KEPT ALL THAT A SECRET EVEN FROM US...
THAT MEANS IT'S COMPLETELY POSSIBLE THAT ONE DAY...
IT'LL BE US ON THE WRONG SIDE OF THOSE GUNS.

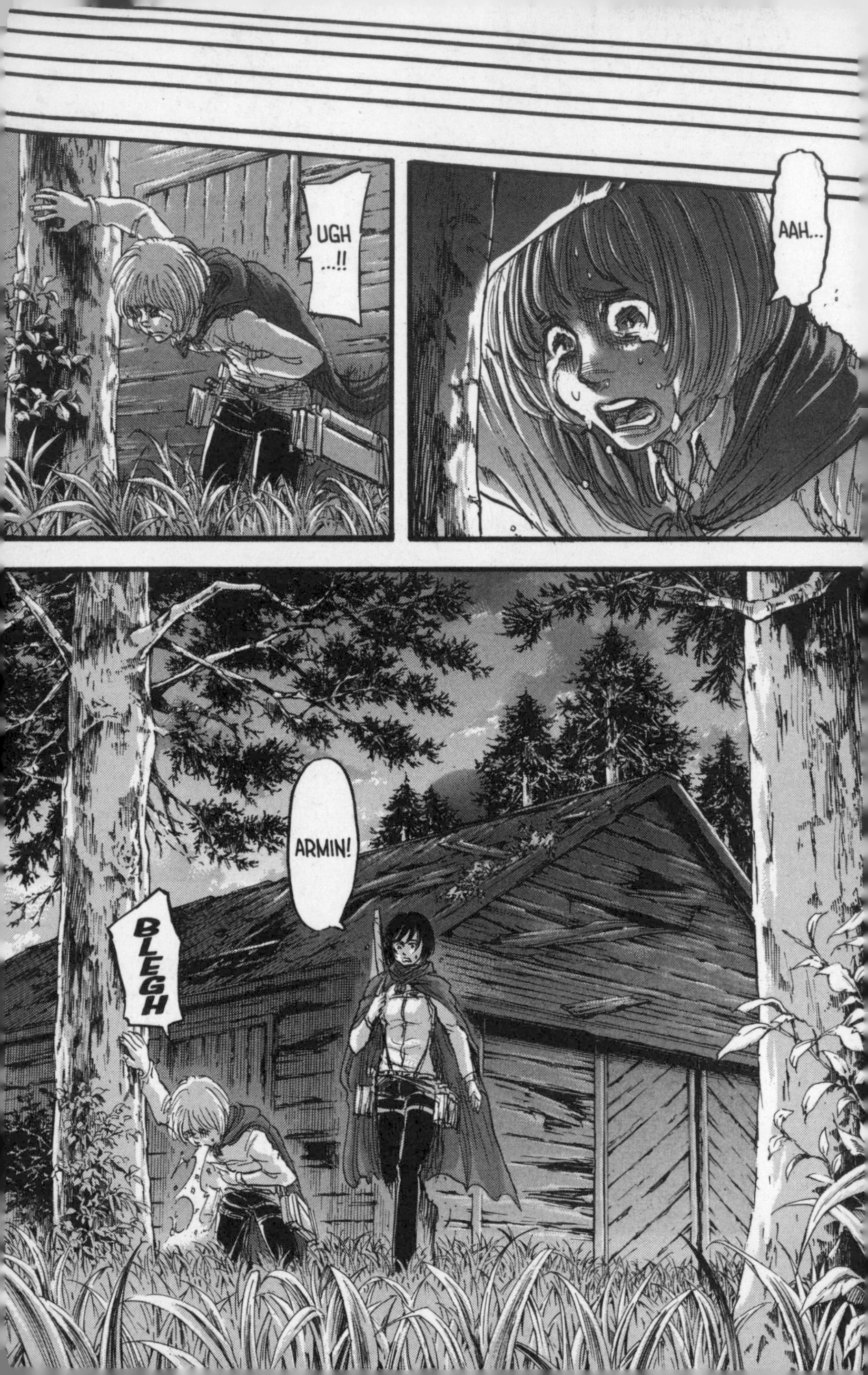
AAH...
UGH ...!!
ARMIN!
BLEGH

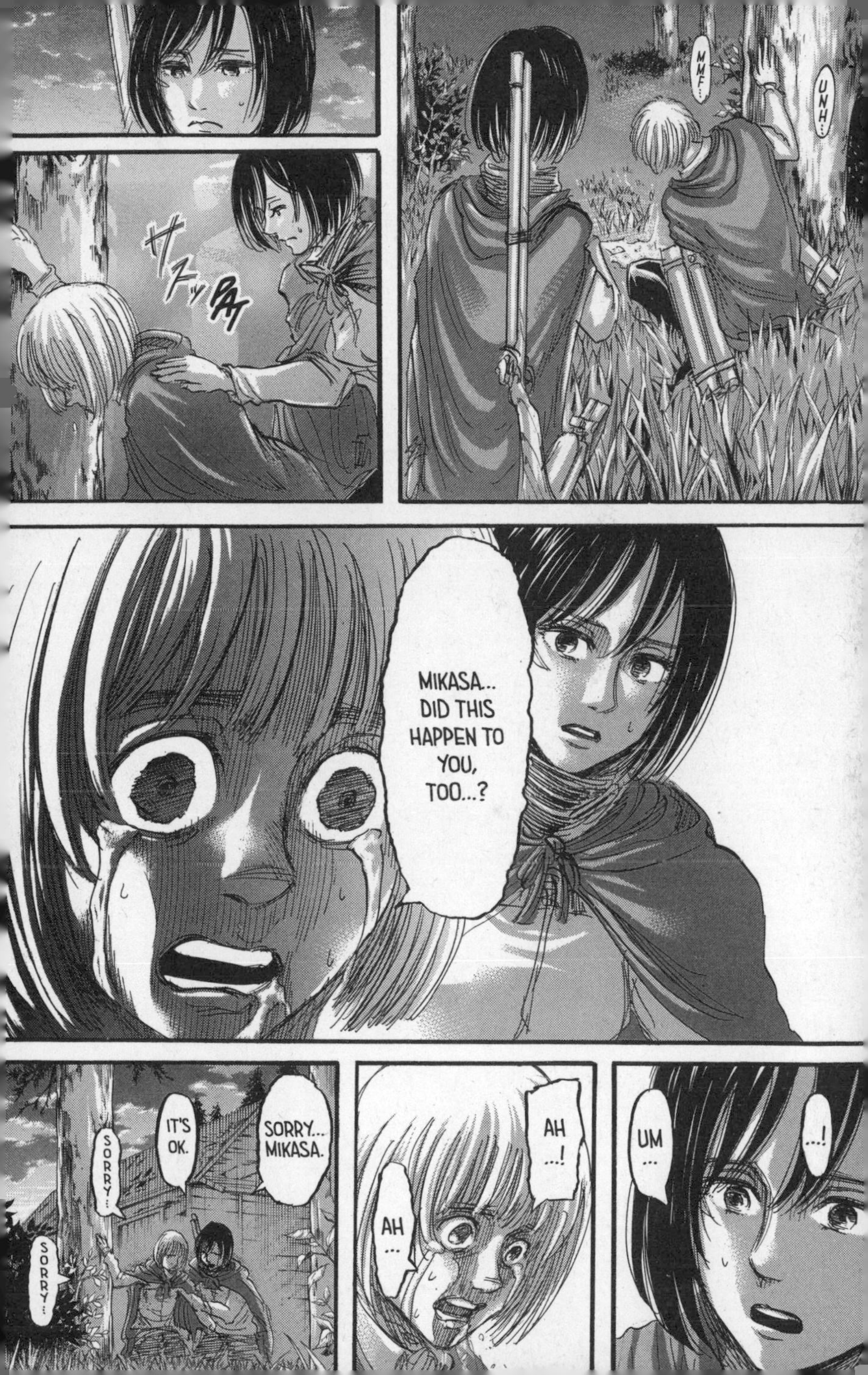
UNH...
MMF...
PAT
MIKASA... DID THIS HAPPEN TO YOU, TOO...?
...!
UM...
AH...!
AH...
SORRY... MIKASA.
IT'S OK.
SORRY...
SORRY...

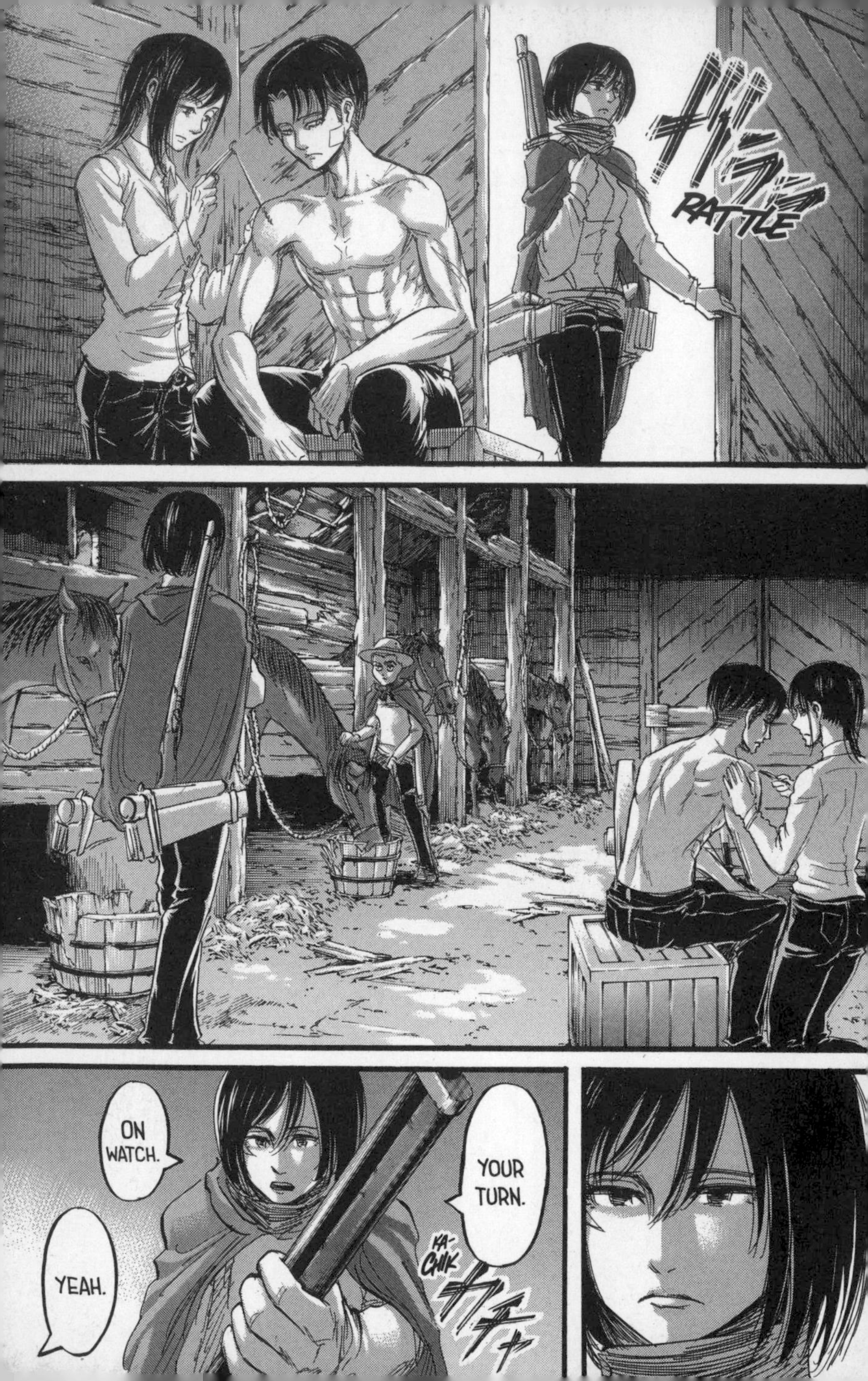
RATTLE
YOUR TURN.
ON WATCH.
KA-CHIK
YEAH.

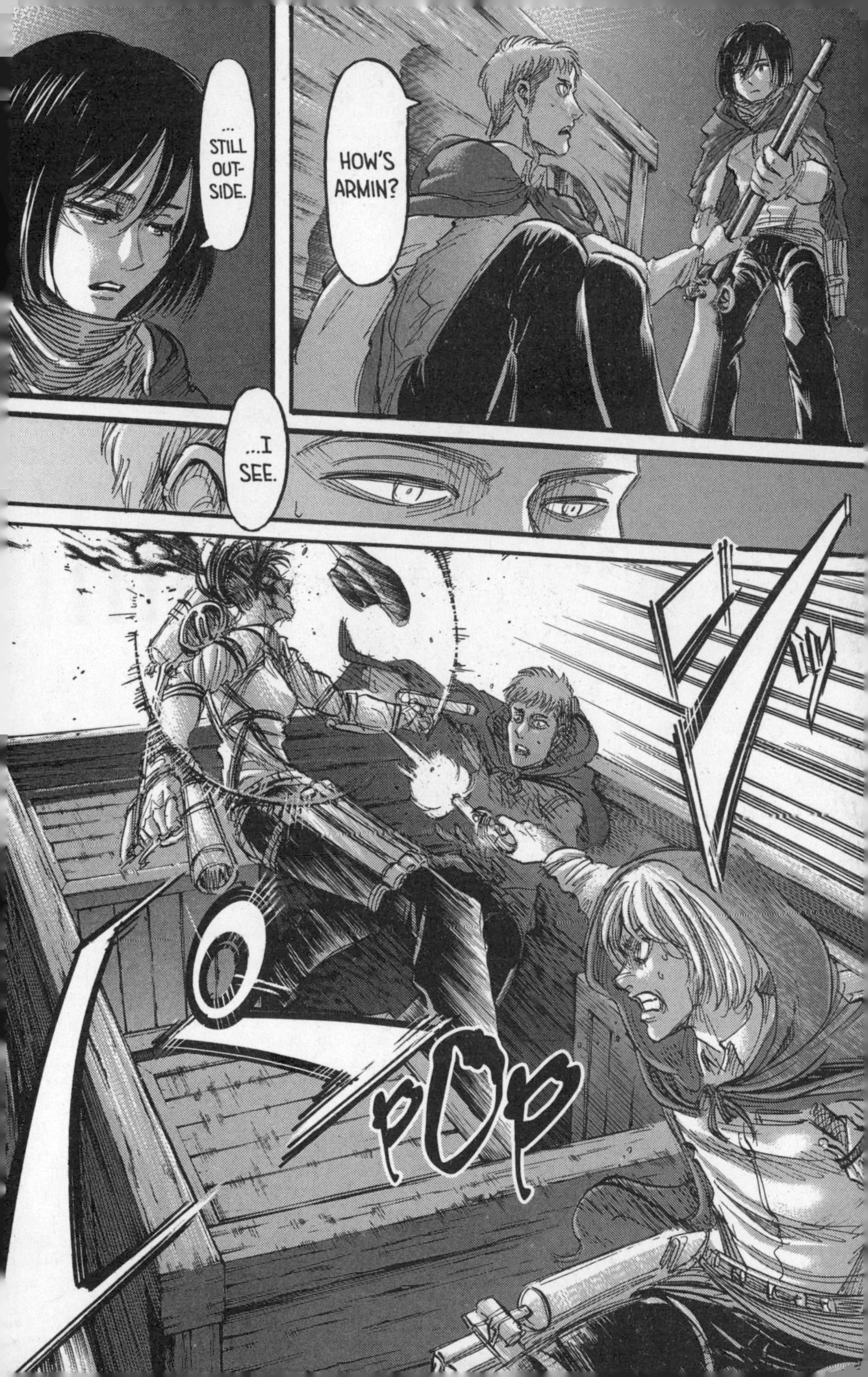
HOW'S ARMIN?
... STILL OUT-SIDE.
...I SEE.
POP

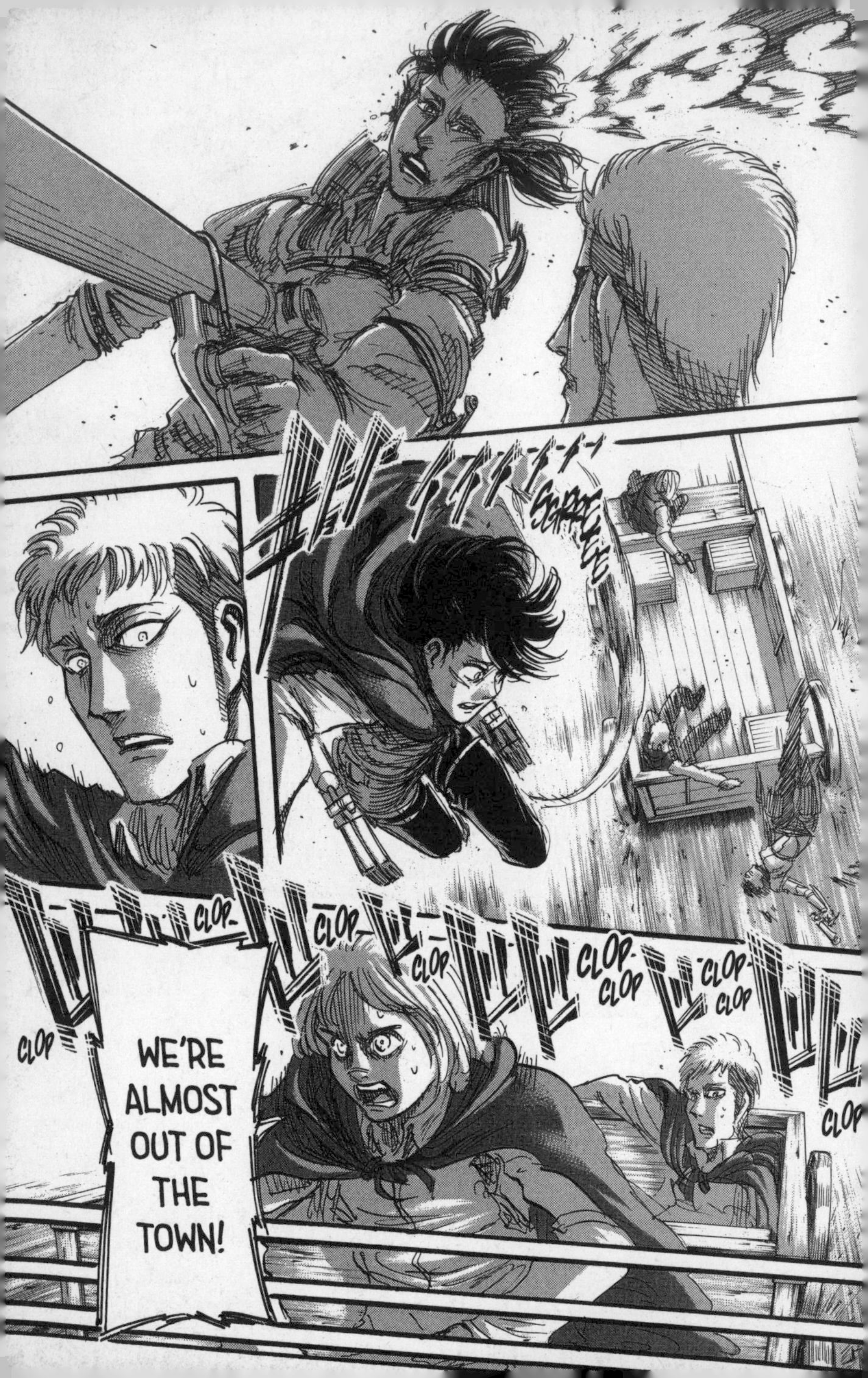
CLOP
CLOP-
CLOP
CLOP-
CLOP
CLOP
CLOP-
CLOP-
CLOP
WE'RE ALMOST OUT OF THE TOWN!

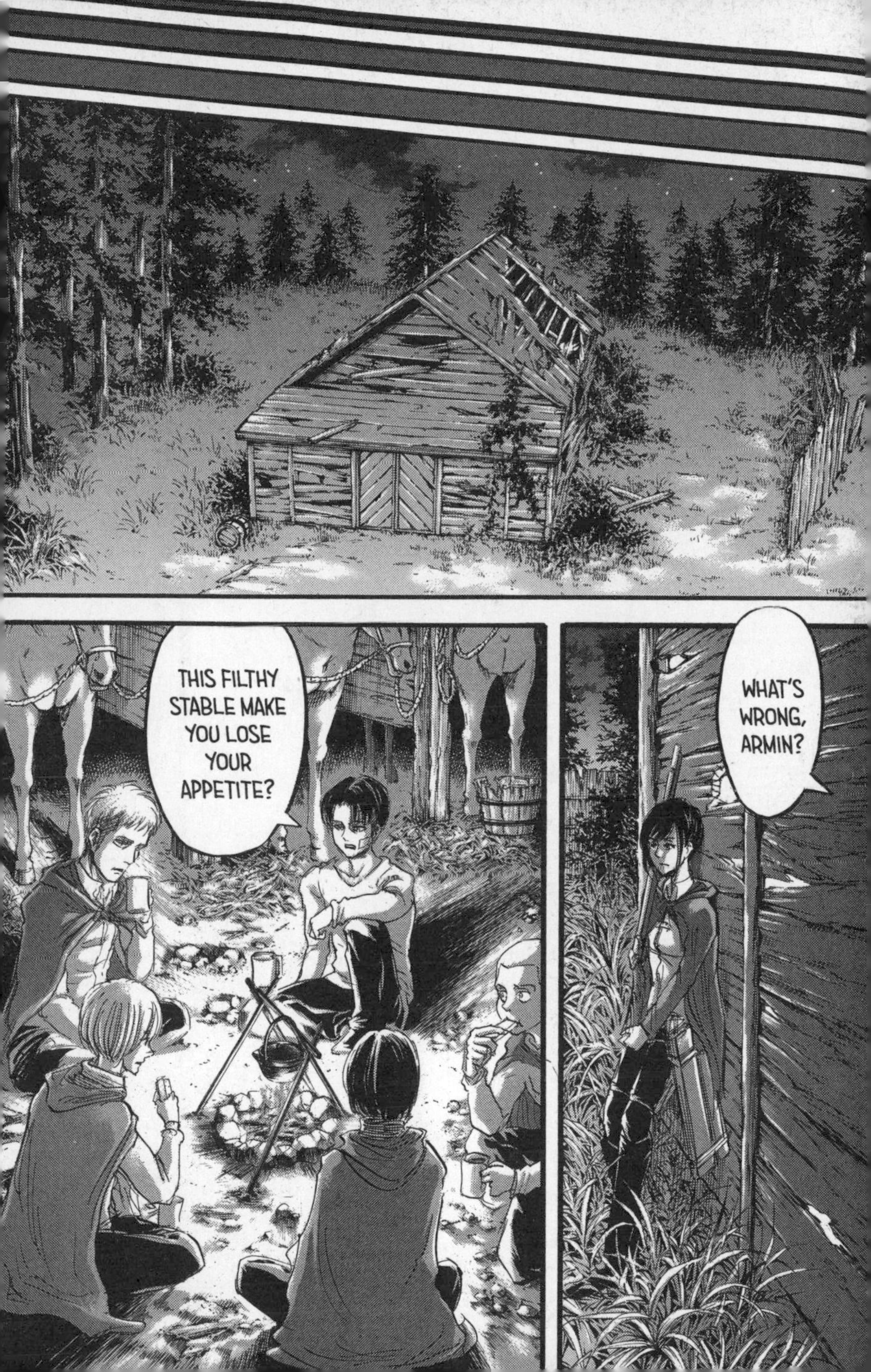
WHAT'S WRONG, ARMIN?
THIS FILTHY STABLE MAKE YOU LOSE YOUR APPETITE?

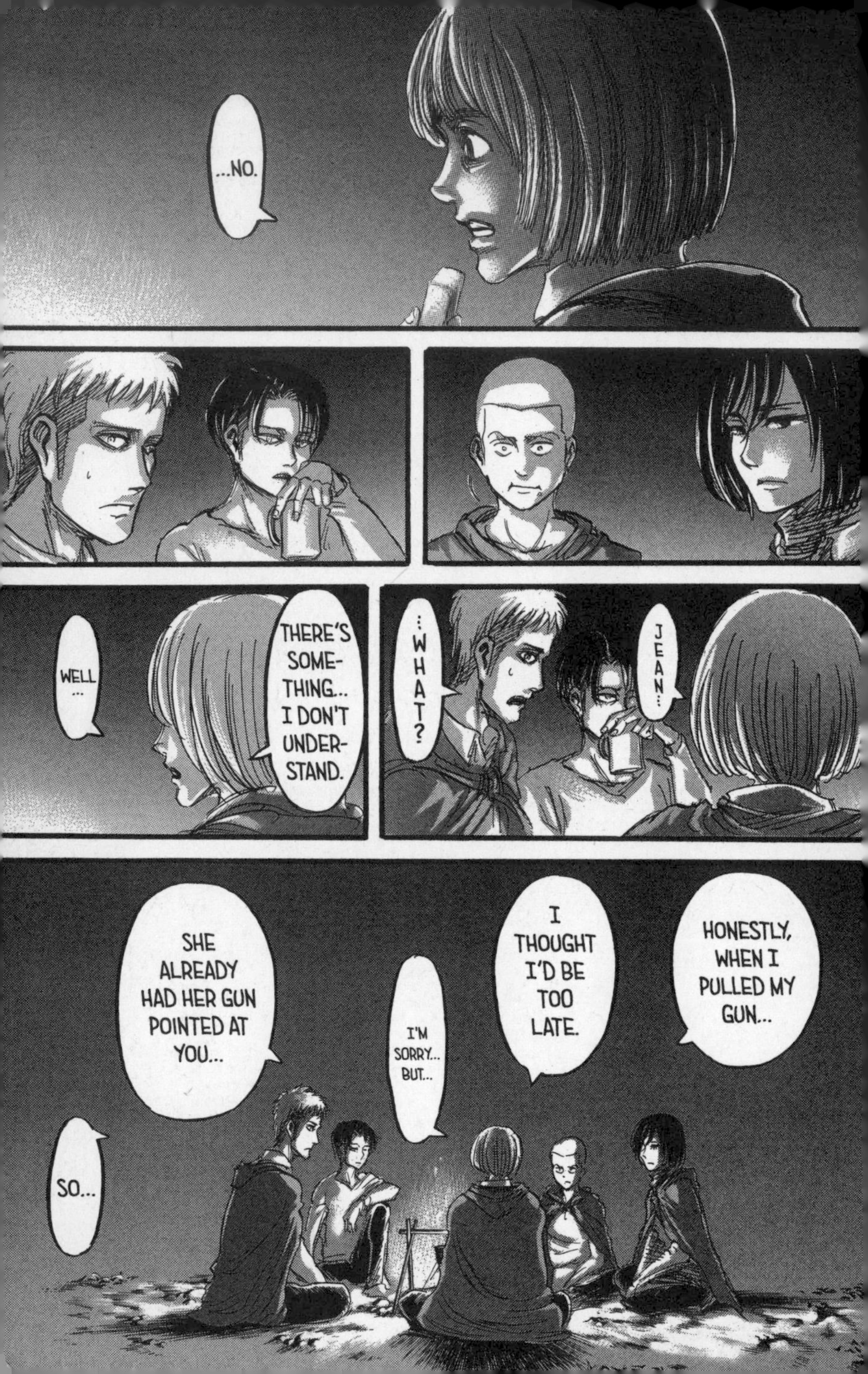
...NO.
JEAN...
...WHAT?
THERE'S SOMETHING... I DON'T UNDERSTAND.
WELL...
HONESTLY, WHEN I PULLED MY GUN...
I THOUGHT I'D BE TOO LATE.
I'M SORRY... BUT...
SHE ALREADY HAD HER GUN POINTED AT YOU...
SO...

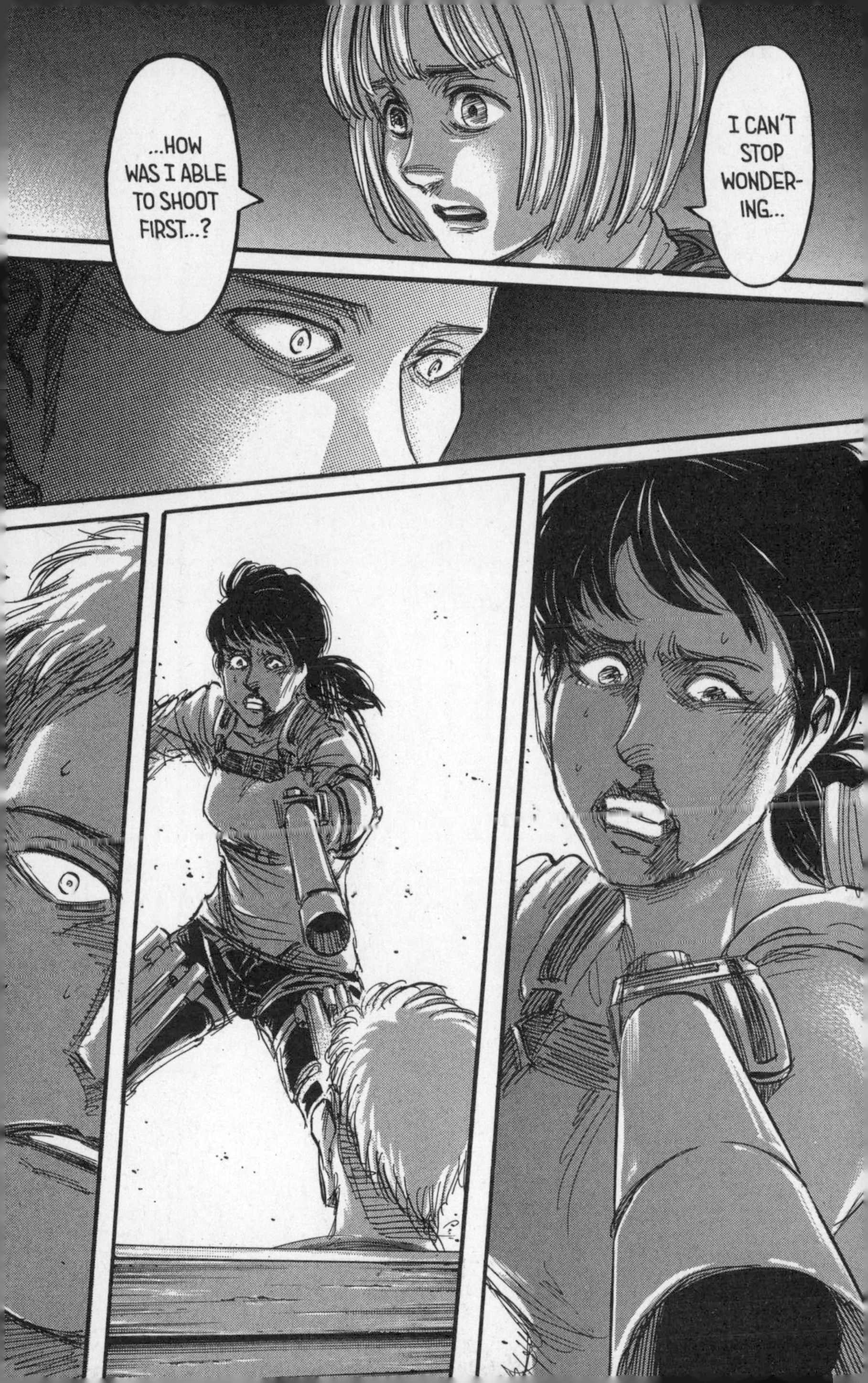
I CAN'T STOP WONDER-ING...
...HOW WAS I ABLE TO SHOOT FIRST...?

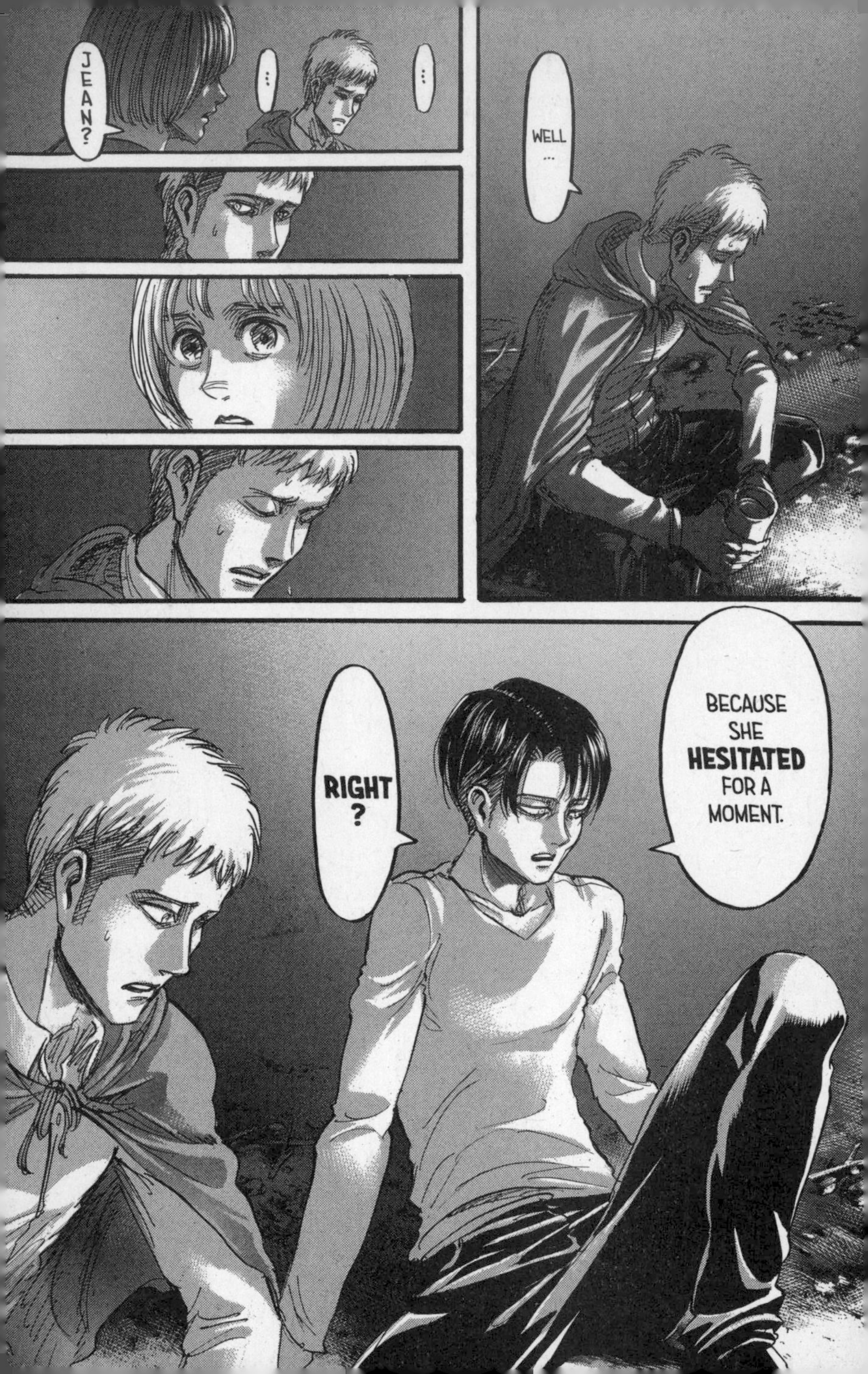
WELL ...
...
...
JEAN?
BECAUSE SHE HESITATED FOR A MOMENT.
RIGHT?

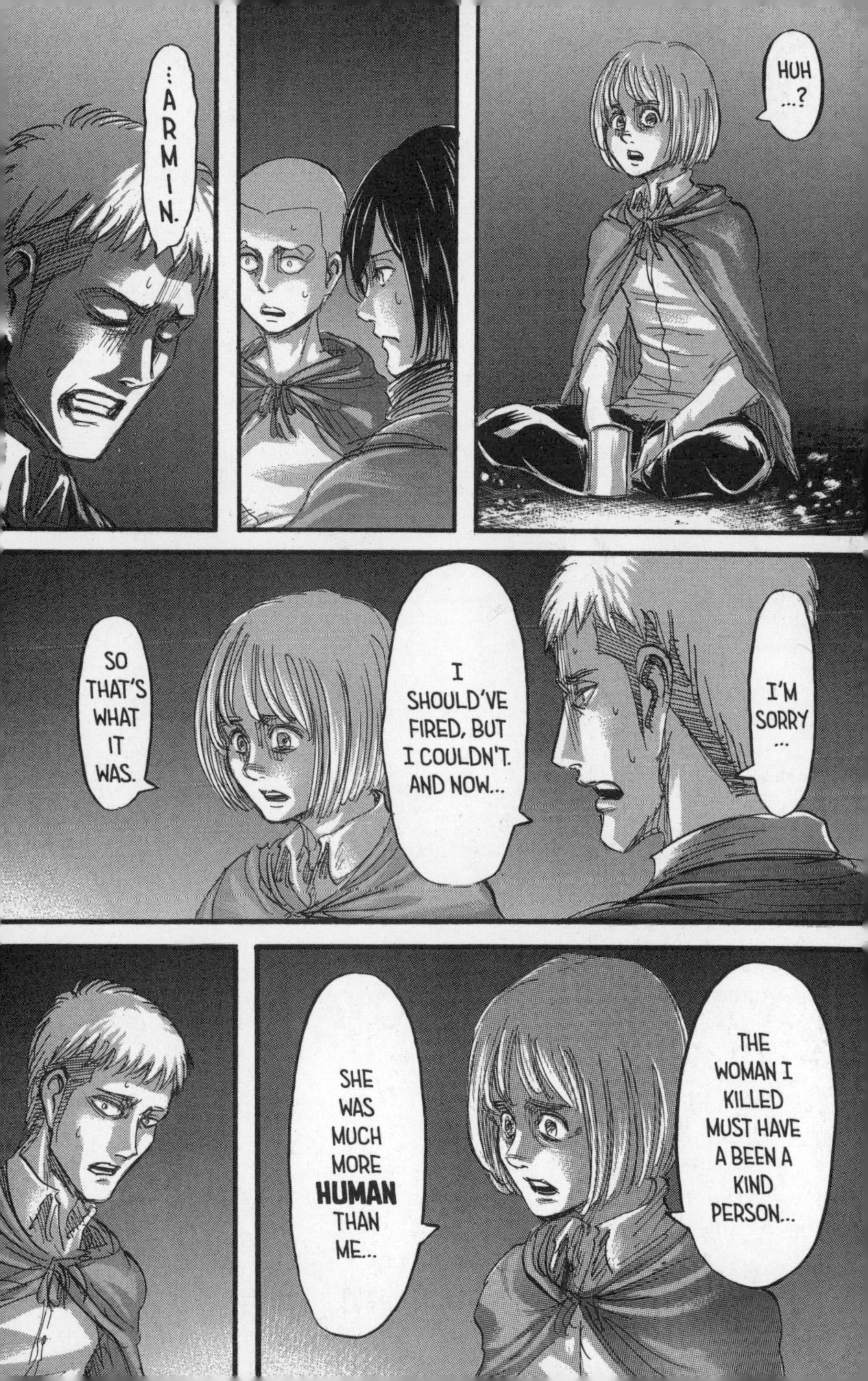
HUH ...?
...ARMIN.
I'M SORRY ...
I SHOULD'VE FIRED, BUT I COULDN'T. AND NOW...
SO THAT'S WHAT IT WAS.
THE WOMAN I KILLED MUST HAVE A BEEN A KIND PERSON...
SHE WAS MUCH MORE **HUMAN** THAN ME...

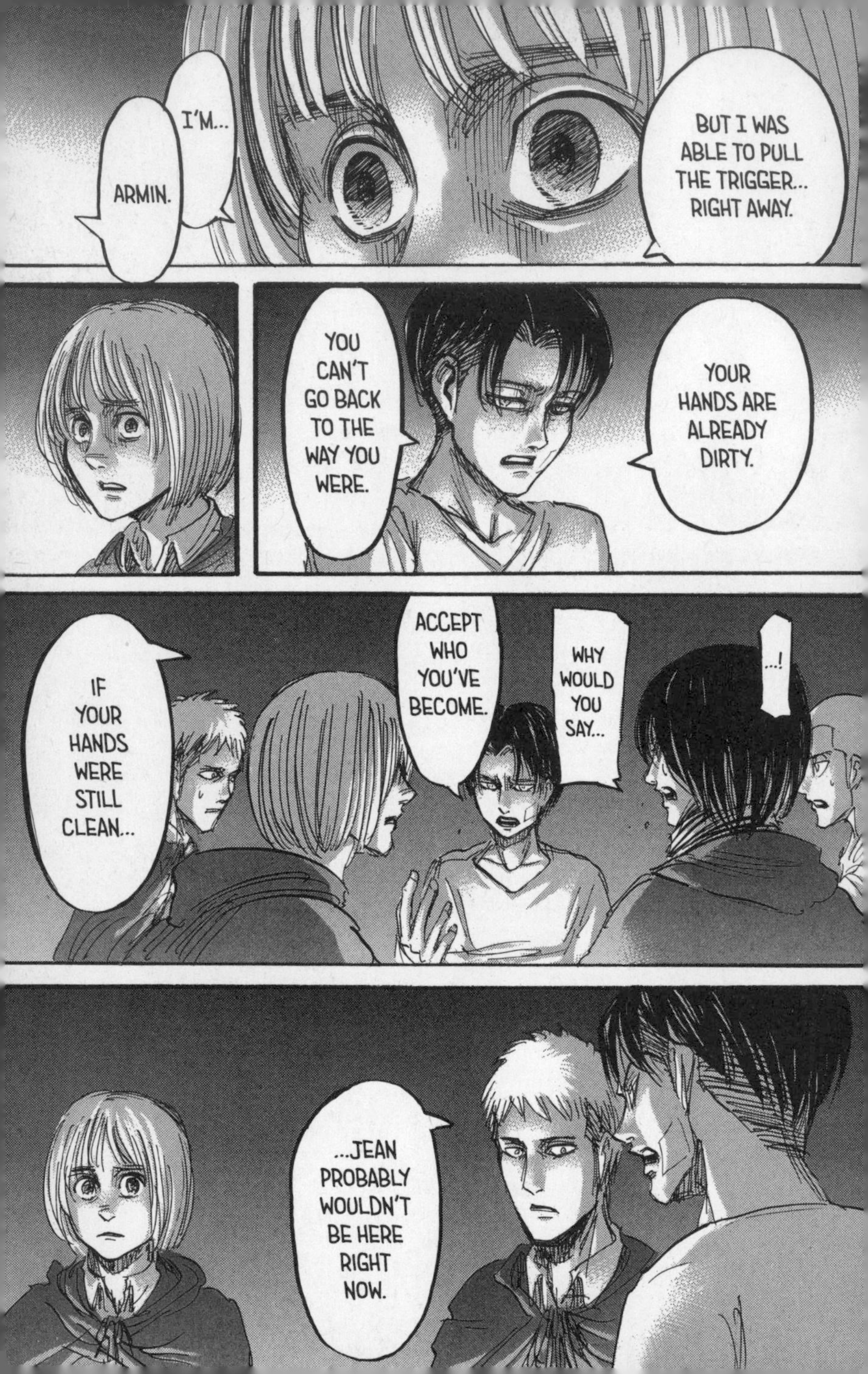
BUT I WAS ABLE TO PULL THE TRIGGER... RIGHT AWAY.
I'M...
ARMIN.
YOUR HANDS ARE ALREADY DIRTY.
YOU CAN'T GO BACK TO THE WAY YOU WERE.
...!
WHY WOULD YOU SAY...
ACCEPT WHO YOU'VE BECOME.
IF YOUR HANDS WERE STILL CLEAN...
...JEAN PROBABLY WOULDN'T BE HERE RIGHT NOW.

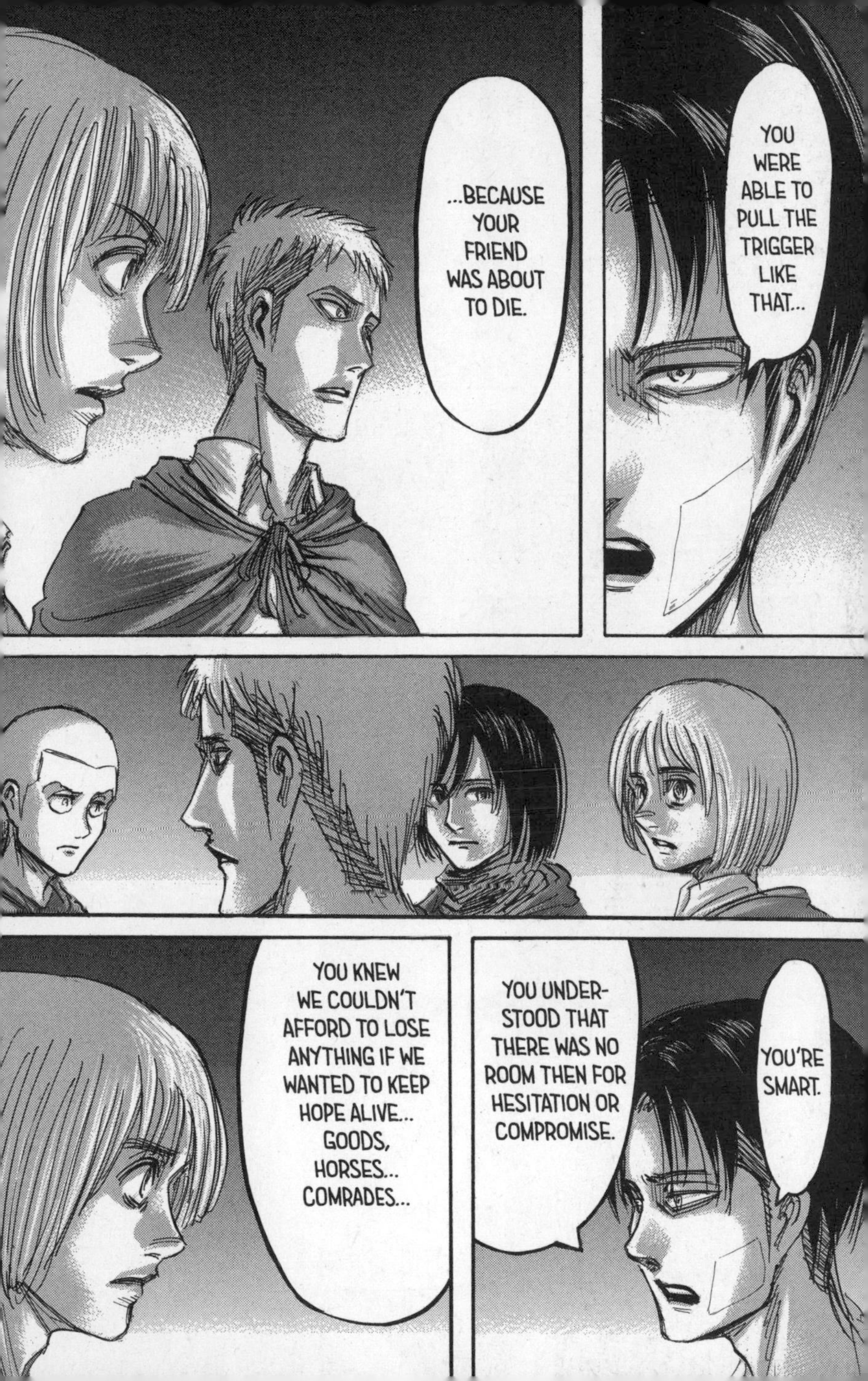
YOU WERE ABLE TO PULL THE TRIGGER LIKE THAT...
...BECAUSE YOUR FRIEND WAS ABOUT TO DIE.
YOU'RE SMART.
YOU UNDER-STOOD THAT THERE WAS NO ROOM THEN FOR HESITATION OR COMPROMISE.
YOU KNEW WE COULDN'T AFFORD TO LOSE ANYTHING IF WE WANTED TO KEEP HOPE ALIVE... GOODS, HORSES... COMRADES...

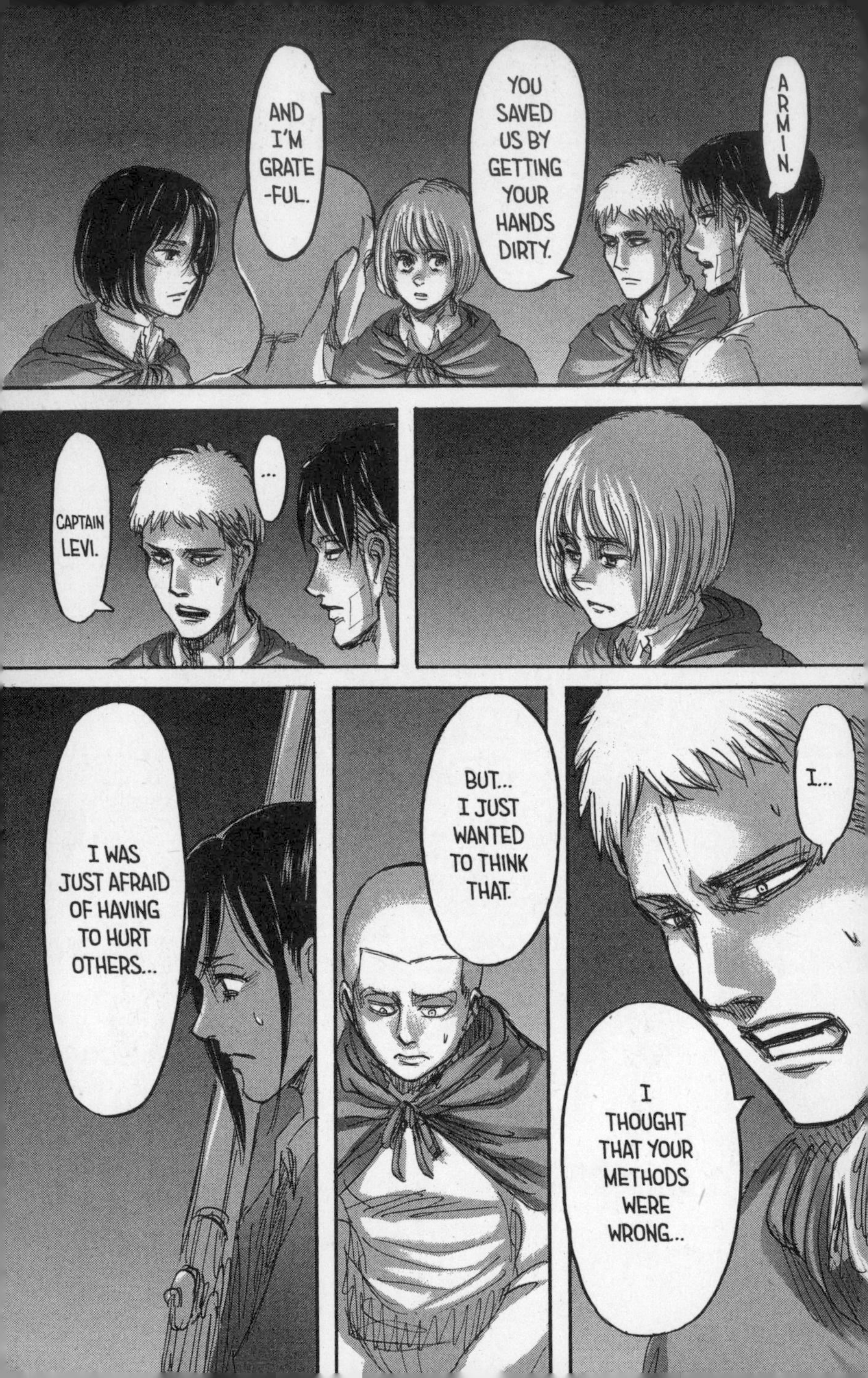
ARMIN.
YOU SAVED US BY GETTING YOUR HANDS DIRTY.
AND I'M GRATEFUL.
...
CAPTAIN LEVI.
I...
I THOUGHT THAT YOUR METHODS WERE WRONG...
BUT... I JUST WANTED TO THINK THAT.
I WAS JUST AFRAID OF HAVING TO HURT OTHERS...

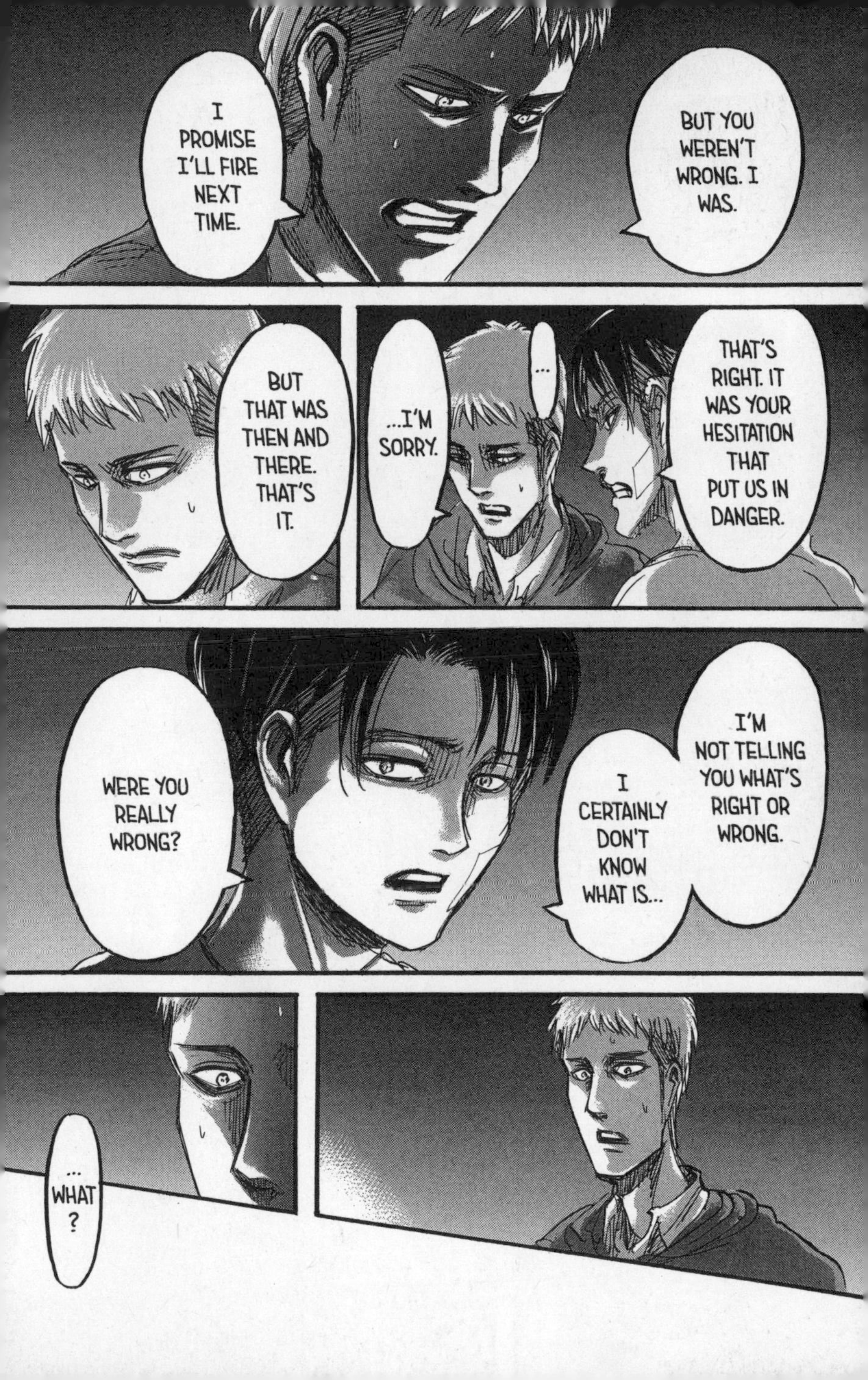
BUT YOU WEREN'T WRONG. I WAS.
I PROMISE I'LL FIRE NEXT TIME.
THAT'S RIGHT. IT WAS YOUR HESITATION THAT PUT US IN DANGER.
...
...I'M SORRY.
BUT THAT WAS THEN AND THERE. THAT'S IT.
I'M NOT TELLING YOU WHAT'S RIGHT OR WRONG.
I CERTAINLY DON'T KNOW WHAT IS...
WERE YOU REALLY WRONG?
...WHAT?

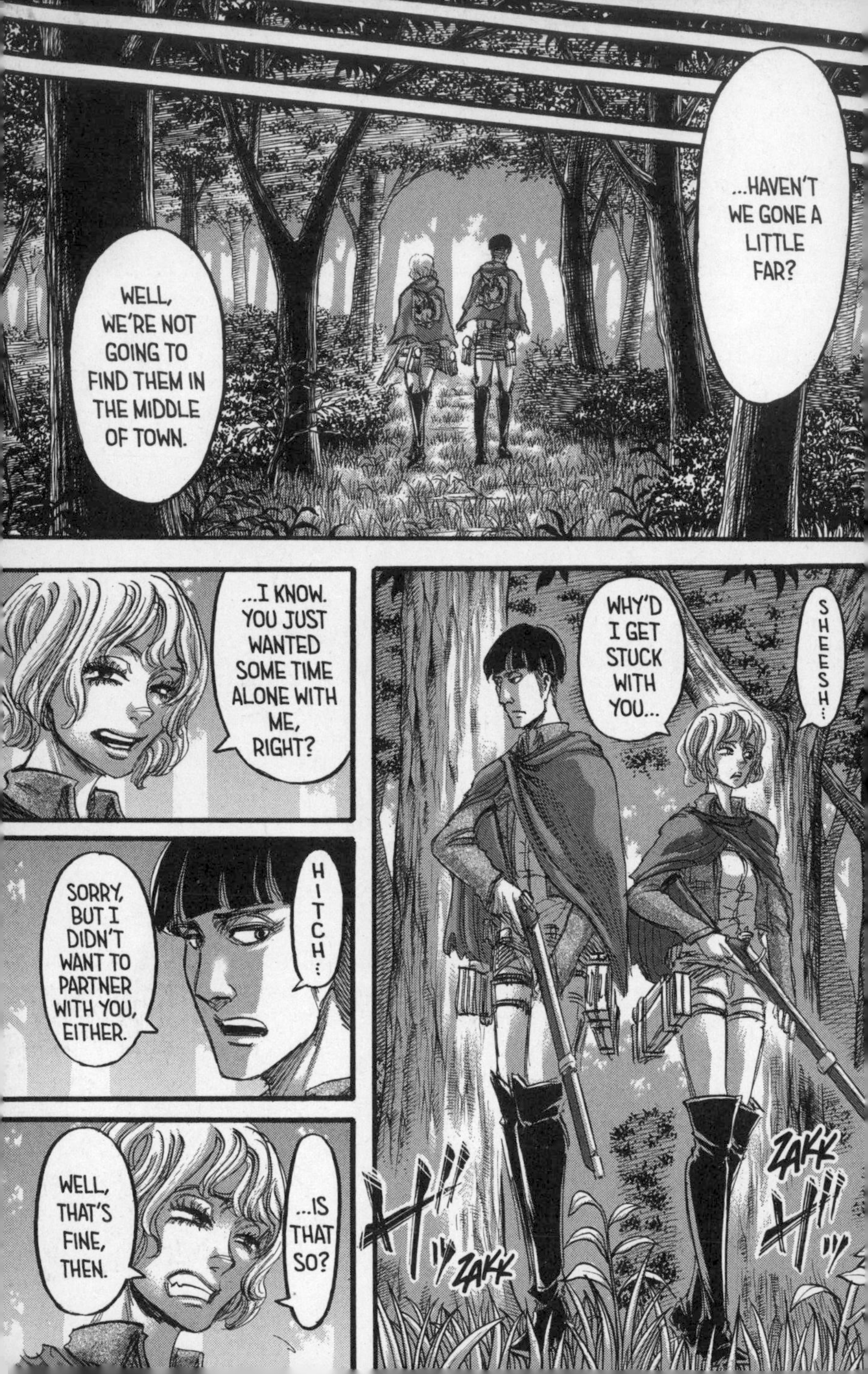
...HAVEN'T WE GONE A LITTLE FAR?
WELL, WE'RE NOT GOING TO FIND THEM IN THE MIDDLE OF TOWN.
SHEESH...
WHY'D I GET STUCK WITH YOU...
ZAKK
ZAKK
...I KNOW. YOU JUST WANTED SOME TIME ALONE WITH ME, RIGHT?
HITCH...
SORRY, BUT I DIDN'T WANT TO PARTNER WITH YOU, EITHER.
...IS THAT SO?
WELL, THAT'S FINE, THEN.

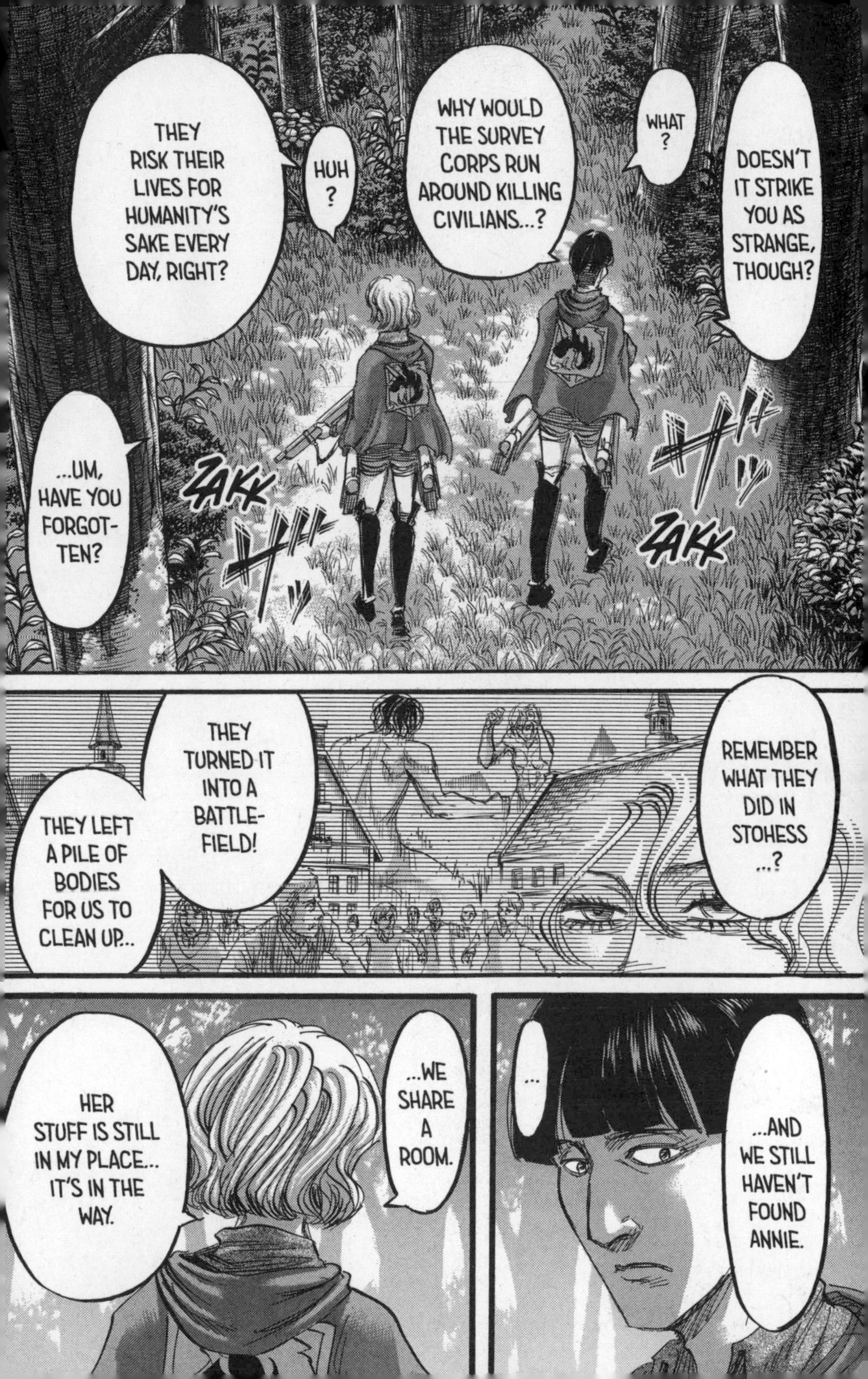
DOESN'T IT STRIKE YOU AS STRANGE, THOUGH?
WHAT?
WHY WOULD THE SURVEY CORPS RUN AROUND KILLING CIVILIANS...?
HUH?
THEY RISK THEIR LIVES FOR HUMANITY'S SAKE EVERY DAY, RIGHT?
ZAKK
ZAKK
...UM, HAVE YOU FORGOTTEN?
REMEMBER WHAT THEY DID IN STOHESS...?
THEY TURNED IT INTO A BATTLEFIELD!
THEY LEFT A PILE OF BODIES FOR US TO CLEAN UP...
...AND WE STILL HAVEN'T FOUND ANNIE.
...
...WE SHARE A ROOM.
HER STUFF IS STILL IN MY PLACE... IT'S IN THE WAY.

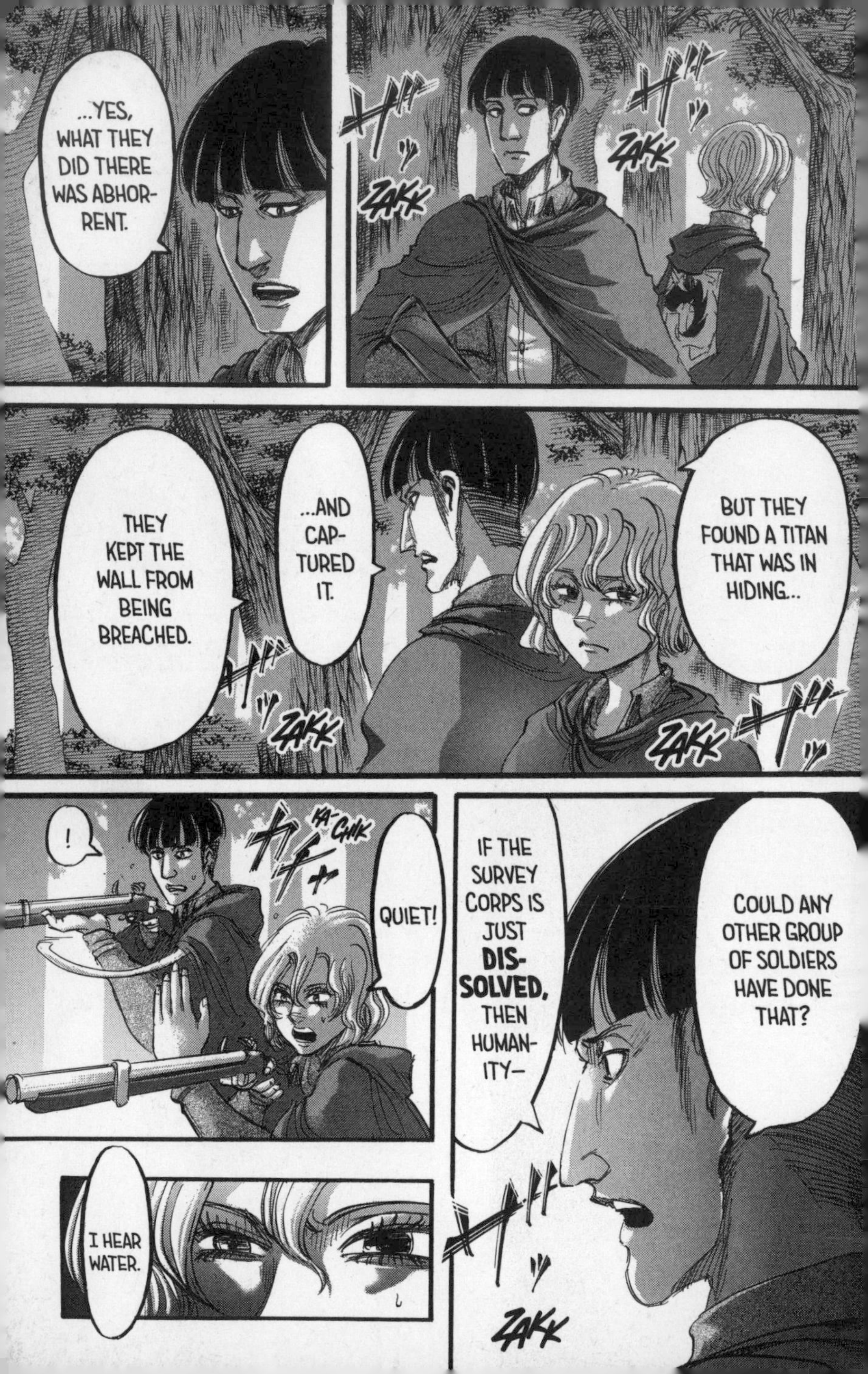
ZAKK
ZAKK
...YES, WHAT THEY DID THERE WAS ABHOR-RENT.
BUT THEY FOUND A TITAN THAT WAS IN HIDING...
ZAKK
...AND CAP-TURED IT.
THEY KEPT THE WALL FROM BEING BREACHED.
ZAKK
COULD ANY OTHER GROUP OF SOLDIERS HAVE DONE THAT?
IF THE SURVEY CORPS IS JUST **DIS-SOLVED,** THEN HUMAN-ITY—
ZAKK
QUIET!
KA-CHIK
!
I HEAR WATER.

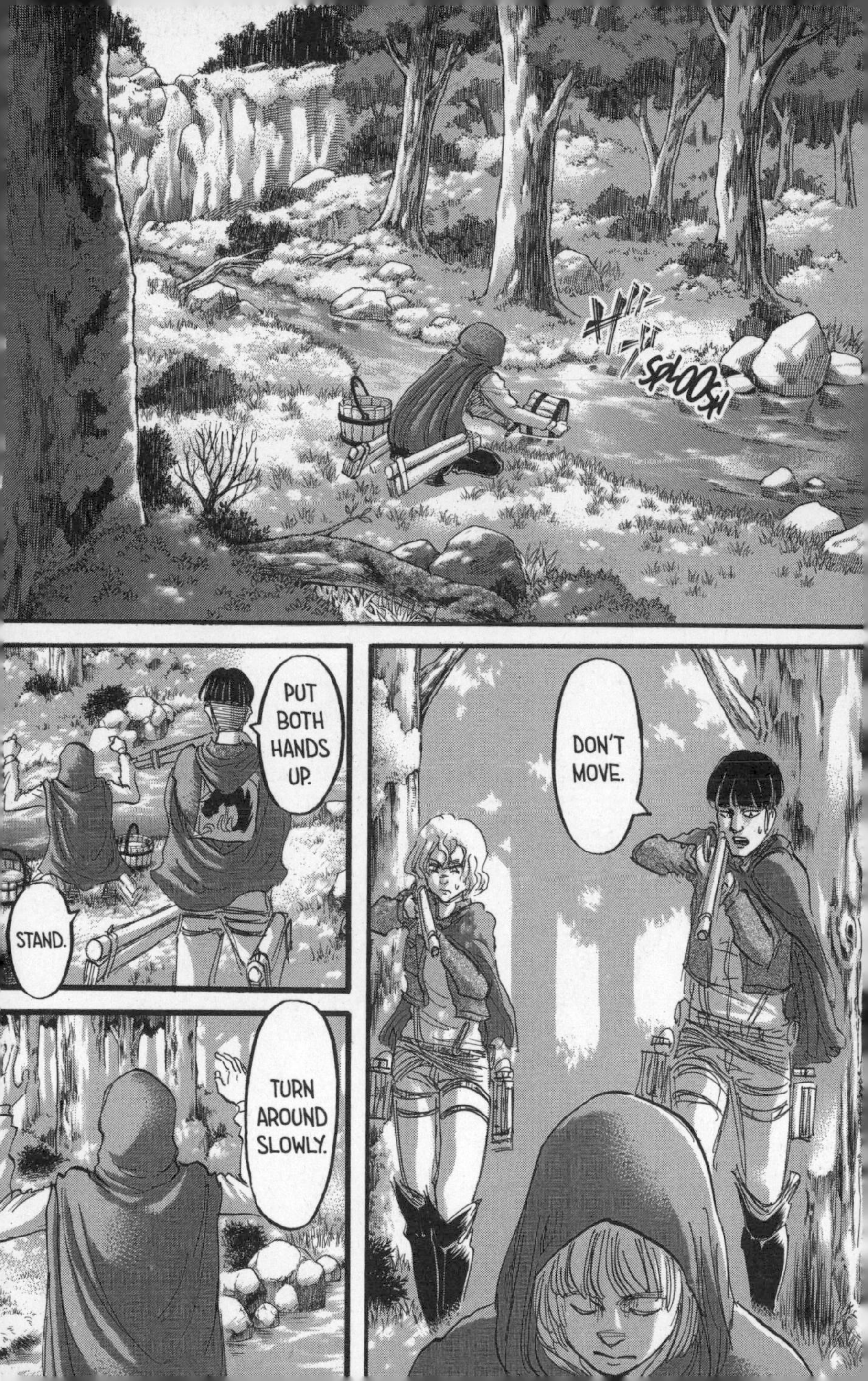
SPLOOSH
DON'T MOVE.
PUT BOTH HANDS UP.
STAND.
TURN AROUND SLOWLY.

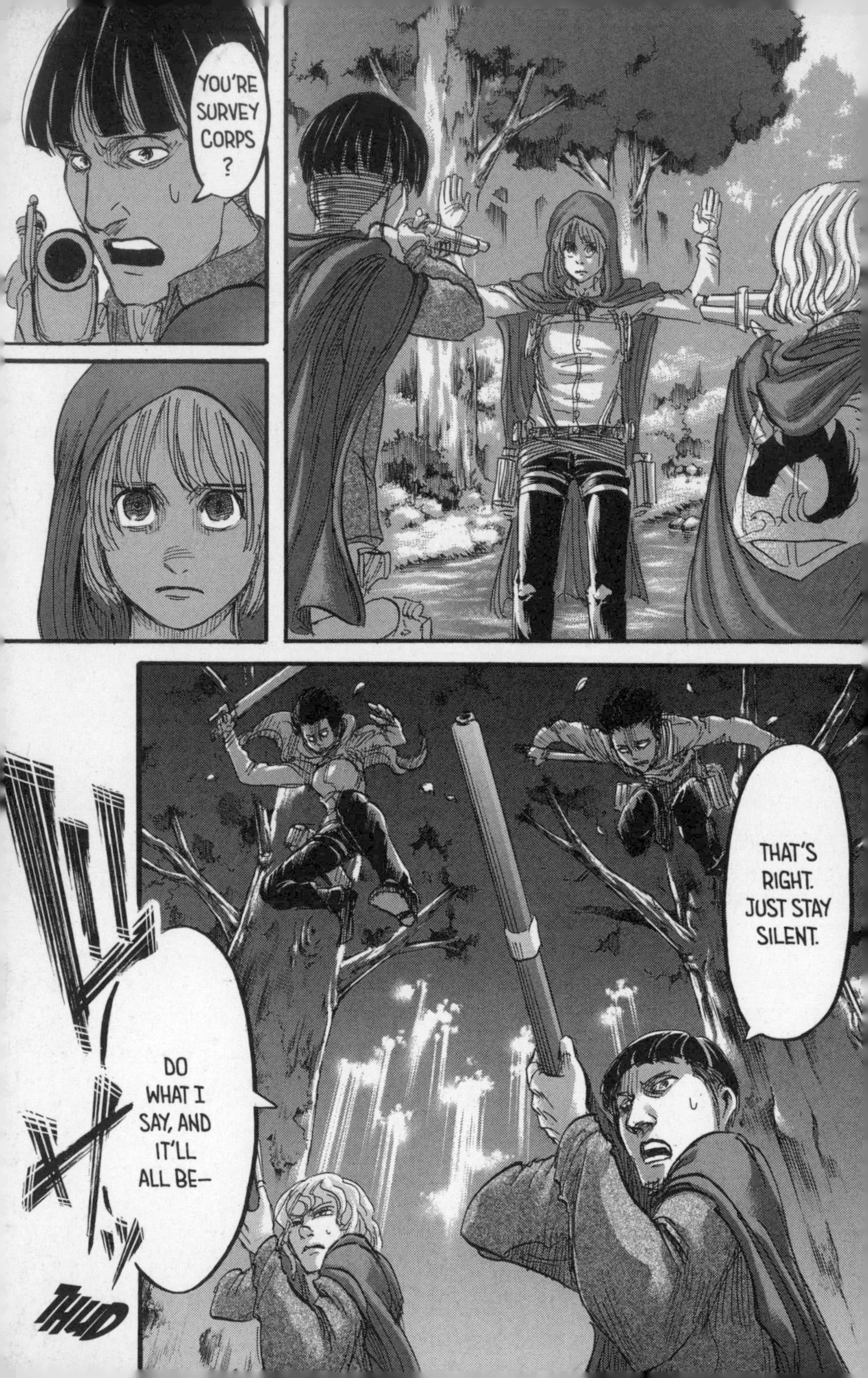
YOU'RE SURVEY CORPS?
THAT'S RIGHT. JUST STAY SILENT.
DO WHAT I SAY, AND IT'LL ALL BE—
THUD

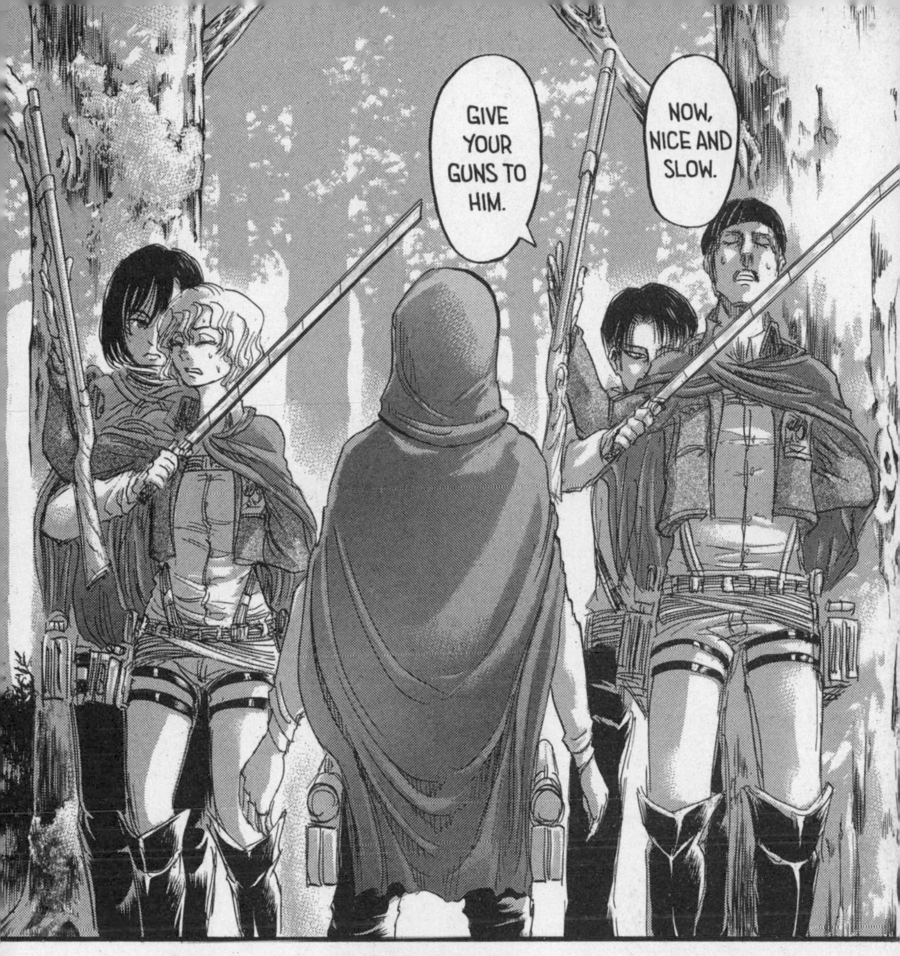
NOW, NICE AND SLOW.
GIVE YOUR GUNS TO HIM.

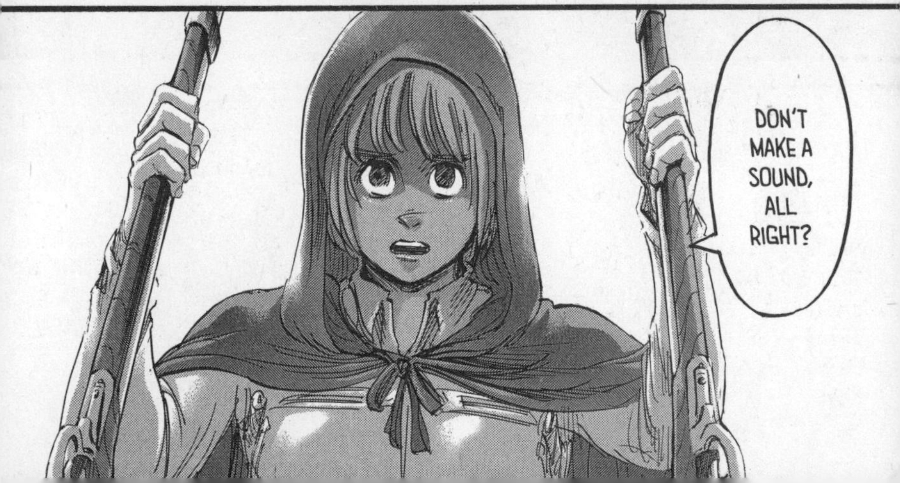
DON'T MAKE A SOUND, ALL RIGHT?

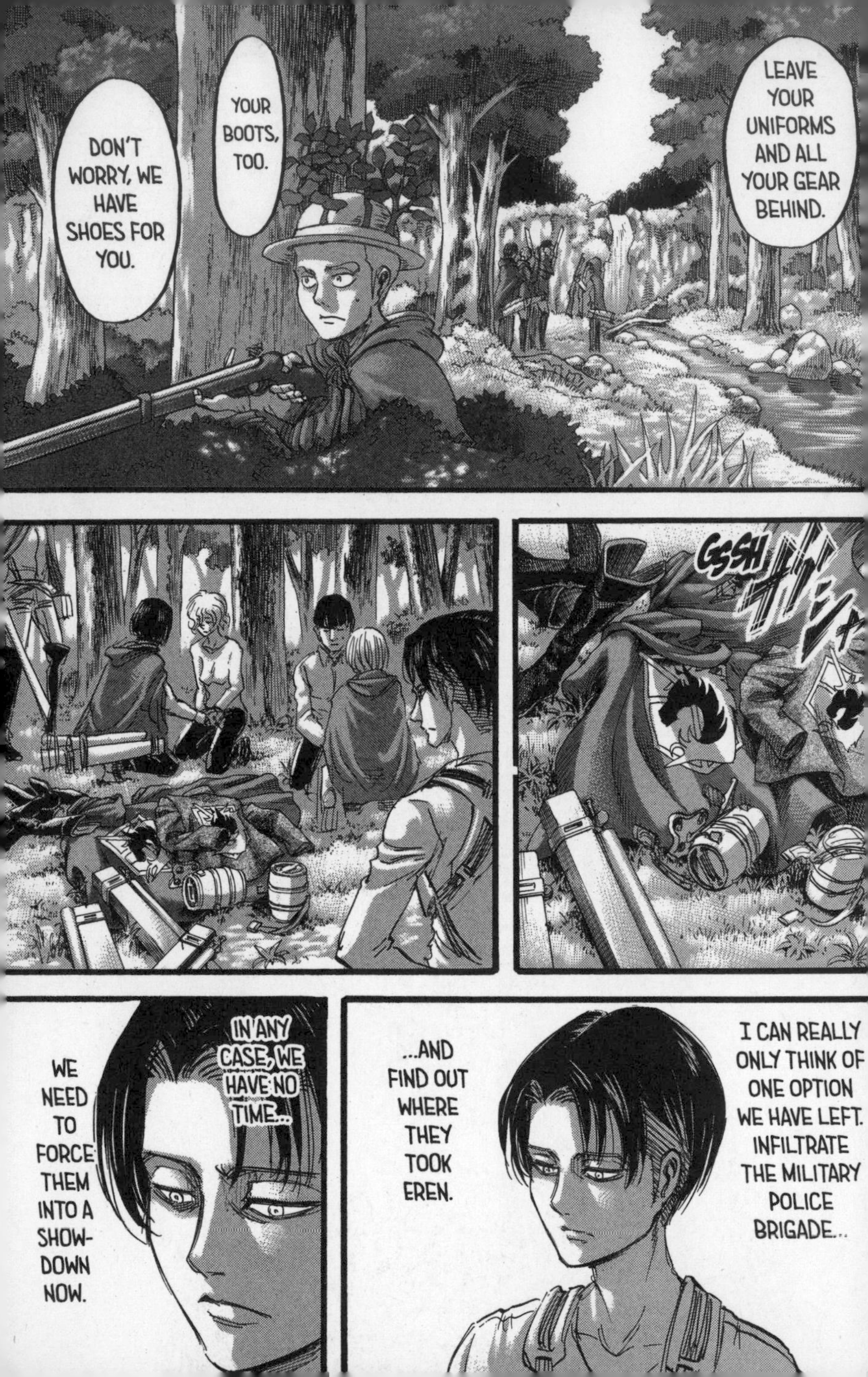
LEAVE YOUR UNIFORMS AND ALL YOUR GEAR BEHIND.
YOUR BOOTS, TOO.
DON'T WORRY, WE HAVE SHOES FOR YOU.
GSSH
I CAN REALLY ONLY THINK OF ONE OPTION WE HAVE LEFT. INFILTRATE THE MILITARY POLICE BRIGADE...
...AND FIND OUT WHERE THEY TOOK EREN.
IN ANY CASE, WE HAVE NO TIME...
WE NEED TO FORCE THEM INTO A SHOW-DOWN NOW.

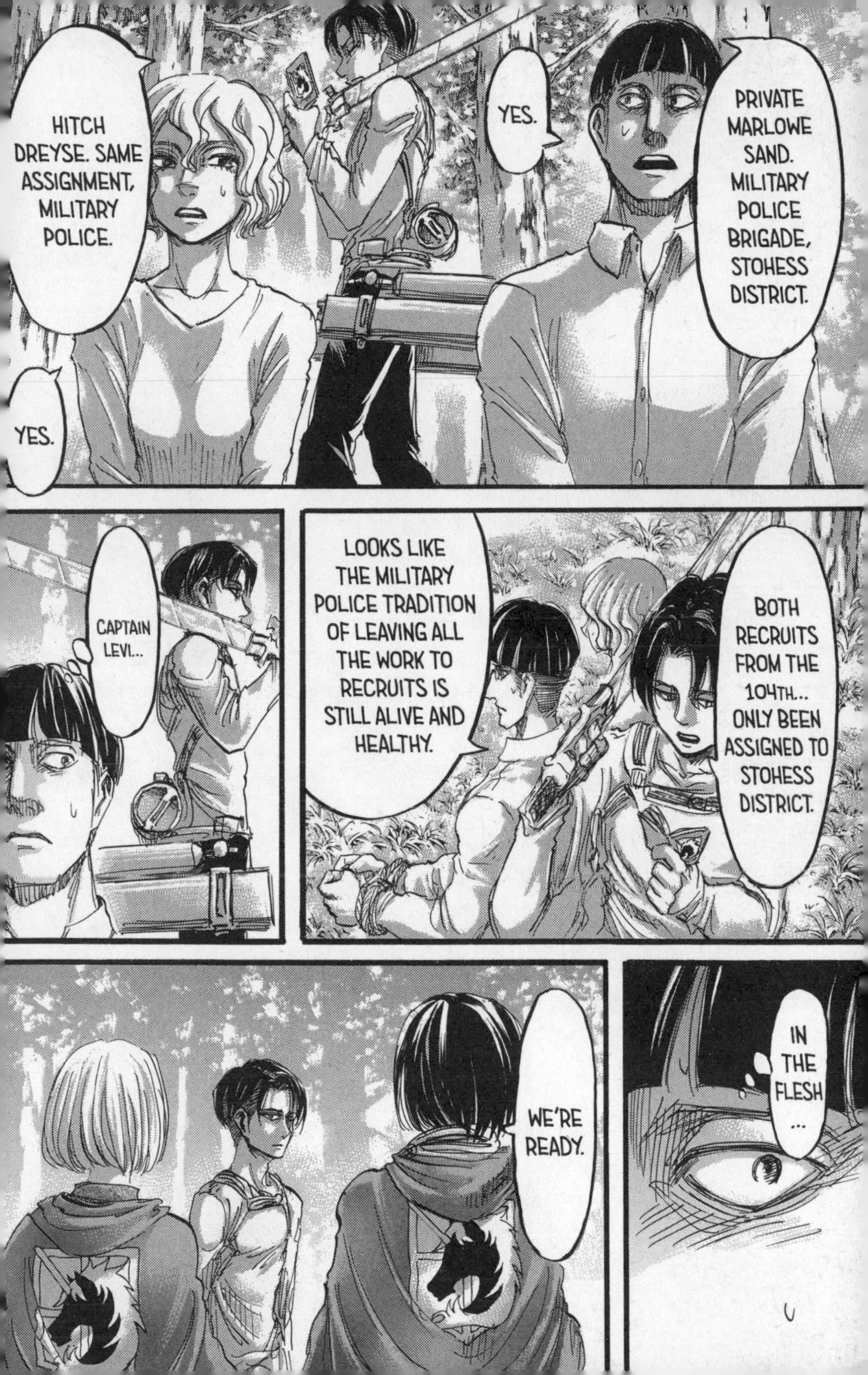
PRIVATE MARLOWE SAND. MILITARY POLICE BRIGADE, STOHESS DISTRICT.
YES.
HITCH DREYSE. SAME ASSIGNMENT, MILITARY POLICE.
YES.
BOTH RECRUITS FROM THE 104TH... ONLY BEEN ASSIGNED TO STOHESS DISTRICT.
LOOKS LIKE THE MILITARY POLICE TRADITION OF LEAVING ALL THE WORK TO RECRUITS IS STILL ALIVE AND HEALTHY.
CAPTAIN LEVI...
IN THE FLESH...
WE'RE READY.

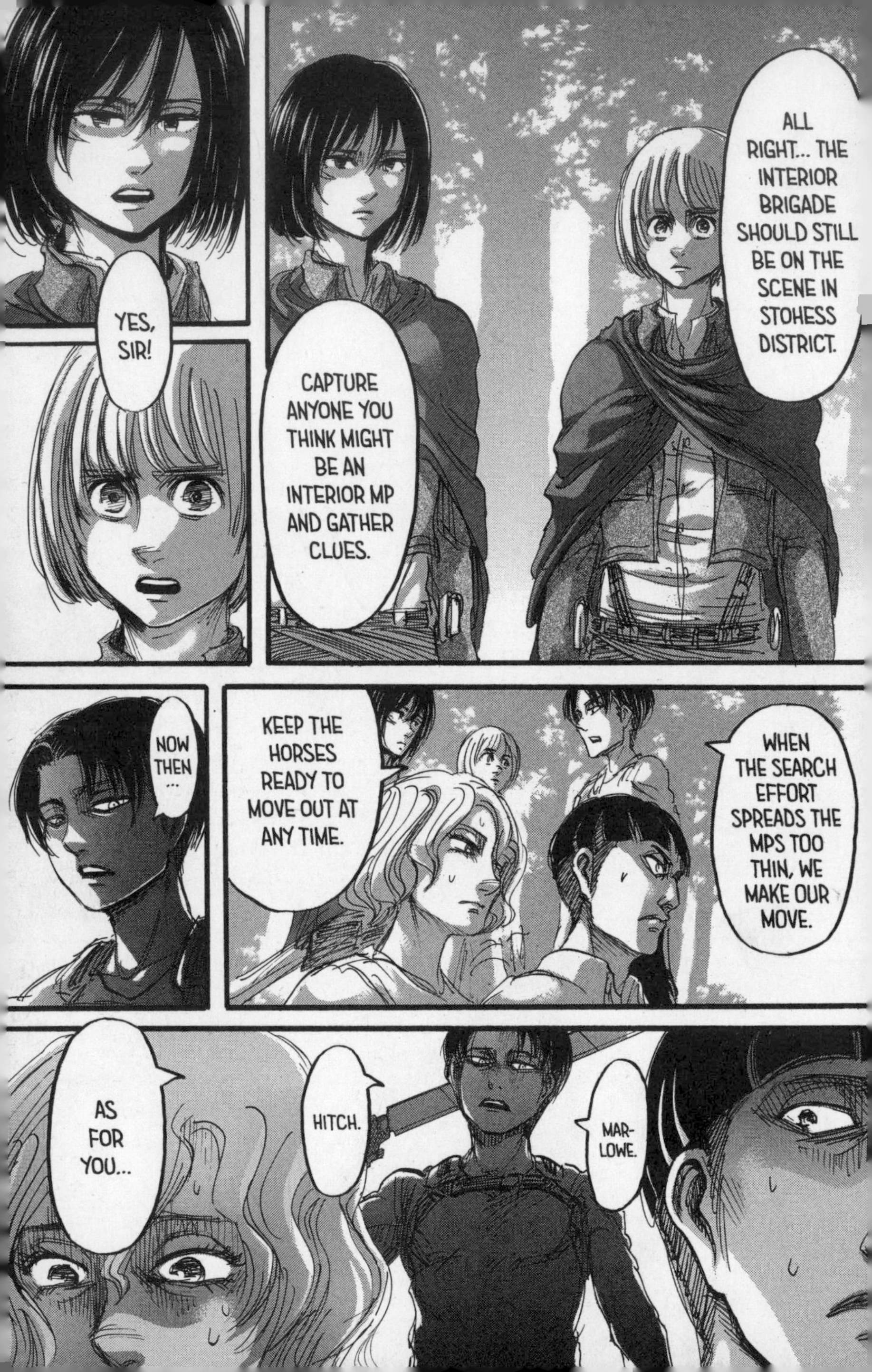
ALL RIGHT... THE INTERIOR BRIGADE SHOULD STILL BE ON THE SCENE IN STOHESS DISTRICT.
CAPTURE ANYONE YOU THINK MIGHT BE AN INTERIOR MP AND GATHER CLUES.
YES, SIR!
WHEN THE SEARCH EFFORT SPREADS THE MPS TOO THIN, WE MAKE OUR MOVE.
KEEP THE HORSES READY TO MOVE OUT AT ANY TIME.
NOW THEN ...
MAR-LOWE.
HITCH.
AS FOR YOU...

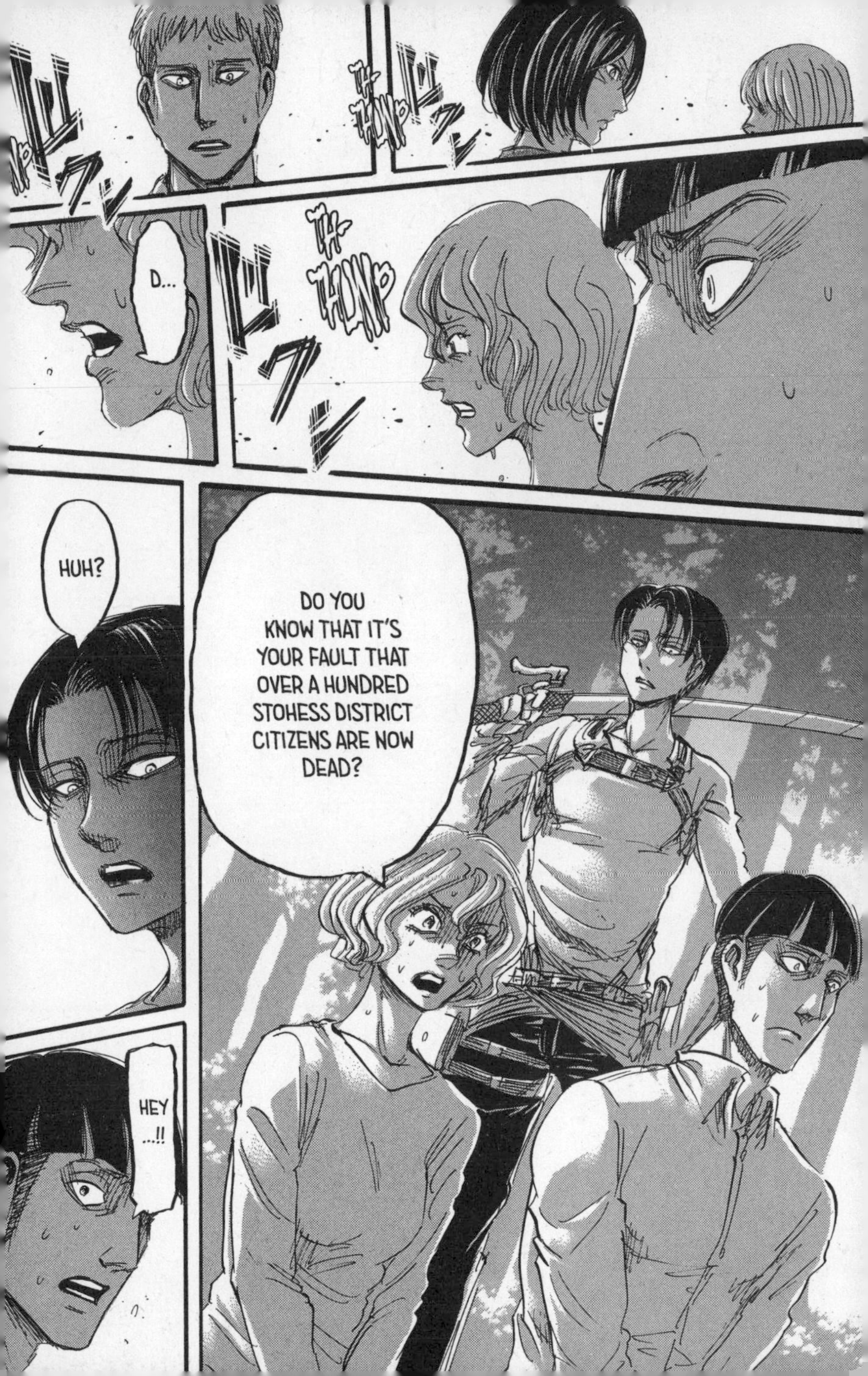
THA-THUMP
THA-THUMP
D...
DO YOU KNOW THAT IT'S YOUR FAULT THAT OVER A HUNDRED STOHESS DISTRICT CITIZENS ARE NOW DEAD?
HUH?
HEY ...!!

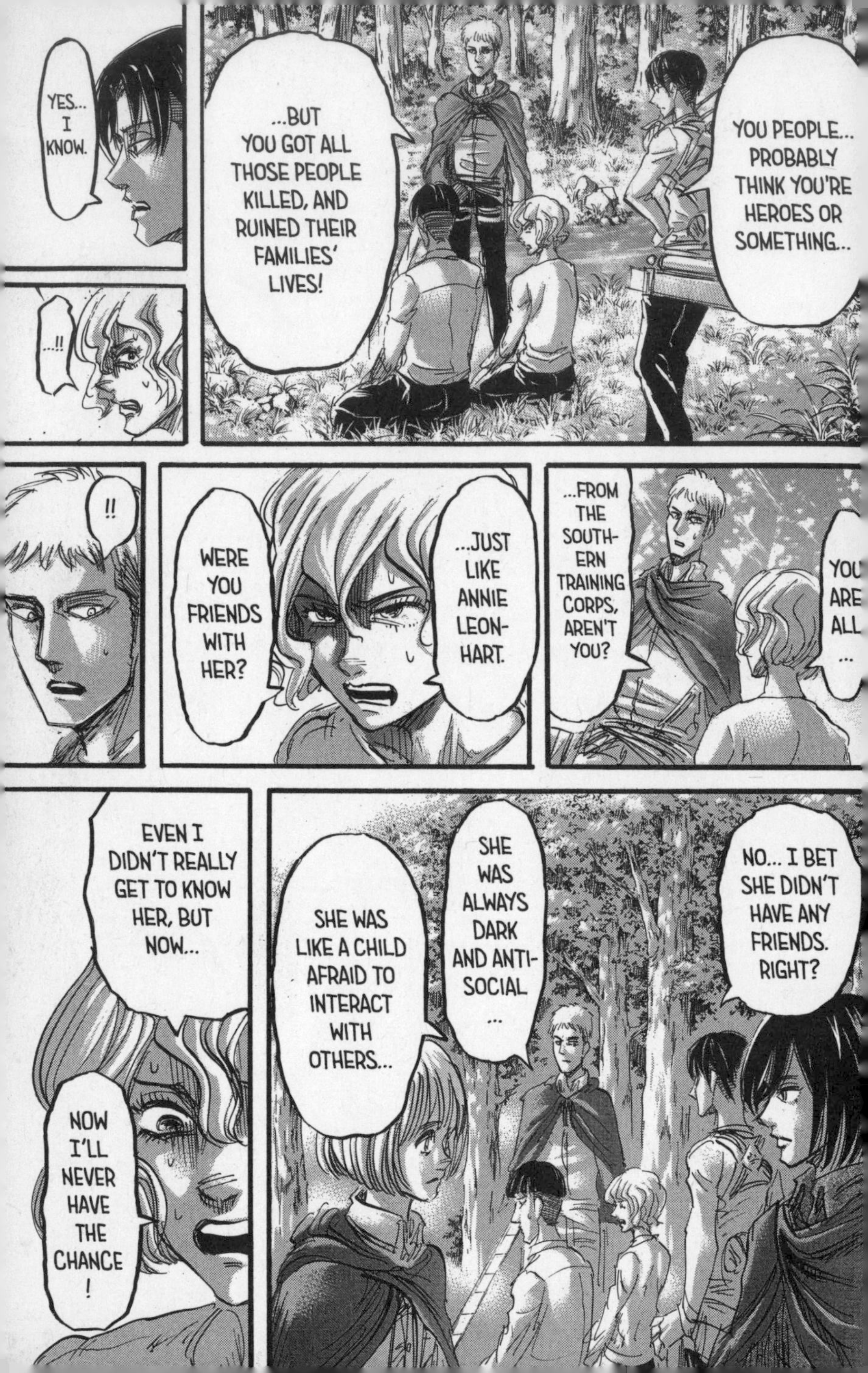
YOU PEOPLE... PROBABLY THINK YOU'RE HEROES OR SOMETHING...
...BUT YOU GOT ALL THOSE PEOPLE KILLED, AND RUINED THEIR FAMILIES' LIVES!
YES... I KNOW.
...!!
YOU ARE ALL ...
...FROM THE SOUTH-ERN TRAINING CORPS, AREN'T YOU?
...JUST LIKE ANNIE LEON-HART.
WERE YOU FRIENDS WITH HER?
!!
NO... I BET SHE DIDN'T HAVE ANY FRIENDS. RIGHT?
SHE WAS ALWAYS DARK AND ANTI-SOCIAL ...
SHE WAS LIKE A CHILD AFRAID TO INTERACT WITH OTHERS...
EVEN I DIDN'T REALLY GET TO KNOW HER, BUT NOW...
NOW I'LL NEVER HAVE THE CHANCE !

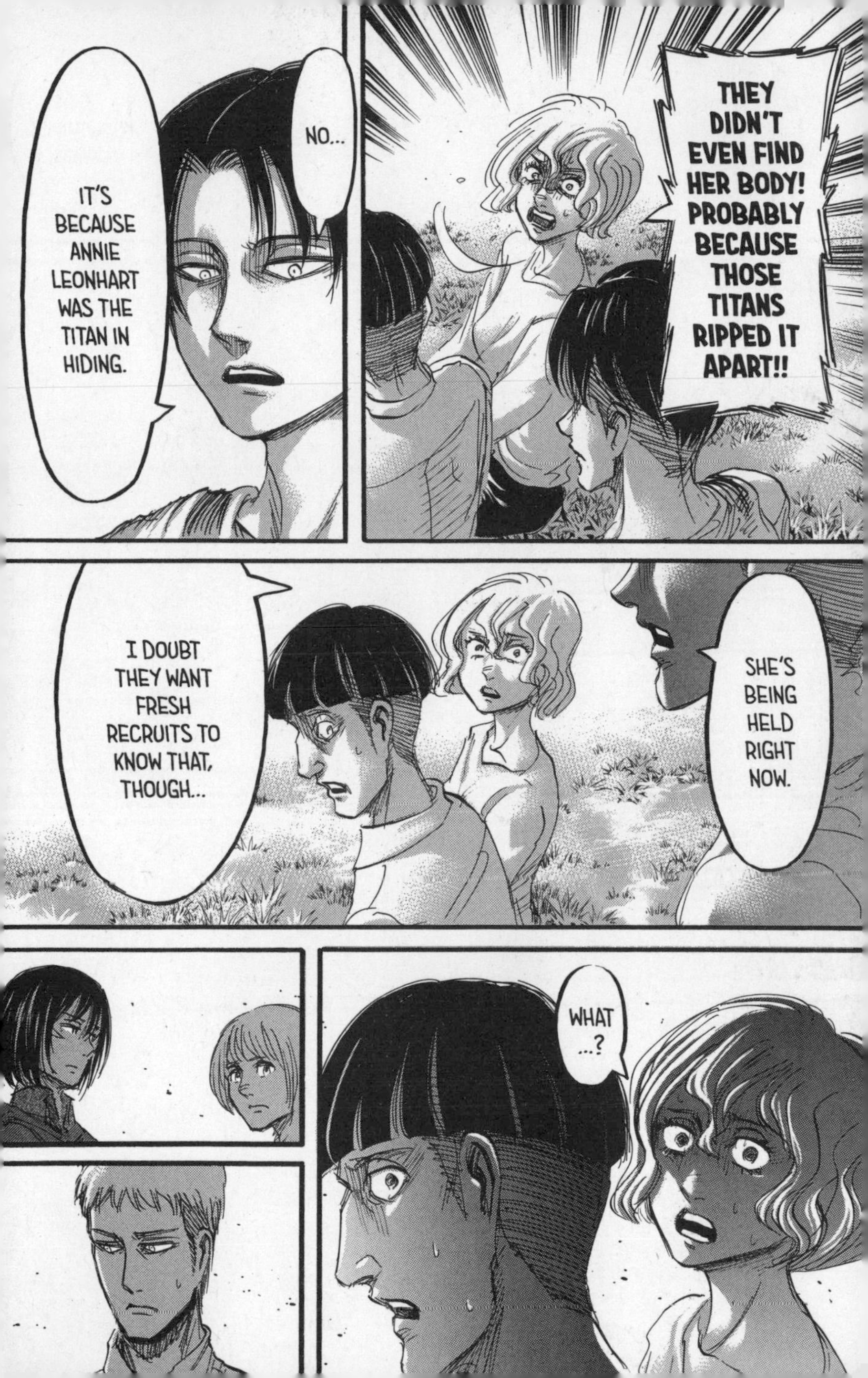
THEY DIDN'T EVEN FIND HER BODY! PROBABLY BECAUSE THOSE TITANS RIPPED IT APART!!
NO...
IT'S BECAUSE ANNIE LEONHART WAS THE TITAN IN HIDING.
SHE'S BEING HELD RIGHT NOW.
I DOUBT THEY WANT FRESH RECRUITS TO KNOW THAT, THOUGH...
WHAT ...?

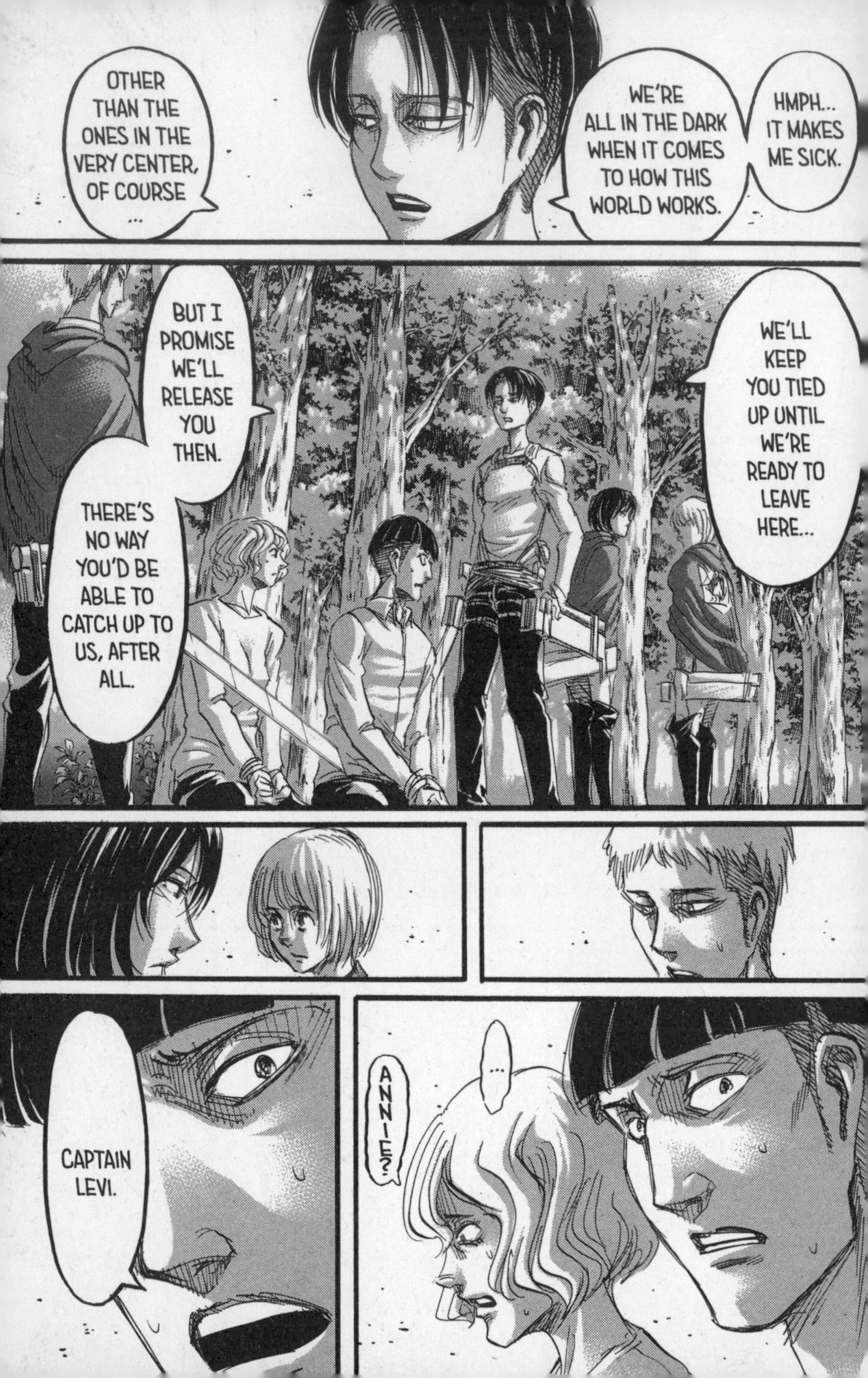
HMPH... IT MAKES ME SICK.
WE'RE ALL IN THE DARK WHEN IT COMES TO HOW THIS WORLD WORKS.
OTHER THAN THE ONES IN THE VERY CENTER, OF COURSE ...
WE'LL KEEP YOU TIED UP UNTIL WE'RE READY TO LEAVE HERE...
BUT I PROMISE WE'LL RELEASE YOU THEN.
THERE'S NO WAY YOU'D BE ABLE TO CATCH UP TO US, AFTER ALL.
...
ANNIE?
CAPTAIN LEVI.

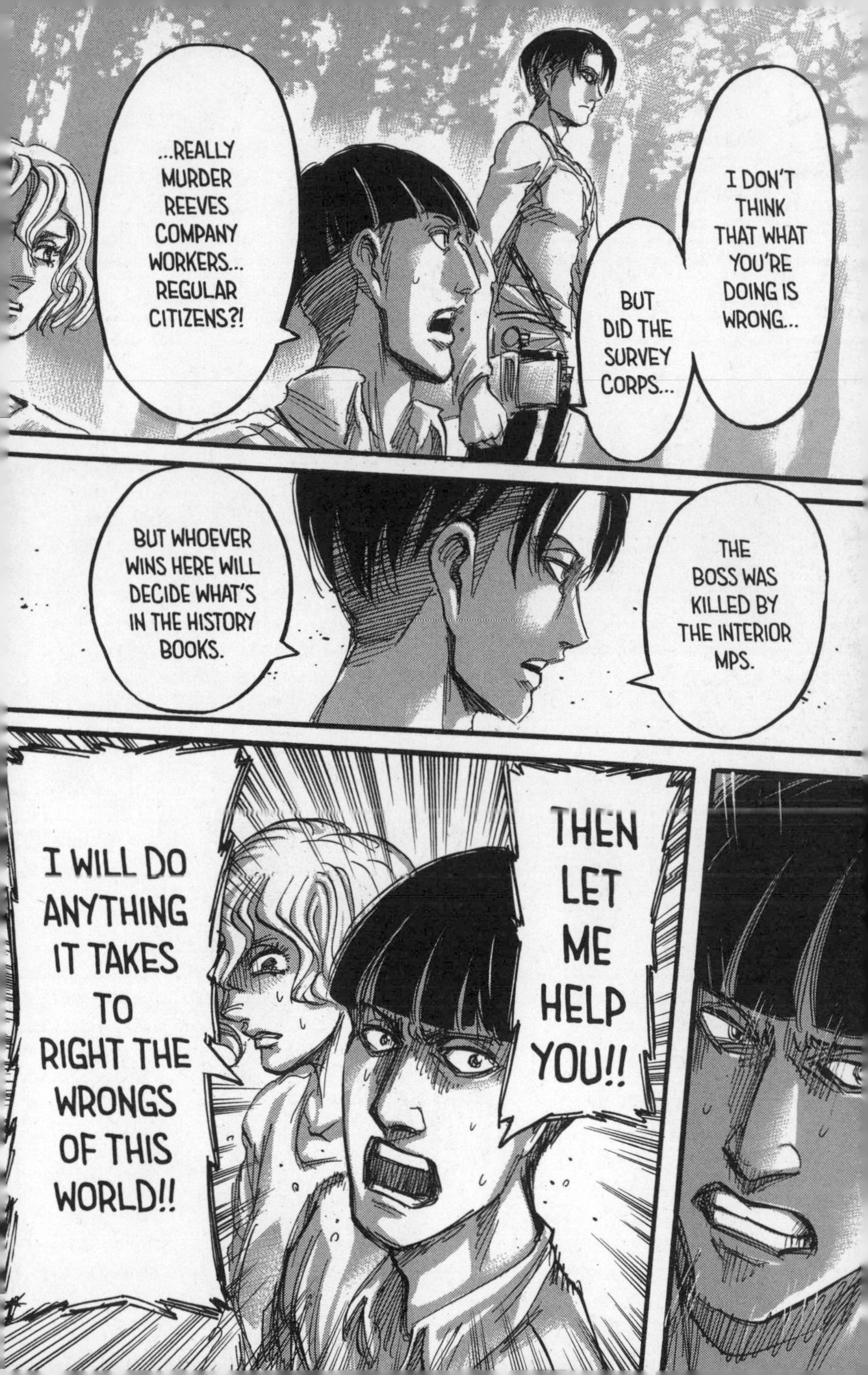
I DON'T THINK THAT WHAT YOU'RE DOING IS WRONG...
BUT DID THE SURVEY CORPS...
...REALLY MURDER REEVES COMPANY WORKERS... REGULAR CITIZENS?!
THE BOSS WAS KILLED BY THE INTERIOR MPS.
BUT WHOEVER WINS HERE WILL DECIDE WHAT'S IN THE HISTORY BOOKS.
THEN LET ME HELP YOU!!
I WILL DO ANYTHING IT TAKES TO RIGHT THE WRONGS OF THIS WORLD!!

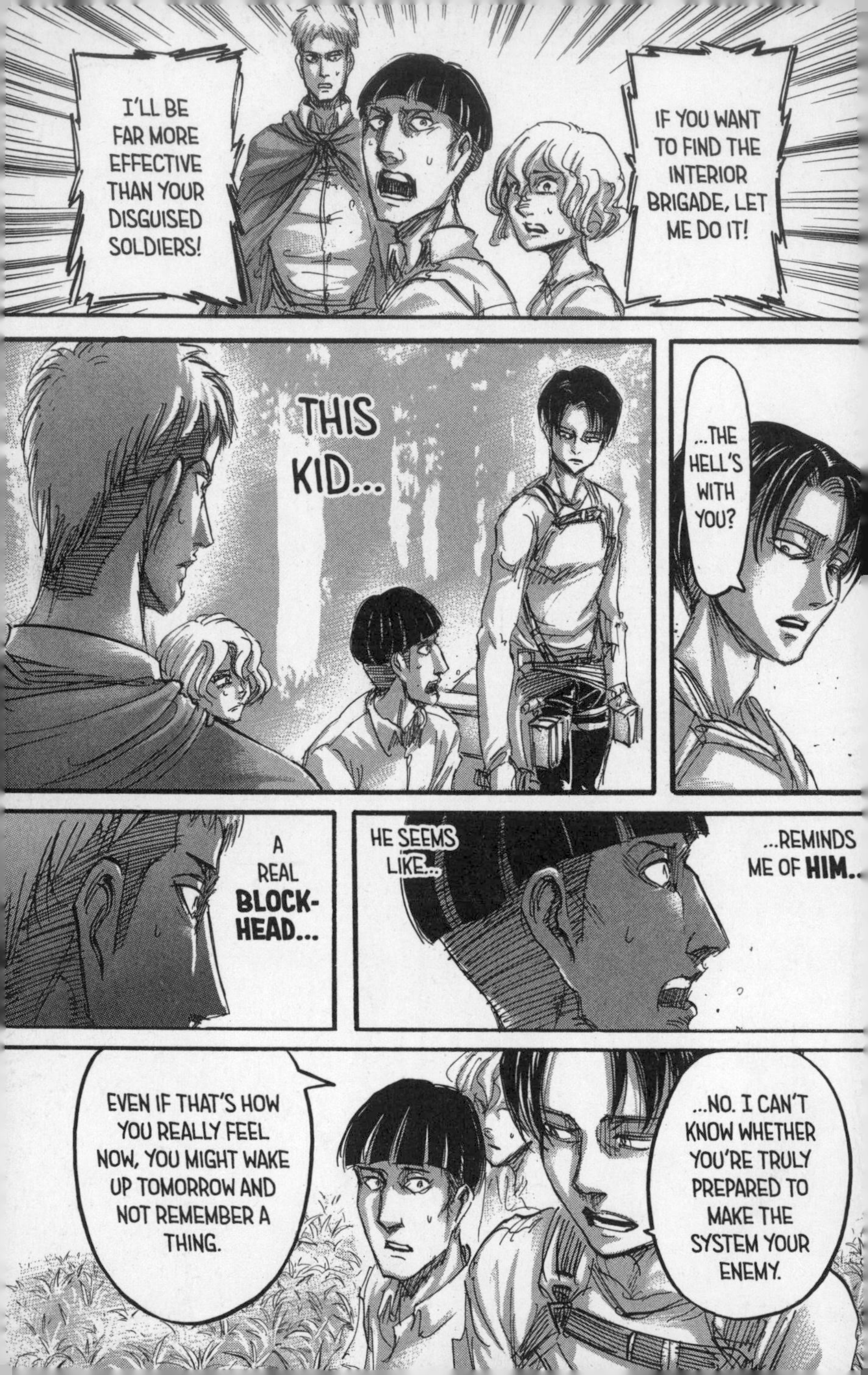
IF YOU WANT TO FIND THE INTERIOR BRIGADE, LET ME DO IT!
I'LL BE FAR MORE EFFECTIVE THAN YOUR DISGUISED SOLDIERS!
...THE HELL'S WITH YOU?
THIS KID...
...REMINDS ME OF **HIM**..
HE SEEMS LIKE...
A REAL **BLOCK-HEAD...**
...NO. I CAN'T KNOW WHETHER YOU'RE TRULY PREPARED TO MAKE THE SYSTEM YOUR ENEMY.
EVEN IF THAT'S HOW YOU REALLY FEEL NOW, YOU MIGHT WAKE UP TOMORROW AND NOT REMEMBER A THING.

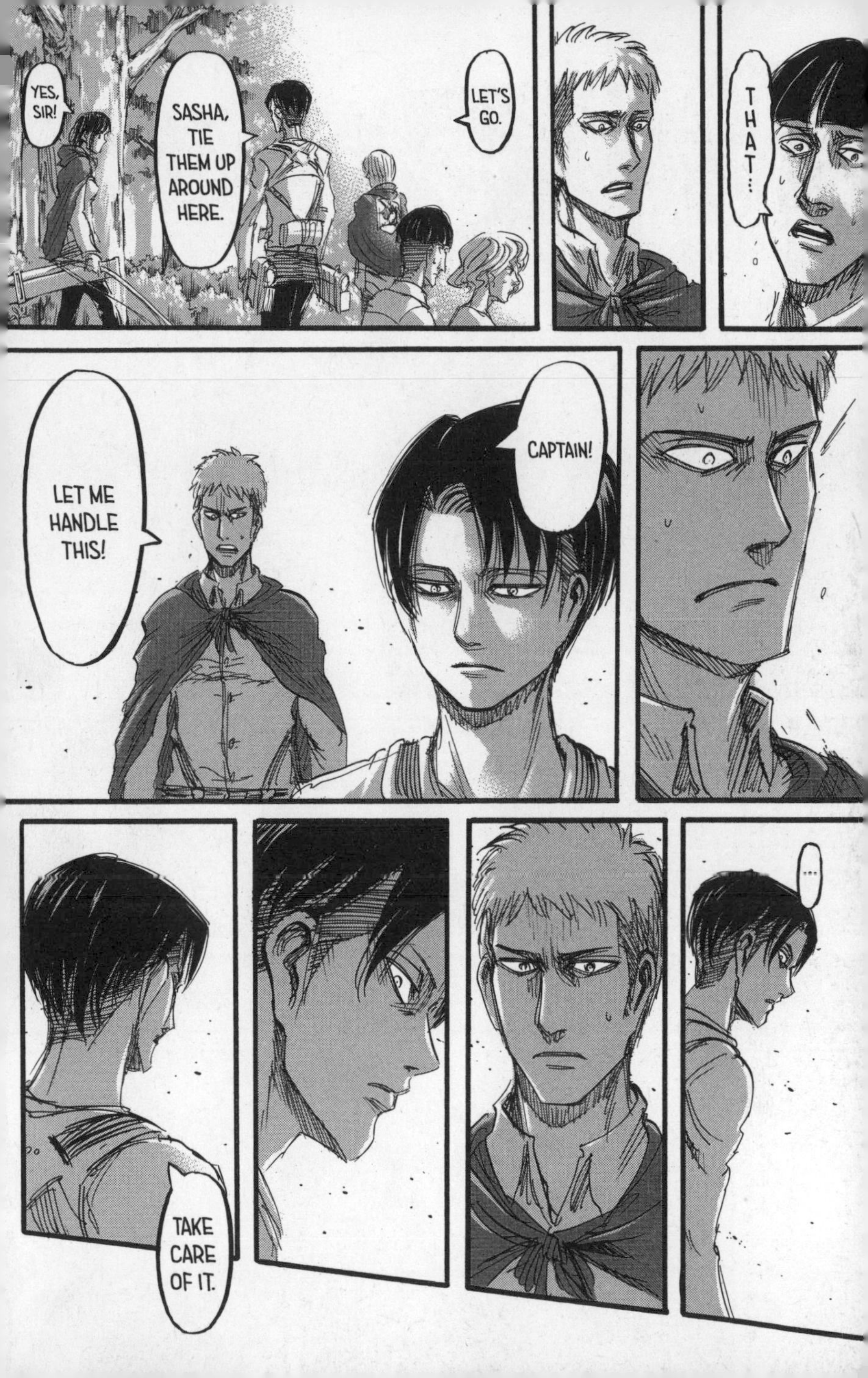
THAT...
LET'S GO.
SASHA, TIE THEM UP AROUND HERE.
YES, SIR!
CAPTAIN!
LET ME HANDLE THIS!
...
TAKE CARE OF IT.

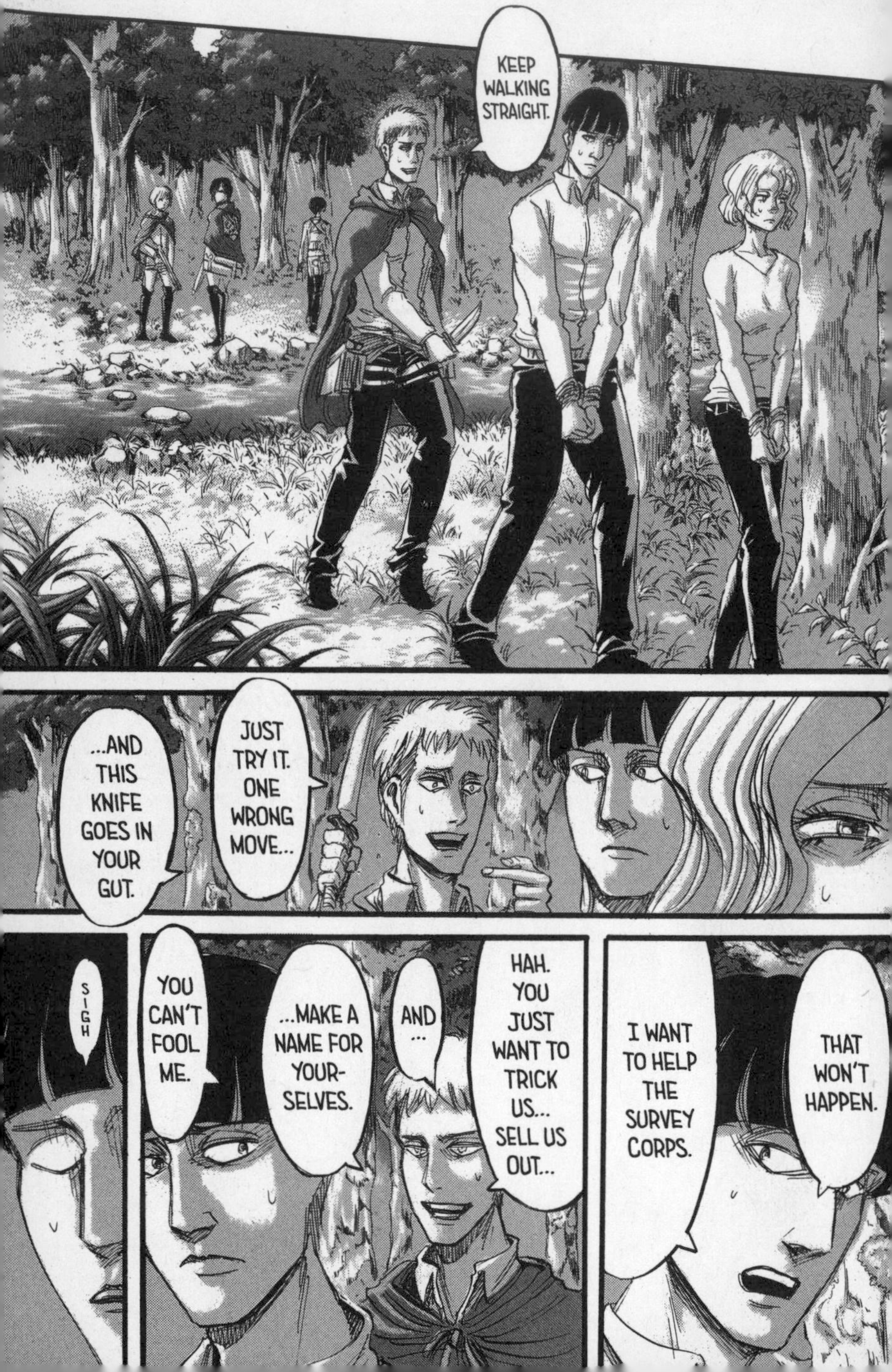
KEEP WALKING STRAIGHT.
JUST TRY IT. ONE WRONG MOVE...
...AND THIS KNIFE GOES IN YOUR GUT.
THAT WON'T HAPPEN.
I WANT TO HELP THE SURVEY CORPS.
HAH. YOU JUST WANT TO TRICK US... SELL US OUT...
AND...
...MAKE A NAME FOR YOUR-SELVES.
YOU CAN'T FOOL ME.
SIGH

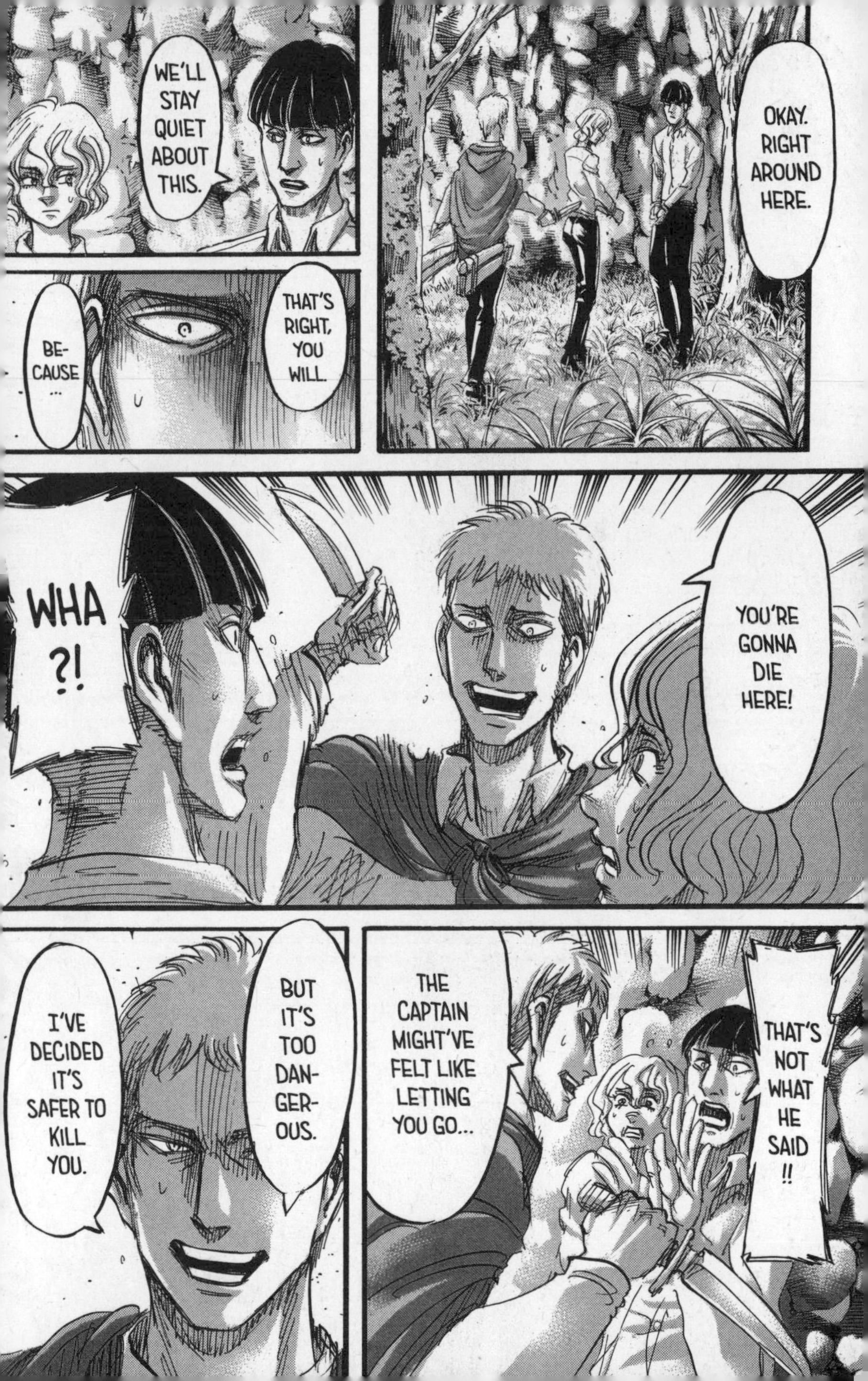
OKAY. RIGHT AROUND HERE.
WE'LL STAY QUIET ABOUT THIS.
THAT'S RIGHT, YOU WILL.
BE-CAUSE ...
YOU'RE GONNA DIE HERE!
WHA ?!
THAT'S NOT WHAT HE SAID !!
THE CAPTAIN MIGHT'VE FELT LIKE LETTING YOU GO...
BUT IT'S TOO DAN-GER-OUS.
I'VE DECIDED IT'S SAFER TO KILL YOU.

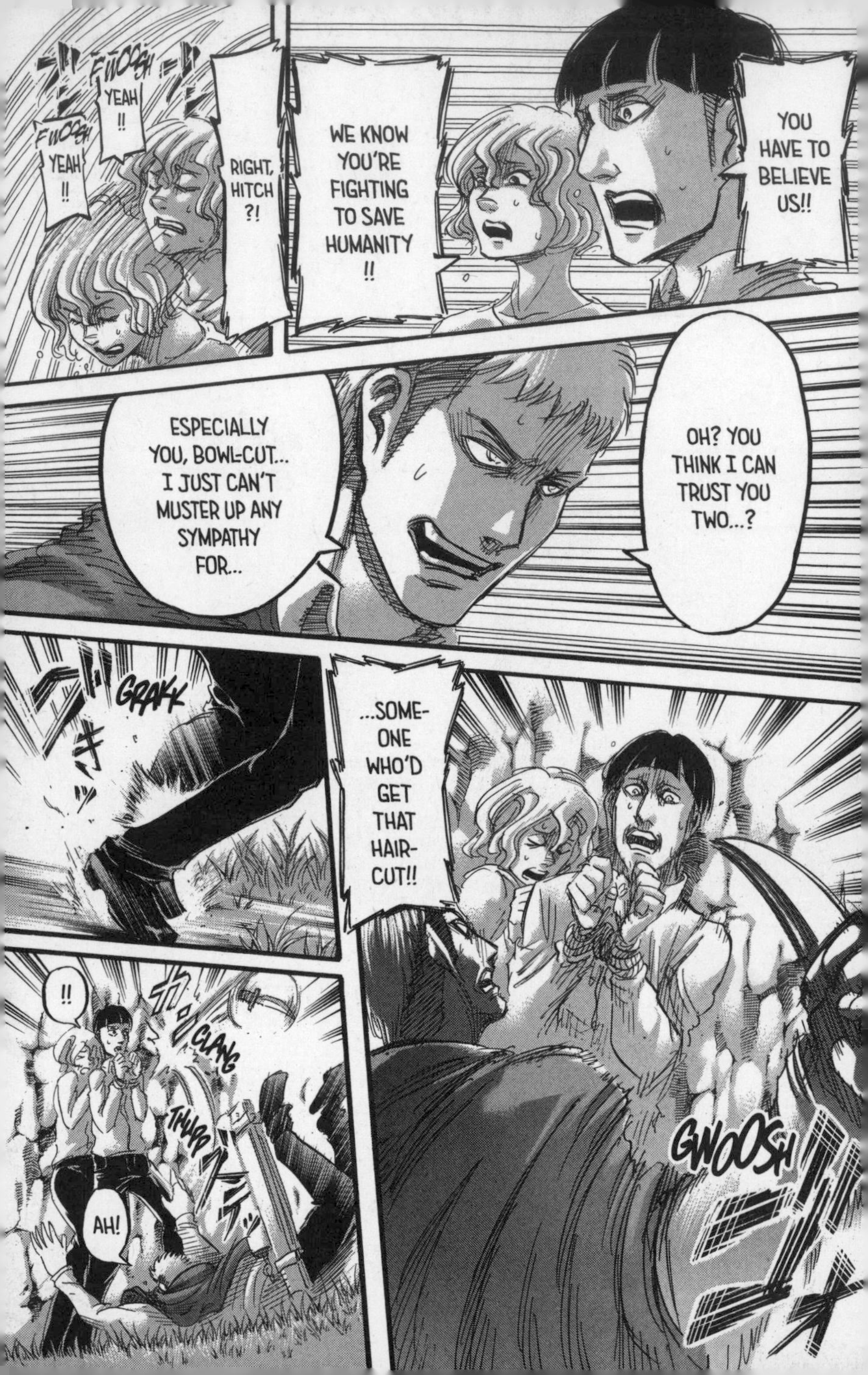
YOU HAVE TO BELIEVE US!!
WE KNOW YOU'RE FIGHTING TO SAVE HUMANITY !!
RIGHT, HITCH ?!
FWOOSH
YEAH !!
FWOOSH
YEAH !!
OH? YOU THINK I CAN TRUST YOU TWO...?
ESPECIALLY YOU, BOWL-CUT... I JUST CAN'T MUSTER UP ANY SYMPATHY FOR...
...SOME-ONE WHO'D GET THAT HAIR-CUT!!
GWOOSH
GRAKK
!!
CLANG
THUPP
AH!

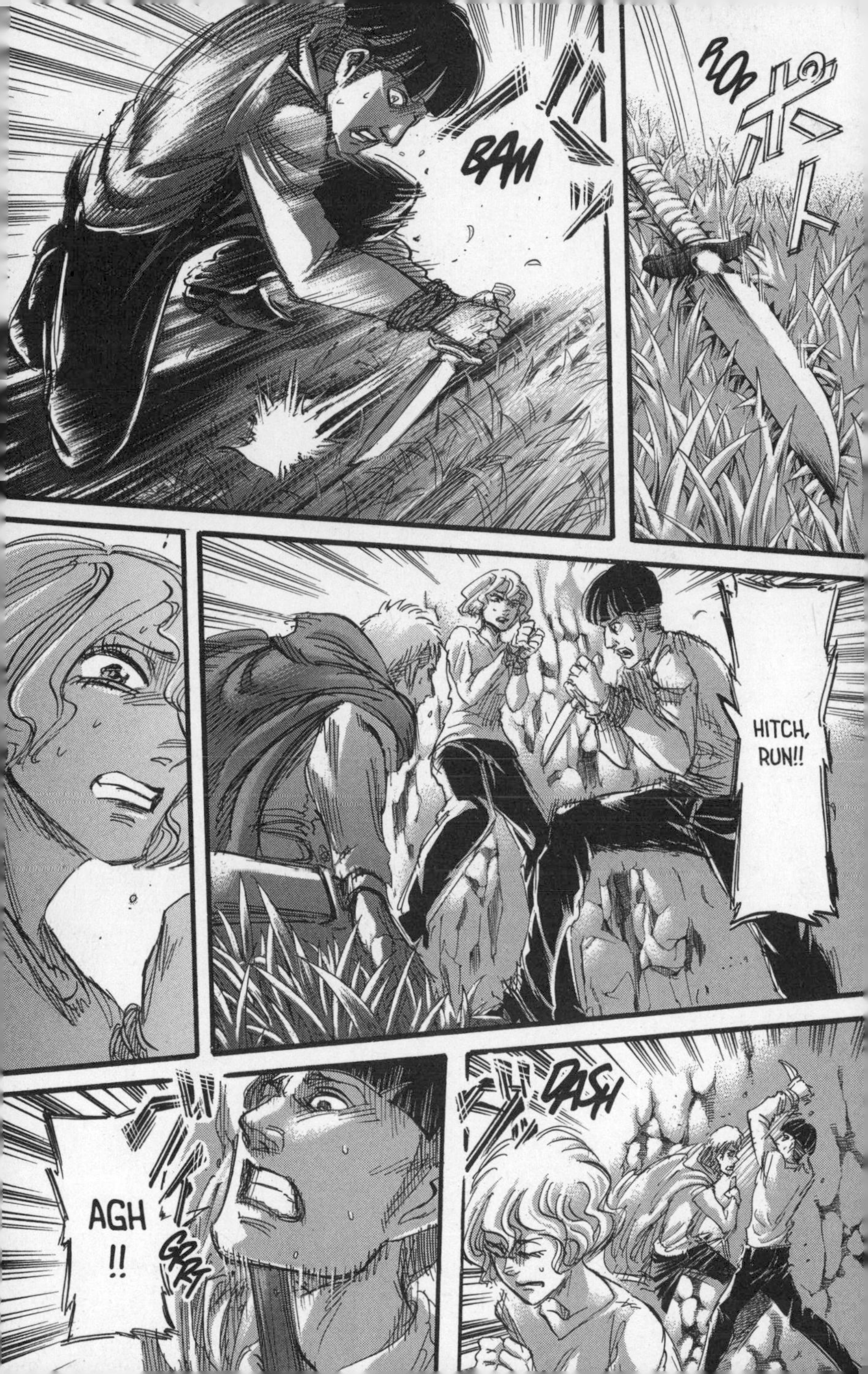
PLOP
BAM
HITCH, RUN!!
DASH
AGH !!

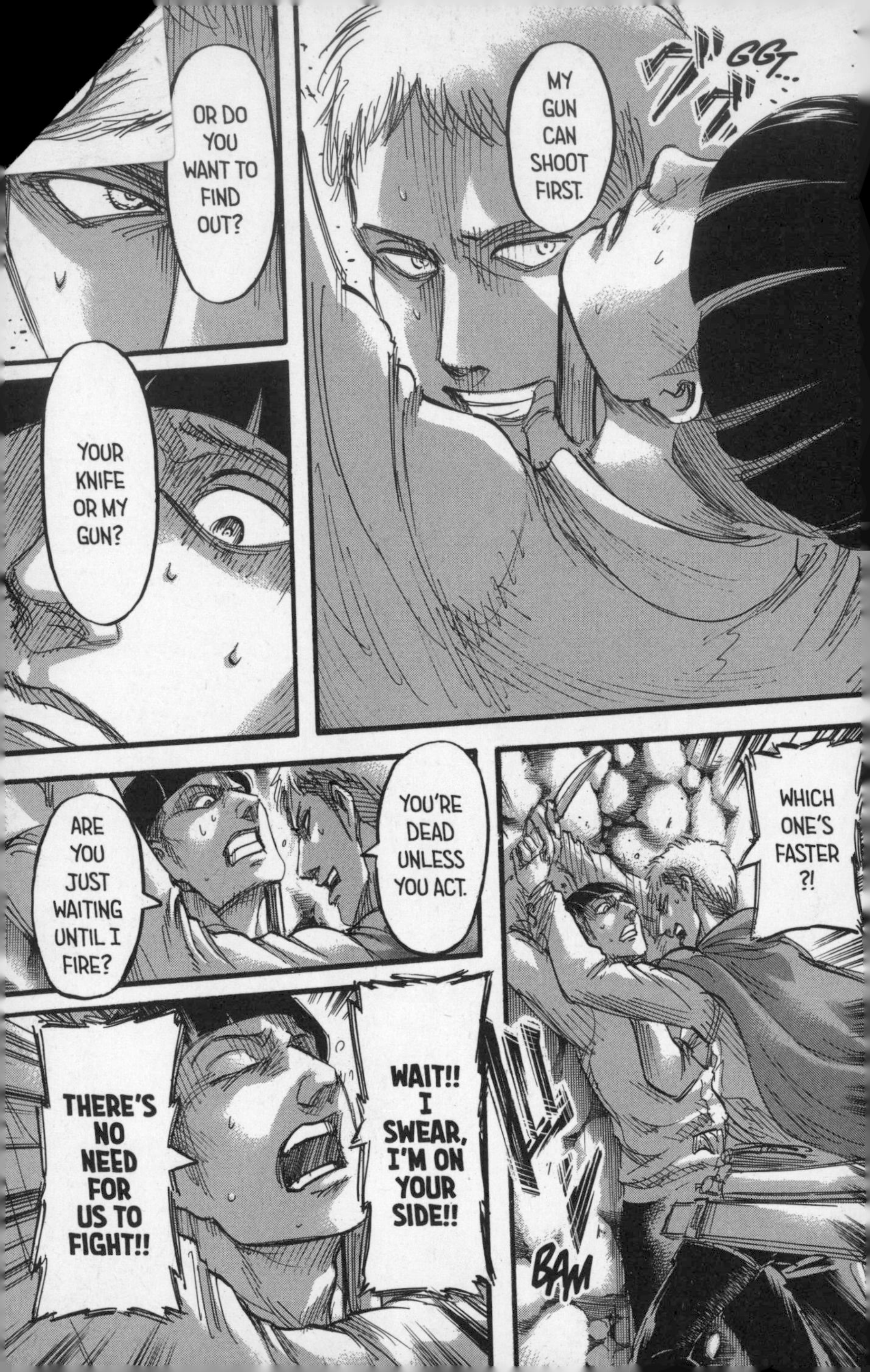
GGT...
MY GUN CAN SHOOT FIRST.
OR DO YOU WANT TO FIND OUT?
YOUR KNIFE OR MY GUN?
WHICH ONE'S FASTER ?!
BAM
YOU'RE DEAD UNLESS YOU ACT.
ARE YOU JUST WAITING UNTIL I FIRE?
WAIT!! I SWEAR, I'M ON YOUR SIDE!!
THERE'S NO NEED FOR US TO FIGHT!!

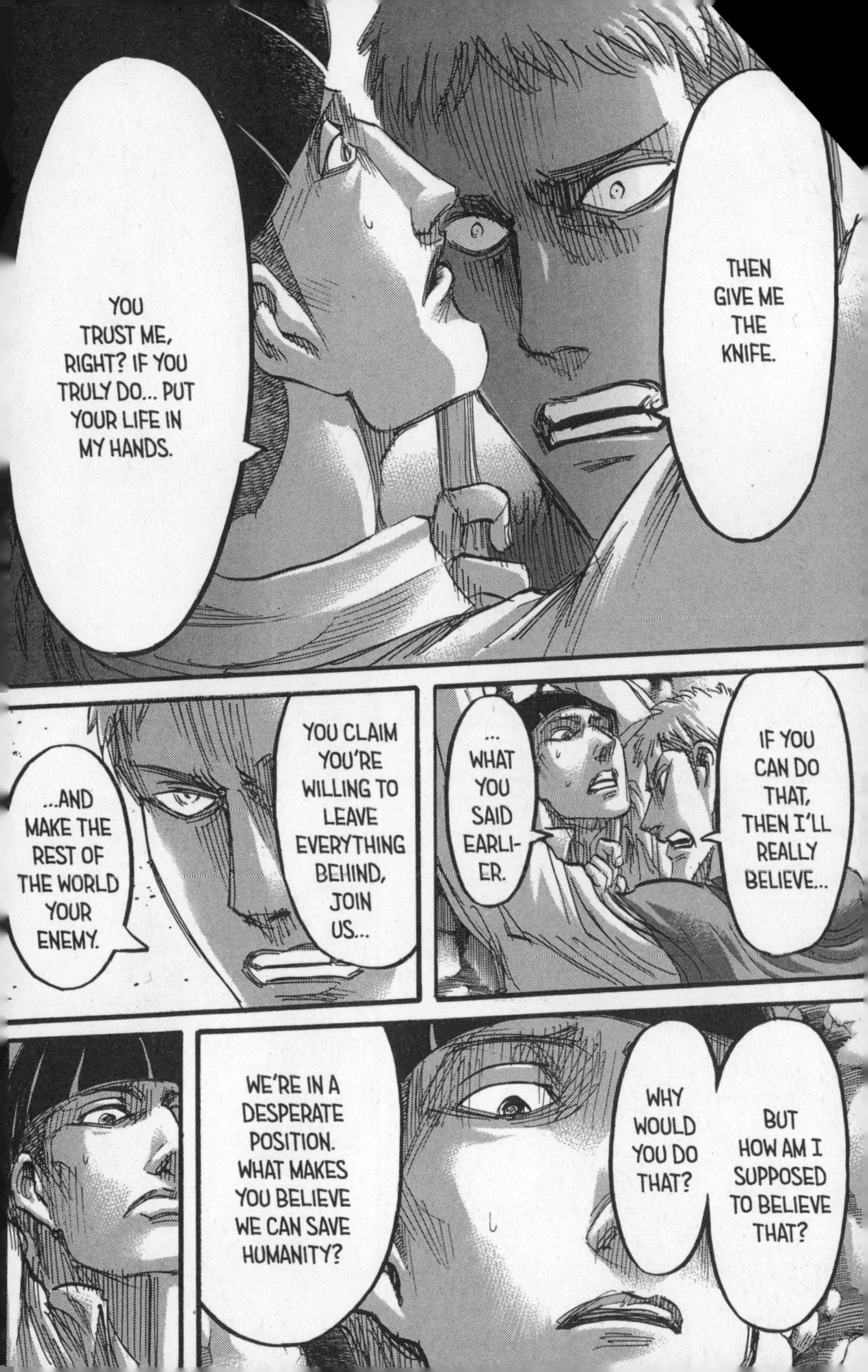
THEN GIVE ME THE KNIFE.
YOU TRUST ME, RIGHT? IF YOU TRULY DO... PUT YOUR LIFE IN MY HANDS.
IF YOU CAN DO THAT, THEN I'LL REALLY BELIEVE...
...WHAT YOU SAID EARLIER.
YOU CLAIM YOU'RE WILLING TO LEAVE EVERYTHING BEHIND, JOIN US...
...AND MAKE THE REST OF THE WORLD YOUR ENEMY.
BUT HOW AM I SUPPOSED TO BELIEVE THAT?
WHY WOULD YOU DO THAT?
WE'RE IN A DESPERATE POSITION. WHAT MAKES YOU BELIEVE WE CAN SAVE HUMANITY?

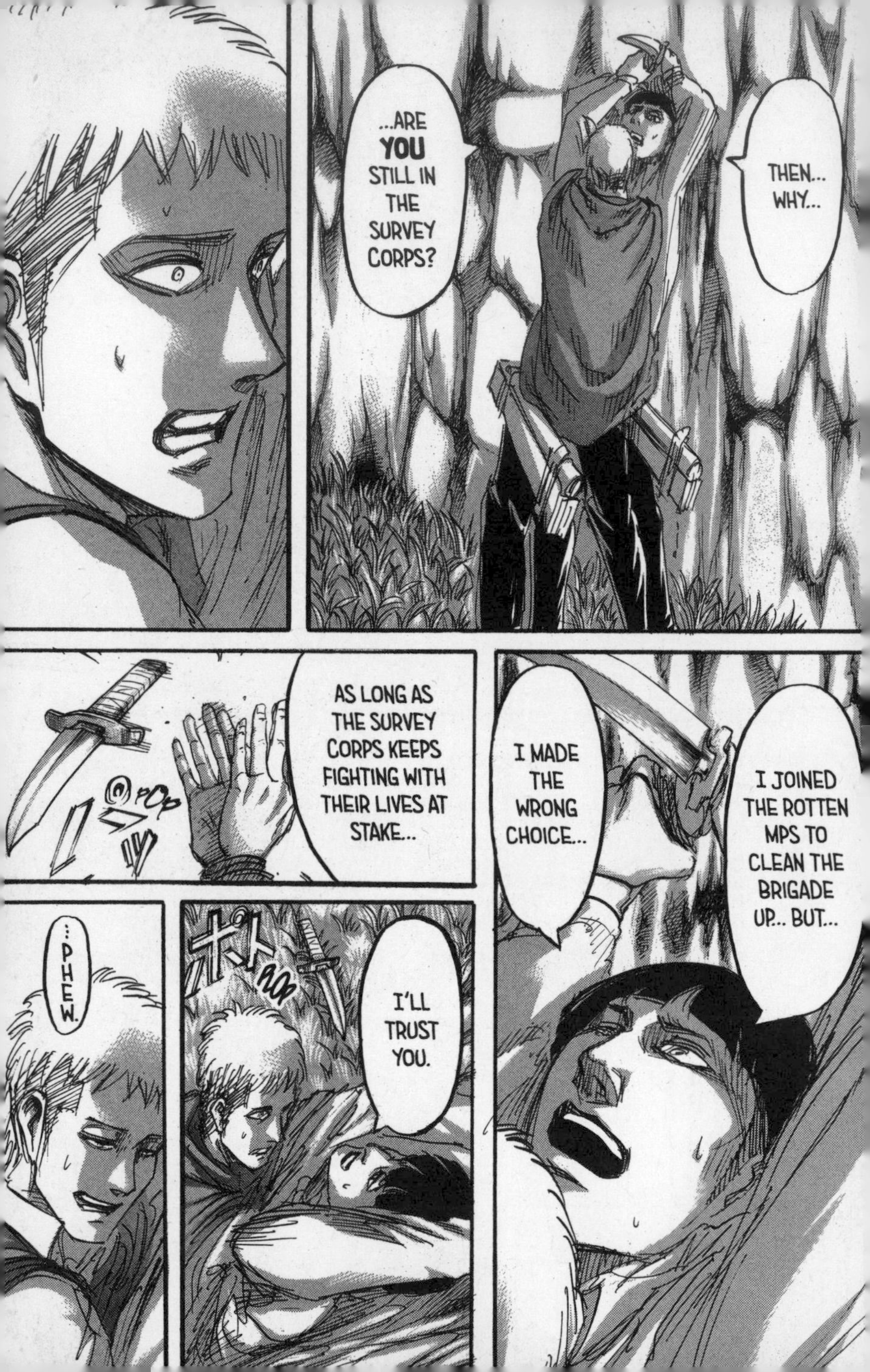
THEN... WHY...
...ARE **YOU** STILL IN THE SURVEY CORPS?
I JOINED THE ROTTEN MPS TO CLEAN THE BRIGADE UP... BUT...
I MADE THE WRONG CHOICE...
AS LONG AS THE SURVEY CORPS KEEPS FIGHTING WITH THEIR LIVES AT STAKE...
POP
I'LL TRUST YOU.
PLOP
...PHEW.

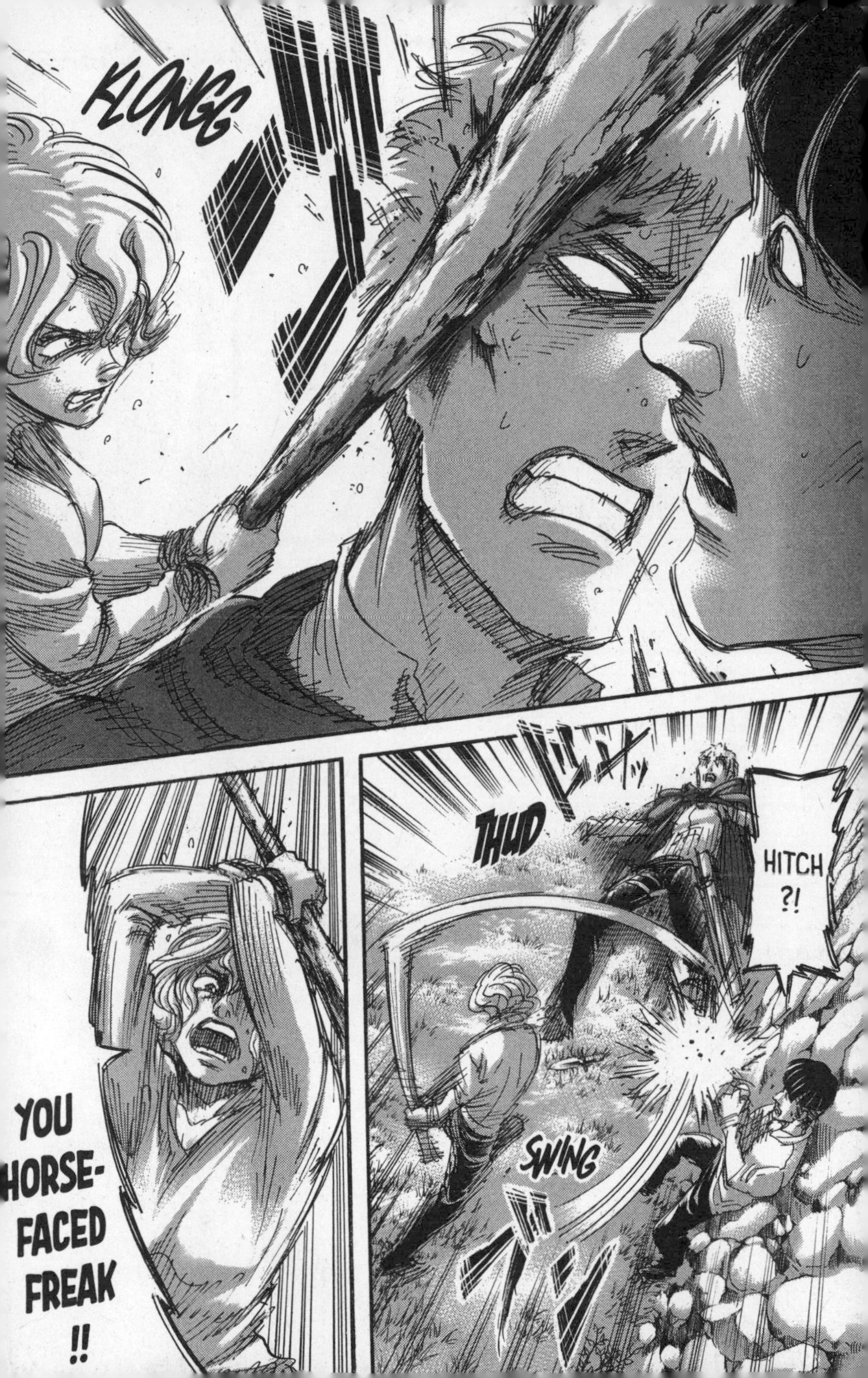
KLONGG
THUD
HITCH ?!
SWING
YOU HORSE-FACED FREAK !!

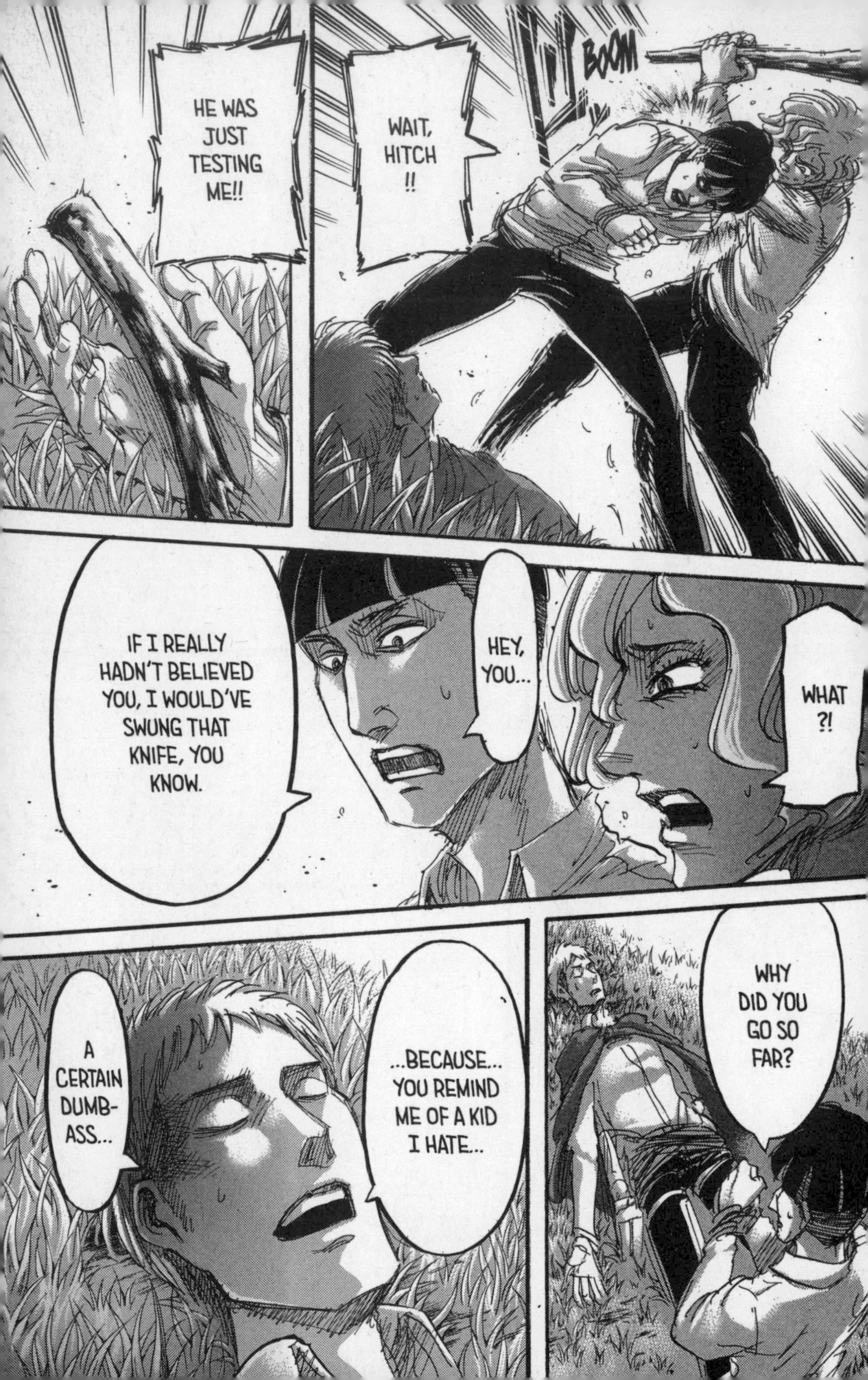
BOOM
WAIT, HITCH !!
HE WAS JUST TESTING ME!!
WHAT ?!
HEY, YOU...
IF I REALLY HADN'T BELIEVED YOU, I WOULD'VE SWUNG THAT KNIFE, YOU KNOW.
WHY DID YOU GO SO FAR?
...BECAUSE... YOU REMIND ME OF A KID I HATE...
A CERTAIN DUMB-ASS...

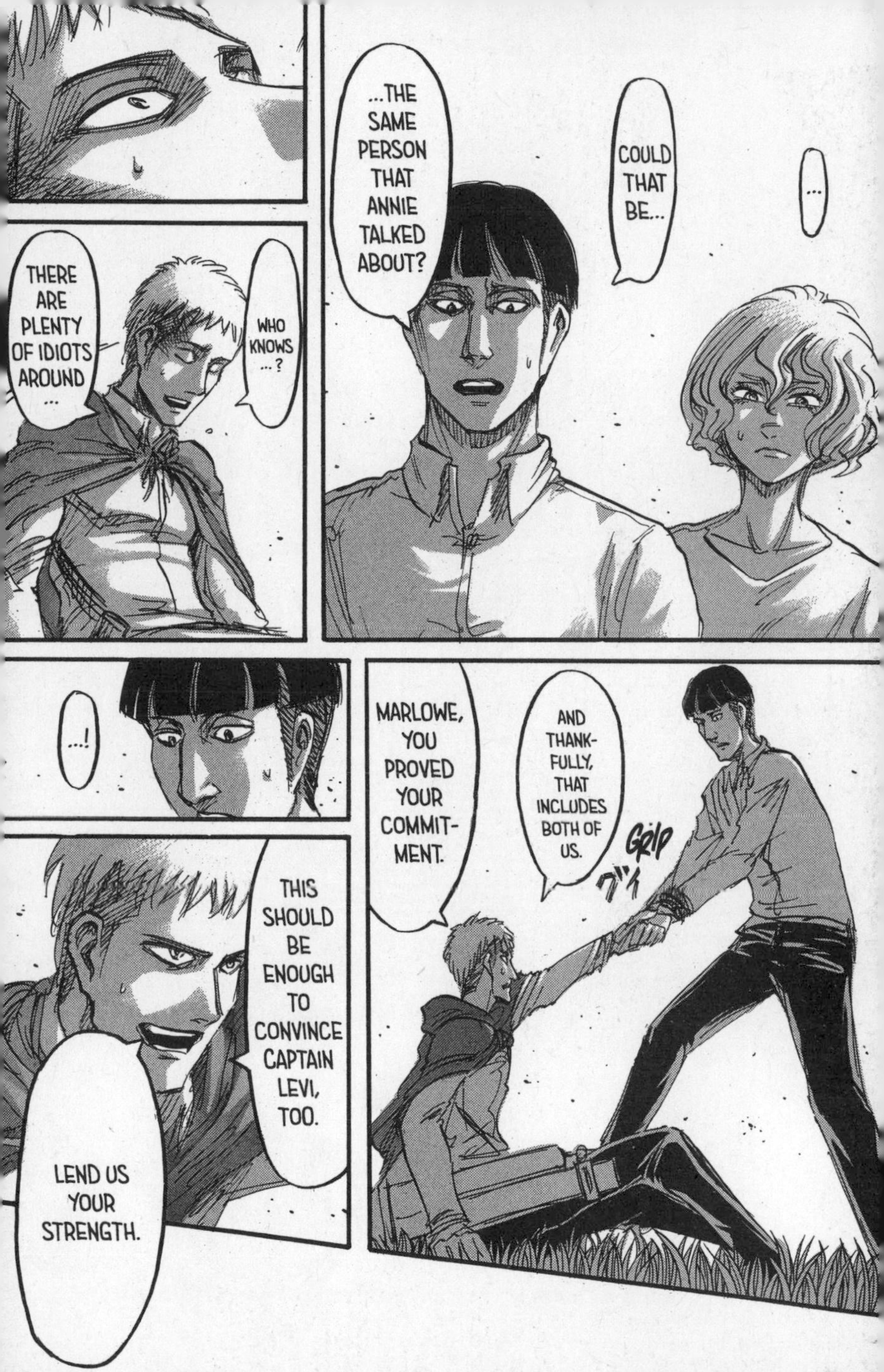
...
COULD THAT BE...
...THE SAME PERSON THAT ANNIE TALKED ABOUT?
WHO KNOWS...?
THERE ARE PLENTY OF IDIOTS AROUND...
AND THANKFULLY, THAT INCLUDES BOTH OF US.
MARLOWE, YOU PROVED YOUR COMMITMENT.
GRIP
...!
THIS SHOULD BE ENOUGH TO CONVINCE CAPTAIN LEVI, TOO.
LEND US YOUR STRENGTH.

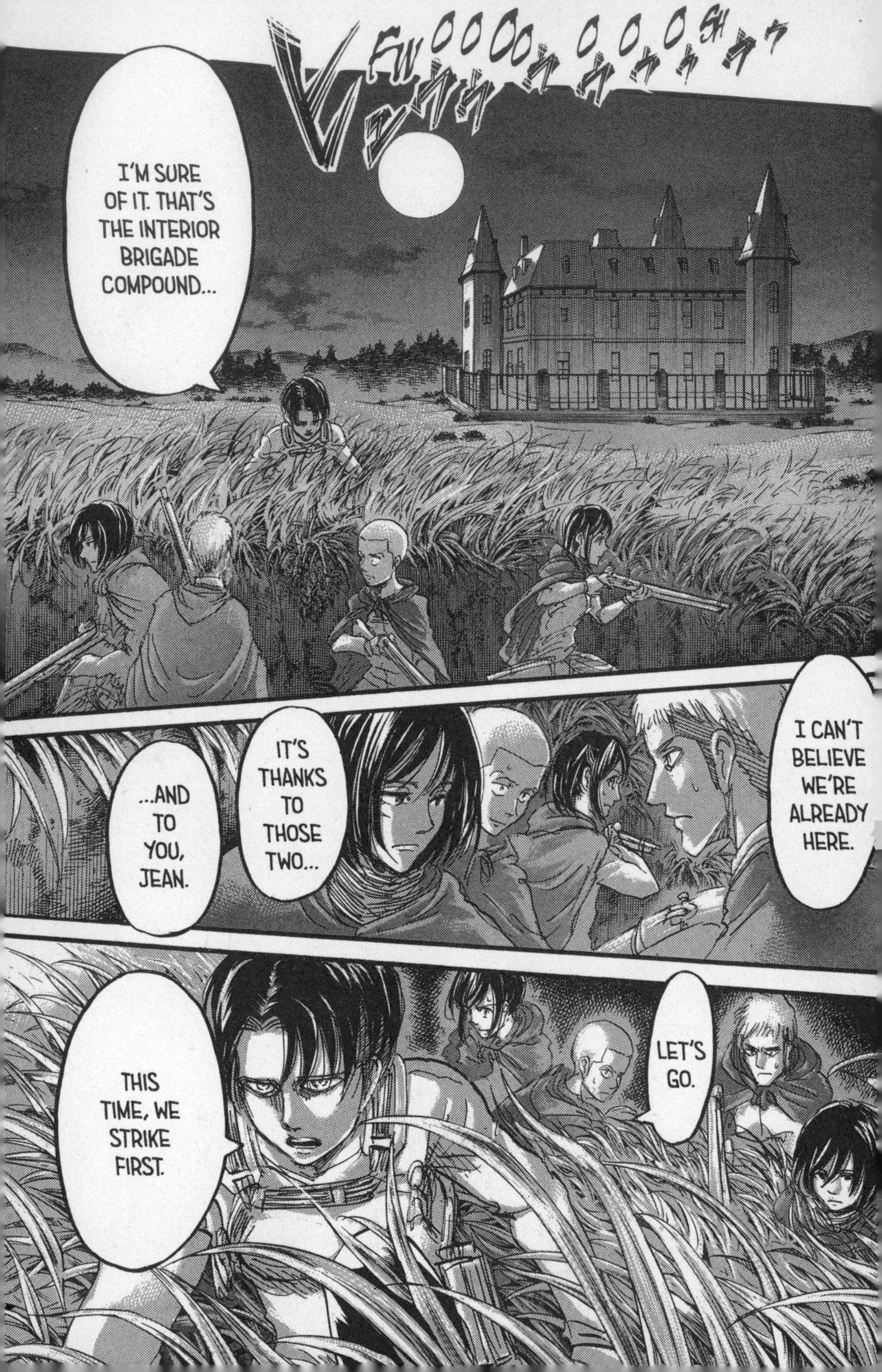
FWOOOOOOOOSH
I'M SURE OF IT. THAT'S THE INTERIOR BRIGADE COMPOUND...
I CAN'T BELIEVE WE'RE ALREADY HERE.
IT'S THANKS TO THOSE TWO...
...AND TO YOU, JEAN.
LET'S GO.
THIS TIME, WE STRIKE FIRST.

ATTACK on TITAN

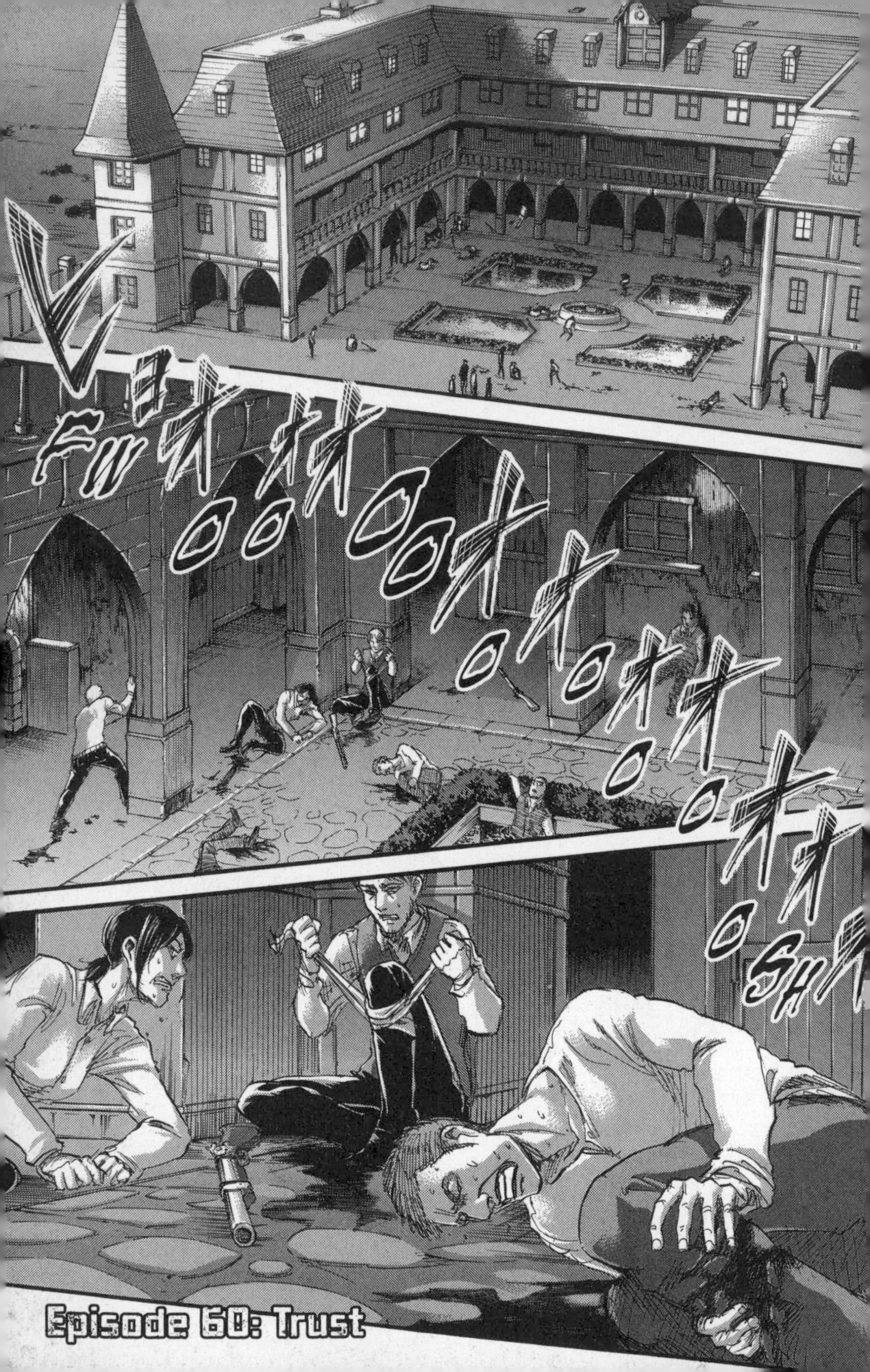
FWOOOOOOOOOSH
Episode 60: Trust

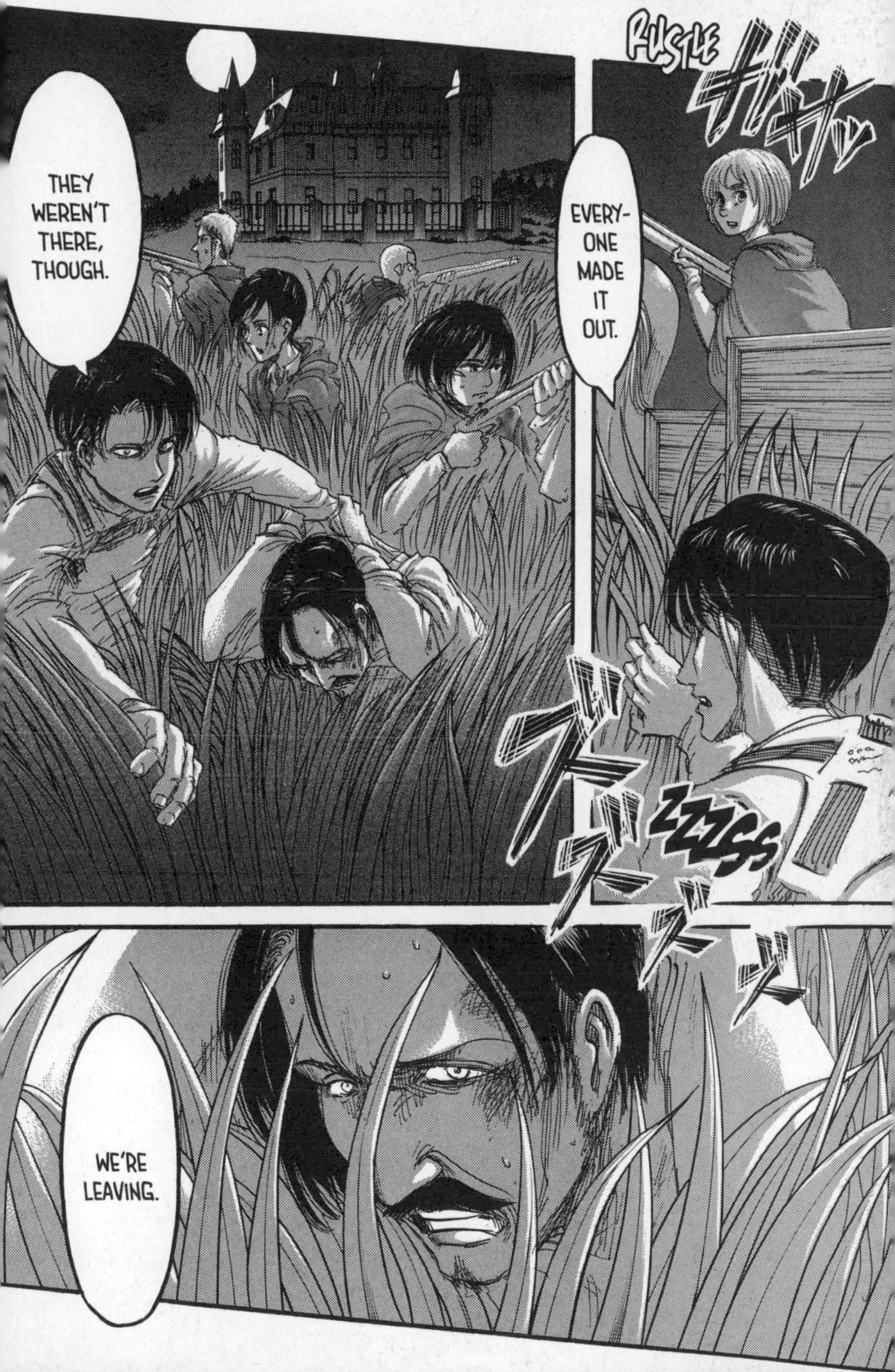
RUSTLE
EVERY-ONE MADE IT OUT.
ZZZSS
THEY WEREN'T THERE, THOUGH.
WE'RE LEAVING.

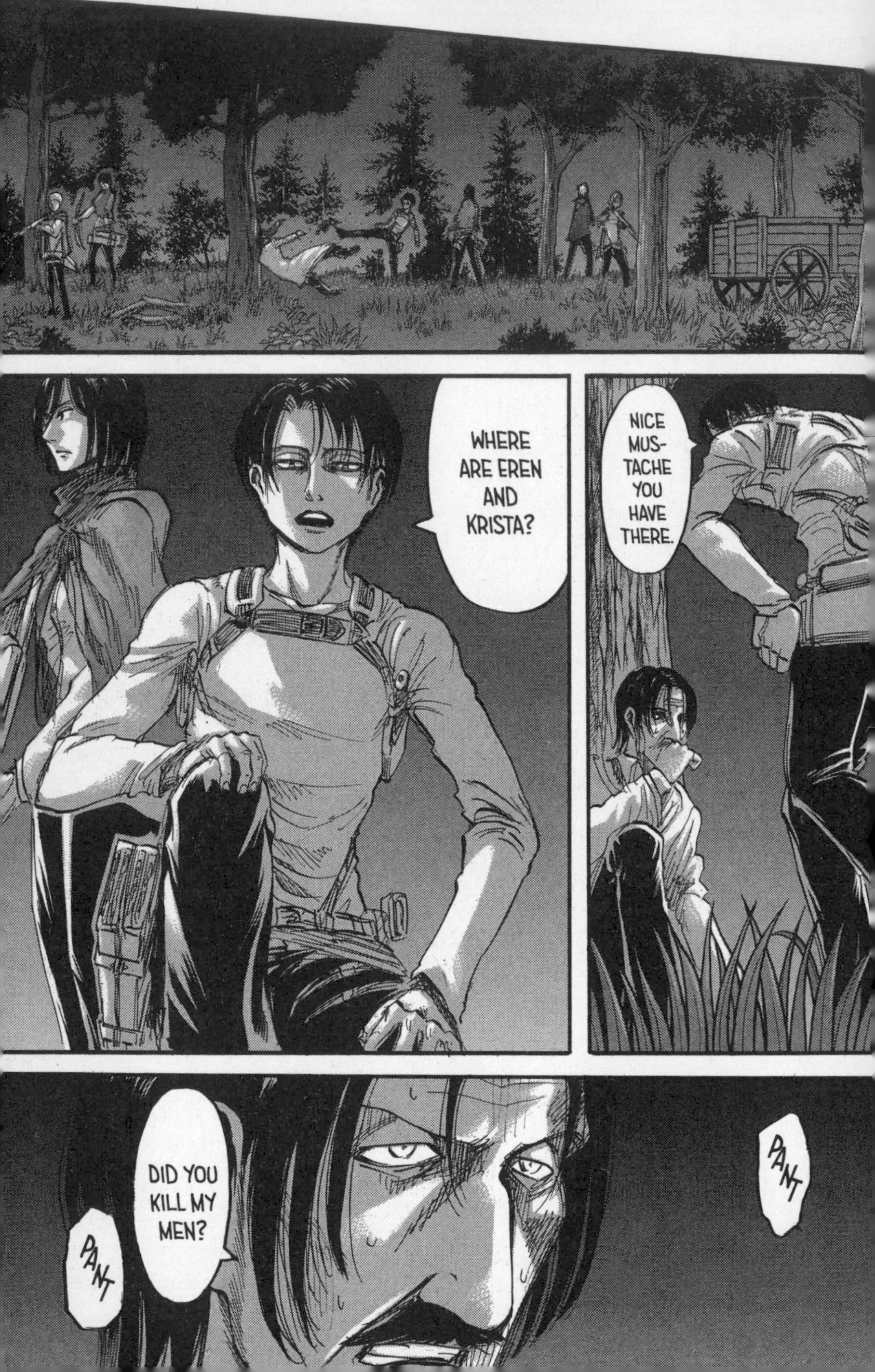
NICE MUS-TACHE YOU HAVE THERE.
WHERE ARE EREN AND KRISTA?
PANT
DID YOU KILL MY MEN?
PANT

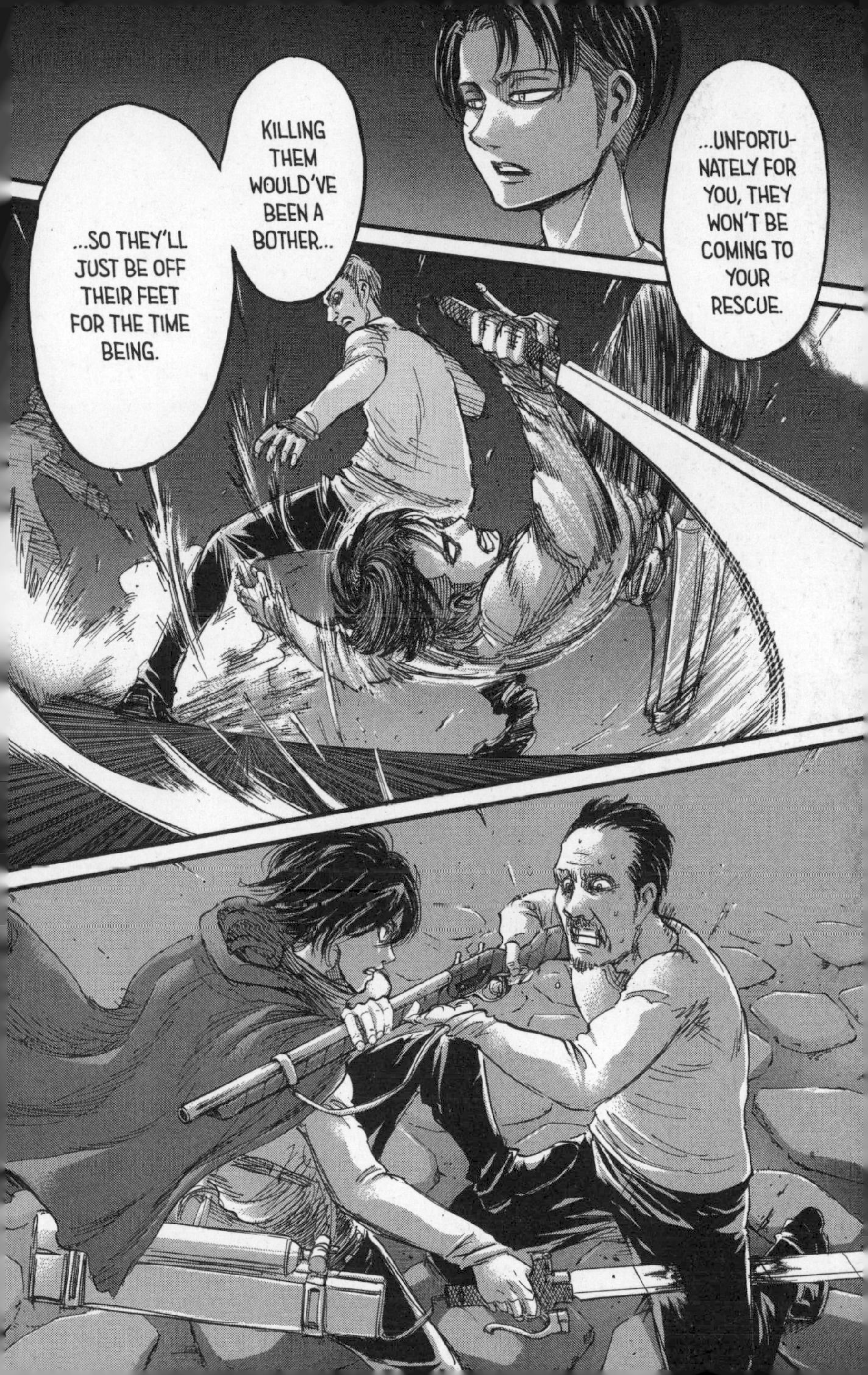
...UNFORTU-NATELY FOR YOU, THEY WON'T BE COMING TO YOUR RESCUE.
KILLING THEM WOULD'VE BEEN A BOTHER...
...SO THEY'LL JUST BE OFF THEIR FEET FOR THE TIME BEING.

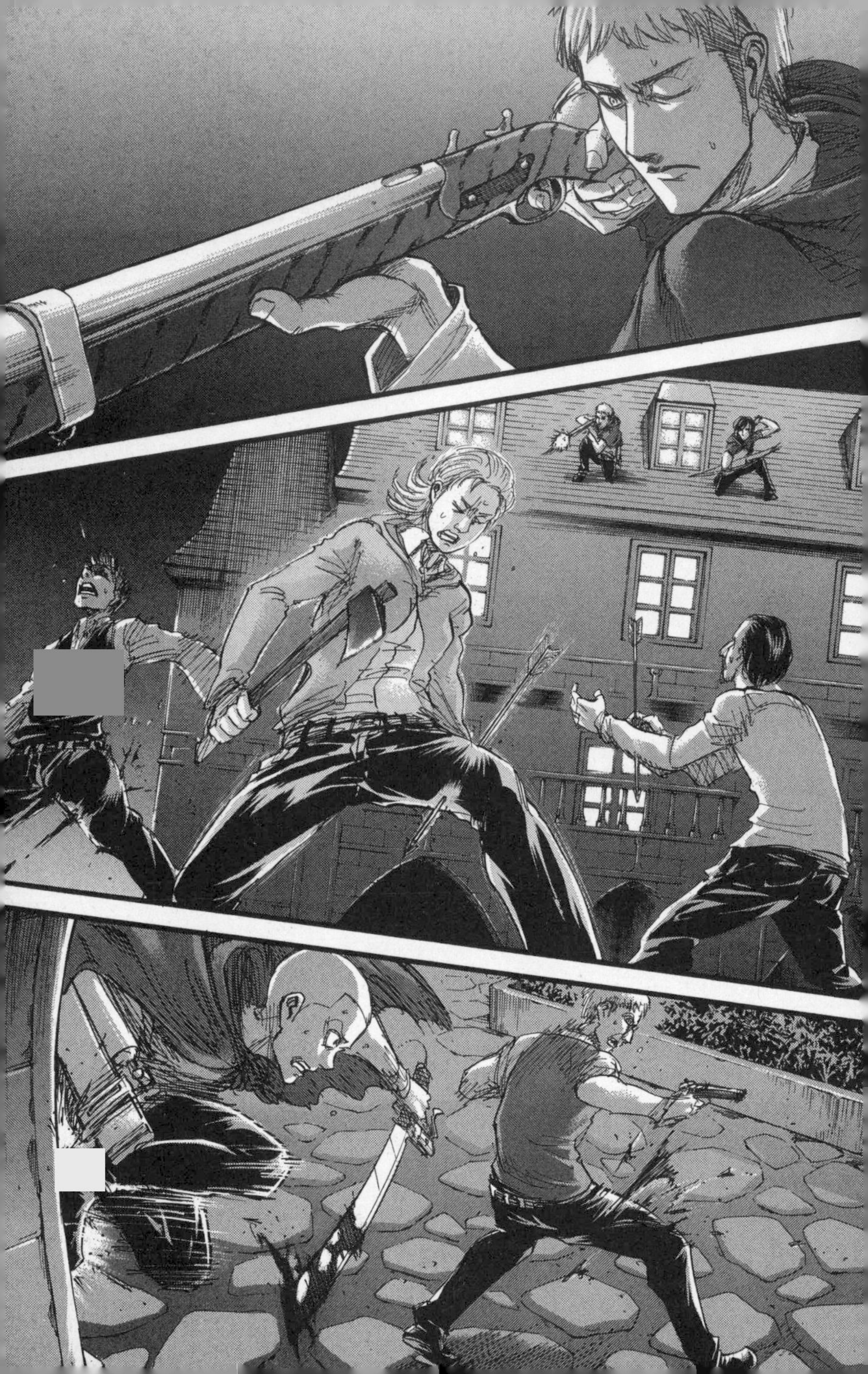

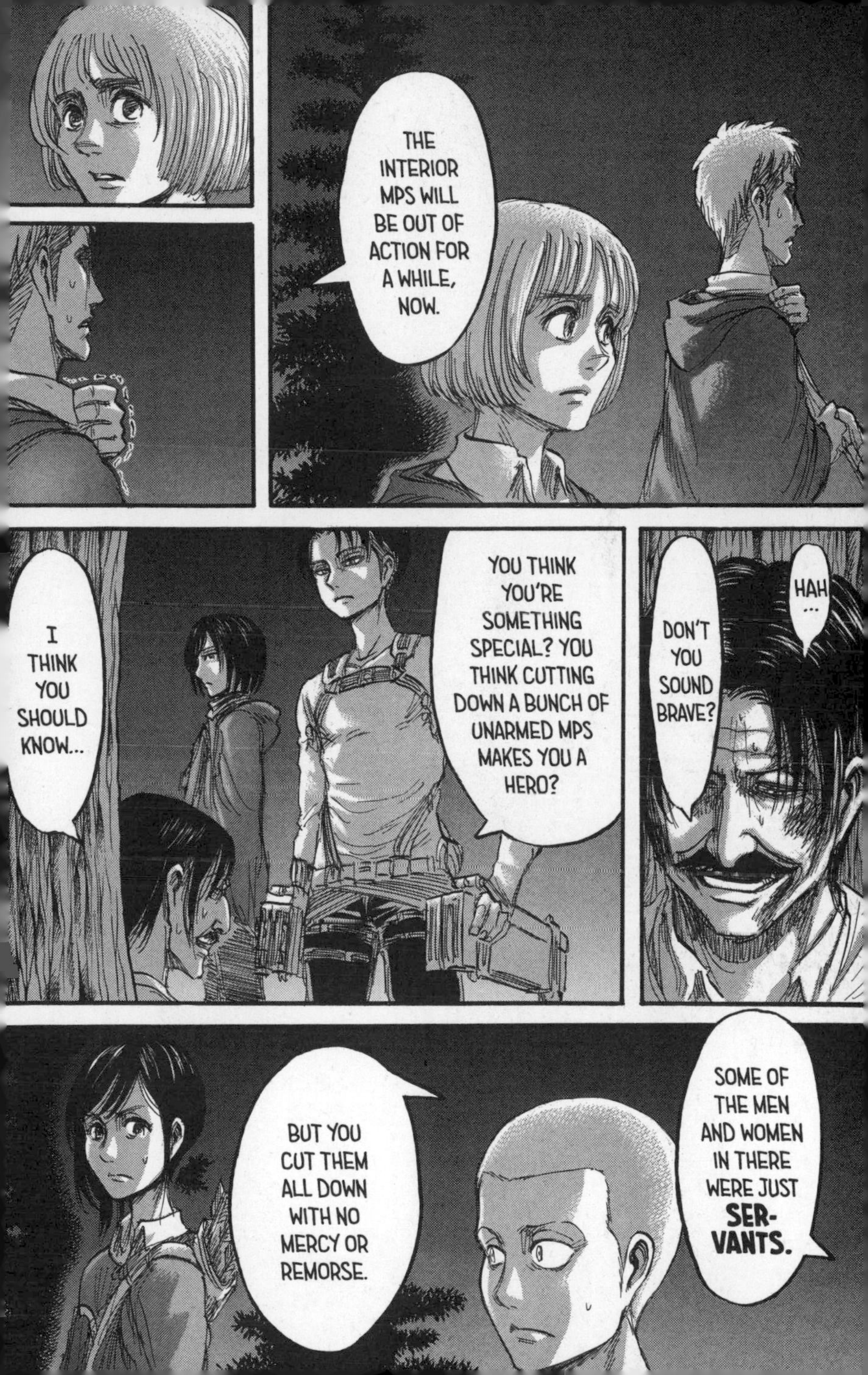
THE INTERIOR MPS WILL BE OUT OF ACTION FOR A WHILE, NOW.
HAH...
DON'T YOU SOUND BRAVE?
YOU THINK YOU'RE SOMETHING SPECIAL? YOU THINK CUTTING DOWN A BUNCH OF UNARMED MPS MAKES YOU A HERO?
I THINK YOU SHOULD KNOW...
SOME OF THE MEN AND WOMEN IN THERE WERE JUST **SER-VANTS.**
BUT YOU CUT THEM ALL DOWN WITH NO MERCY OR REMORSE.

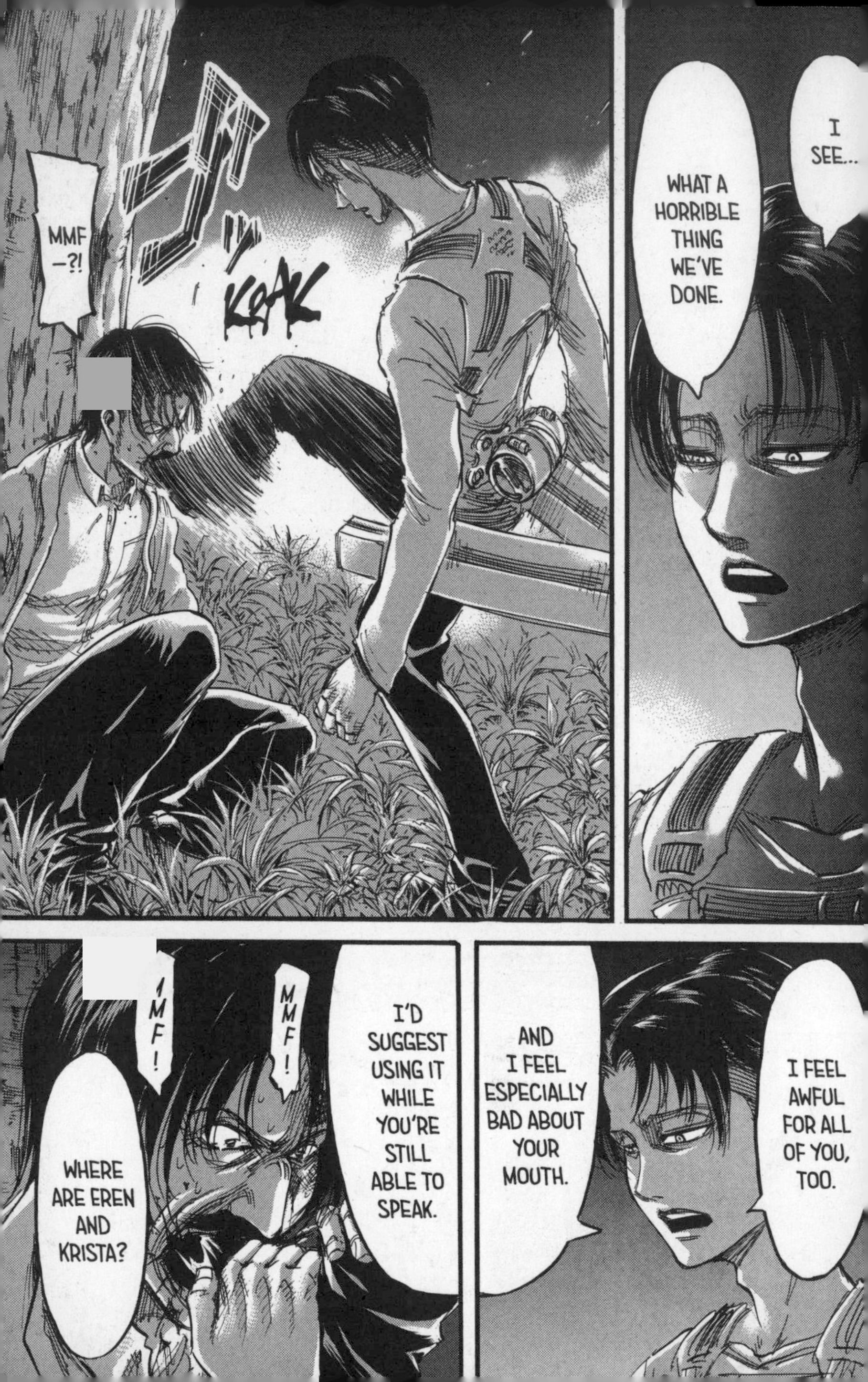
I SEE...
WHAT A HORRIBLE THING WE'VE DONE.
KRAK
MMF—?!
I FEEL AWFUL FOR ALL OF YOU, TOO.
AND I FEEL ESPECIALLY BAD ABOUT YOUR MOUTH.
I'D SUGGEST USING IT WHILE YOU'RE STILL ABLE TO SPEAK.
MMF!
MF!
WHERE ARE EREN AND KRISTA?

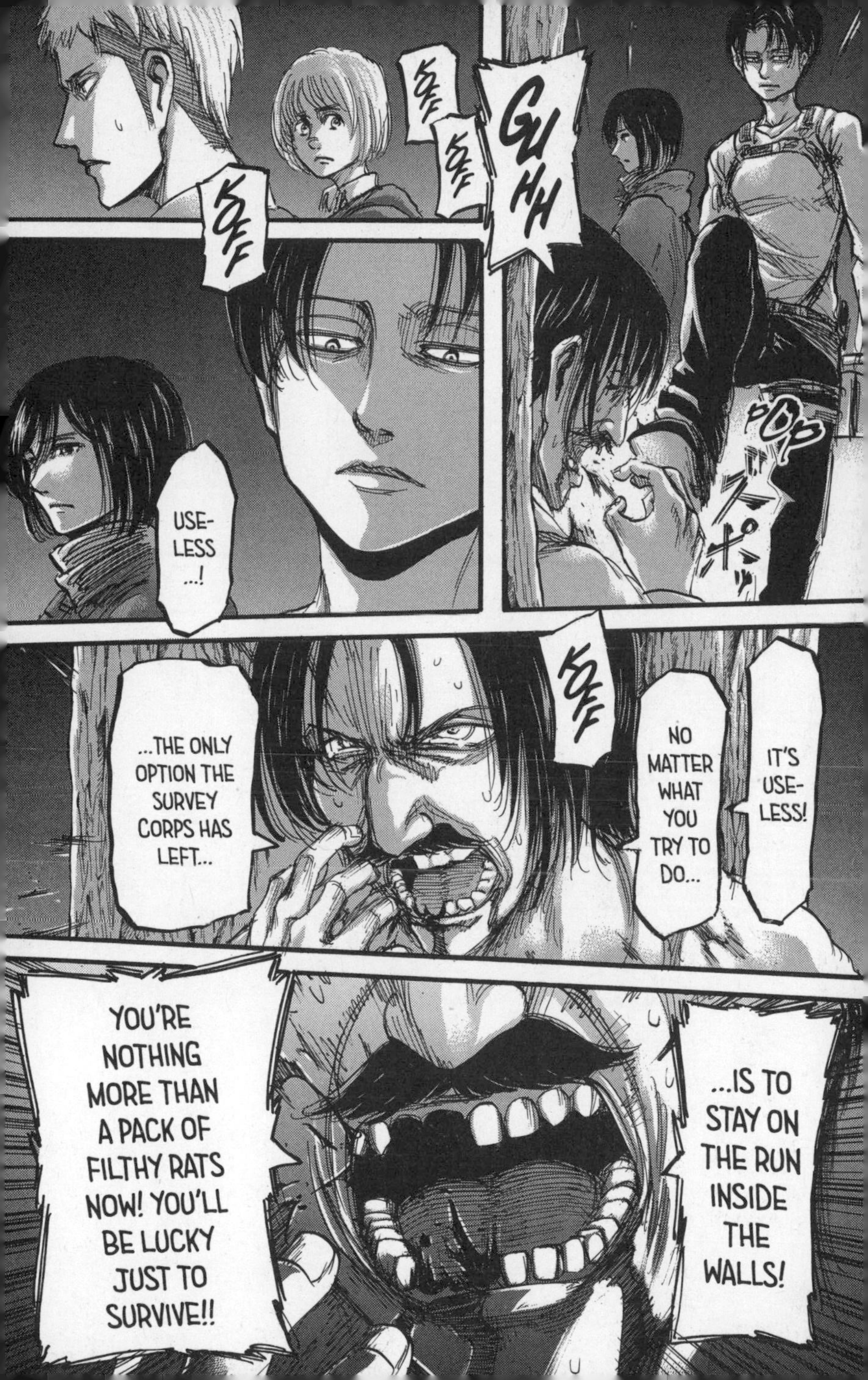
GUHH
POP
KOFF
KOFF
KOFF
USE-
LESS
...!
IT'S
USE-
LESS!
NO
MATTER
WHAT
YOU
TRY TO
DO...
KOFF
...THE ONLY
OPTION THE
SURVEY
CORPS HAS
LEFT...
...IS TO
STAY ON
THE RUN
INSIDE
THE
WALLS!
YOU'RE
NOTHING
MORE THAN
A PACK OF
FILTHY RATS
NOW! YOU'LL
BE LUCKY
JUST TO
SURVIVE!!

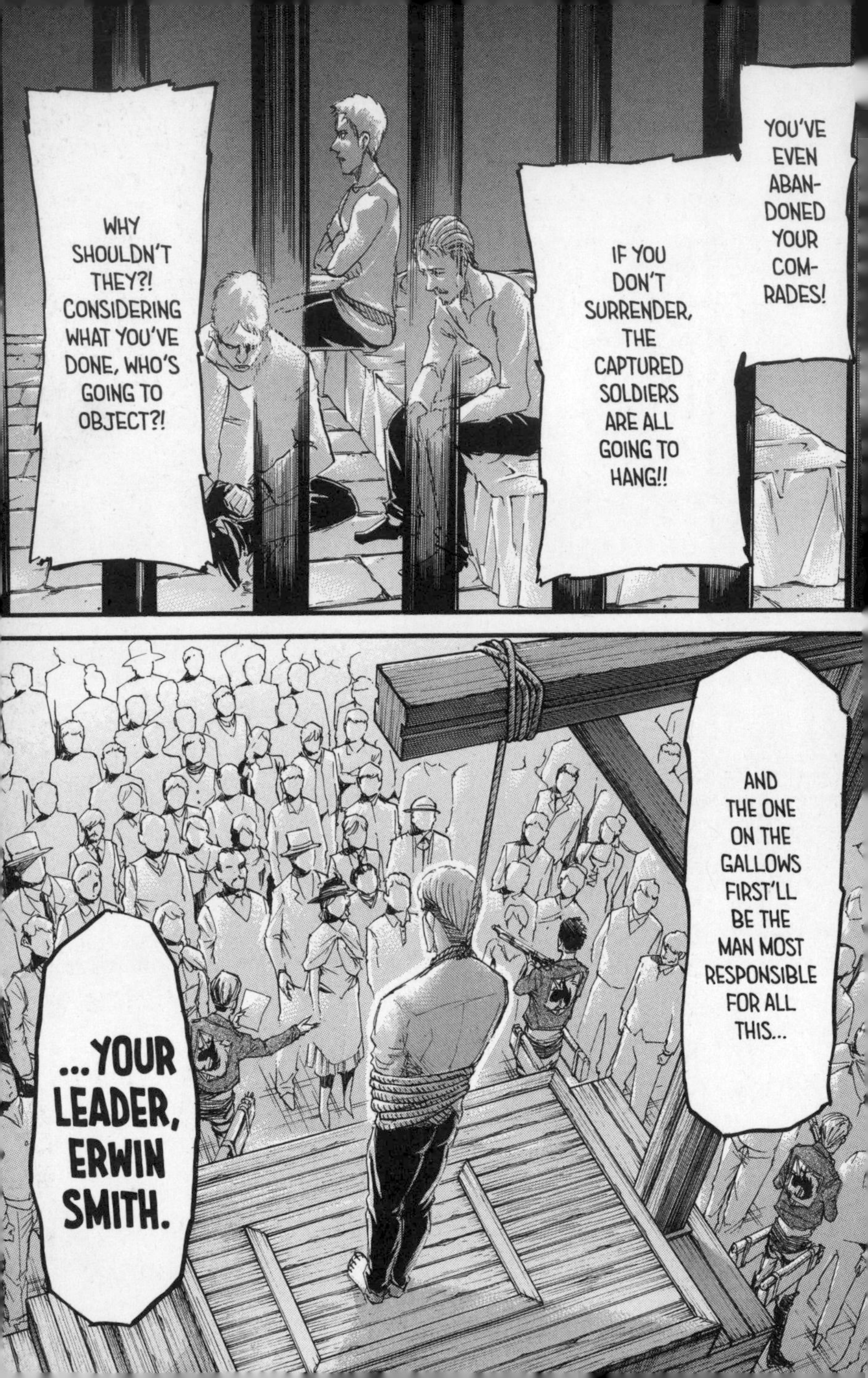
YOU'VE EVEN ABANDONED YOUR COMRADES!
IF YOU DON'T SURRENDER, THE CAPTURED SOLDIERS ARE ALL GOING TO HANG!!
WHY SHOULDN'T THEY?! CONSIDERING WHAT YOU'VE DONE, WHO'S GOING TO OBJECT?!
AND THE ONE ON THE GALLOWS FIRST'LL BE THE MAN MOST RESPONSIBLE FOR ALL THIS...
...YOUR LEADER, ERWIN SMITH.

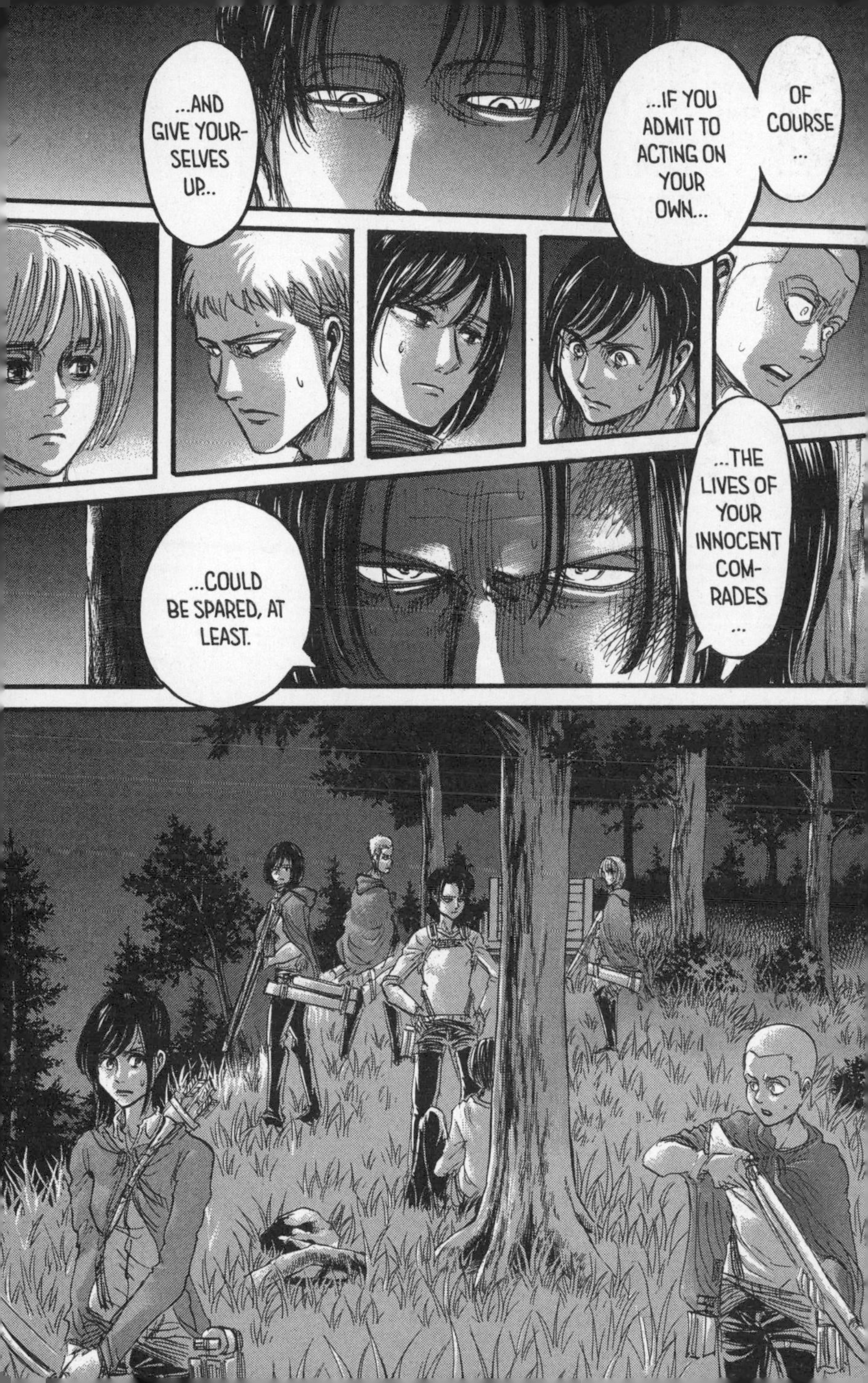
OF COURSE ...
...IF YOU ADMIT TO ACTING ON YOUR OWN...
...AND GIVE YOUR-SELVES UP...
...THE LIVES OF YOUR INNOCENT COM-RADES ...
...COULD BE SPARED, AT LEAST.

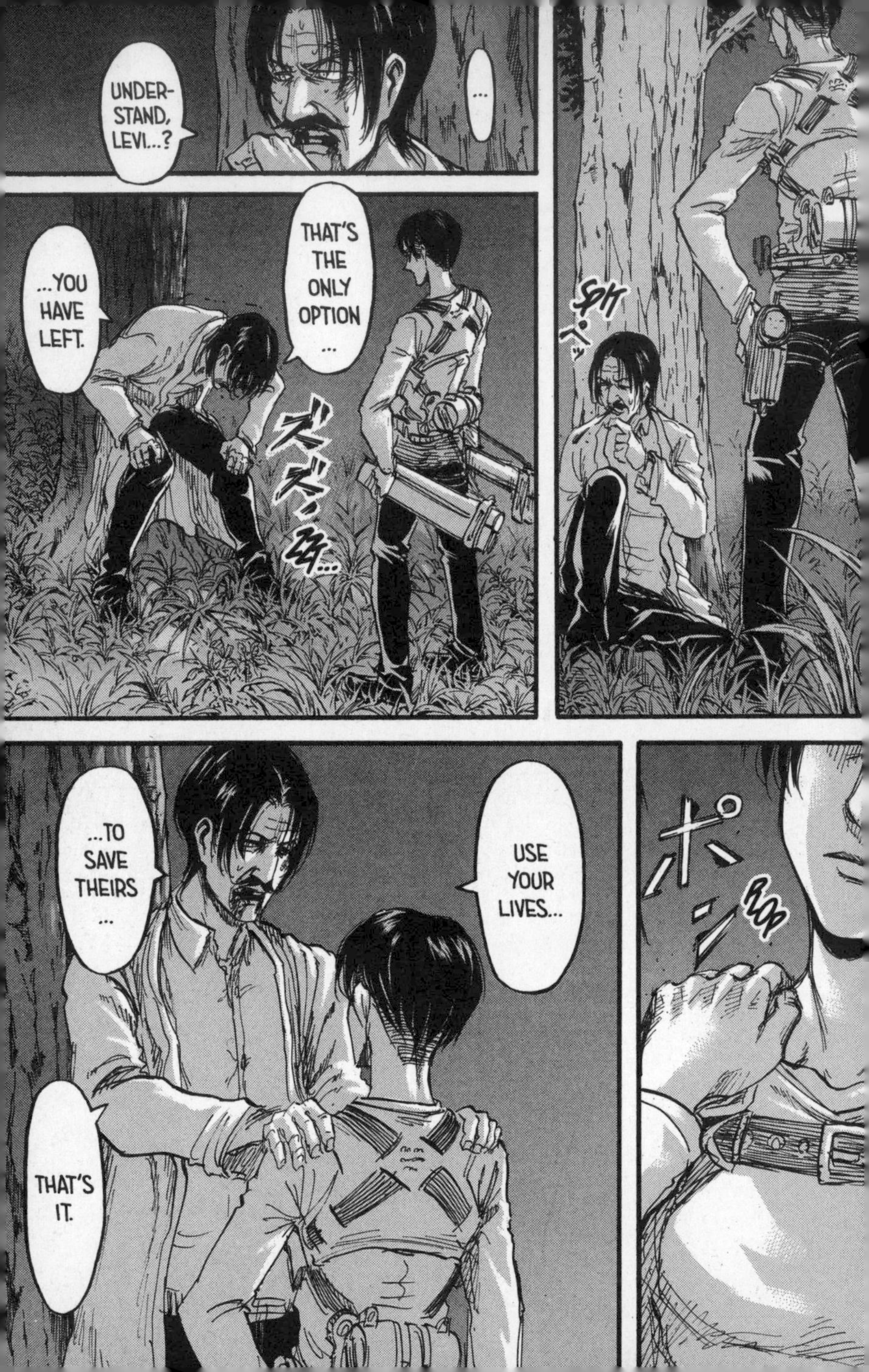
SPK
...
UNDER-STAND, LEVI...?
THAT'S THE ONLY OPTION ...
...YOU HAVE LEFT.
USE YOUR LIVES...
...TO SAVE THEIRS ...
THAT'S IT.

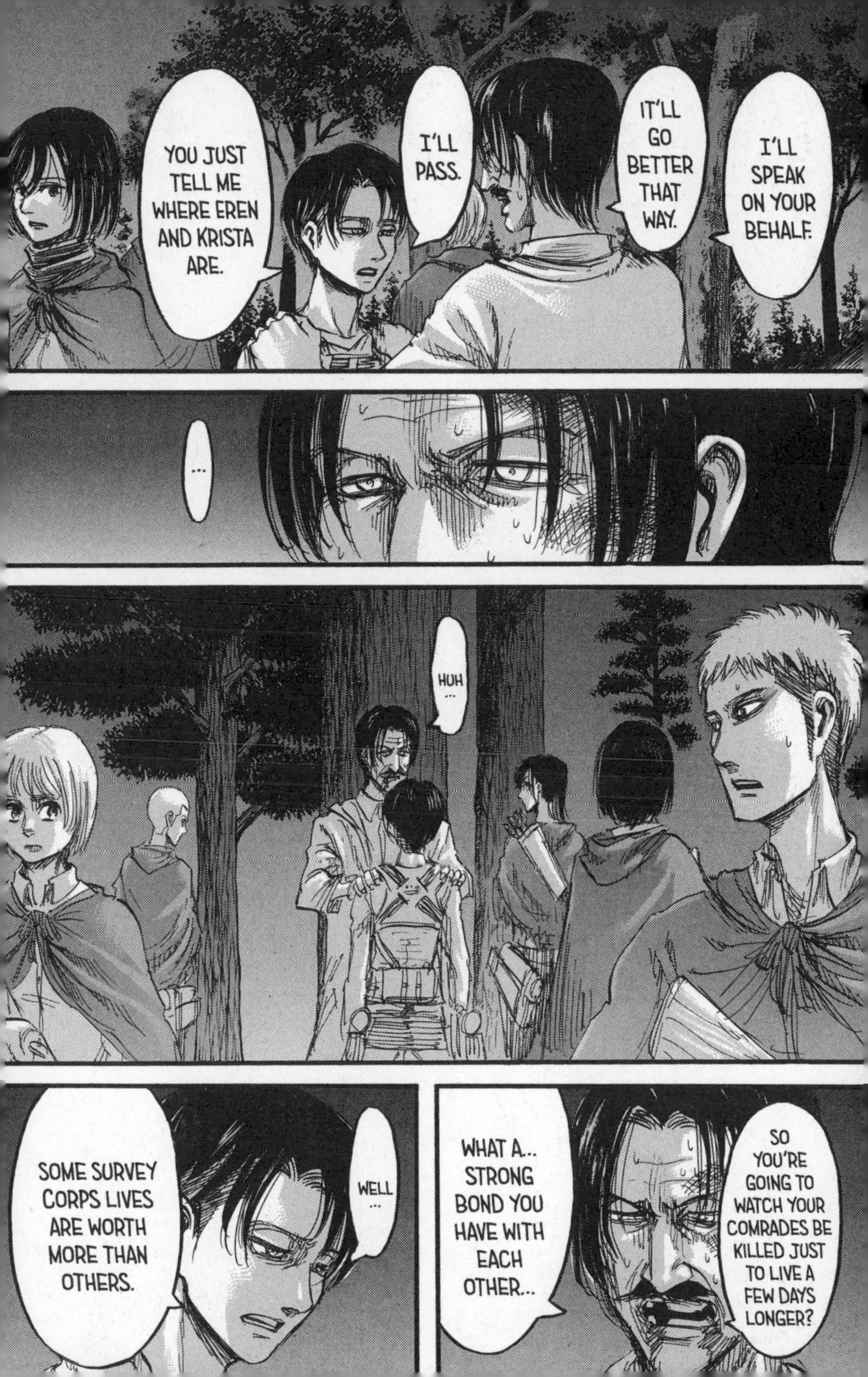
I'LL SPEAK ON YOUR BEHALF.
IT'LL GO BETTER THAT WAY.
I'LL PASS.
YOU JUST TELL ME WHERE EREN AND KRISTA ARE.
...
HUH...
SO YOU'RE GOING TO WATCH YOUR COMRADES BE KILLED JUST TO LIVE A FEW DAYS LONGER?
WHAT A... STRONG BOND YOU HAVE WITH EACH OTHER...
WELL...
SOME SURVEY CORPS LIVES ARE WORTH MORE THAN OTHERS.

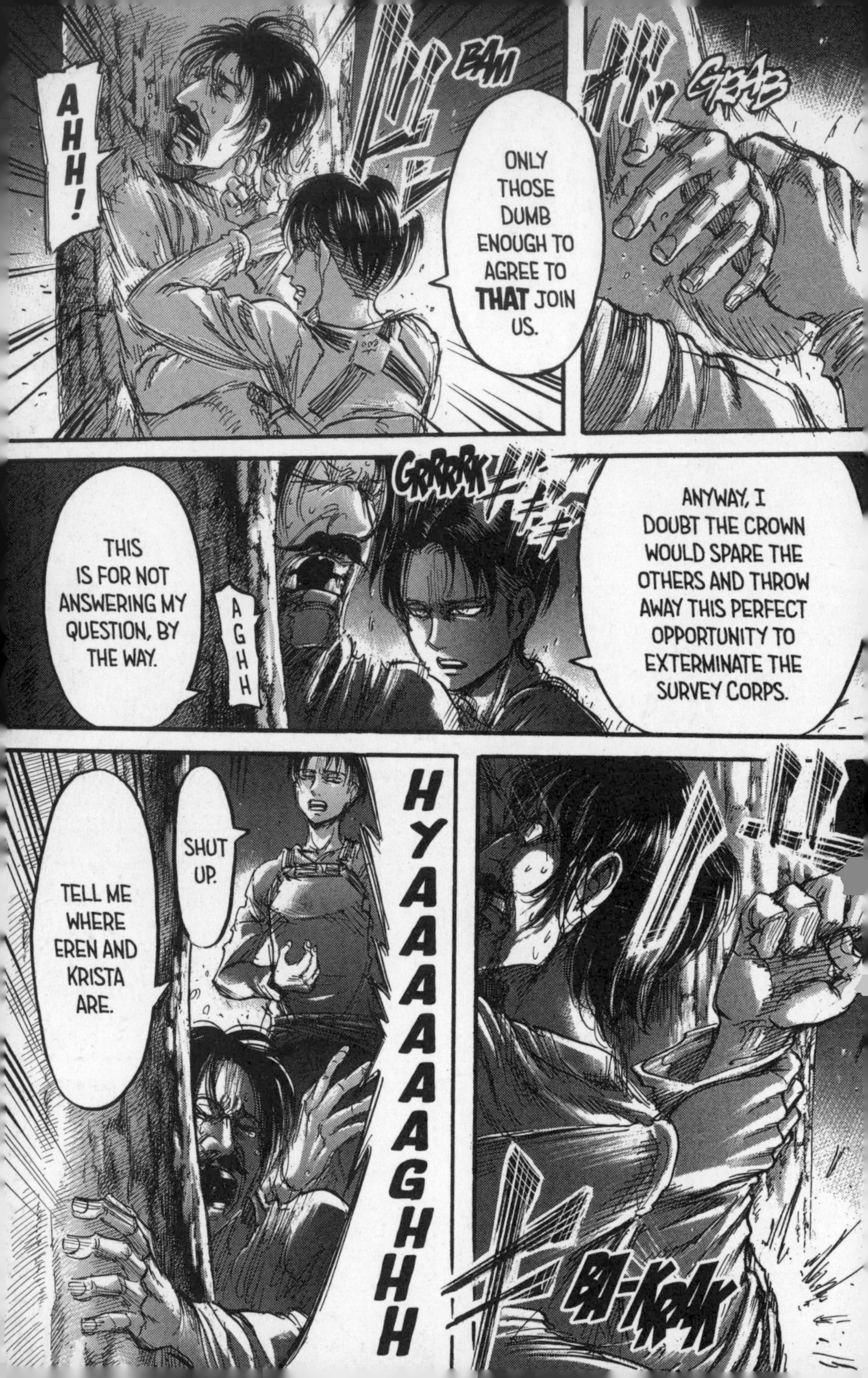
GRAB
BAM
ONLY THOSE DUMB ENOUGH TO AGREE TO THAT JOIN US.
AHH!
GRRRRK
ANYWAY, I DOUBT THE CROWN WOULD SPARE THE OTHERS AND THROW AWAY THIS PERFECT OPPORTUNITY TO EXTERMINATE THE SURVEY CORPS.
AGHH
THIS IS FOR NOT ANSWERING MY QUESTION, BY THE WAY.
BA-KRAK
HYAAAAAAGHHH
SHUT UP.
TELL ME WHERE EREN AND KRISTA ARE.

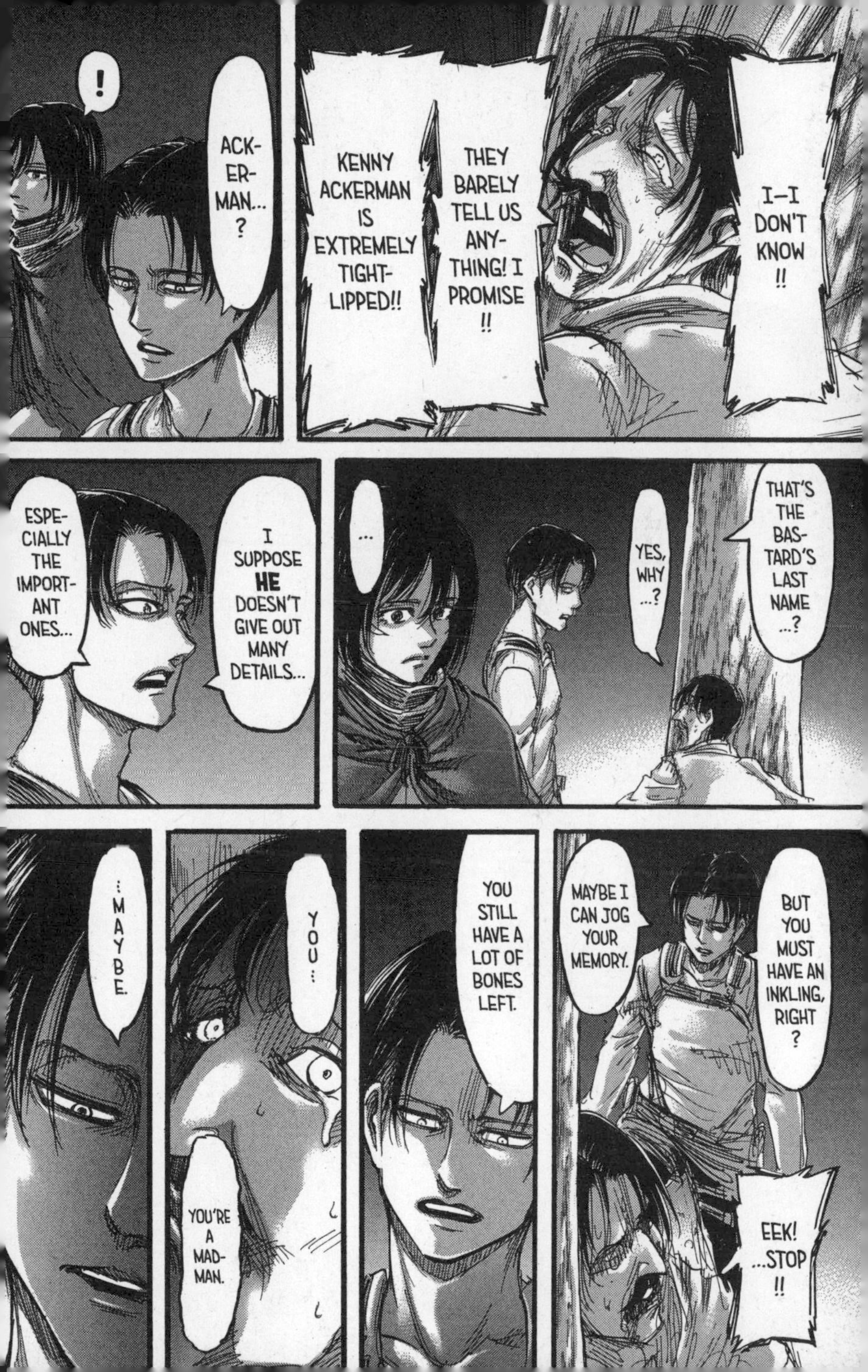
I—I DON'T KNOW !!
THEY BARELY TELL US ANYTHING! I PROMISE !!
KENNY ACKERMAN IS EXTREMELY TIGHT-LIPPED!!
ACKERMAN...?
!
THAT'S THE BASTARD'S LAST NAME...?
YES, WHY...?
...
I SUPPOSE **HE** DOESN'T GIVE OUT MANY DETAILS...
ESPECIALLY THE IMPORTANT ONES...
BUT YOU MUST HAVE AN INKLING, RIGHT?
MAYBE I CAN JOG YOUR MEMORY.
EEK! ...STOP !!
YOU STILL HAVE A LOT OF BONES LEFT.
YOU...
YOU'RE A MADMAN.
...MAYBE.

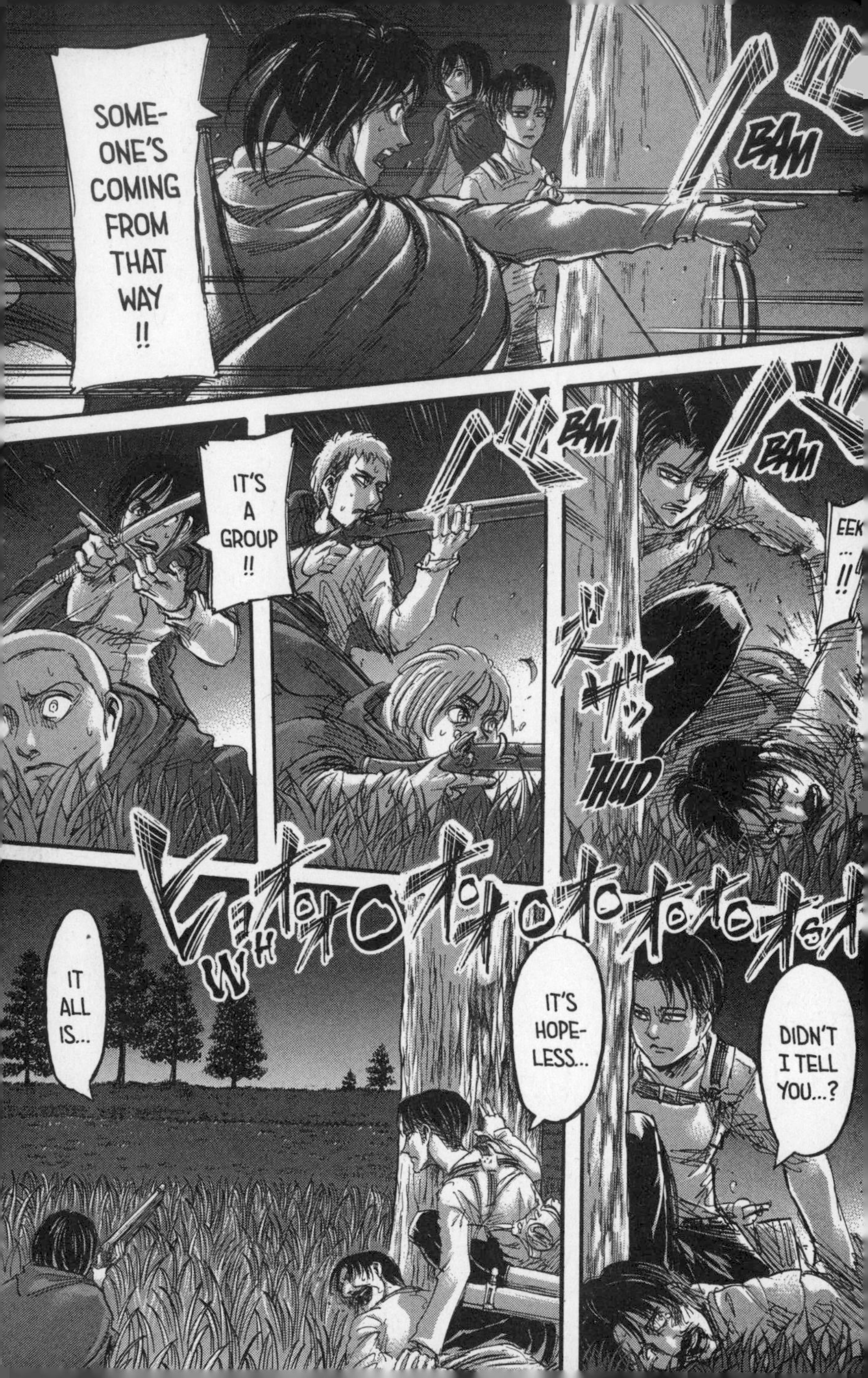
BAM
SOME-ONE'S COMING FROM THAT WAY !!
BAM
EEK ... !!
THUD
BAM
IT'S A GROUP !!
DIDN'T I TELL YOU...?
IT'S HOPE-LESS...
IT ALL IS...

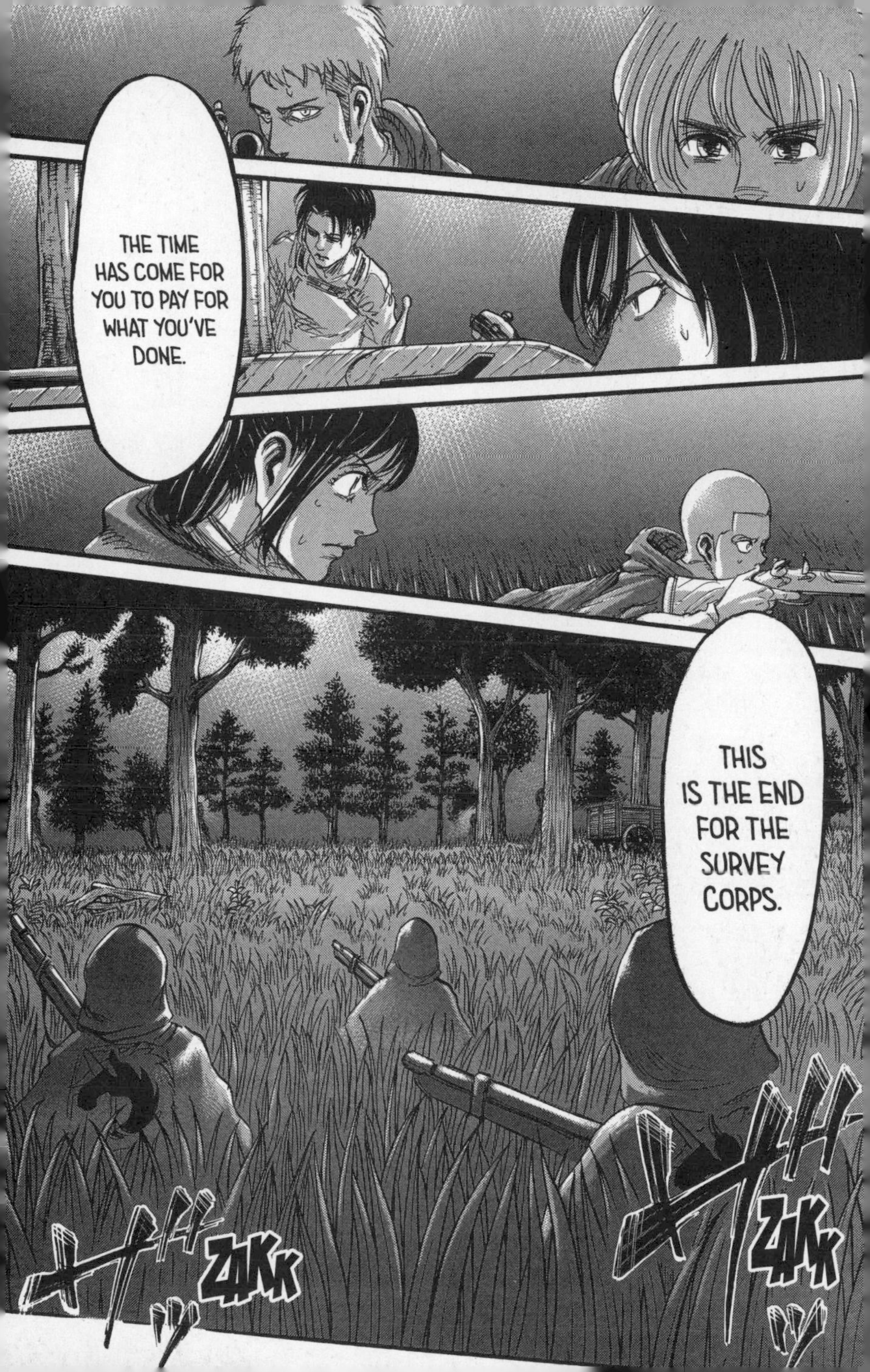
THE TIME HAS COME FOR YOU TO PAY FOR WHAT YOU'VE DONE.
THIS IS THE END FOR THE SURVEY CORPS.
ZAKK
ZAKK

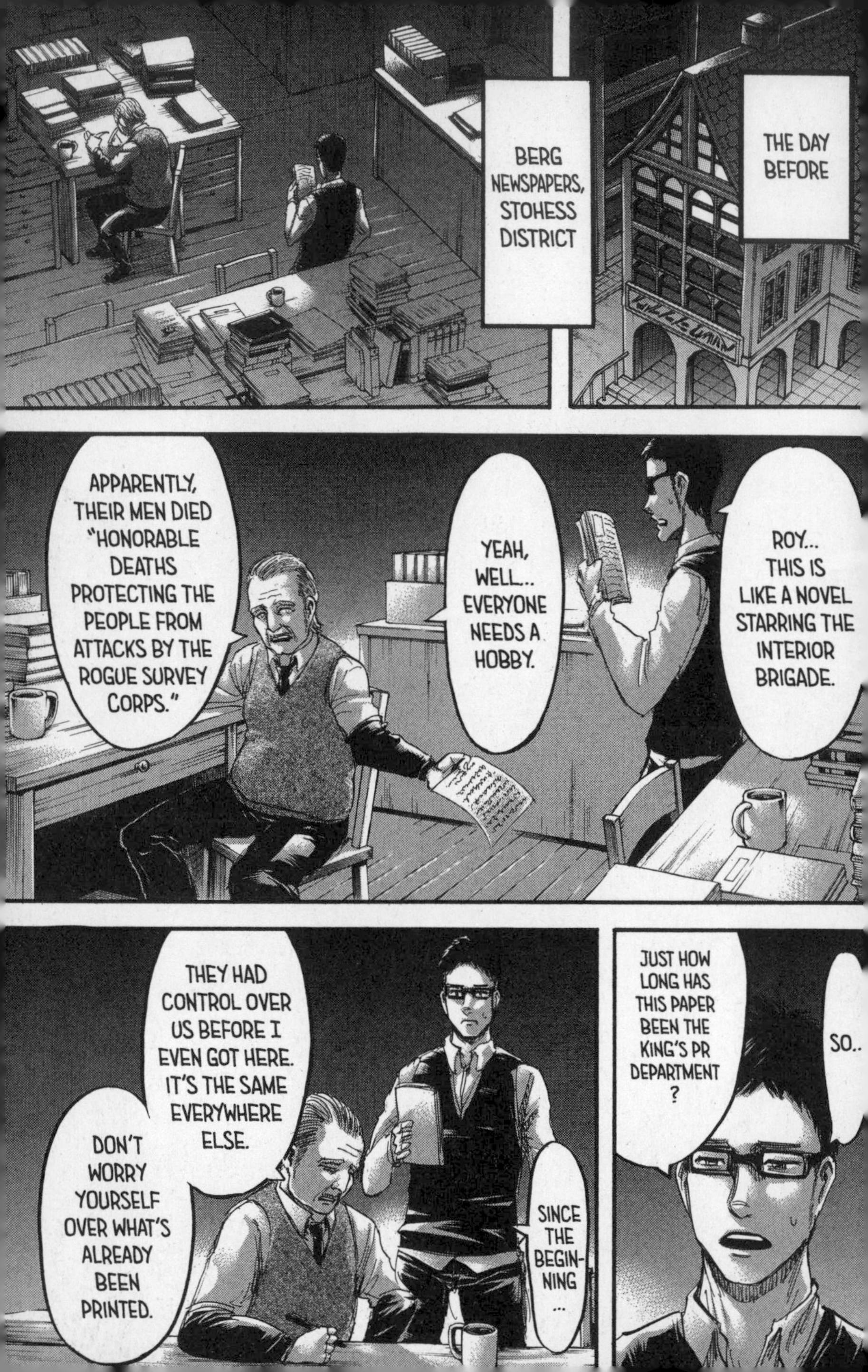
THE DAY BEFORE
BERG NEWSPAPERS, STOHESS DISTRICT
ROY... THIS IS LIKE A NOVEL STARRING THE INTERIOR BRIGADE.
YEAH, WELL... EVERYONE NEEDS A HOBBY.
APPARENTLY, THEIR MEN DIED "HONORABLE DEATHS PROTECTING THE PEOPLE FROM ATTACKS BY THE ROGUE SURVEY CORPS."
SO..
JUST HOW LONG HAS THIS PAPER BEEN THE KING'S PR DEPARTMENT ?
SINCE THE BEGIN-NING ...
THEY HAD CONTROL OVER US BEFORE I EVEN GOT HERE. IT'S THE SAME EVERYWHERE ELSE.
DON'T WORRY YOURSELF OVER WHAT'S ALREADY BEEN PRINTED.

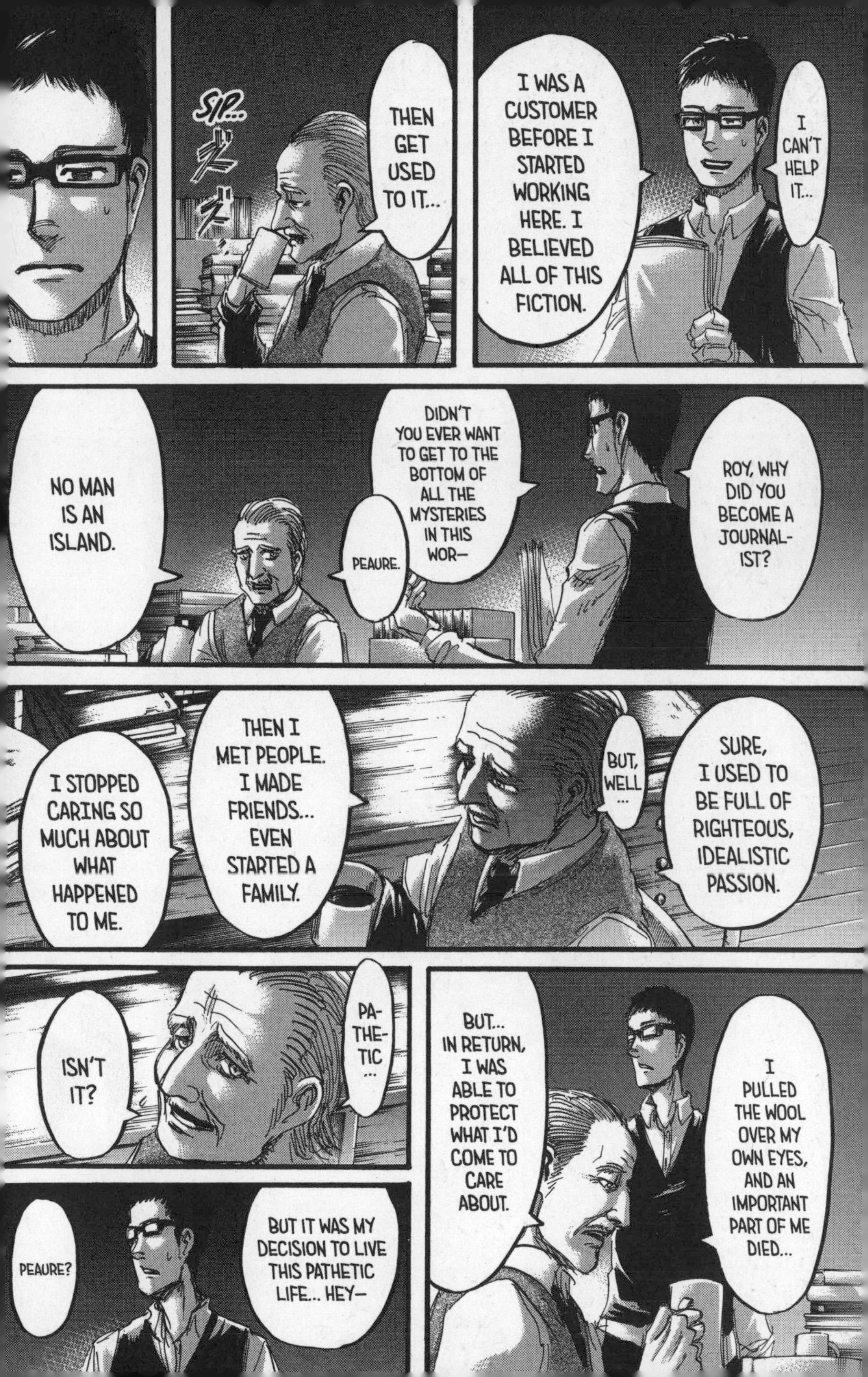
I CAN'T HELP IT...
I WAS A CUSTOMER BEFORE I STARTED WORKING HERE. I BELIEVED ALL OF THIS FICTION.
THEN GET USED TO IT...
SIP...
ROY, WHY DID YOU BECOME A JOURNAL-IST?
DIDN'T YOU EVER WANT TO GET TO THE BOTTOM OF ALL THE MYSTERIES IN THIS WOR—
PEAURE.
NO MAN IS AN ISLAND.
SURE, I USED TO BE FULL OF RIGHTEOUS, IDEALISTIC PASSION.
BUT, WELL...
THEN I MET PEOPLE. I MADE FRIENDS... EVEN STARTED A FAMILY.
I STOPPED CARING SO MUCH ABOUT WHAT HAPPENED TO ME.
I PULLED THE WOOL OVER MY OWN EYES, AND AN IMPORTANT PART OF ME DIED...
BUT... IN RETURN, I WAS ABLE TO PROTECT WHAT I'D COME TO CARE ABOUT.
PA-THE-TIC...
ISN'T IT?
BUT IT WAS MY DECISION TO LIVE THIS PATHETIC LIFE... HEY—
PEAURE?

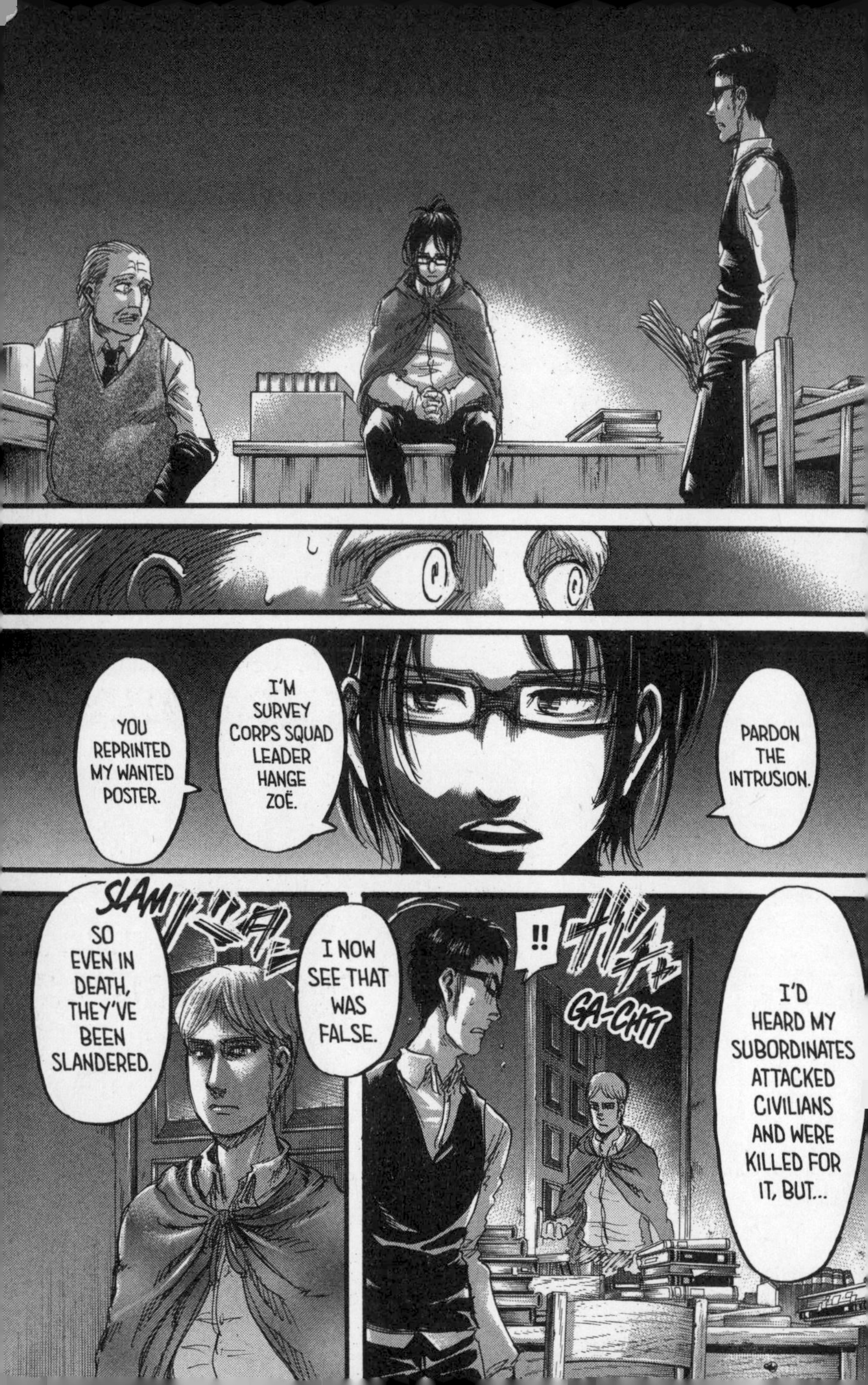
PARDON THE INTRUSION.
I'M SURVEY CORPS SQUAD LEADER HANGE ZOË.
YOU REPRINTED MY WANTED POSTER.
I'D HEARD MY SUBORDINATES ATTACKED CIVILIANS AND WERE KILLED FOR IT, BUT...
!!
GA-CHI
I NOW SEE THAT WAS FALSE.
SLAM
SO EVEN IN DEATH, THEY'VE BEEN SLANDERED.

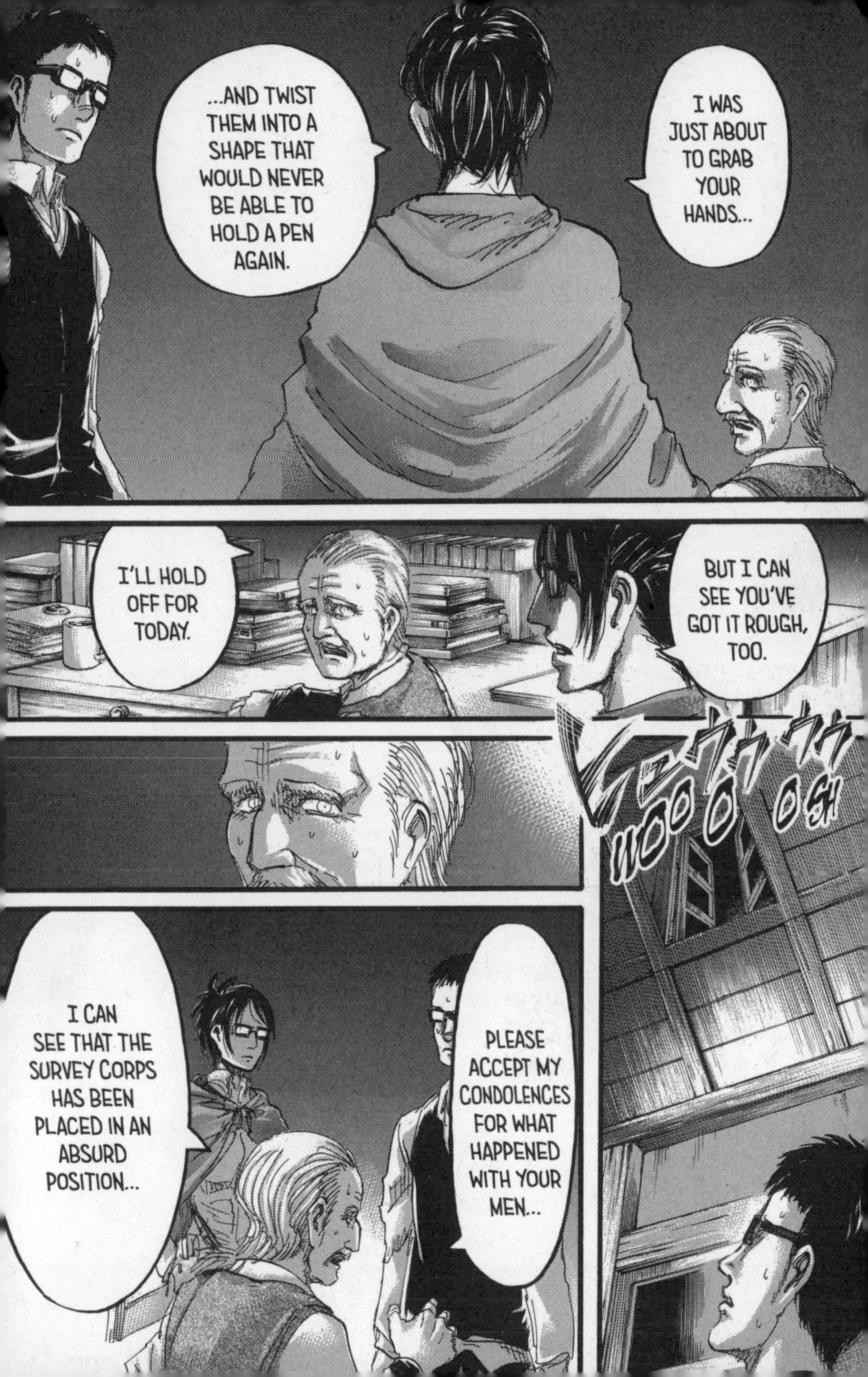
I WAS JUST ABOUT TO GRAB YOUR HANDS...
...AND TWIST THEM INTO A SHAPE THAT WOULD NEVER BE ABLE TO HOLD A PEN AGAIN.
BUT I CAN SEE YOU'VE GOT IT ROUGH, TOO.
I'LL HOLD OFF FOR TODAY.
WOOOOOSH
PLEASE ACCEPT MY CONDOLENCES FOR WHAT HAPPENED WITH YOUR MEN...
I CAN SEE THAT THE SURVEY CORPS HAS BEEN PLACED IN AN ABSURD POSITION...

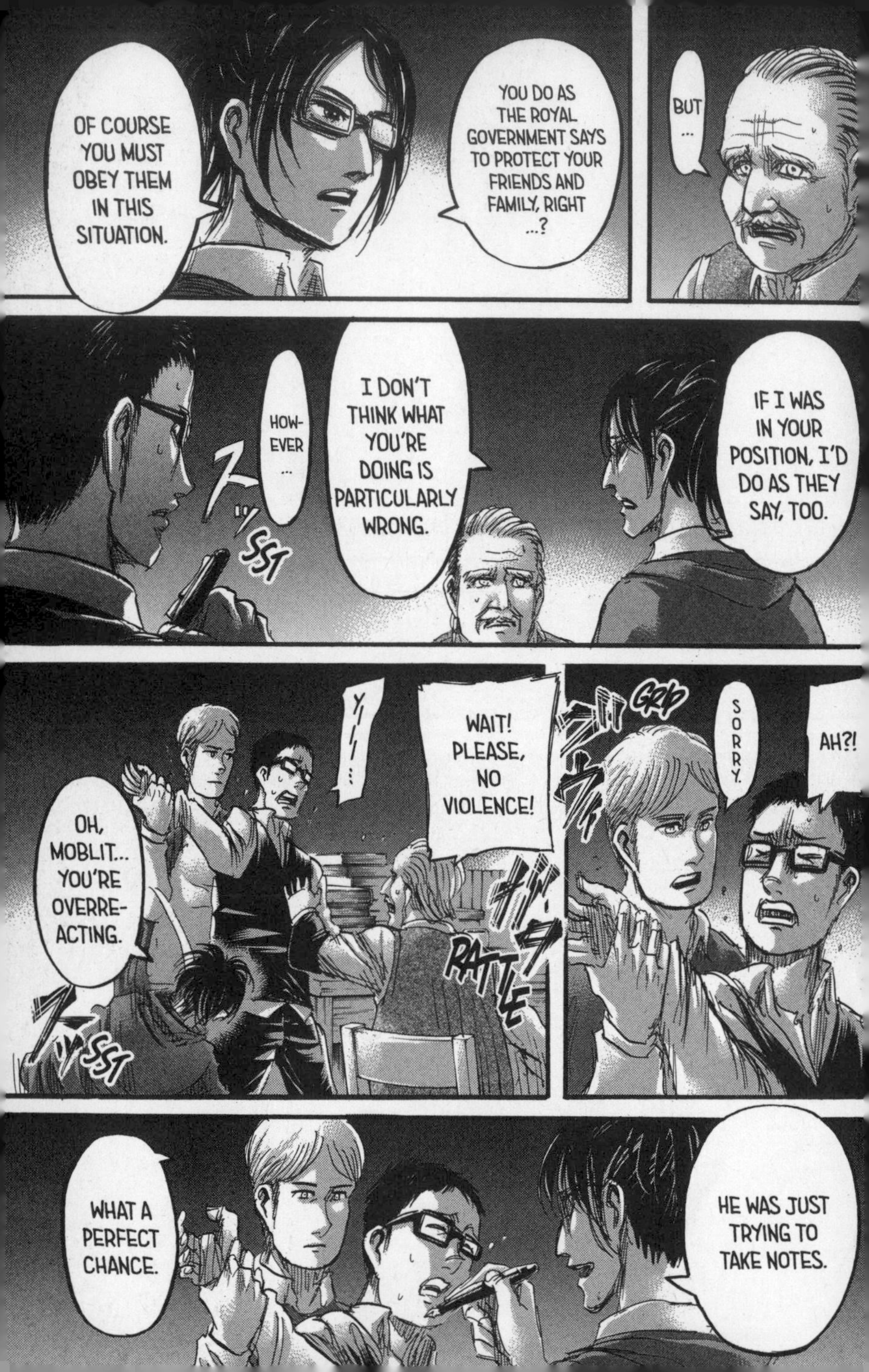
BUT ...
YOU DO AS THE ROYAL GOVERNMENT SAYS TO PROTECT YOUR FRIENDS AND FAMILY, RIGHT ...?
OF COURSE YOU MUST OBEY THEM IN THIS SITUATION.
IF I WAS IN YOUR POSITION, I'D DO AS THEY SAY, TOO.
I DON'T THINK WHAT YOU'RE DOING IS PARTICULARLY WRONG.
HOW-EVER ...
SSST
AH?!
SORRY.
GRIP
WAIT! PLEASE, NO VIOLENCE!
Y---...
RATTLE
OH, MOBLIT... YOU'RE OVERRE-ACTING.
SSST
HE WAS JUST TRYING TO TAKE NOTES.
WHAT A PERFECT CHANCE.

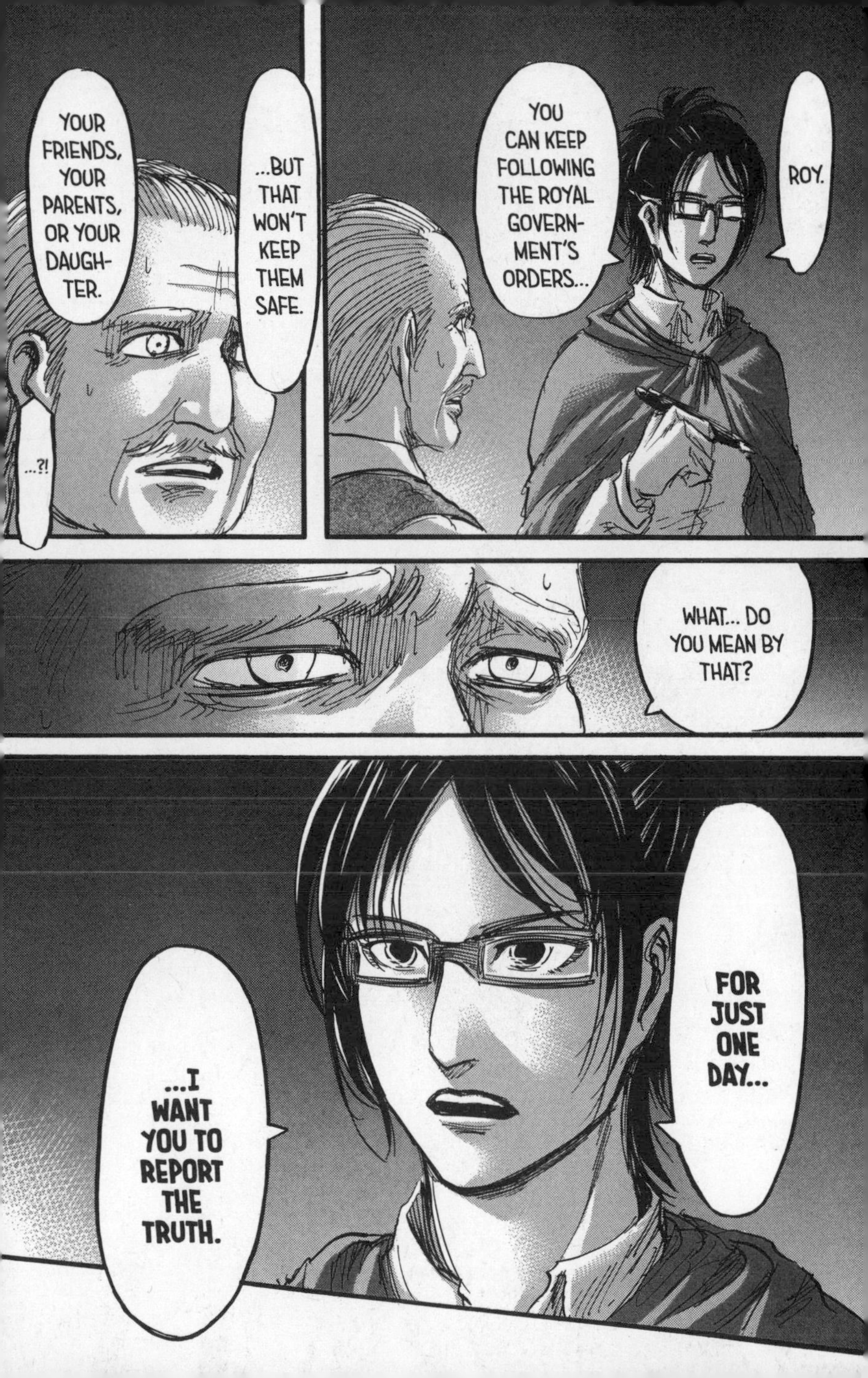
ROY.
YOU CAN KEEP FOLLOWING THE ROYAL GOVERN-MENT'S ORDERS...
...BUT THAT WON'T KEEP THEM SAFE.
YOUR FRIENDS, YOUR PARENTS, OR YOUR DAUGH-TER.
...?!
WHAT... DO YOU MEAN BY THAT?
FOR JUST ONE DAY...
...I WANT YOU TO REPORT THE TRUTH.

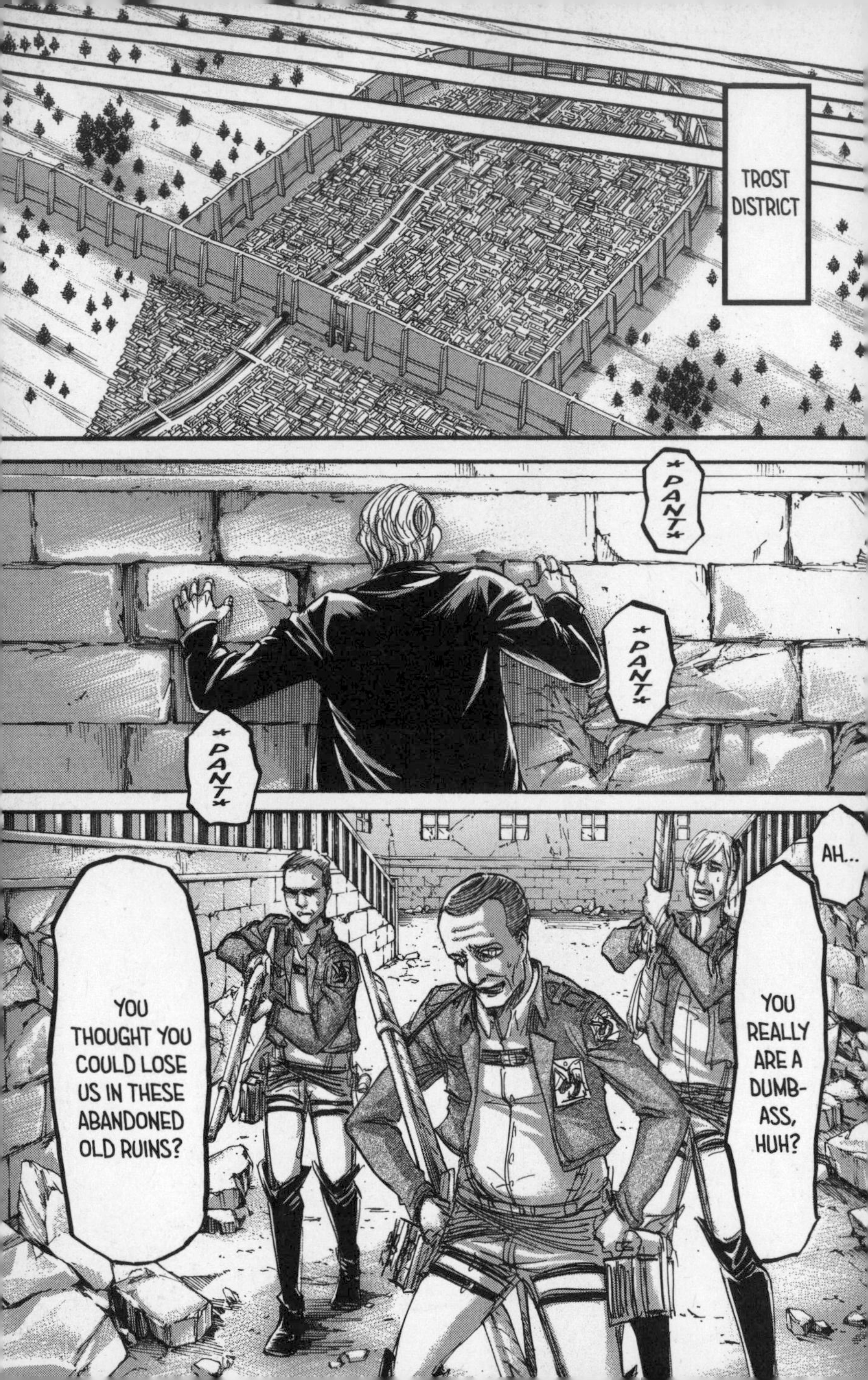
TROST DISTRICT
*PANT*
*PANT*
*PANT*
AH...
YOU REALLY ARE A DUMB-ASS, HUH?
YOU THOUGHT YOU COULD LOSE US IN THESE ABANDONED OLD RUINS?

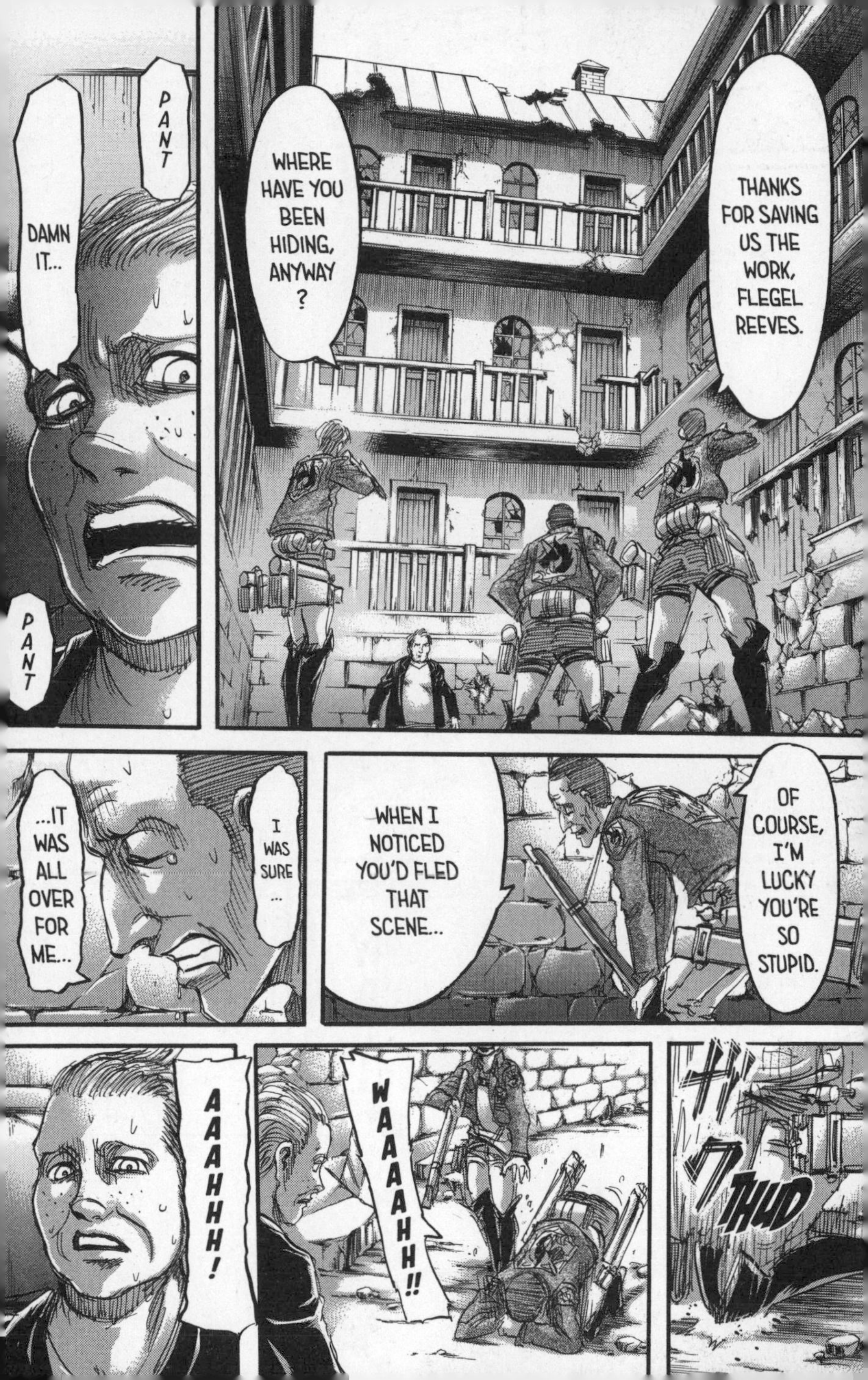
THANKS FOR SAVING US THE WORK, FLEGEL REEVES.
WHERE HAVE YOU BEEN HIDING, ANYWAY?
PANT
DAMN IT...
PANT
OF COURSE, I'M LUCKY YOU'RE SO STUPID.
WHEN I NOTICED YOU'D FLED THAT SCENE...
I WAS SURE...
...IT WAS ALL OVER FOR ME...
THUD
WAAAAAHH!!
AAAAHHH!

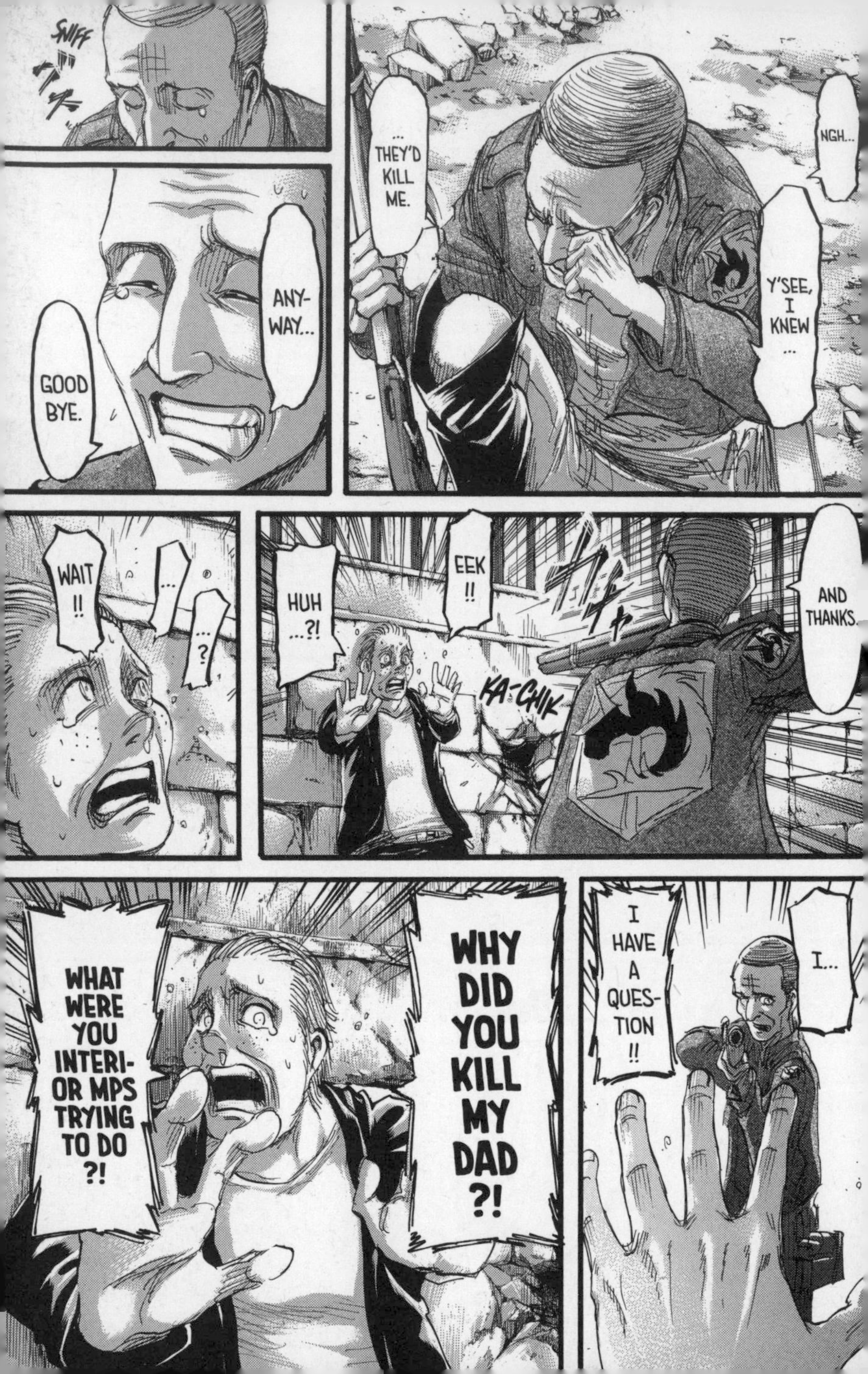
NGH...
Y'SEE, I KNEW ...
... THEY'D KILL ME.
SNIFF
ANY-WAY...
GOOD BYE.
AND THANKS.
KA-CHIK
EEK !!
HUH ...?!
...
...?
WAIT !!
I...
I HAVE A QUES-TION !!
WHY DID YOU KILL MY DAD ?!
WHAT WERE YOU INTERI-OR MPS TRYING TO DO ?!

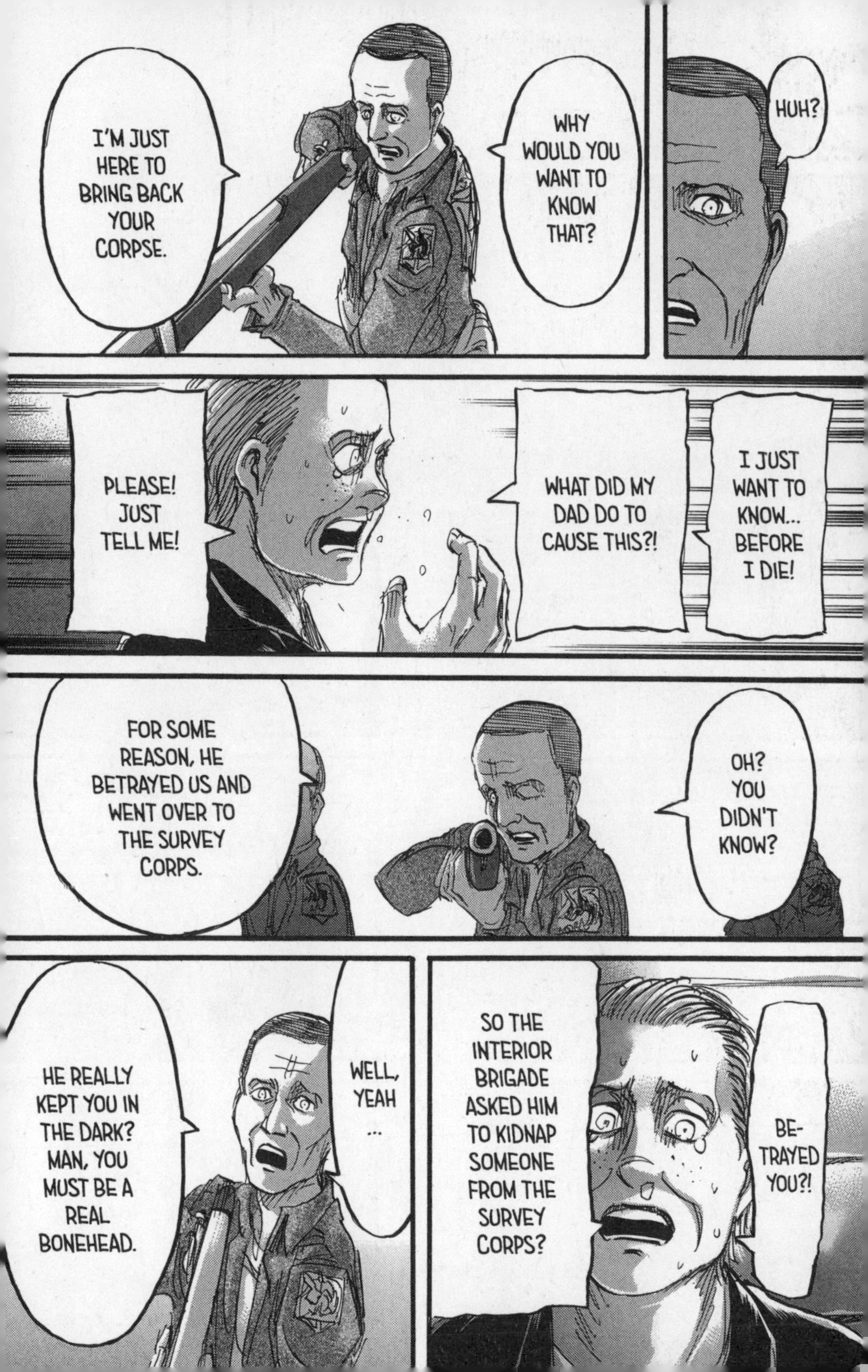
HUH?
WHY WOULD YOU WANT TO KNOW THAT?
I'M JUST HERE TO BRING BACK YOUR CORPSE.
I JUST WANT TO KNOW... BEFORE I DIE!
WHAT DID MY DAD DO TO CAUSE THIS?!
PLEASE! JUST TELL ME!
OH? YOU DIDN'T KNOW?
FOR SOME REASON, HE BETRAYED US AND WENT OVER TO THE SURVEY CORPS.
BE-TRAYED YOU?!
SO THE INTERIOR BRIGADE ASKED HIM TO KIDNAP SOMEONE FROM THE SURVEY CORPS?
WELL, YEAH ...
HE REALLY KEPT YOU IN THE DARK? MAN, YOU MUST BE A REAL BONEHEAD.

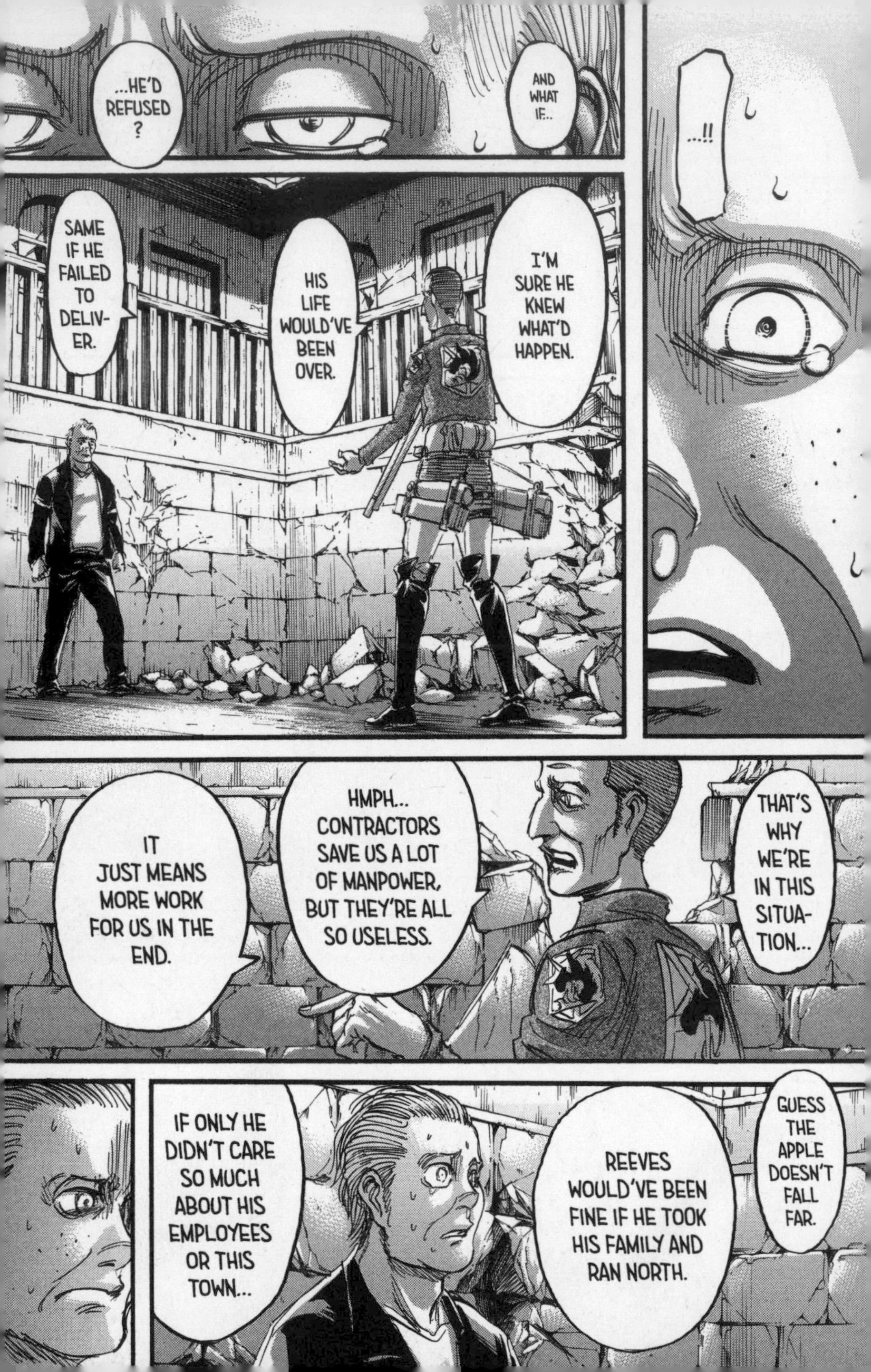
...!!
AND WHAT IF..
...HE'D REFUSED?
I'M SURE HE KNEW WHAT'D HAPPEN.
HIS LIFE WOULD'VE BEEN OVER.
SAME IF HE FAILED TO DELIV-ER.
THAT'S WHY WE'RE IN THIS SITUA-TION...
HMPH... CONTRACTORS SAVE US A LOT OF MANPOWER, BUT THEY'RE ALL SO USELESS.
IT JUST MEANS MORE WORK FOR US IN THE END.
GUESS THE APPLE DOESN'T FALL FAR.
REEVES WOULD'VE BEEN FINE IF HE TOOK HIS FAMILY AND RAN NORTH.
IF ONLY HE DIDN'T CARE SO MUCH ABOUT HIS EMPLOYEES OR THIS TOWN...

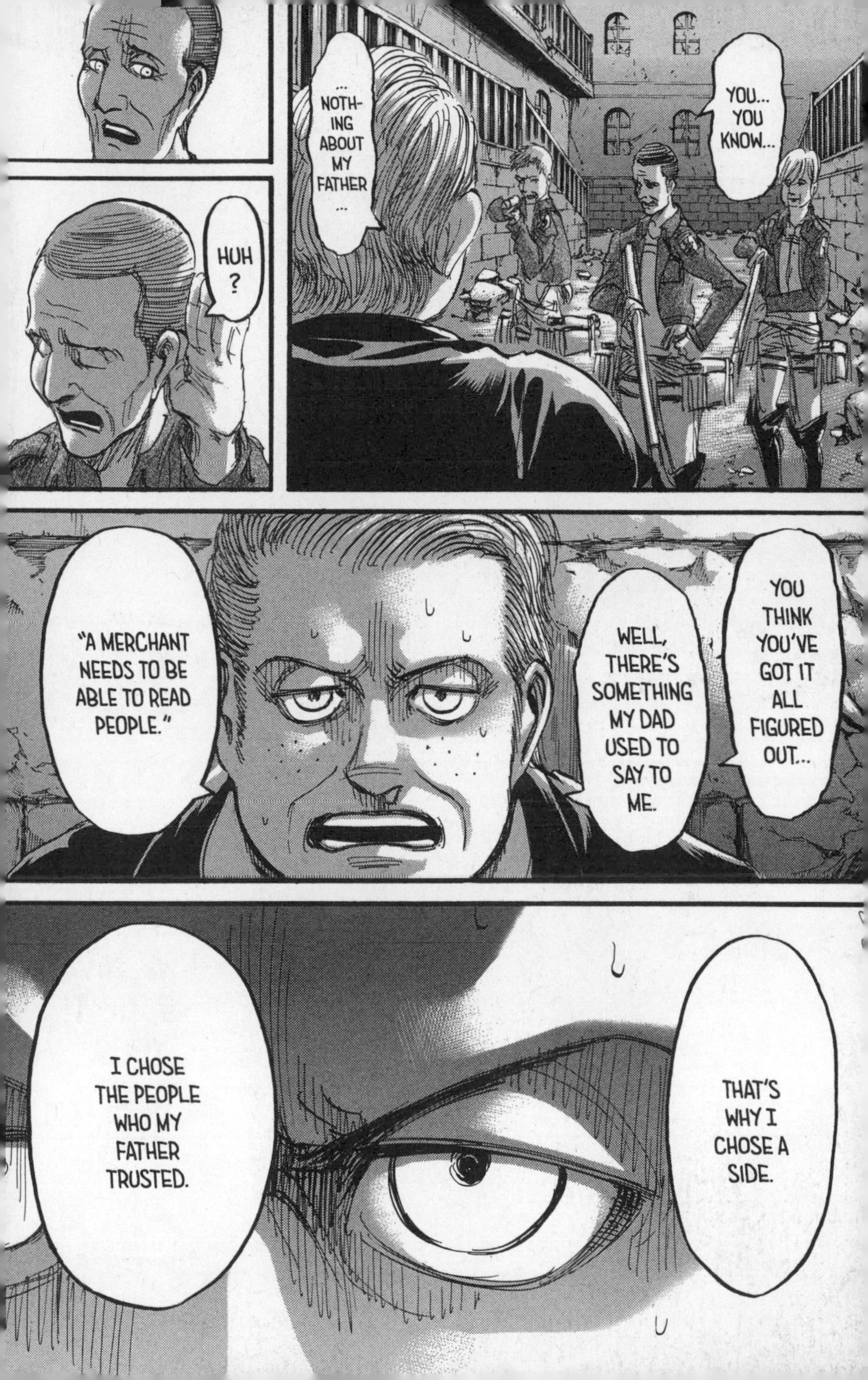
YOU... YOU KNOW...
... NOTH-ING ABOUT MY FATHER ...
HUH ?
YOU THINK YOU'VE GOT IT ALL FIGURED OUT...
WELL, THERE'S SOMETHING MY DAD USED TO SAY TO ME.
"A MERCHANT NEEDS TO BE ABLE TO READ PEOPLE."
THAT'S WHY I CHOSE A SIDE.
I CHOSE THE PEOPLE WHO MY FATHER TRUSTED.

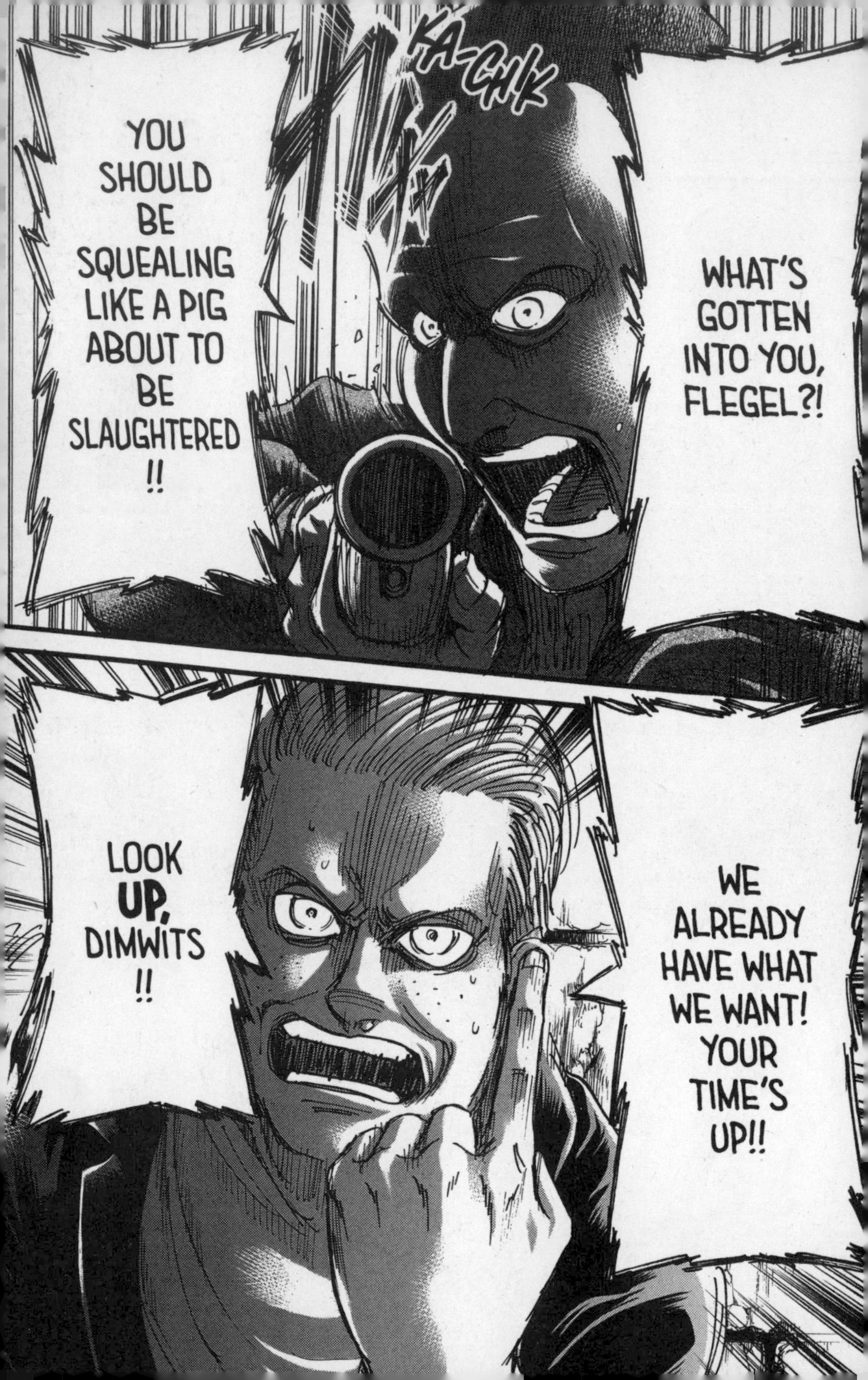
KA-CHIK
WHAT'S GOTTEN INTO YOU, FLEGEL?!
YOU SHOULD BE SQUEALING LIKE A PIG ABOUT TO BE SLAUGHTERED !!
WE ALREADY HAVE WHAT WE WANT! YOUR TIME'S UP!!
LOOK **UP,** DIMWITS !!

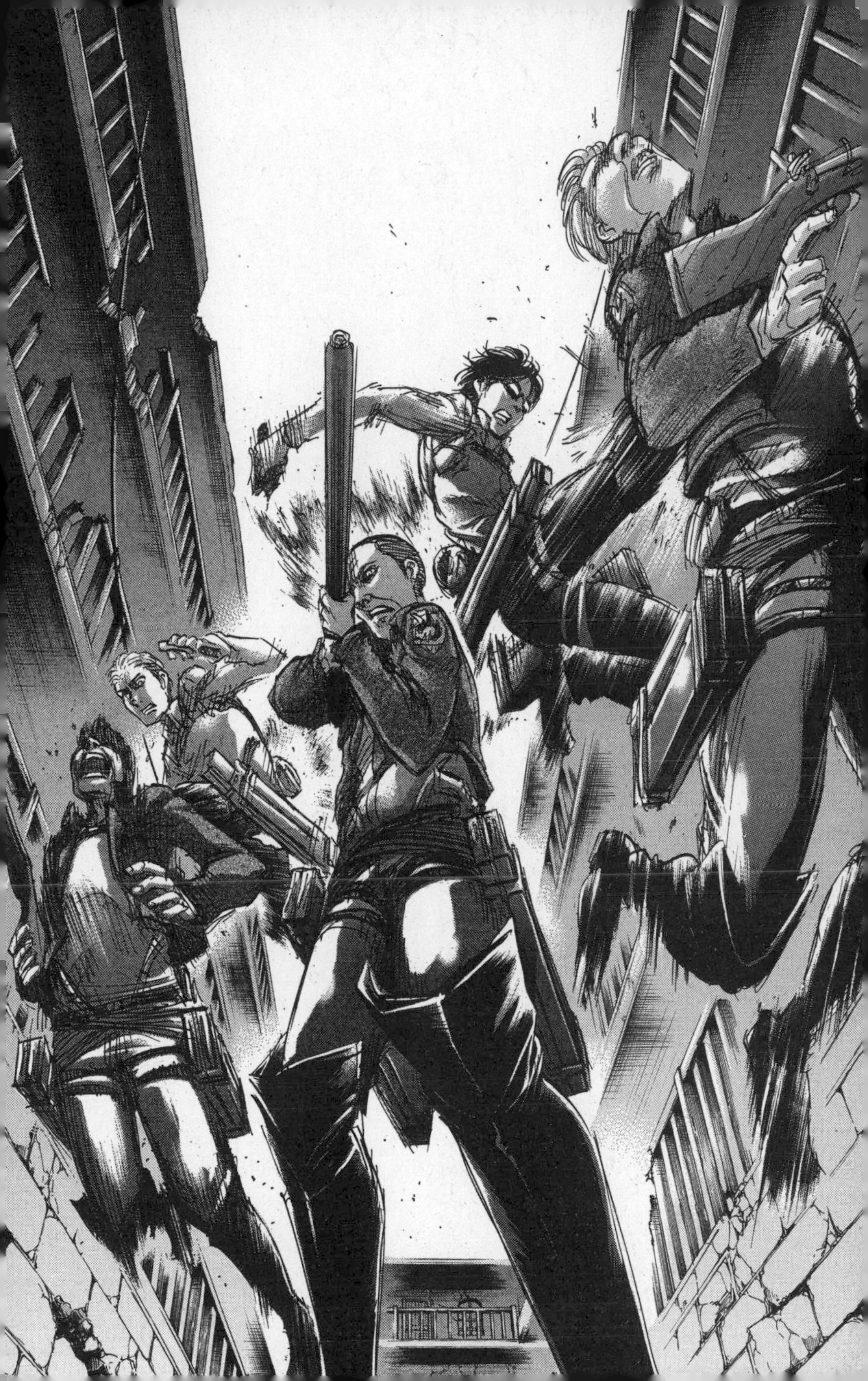

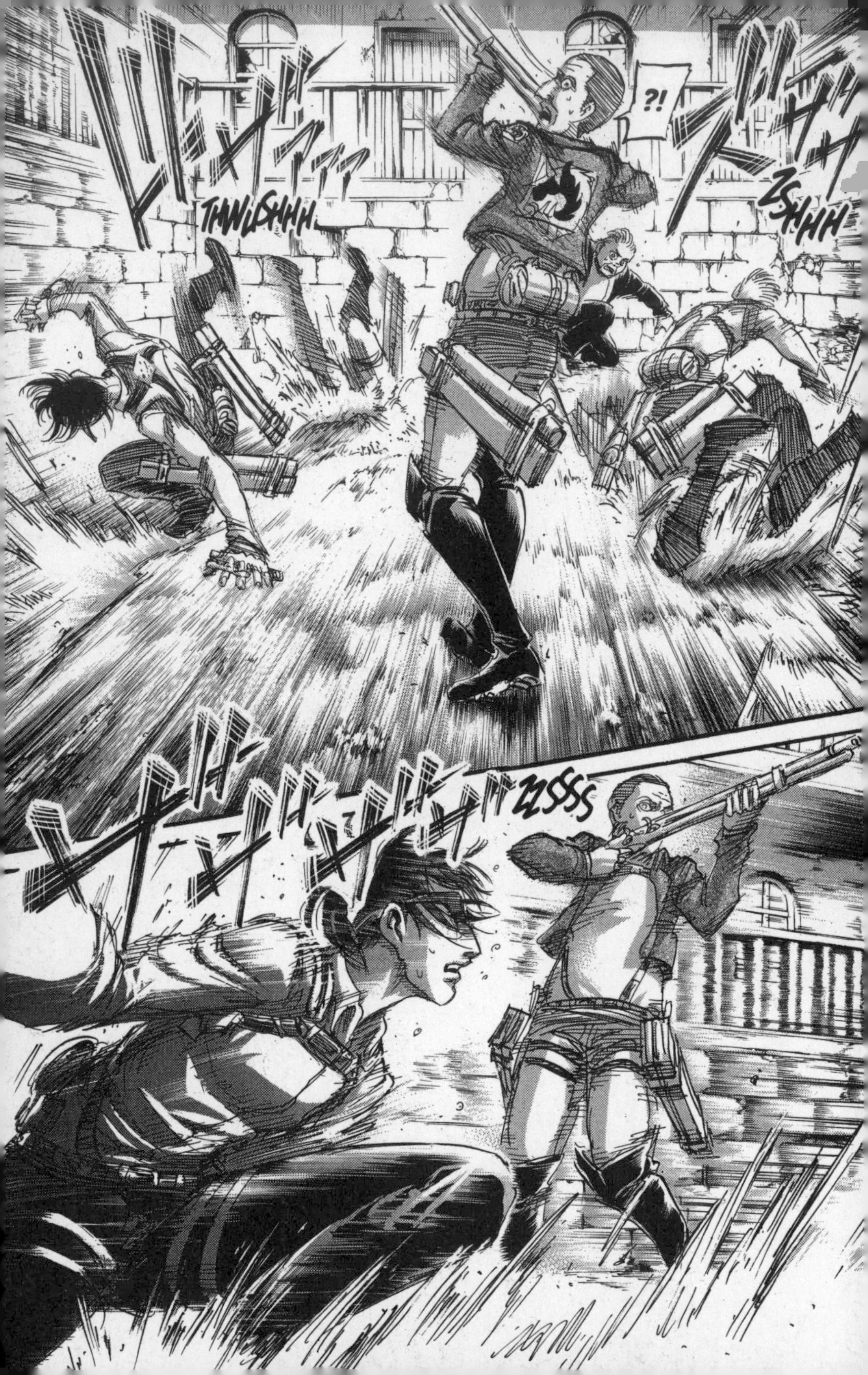
?!
ZSHHH
THWUSHHH
ZZSSSS

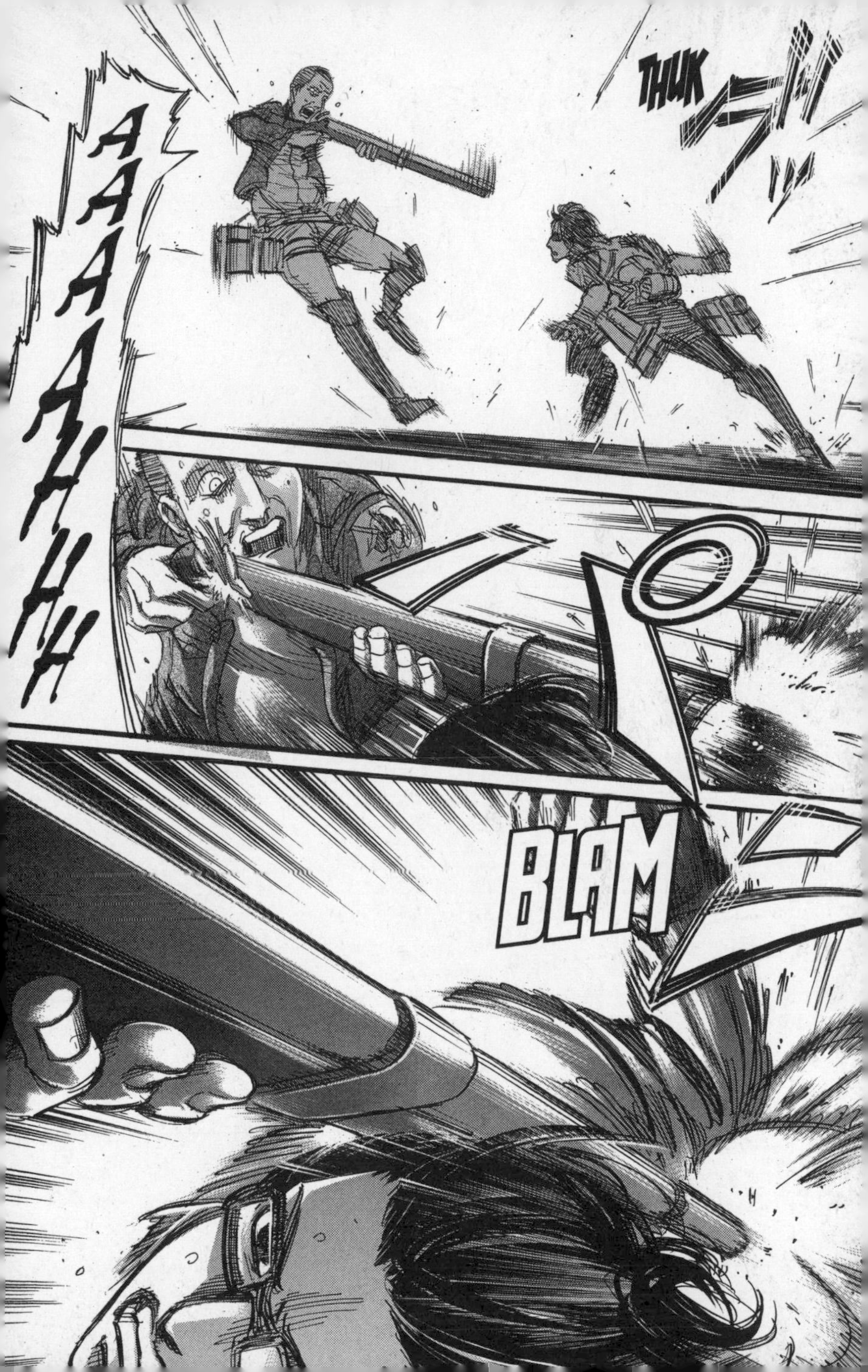
THUK
AAAAHHH
BLAM

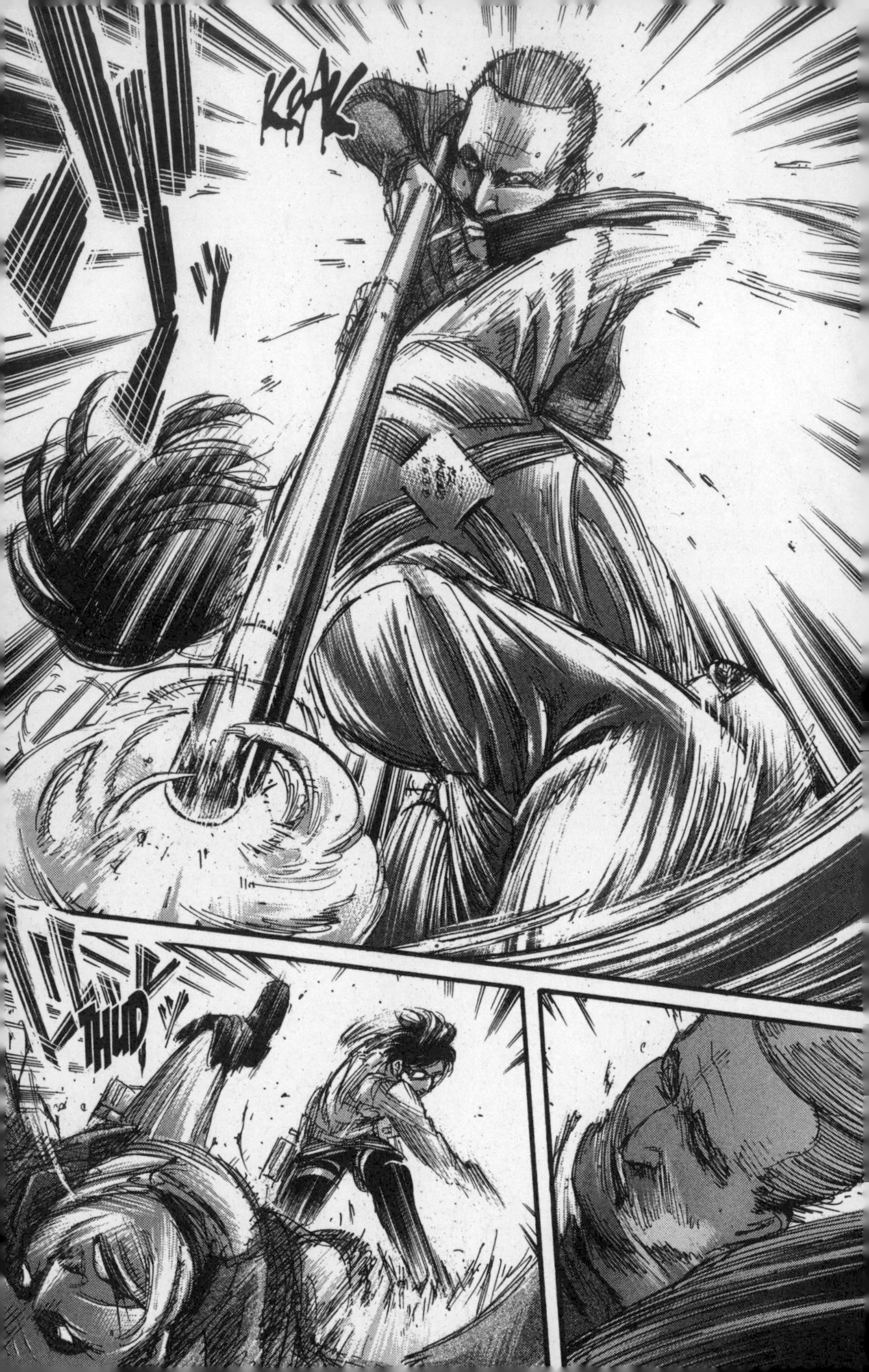
KRAK
THUD

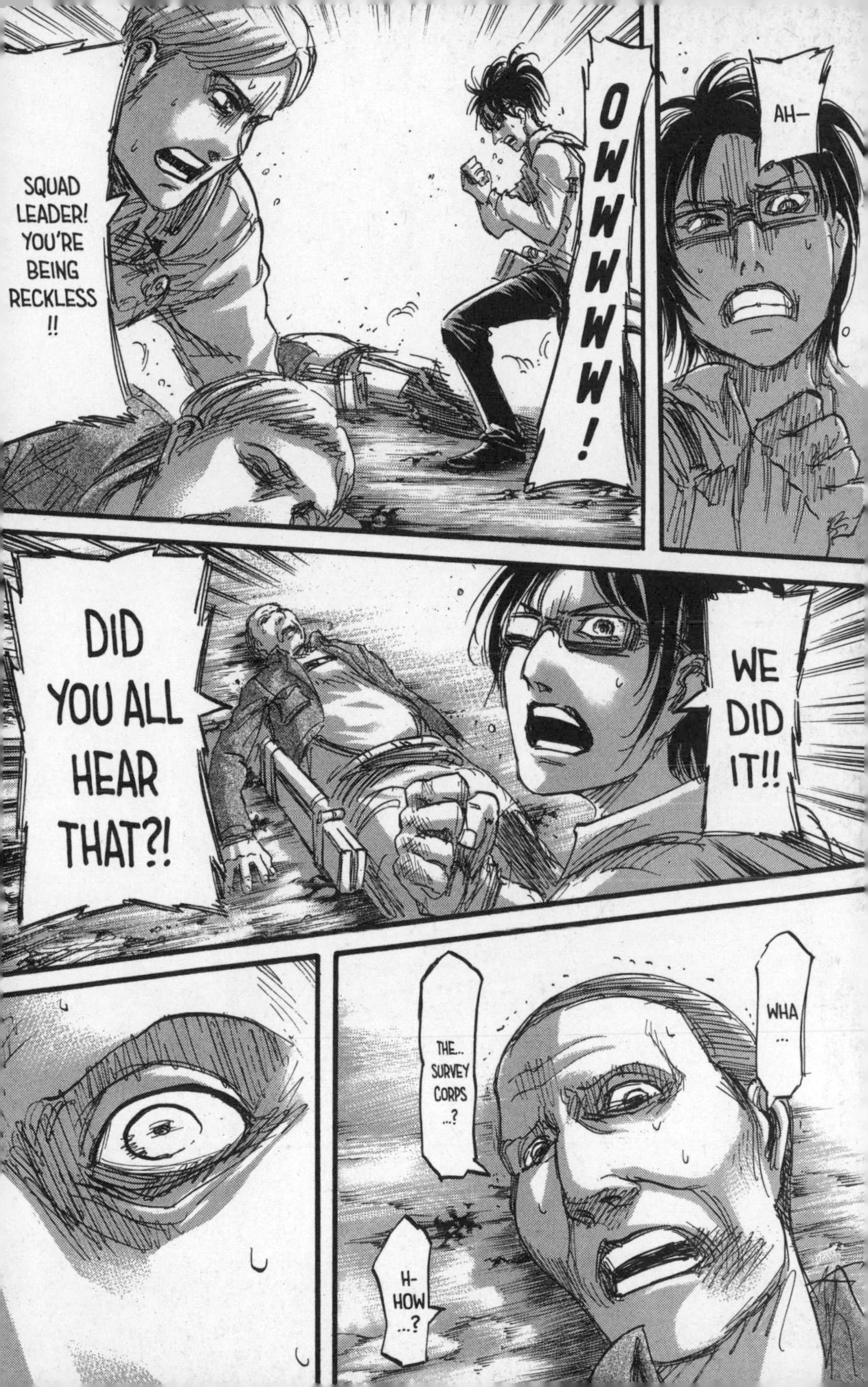
AH—
OWWWWW!
SQUAD LEADER! YOU'RE BEING RECKLESS!!
WE DID IT!!
DID YOU ALL HEAR THAT?!
WHA...
THE.. SURVEY CORPS ...?
H-HOW ...?

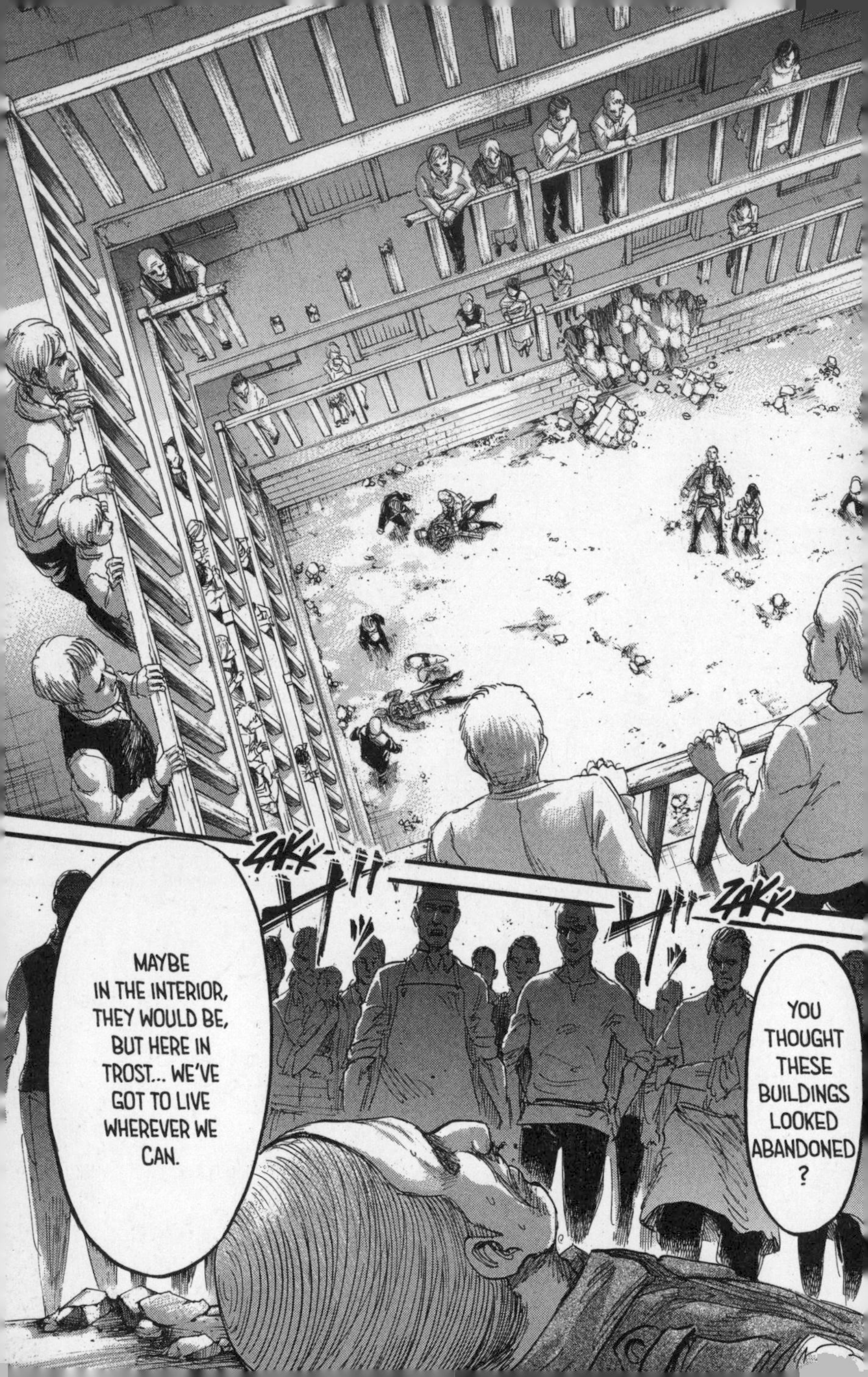
ZAK-K
ZAK-K
YOU THOUGHT THESE BUILDINGS LOOKED ABANDONED?
MAYBE IN THE INTERIOR, THEY WOULD BE, BUT HERE IN TROST... WE'VE GOT TO LIVE WHEREVER WE CAN.

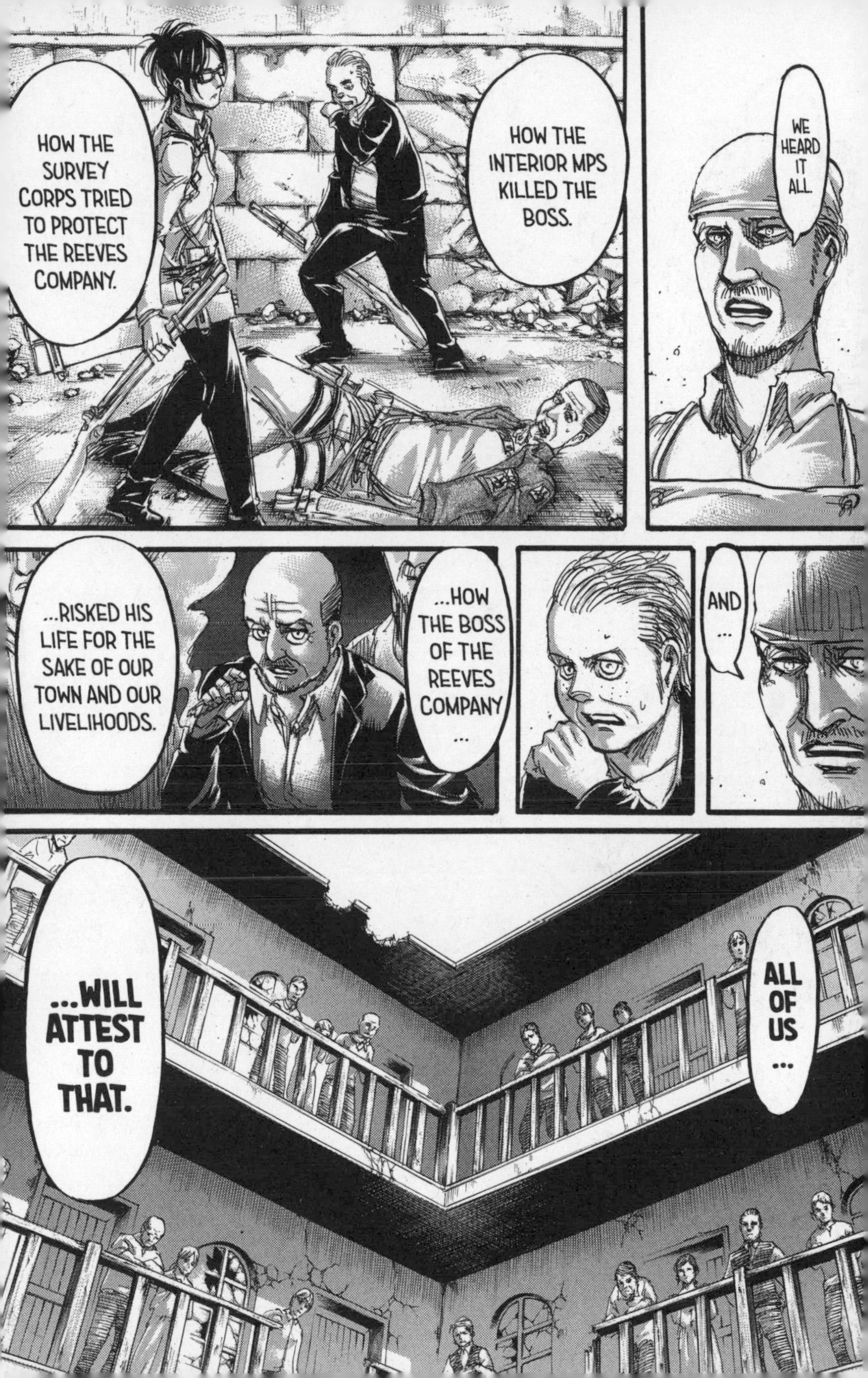
WE HEARD IT ALL.
HOW THE INTERIOR MPS KILLED THE BOSS.
HOW THE SURVEY CORPS TRIED TO PROTECT THE REEVES COMPANY.
AND ...
...HOW THE BOSS OF THE REEVES COMPANY ...
...RISKED HIS LIFE FOR THE SAKE OF OUR TOWN AND OUR LIVELIHOODS.
ALL OF US ...
...WILL ATTEST TO THAT.

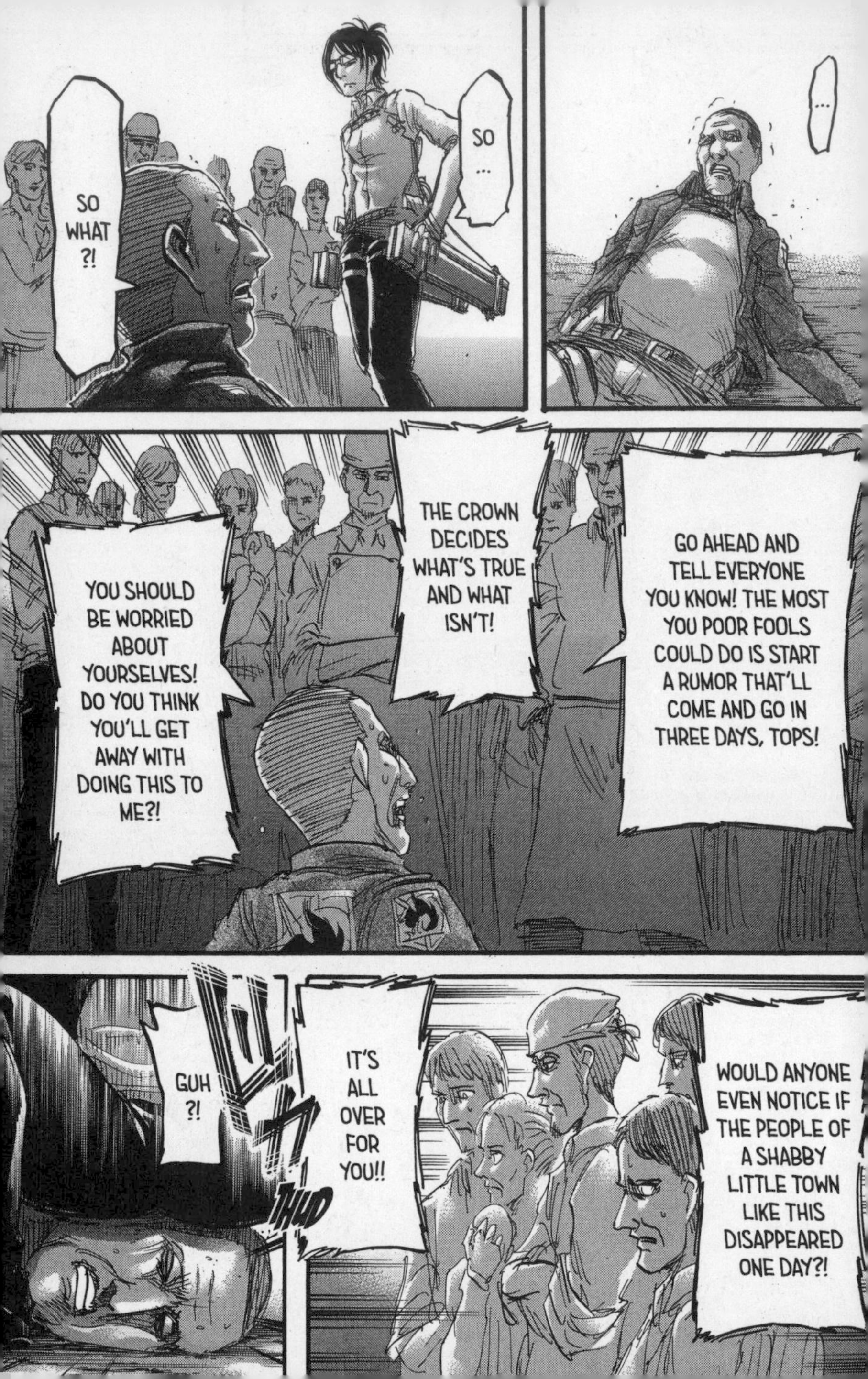
...
SO ...
SO WHAT?!
GO AHEAD AND TELL EVERYONE YOU KNOW! THE MOST YOU POOR FOOLS COULD DO IS START A RUMOR THAT'LL COME AND GO IN THREE DAYS, TOPS!
THE CROWN DECIDES WHAT'S TRUE AND WHAT ISN'T!
YOU SHOULD BE WORRIED ABOUT YOURSELVES! DO YOU THINK YOU'LL GET AWAY WITH DOING THIS TO ME?!
WOULD ANYONE EVEN NOTICE IF THE PEOPLE OF A SHABBY LITTLE TOWN LIKE THIS DISAPPEARED ONE DAY?!
IT'S ALL OVER FOR YOU!!
GUH?!
THUD

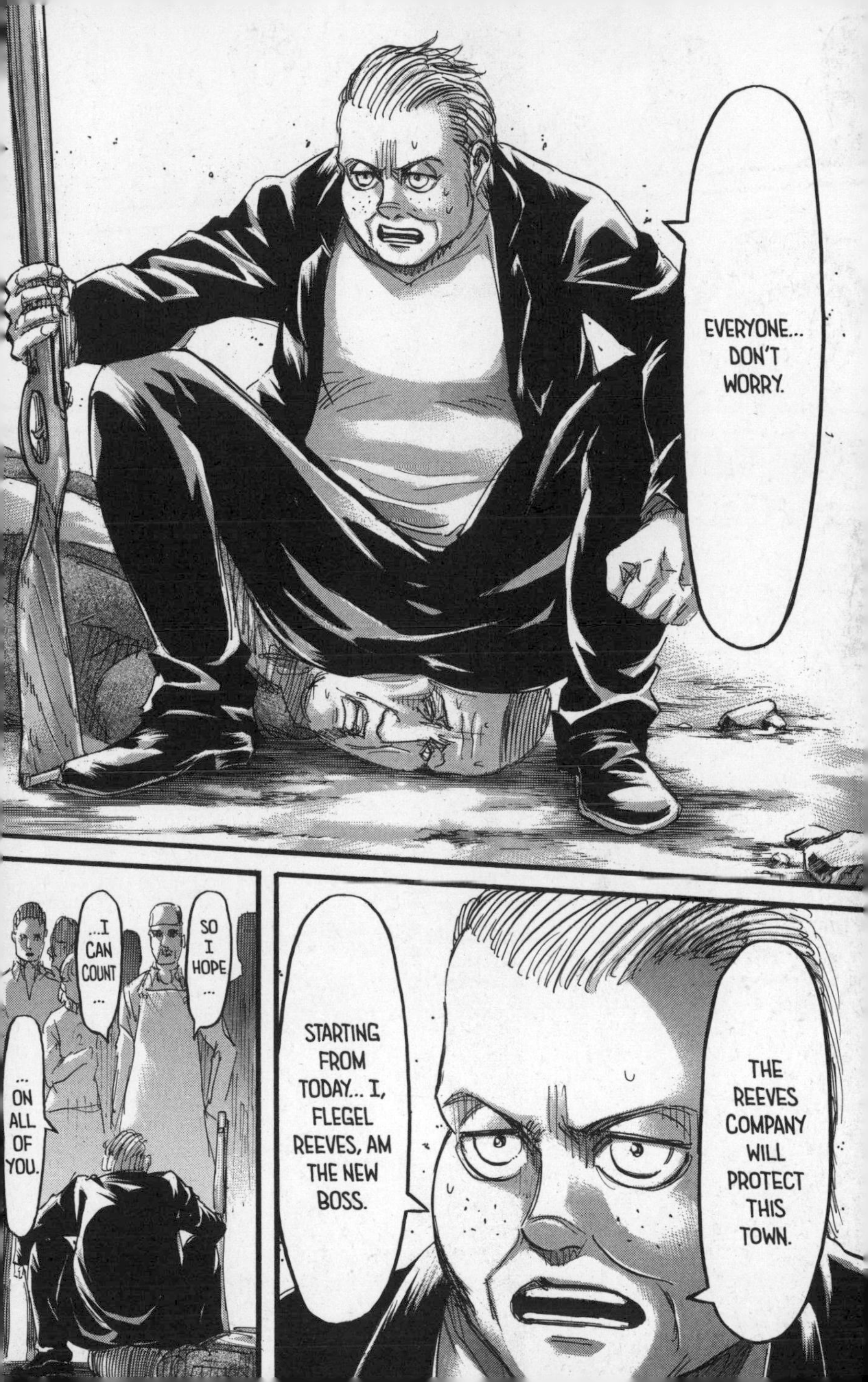
EVERYONE... DON'T WORRY.
THE REEVES COMPANY WILL PROTECT THIS TOWN.
STARTING FROM TODAY... I, FLEGEL REEVES, AM THE NEW BOSS.
SO I HOPE ...
...I CAN COUNT ...
... ON ALL OF YOU.

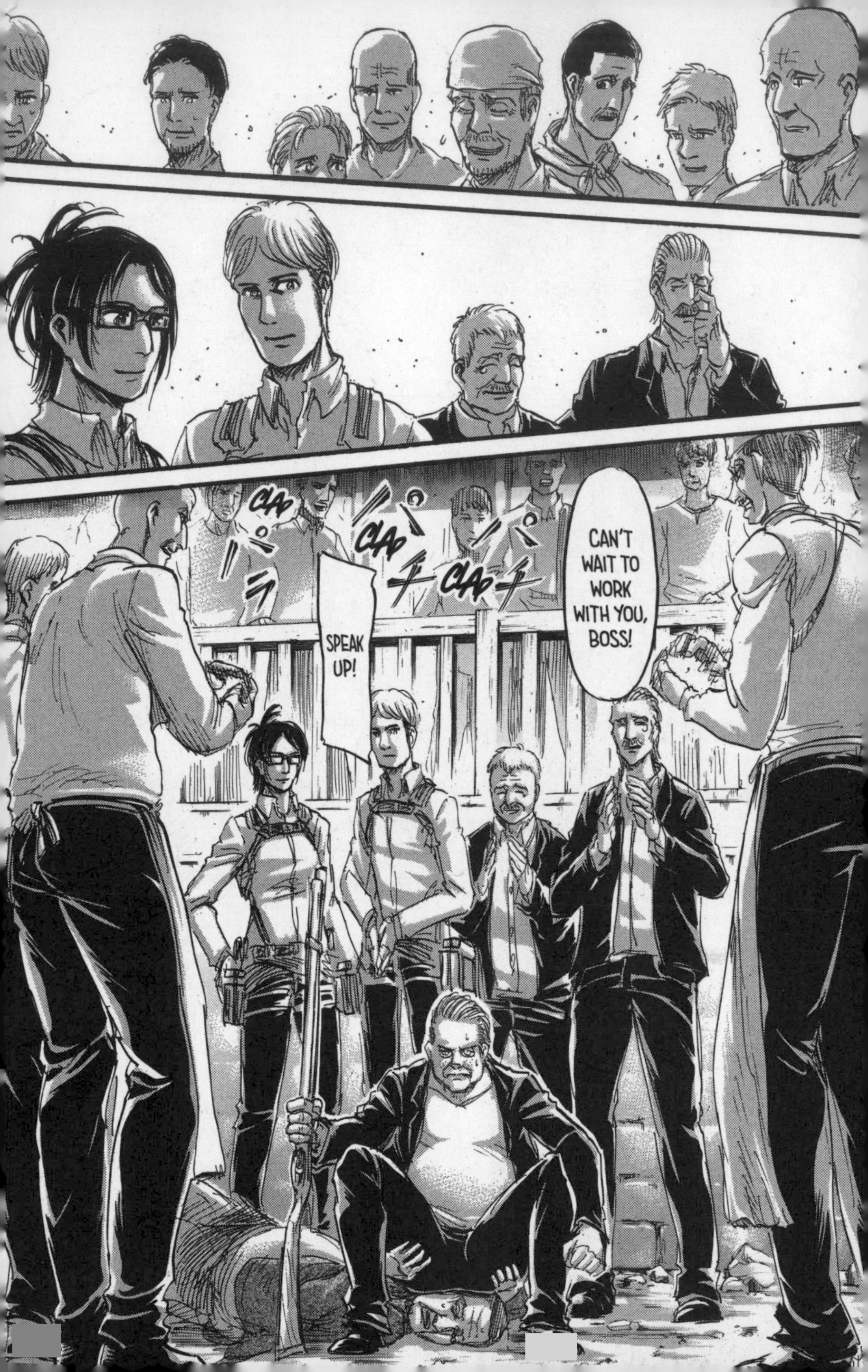
CLAP
CLAP
CLAP
CAN'T WAIT TO WORK WITH YOU, BOSS!
SPEAK UP!

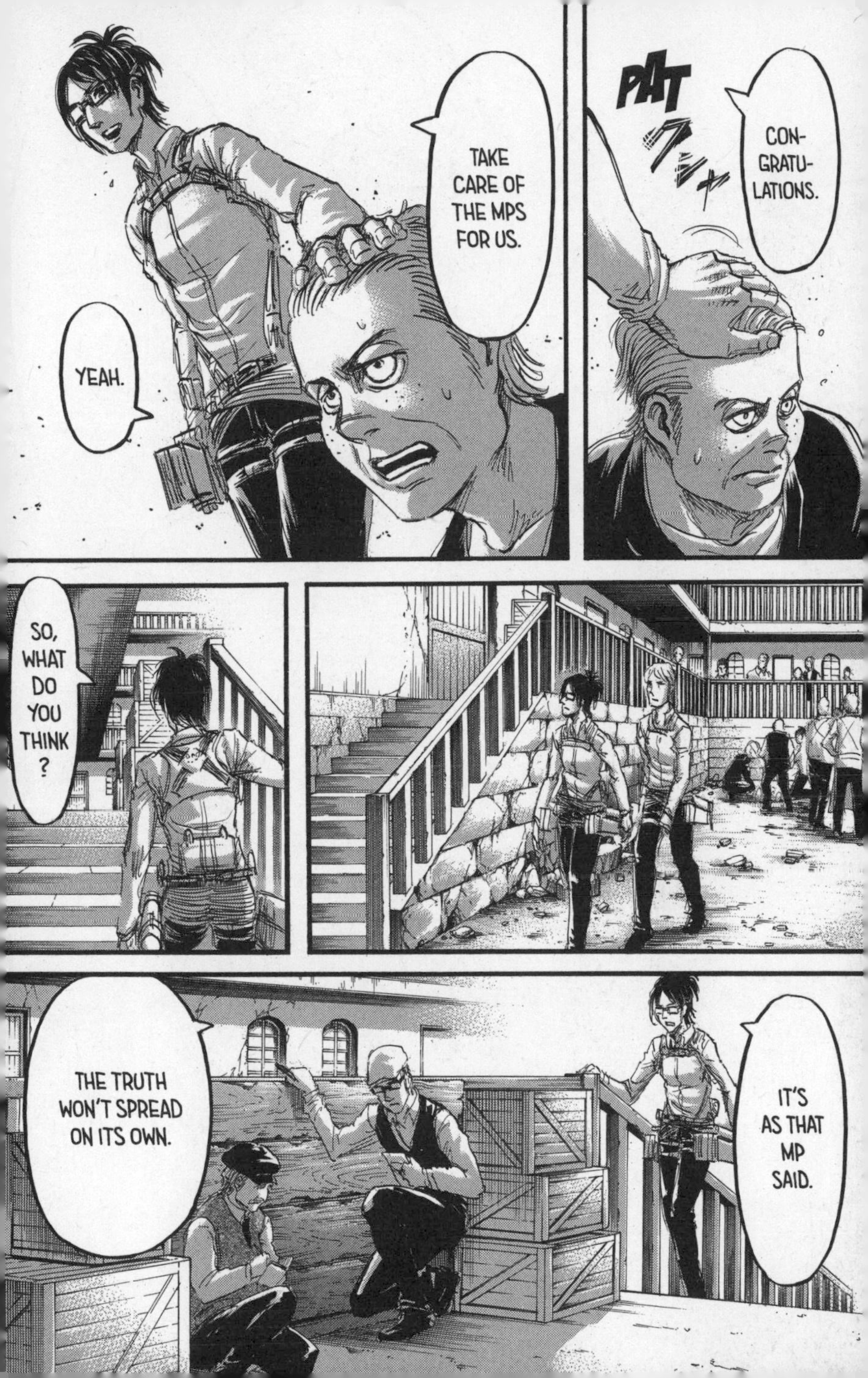
PAT
CON-GRATU-LATIONS.
TAKE CARE OF THE MPS FOR US.
YEAH.
SO, WHAT DO YOU THINK?
IT'S AS THAT MP SAID.
THE TRUTH WON'T SPREAD ON ITS OWN.

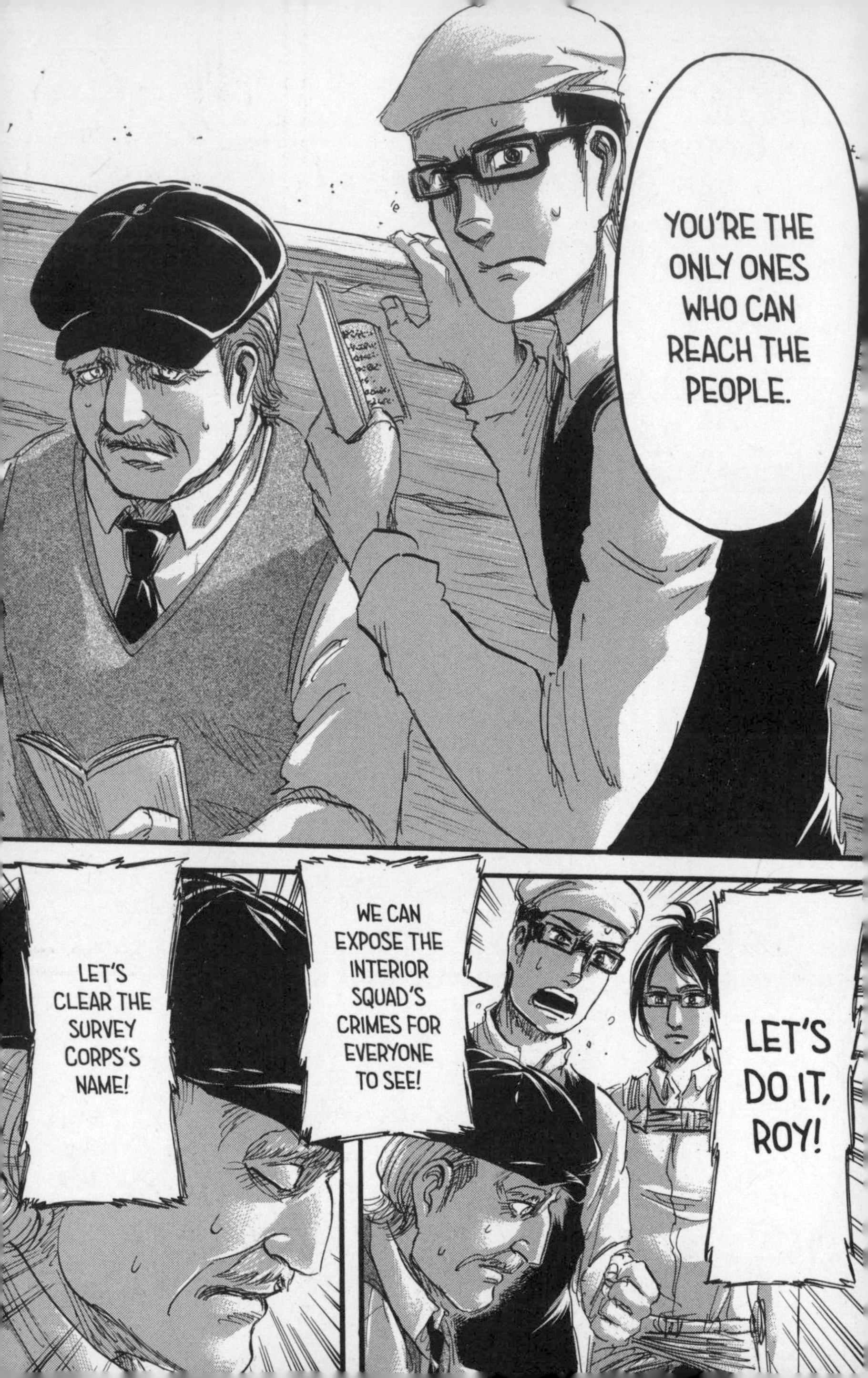
YOU'RE THE ONLY ONES WHO CAN REACH THE PEOPLE.
LET'S DO IT, ROY!
WE CAN EXPOSE THE INTERIOR SQUAD'S CRIMES FOR EVERYONE TO SEE!
LET'S CLEAR THE SURVEY CORPS'S NAME!

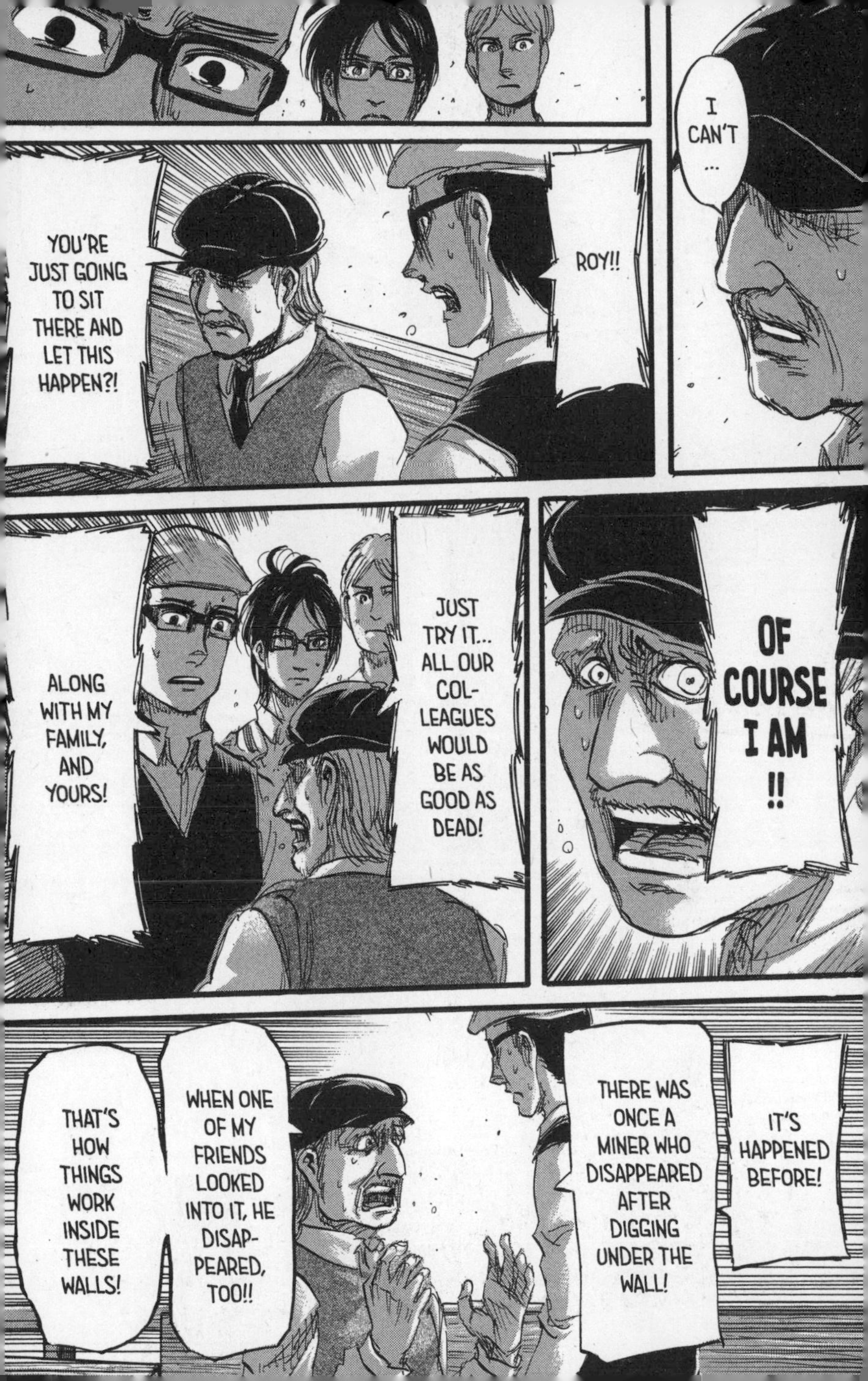
I CAN'T ...
ROY!!
YOU'RE JUST GOING TO SIT THERE AND LET THIS HAPPEN?!
OF COURSE I AM!!
JUST TRY IT... ALL OUR COL-LEAGUES WOULD BE AS GOOD AS DEAD!
ALONG WITH MY FAMILY, AND YOURS!
IT'S HAPPENED BEFORE!
THERE WAS ONCE A MINER WHO DISAPPEARED AFTER DIGGING UNDER THE WALL!
WHEN ONE OF MY FRIENDS LOOKED INTO IT, HE DISAP-PEARED, TOO!!
THAT'S HOW THINGS WORK INSIDE THESE WALLS!

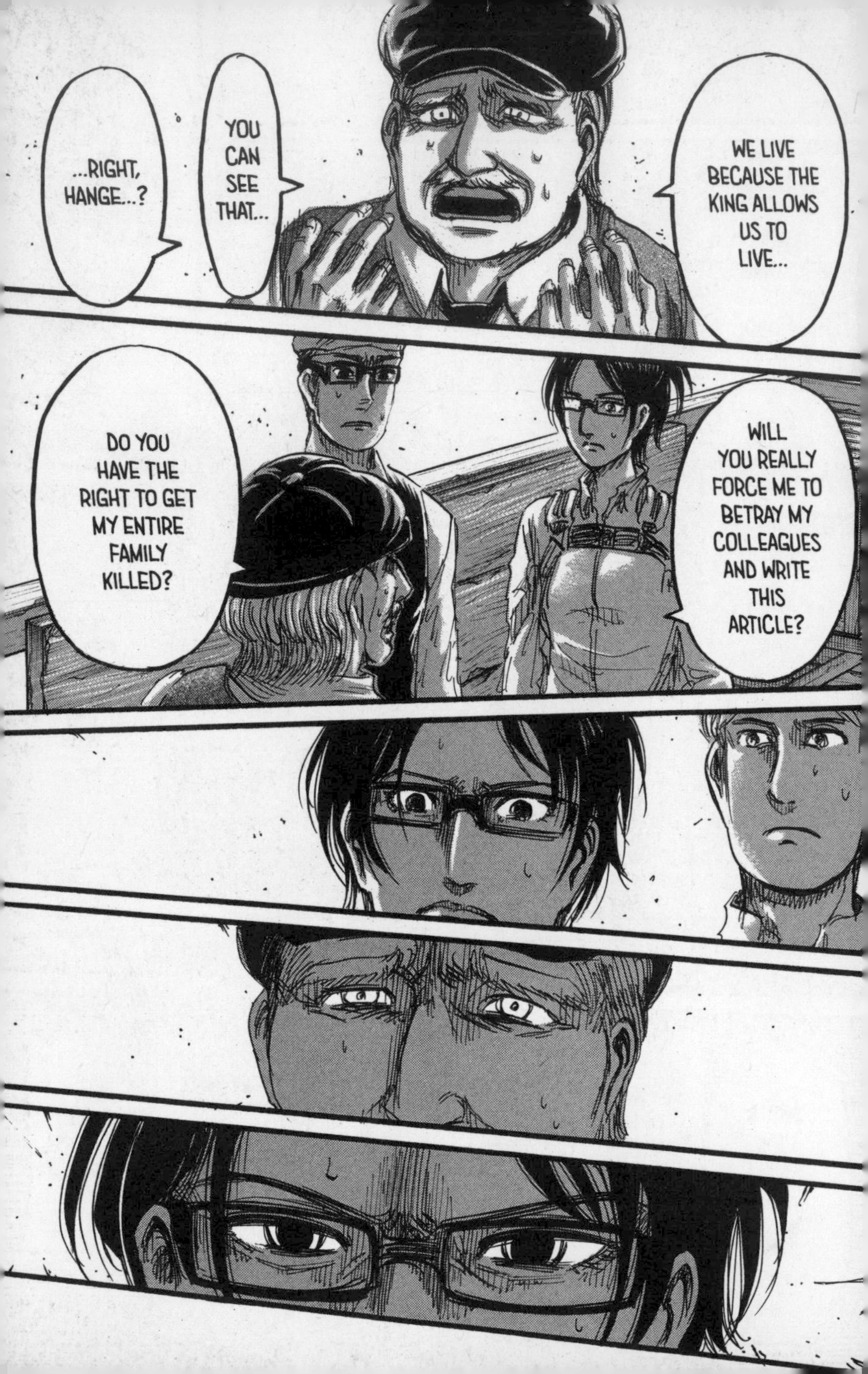
WE LIVE BECAUSE THE KING ALLOWS US TO LIVE...
YOU CAN SEE THAT...
...RIGHT, HANGE...?
WILL YOU REALLY FORCE ME TO BETRAY MY COLLEAGUES AND WRITE THIS ARTICLE?
DO YOU HAVE THE RIGHT TO GET MY ENTIRE FAMILY KILLED?

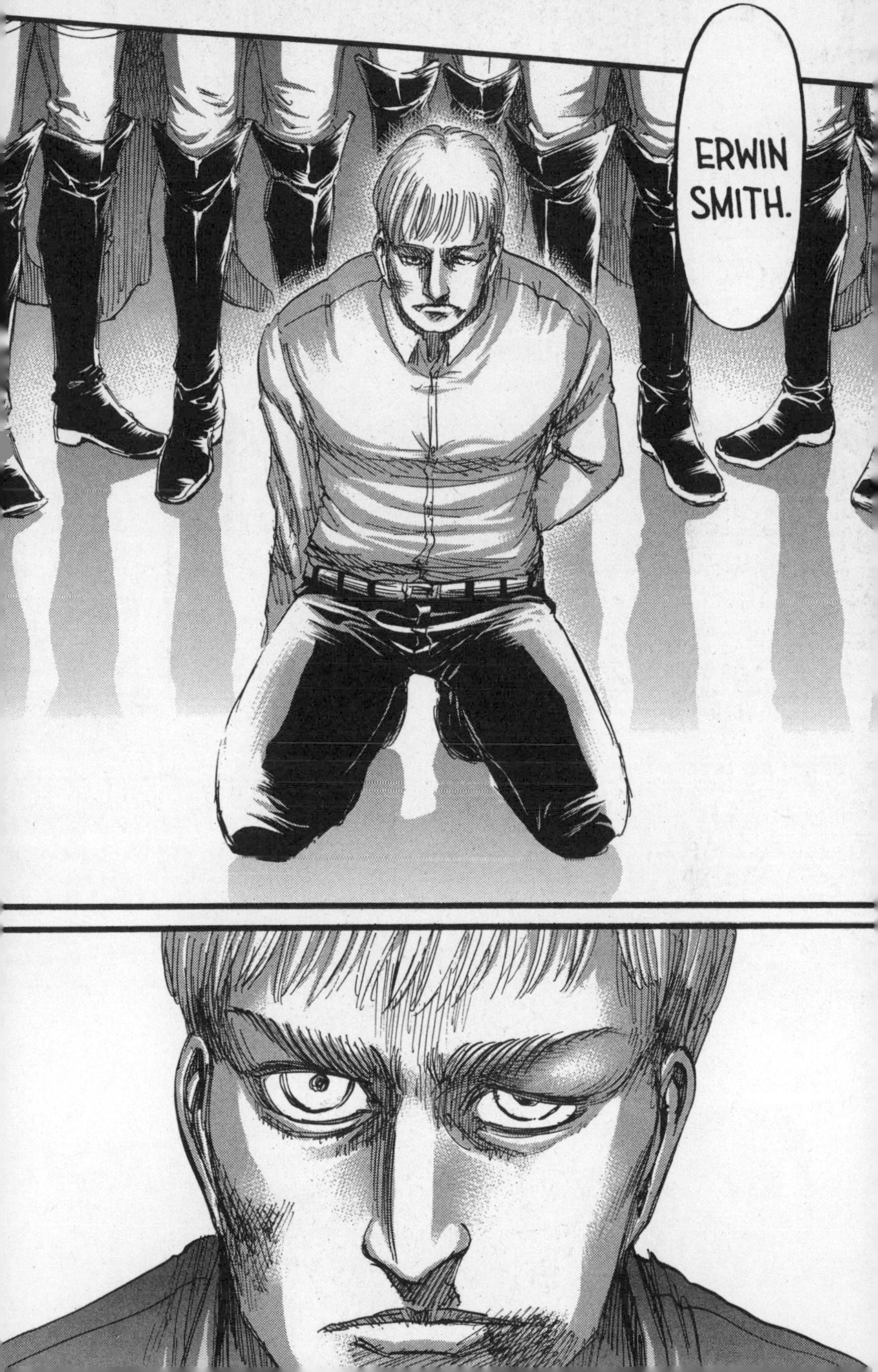
ERWIN SMITH.

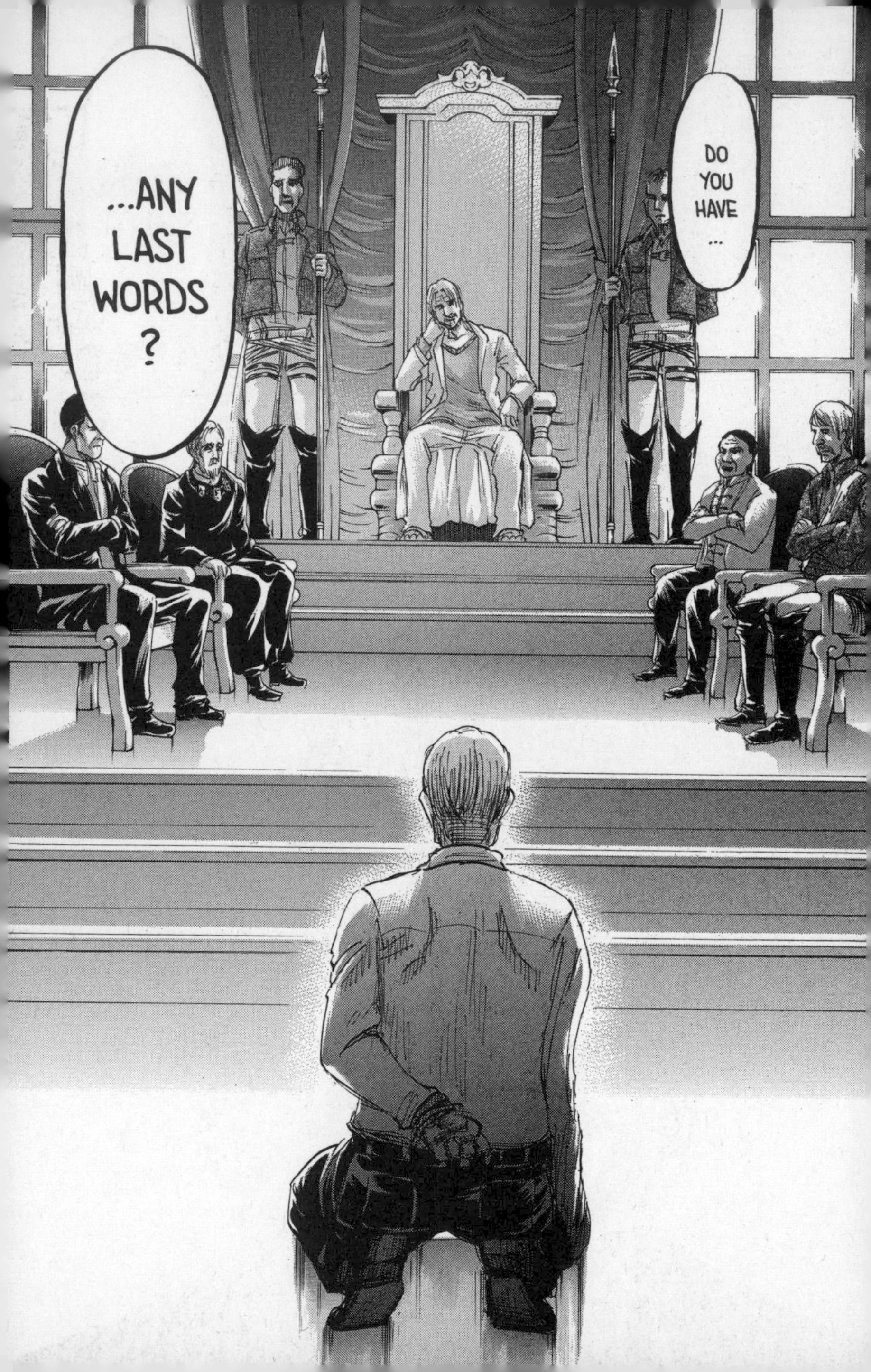
DO YOU HAVE ...
...ANY LAST WORDS ?

ATTACK on TITAN

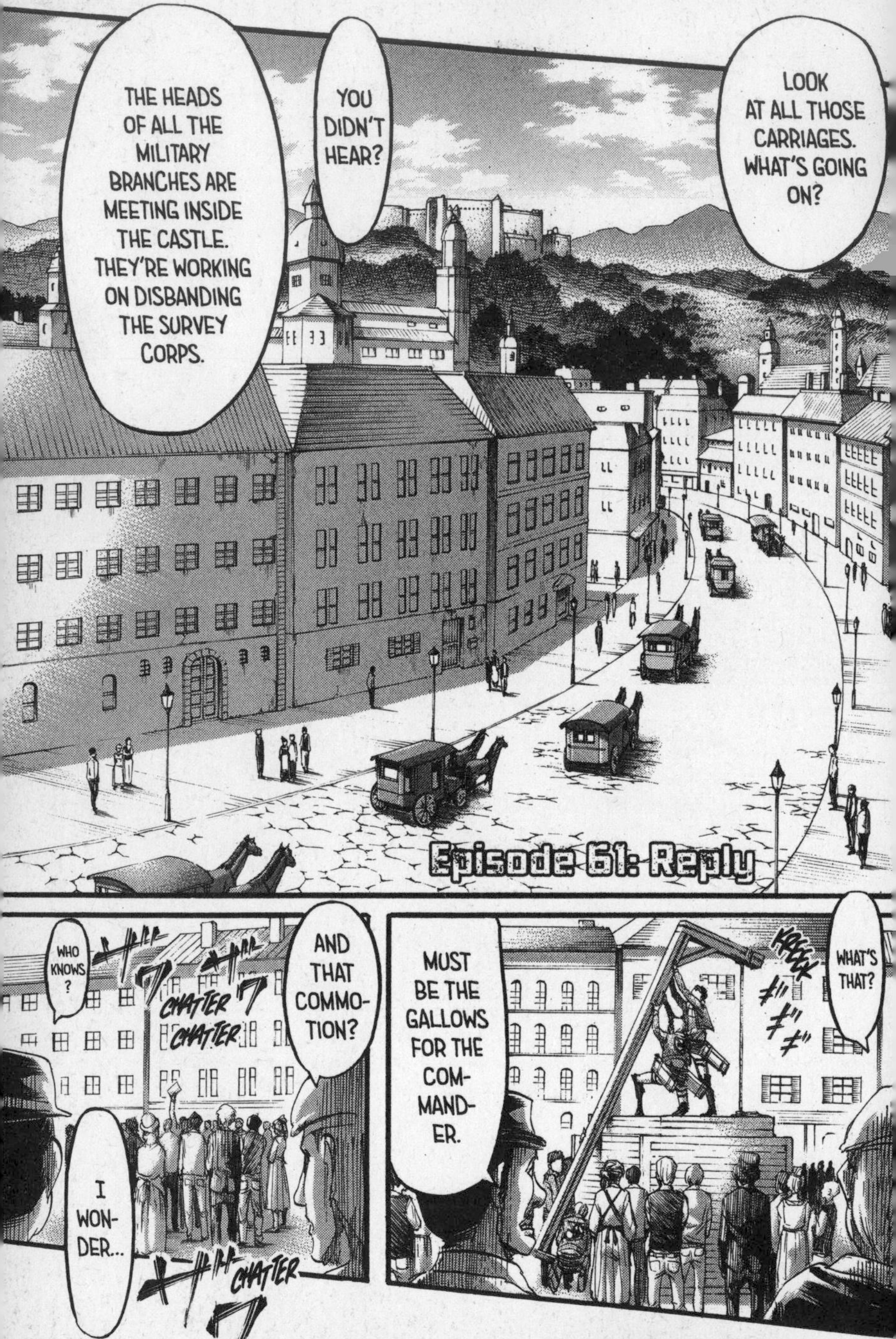

LOOK AT ALL THOSE CARRIAGES. WHAT'S GOING ON?
YOU DIDN'T HEAR?
THE HEADS OF ALL THE MILITARY BRANCHES ARE MEETING INSIDE THE CASTLE. THEY'RE WORKING ON DISBANDING THE SURVEY CORPS.
Episode 61: Reply
WHAT'S THAT?
KREEK
MUST BE THE GALLOWS FOR THE COMMANDER.
AND THAT COMMOTION?
WHO KNOWS?
CHATTER CHATTER
I WONDER...
CHATTER

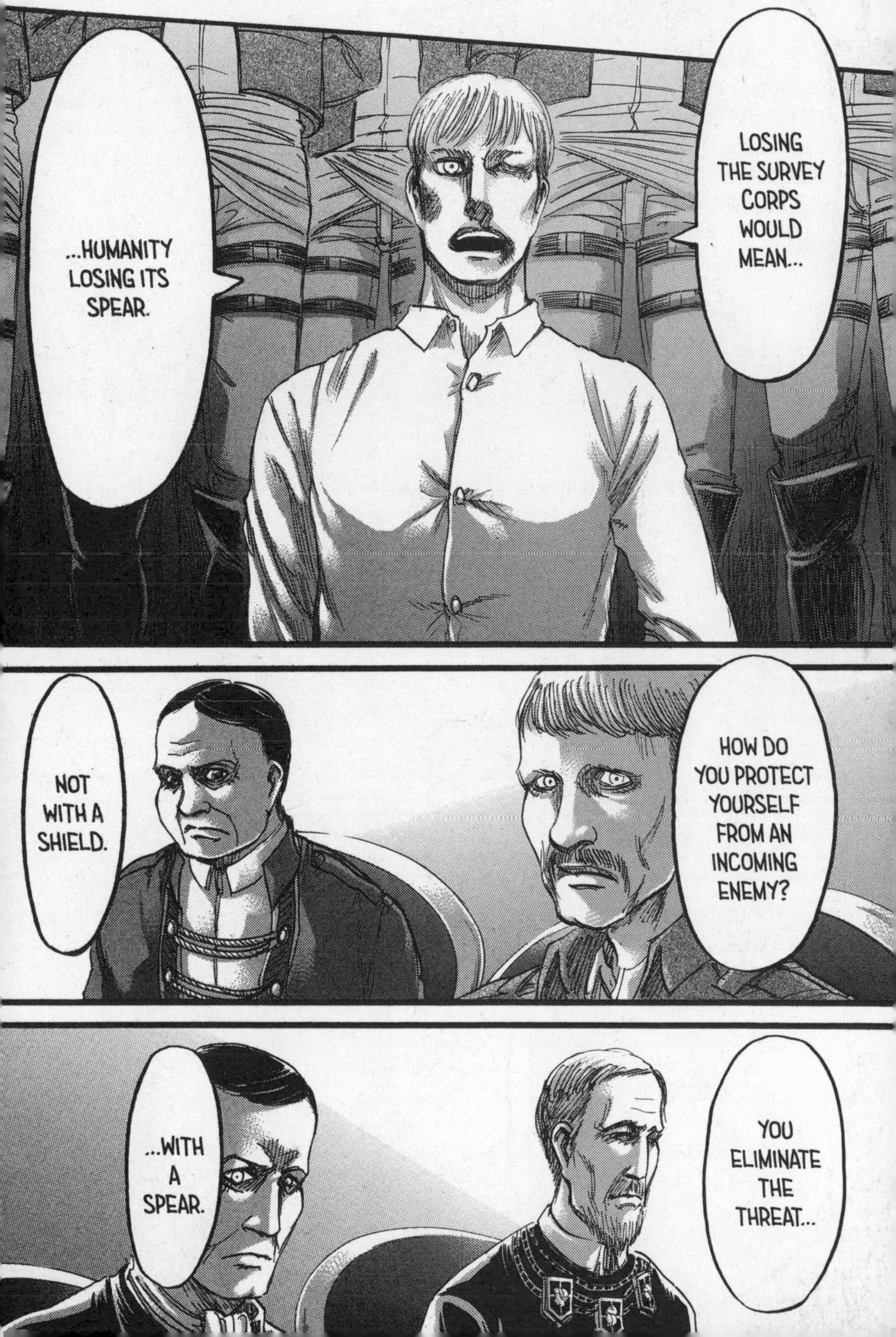
LOSING THE SURVEY CORPS WOULD MEAN...
...HUMANITY LOSING ITS SPEAR.
HOW DO YOU PROTECT YOURSELF FROM AN INCOMING ENEMY?
NOT WITH A SHIELD.
YOU ELIMINATE THE THREAT...
...WITH A SPEAR.

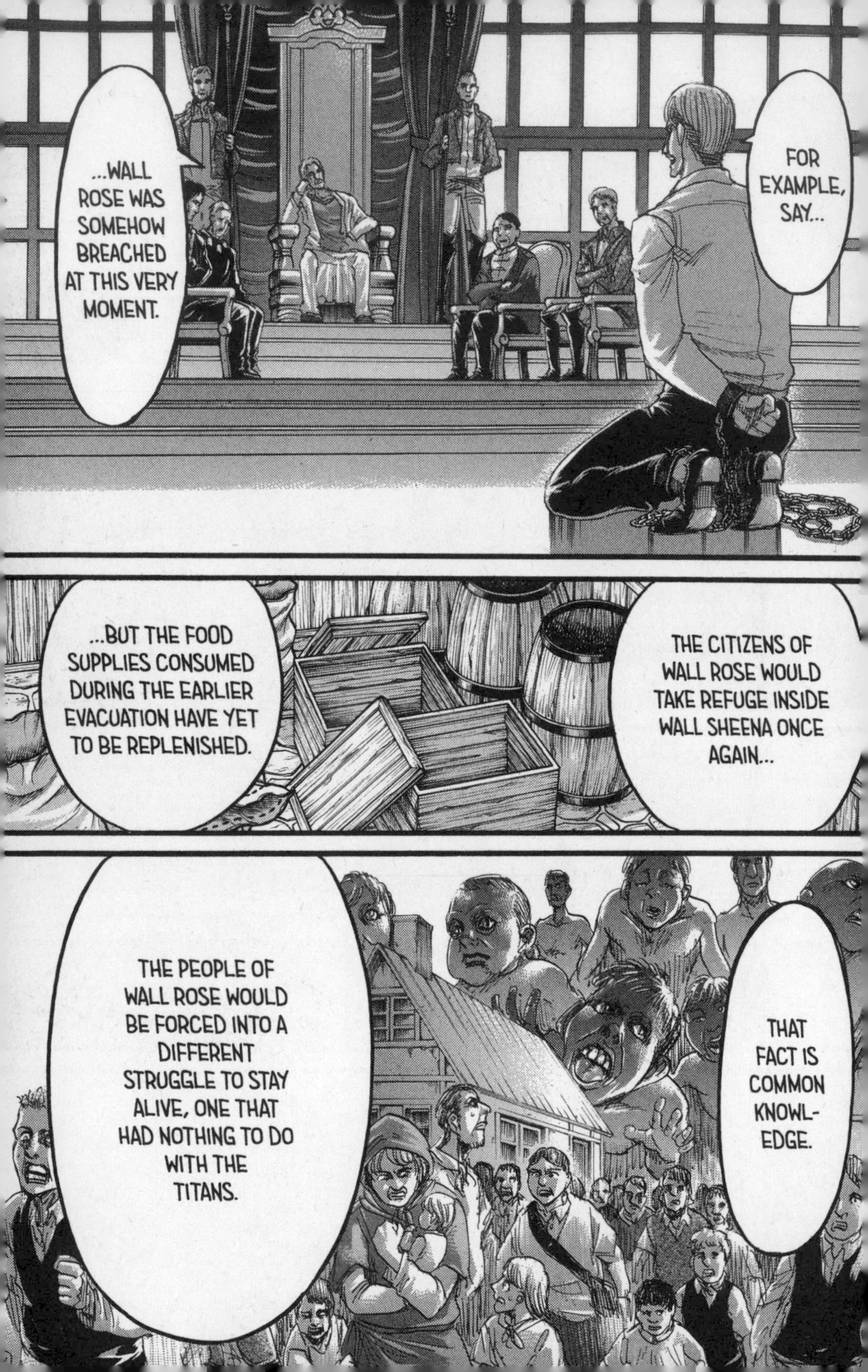
FOR EXAMPLE, SAY...
...WALL ROSE WAS SOMEHOW BREACHED AT THIS VERY MOMENT.
THE CITIZENS OF WALL ROSE WOULD TAKE REFUGE INSIDE WALL SHEENA ONCE AGAIN...
...BUT THE FOOD SUPPLIES CONSUMED DURING THE EARLIER EVACUATION HAVE YET TO BE REPLENISHED.
THAT FACT IS COMMON KNOWL-EDGE.
THE PEOPLE OF WALL ROSE WOULD BE FORCED INTO A DIFFERENT STRUGGLE TO STAY ALIVE, ONE THAT HAD NOTHING TO DO WITH THE TITANS.

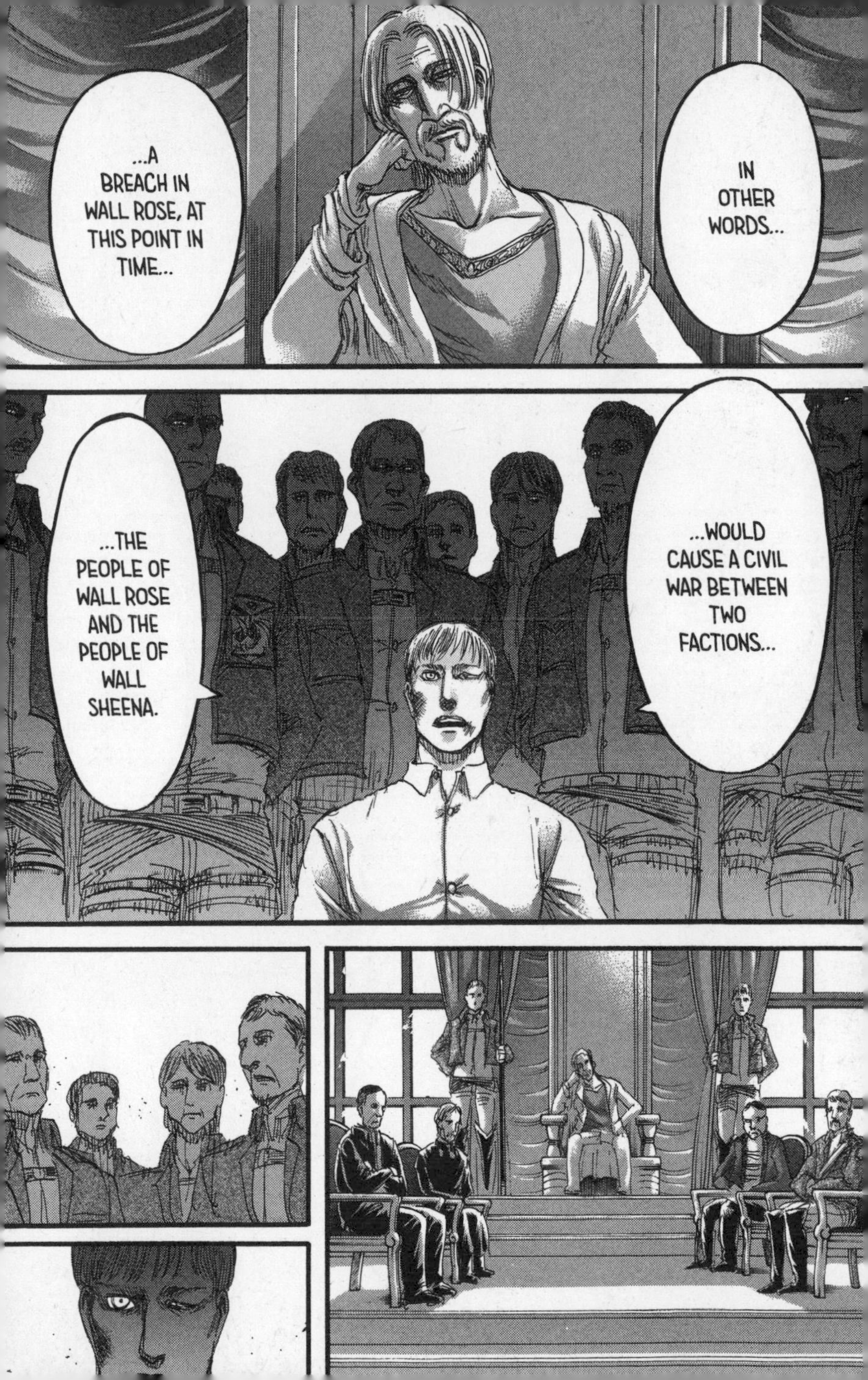
IN OTHER WORDS...
...A BREACH IN WALL ROSE, AT THIS POINT IN TIME...
...WOULD CAUSE A CIVIL WAR BETWEEN TWO FACTIONS...
...THE PEOPLE OF WALL ROSE AND THE PEOPLE OF WALL SHEENA.

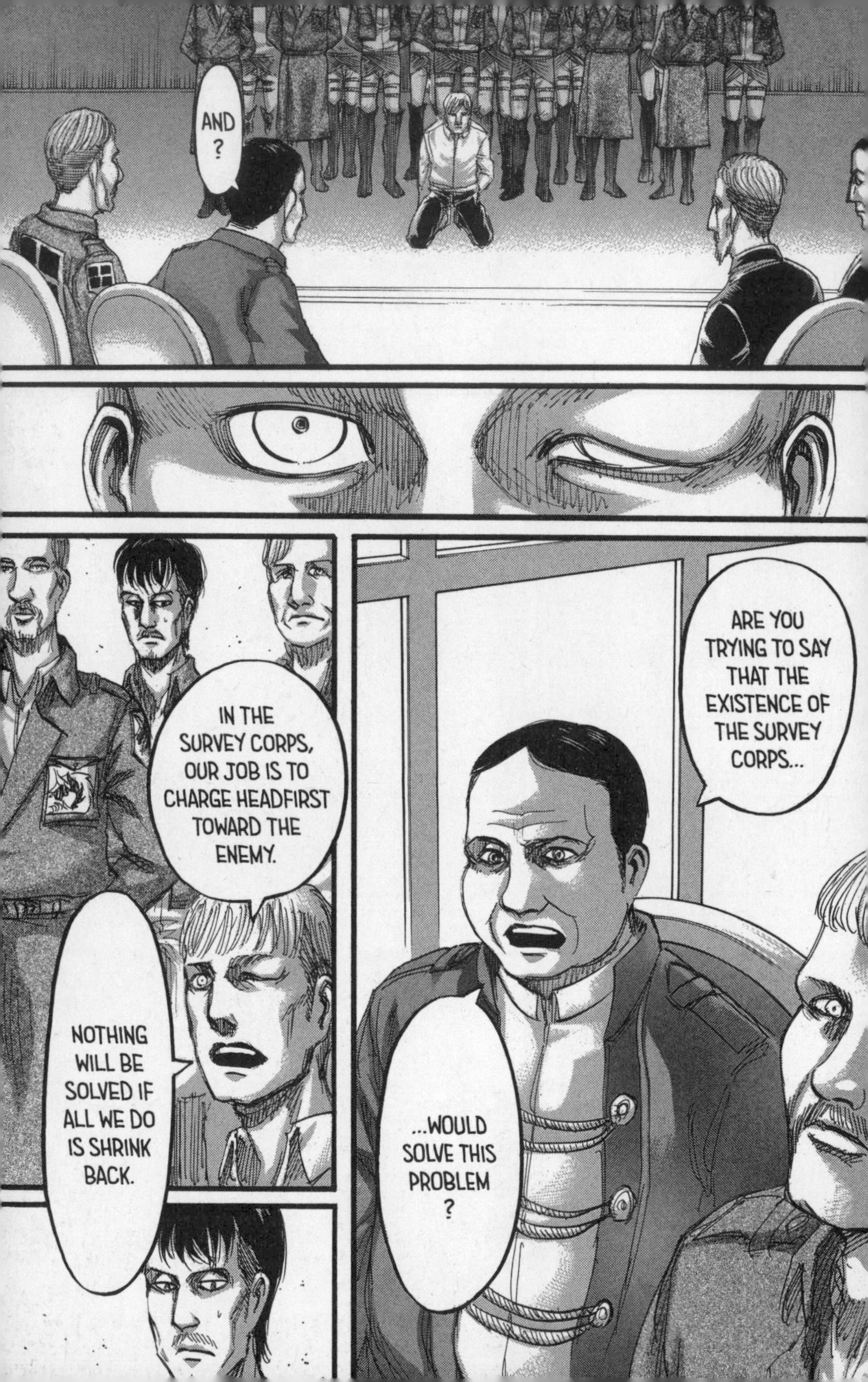
AND ?
ARE YOU TRYING TO SAY THAT THE EXISTENCE OF THE SURVEY CORPS...
...WOULD SOLVE THIS PROBLEM ?
IN THE SURVEY CORPS, OUR JOB IS TO CHARGE HEADFIRST TOWARD THE ENEMY.
NOTHING WILL BE SOLVED IF ALL WE DO IS SHRINK BACK.

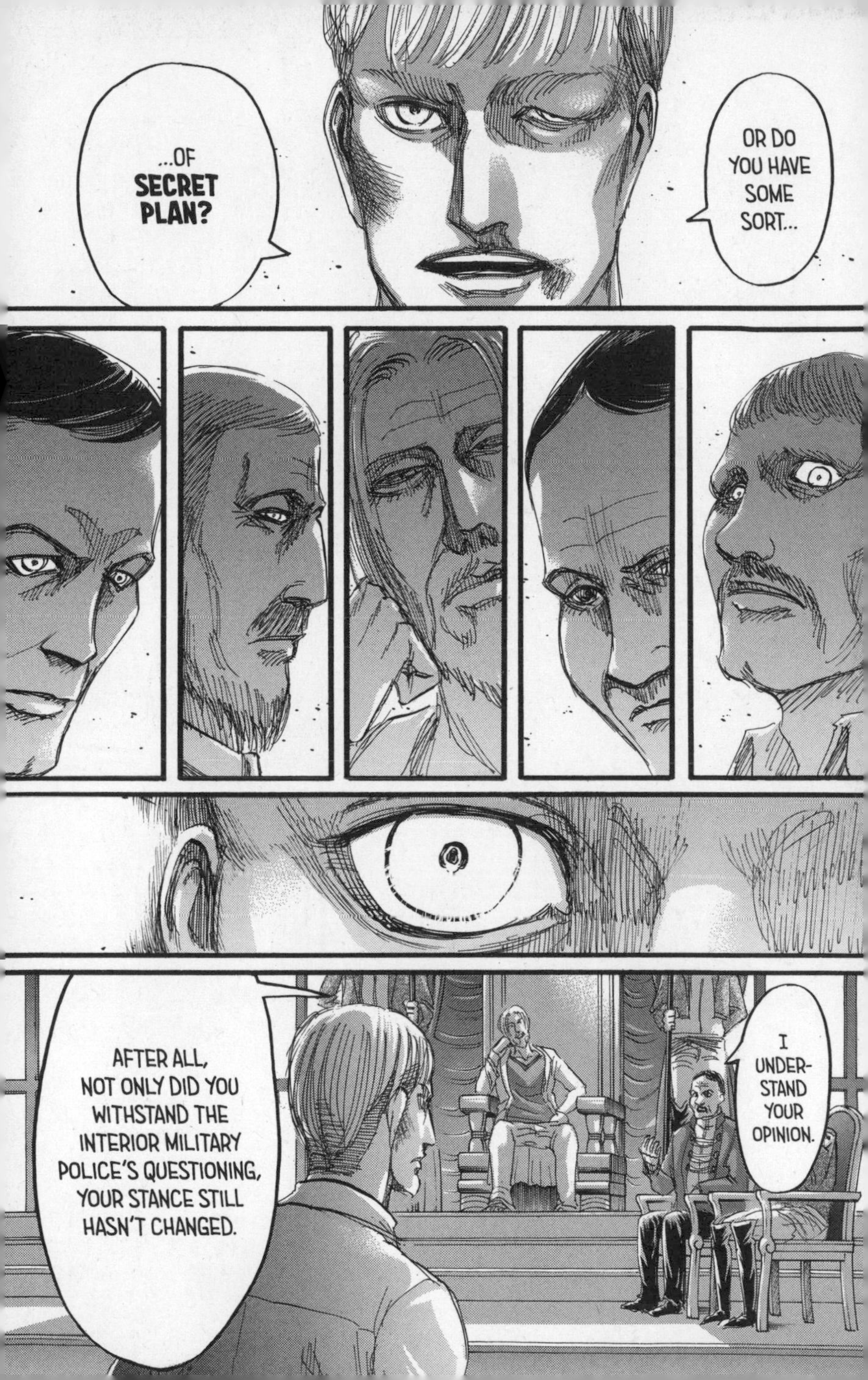
OR DO YOU HAVE SOME SORT...
...OF SECRET PLAN?
I UNDER-STAND YOUR OPINION.
AFTER ALL, NOT ONLY DID YOU WITHSTAND THE INTERIOR MILITARY POLICE'S QUESTIONING, YOUR STANCE STILL HASN'T CHANGED.

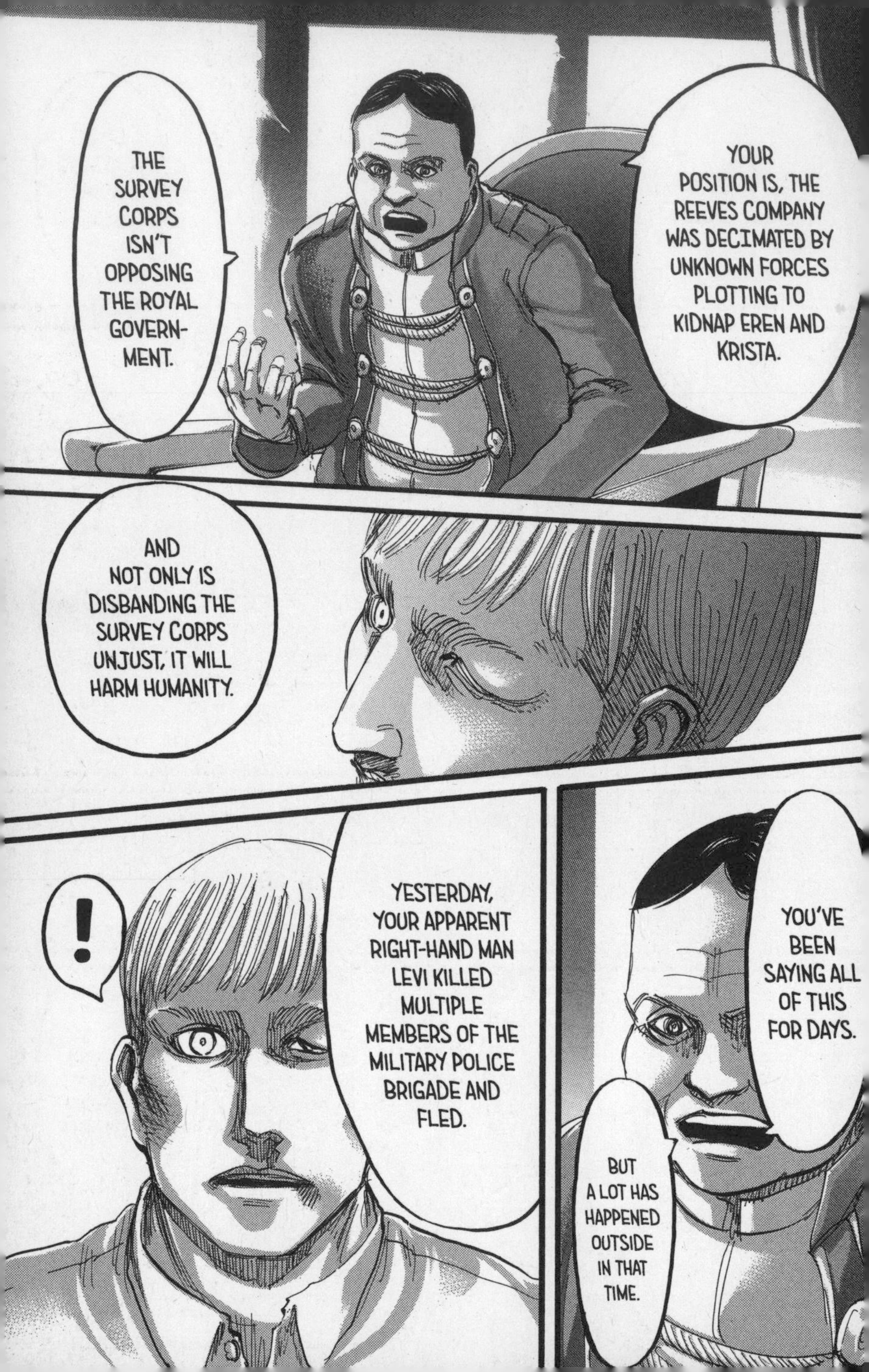
YOUR POSITION IS, THE REEVES COMPANY WAS DECIMATED BY UNKNOWN FORCES PLOTTING TO KIDNAP EREN AND KRISTA.
THE SURVEY CORPS ISN'T OPPOSING THE ROYAL GOVERN-MENT.
AND NOT ONLY IS DISBANDING THE SURVEY CORPS UNJUST, IT WILL HARM HUMANITY.
YOU'VE BEEN SAYING ALL OF THIS FOR DAYS.
BUT A LOT HAS HAPPENED OUTSIDE IN THAT TIME.
YESTERDAY, YOUR APPARENT RIGHT-HAND MAN LEVI KILLED MULTIPLE MEMBERS OF THE MILITARY POLICE BRIGADE AND FLED.
!

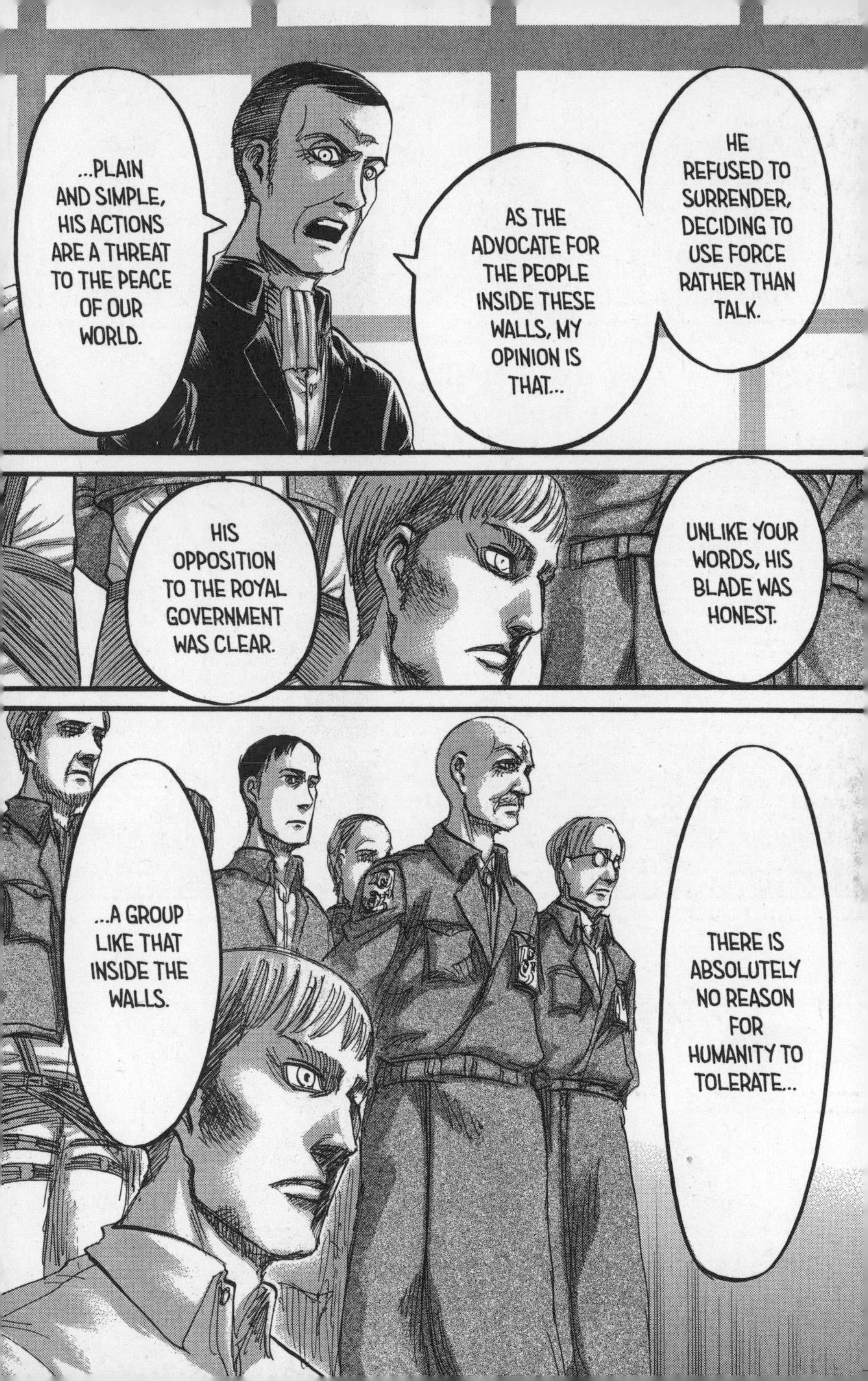
HE REFUSED TO SURRENDER, DECIDING TO USE FORCE RATHER THAN TALK.
AS THE ADVOCATE FOR THE PEOPLE INSIDE THESE WALLS, MY OPINION IS THAT...
...PLAIN AND SIMPLE, HIS ACTIONS ARE A THREAT TO THE PEACE OF OUR WORLD.
UNLIKE YOUR WORDS, HIS BLADE WAS HONEST.
HIS OPPOSITION TO THE ROYAL GOVERNMENT WAS CLEAR.
THERE IS ABSOLUTELY NO REASON FOR HUMANITY TO TOLERATE...
...A GROUP LIKE THAT INSIDE THE WALLS.

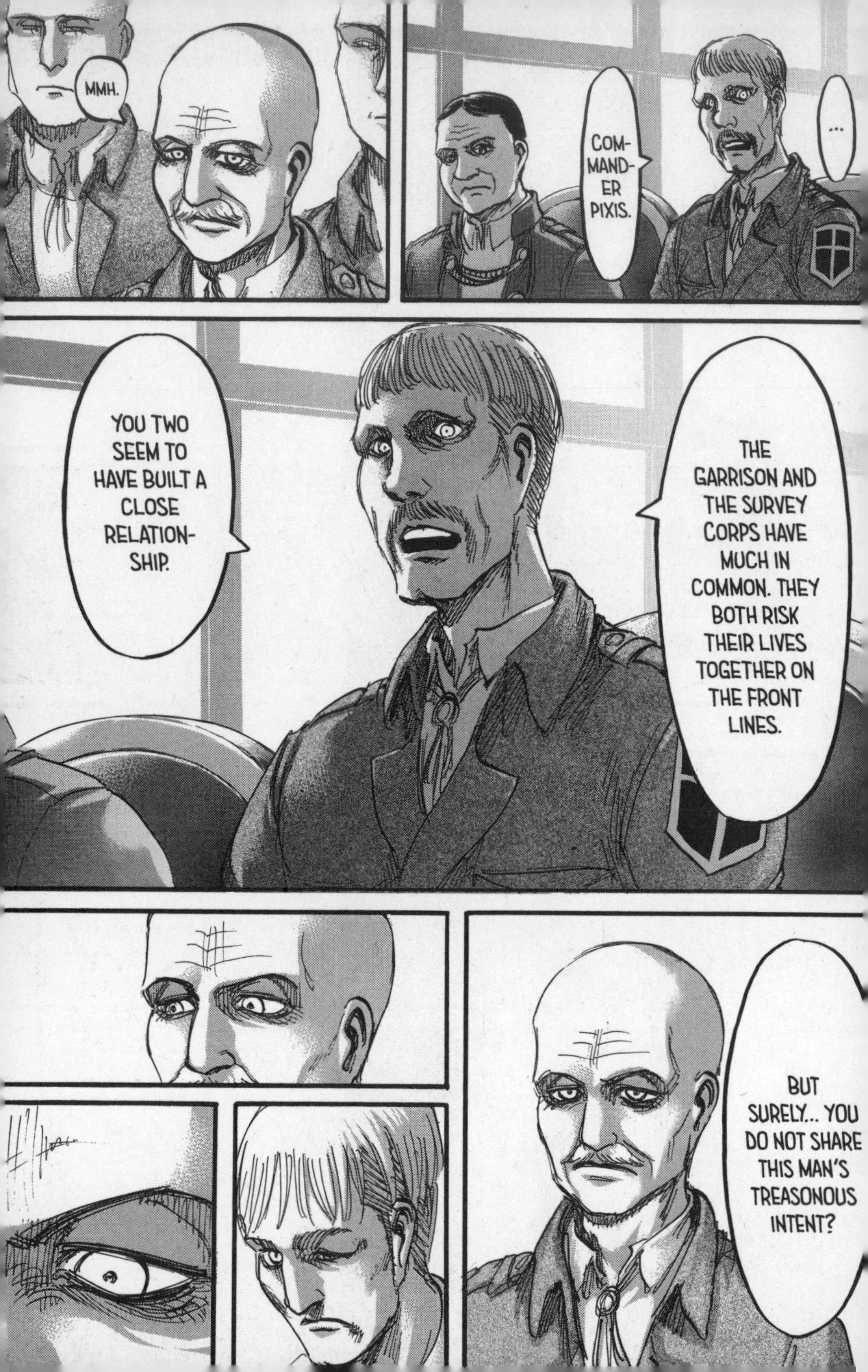
...
COM-MAND-ER PIXIS.
MMH.
THE GARRISON AND THE SURVEY CORPS HAVE MUCH IN COMMON. THEY BOTH RISK THEIR LIVES TOGETHER ON THE FRONT LINES.
YOU TWO SEEM TO HAVE BUILT A CLOSE RELATION-SHIP.
BUT SURELY... YOU DO NOT SHARE THIS MAN'S TREASONOUS INTENT?

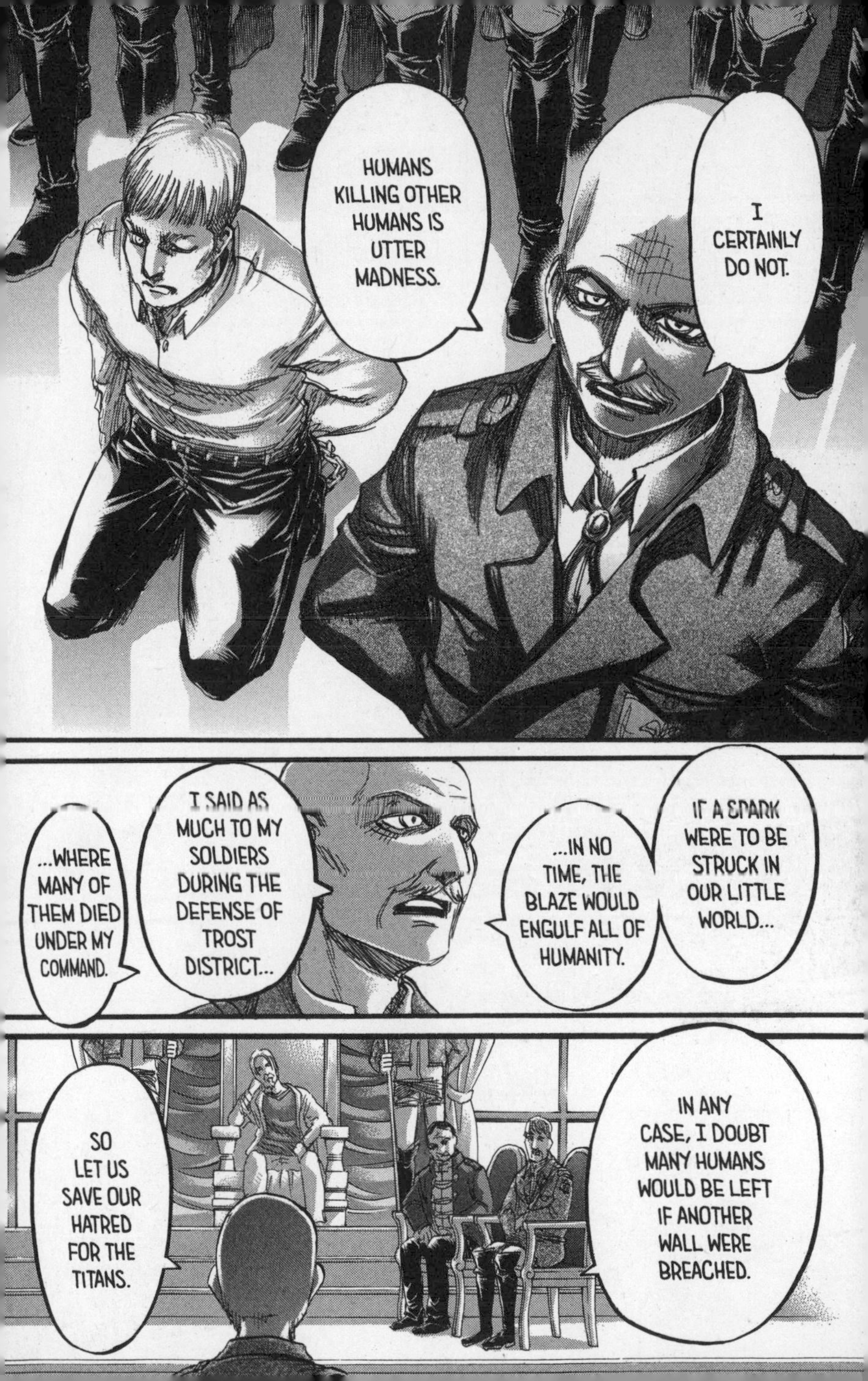
I CERTAINLY DO NOT.
HUMANS KILLING OTHER HUMANS IS UTTER MADNESS.
IF A SPARK WERE TO BE STRUCK IN OUR LITTLE WORLD...
...IN NO TIME, THE BLAZE WOULD ENGULF ALL OF HUMANITY.
I SAID AS MUCH TO MY SOLDIERS DURING THE DEFENSE OF TROST DISTRICT...
...WHERE MANY OF THEM DIED UNDER MY COMMAND.
IN ANY CASE, I DOUBT MANY HUMANS WOULD BE LEFT IF ANOTHER WALL WERE BREACHED.
SO LET US SAVE OUR HATRED FOR THE TITANS.

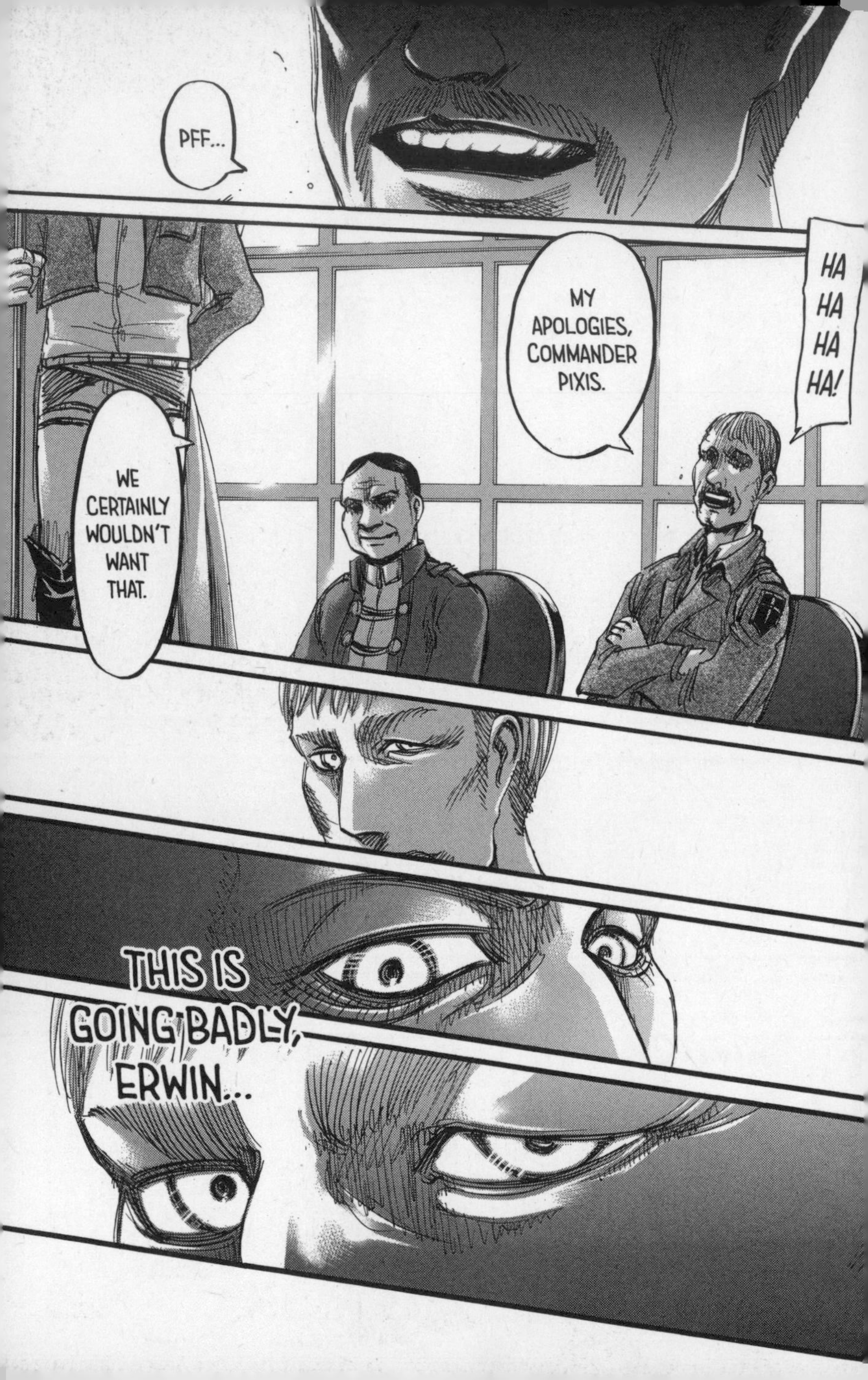
PFF...
HA HA HA HA!
MY APOLOGIES, COMMANDER PIXIS.
WE CERTAINLY WOULDN'T WANT THAT.
THIS IS GOING BADLY, ERWIN...

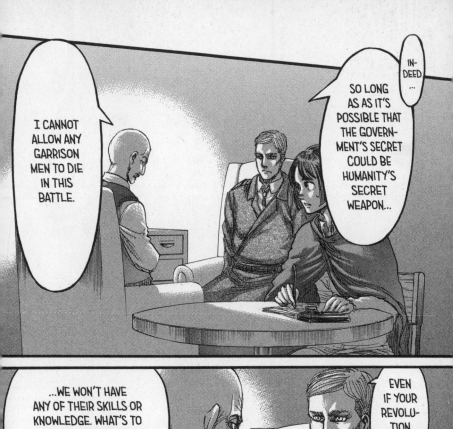

I CANNOT ALLOW ANY GARRISON MEN TO DIE IN THIS BATTLE.

SO LONG AS AS IT'S POSSIBLE THAT THE GOVERNMENT'S SECRET COULD BE HUMANITY'S SECRET WEAPON...

IN-DEED...

...WE WON'T HAVE ANY OF THEIR SKILLS OR KNOWLEDGE. WHAT'S TO SAY WE'LL BE ABLE TO TAKE THEIR PLACES SUCCESSFULLY?

EVEN IF YOUR REVOLUTION SUCCEEDS...

...THEN THIS REVOLUTION RUNS THE RISK OF LOSING ALL OF THAT...

...FOREVER.

...IF IT'S TRUE THAT THEY BUILT THE WALL OF TITANS AND ALTERED HUMANITY'S MEMORIES...

IN SHORT...

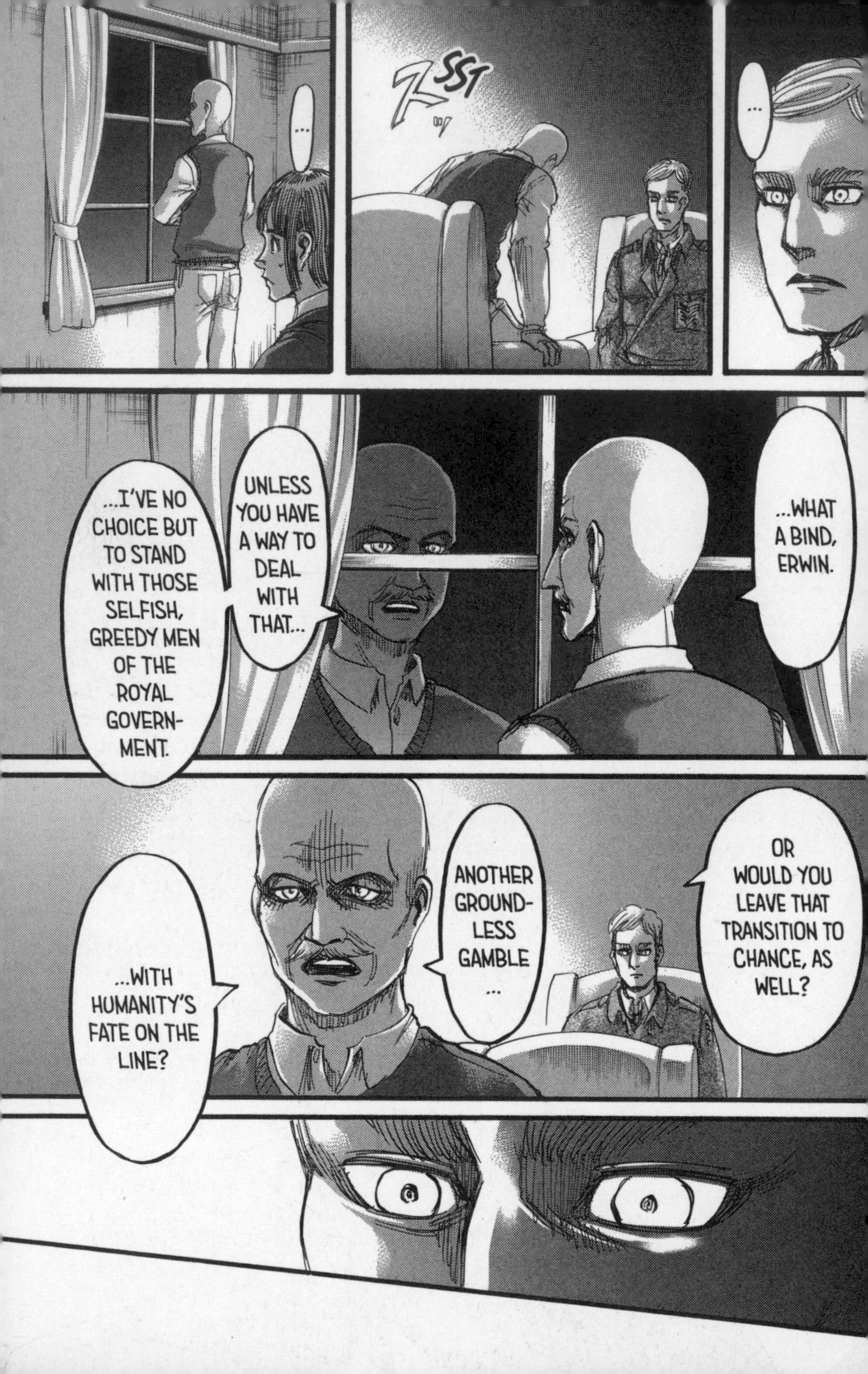
...
ZSST
...
...WHAT A BIND, ERWIN.
UNLESS YOU HAVE A WAY TO DEAL WITH THAT...
...I'VE NO CHOICE BUT TO STAND WITH THOSE SELFISH, GREEDY MEN OF THE ROYAL GOVERN-MENT.
OR WOULD YOU LEAVE THAT TRANSITION TO CHANCE, AS WELL?
ANOTHER GROUND-LESS GAMBLE ...
...WITH HUMANITY'S FATE ON THE LINE?

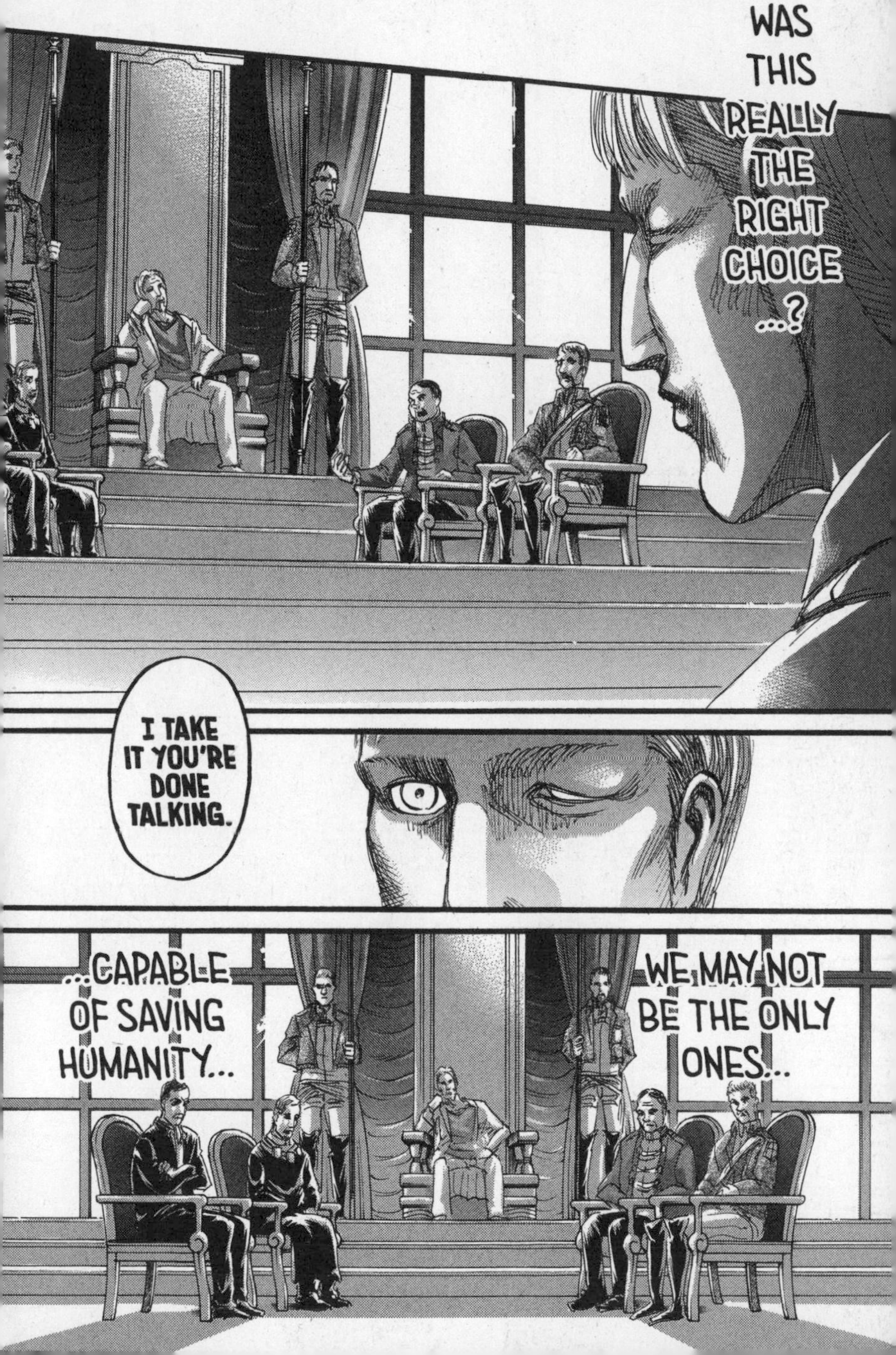
WAS THIS REALLY THE RIGHT CHOICE ...?
I TAKE IT YOU'RE DONE TALKING.
WE MAY NOT BE THE ONLY ONES...
...CAPABLE OF SAVING HUMANITY...

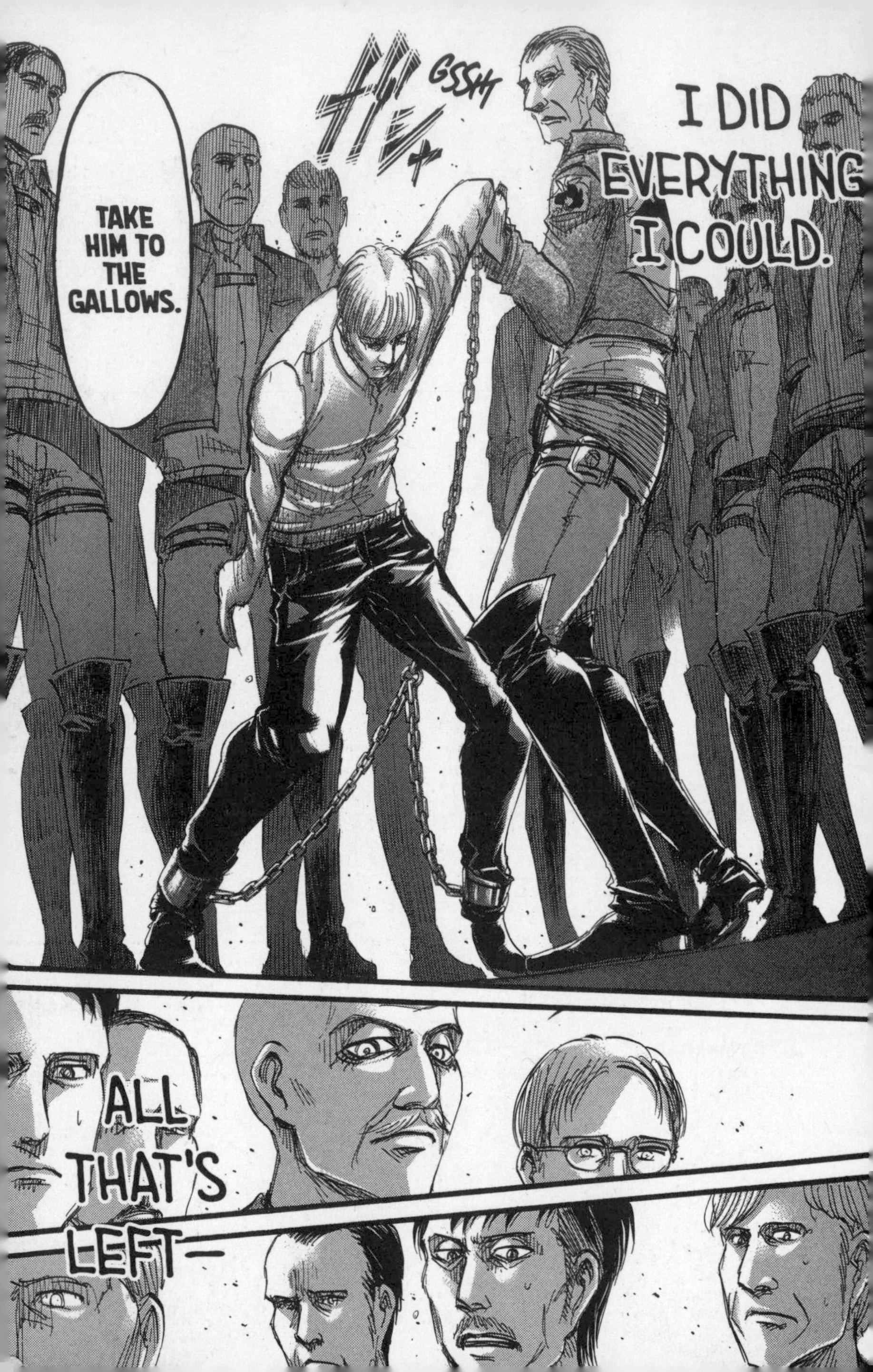
I DID EVERYTHING I COULD.
GSSH
TAKE HIM TO THE GALLOWS.
ALL THAT'S LEFT—

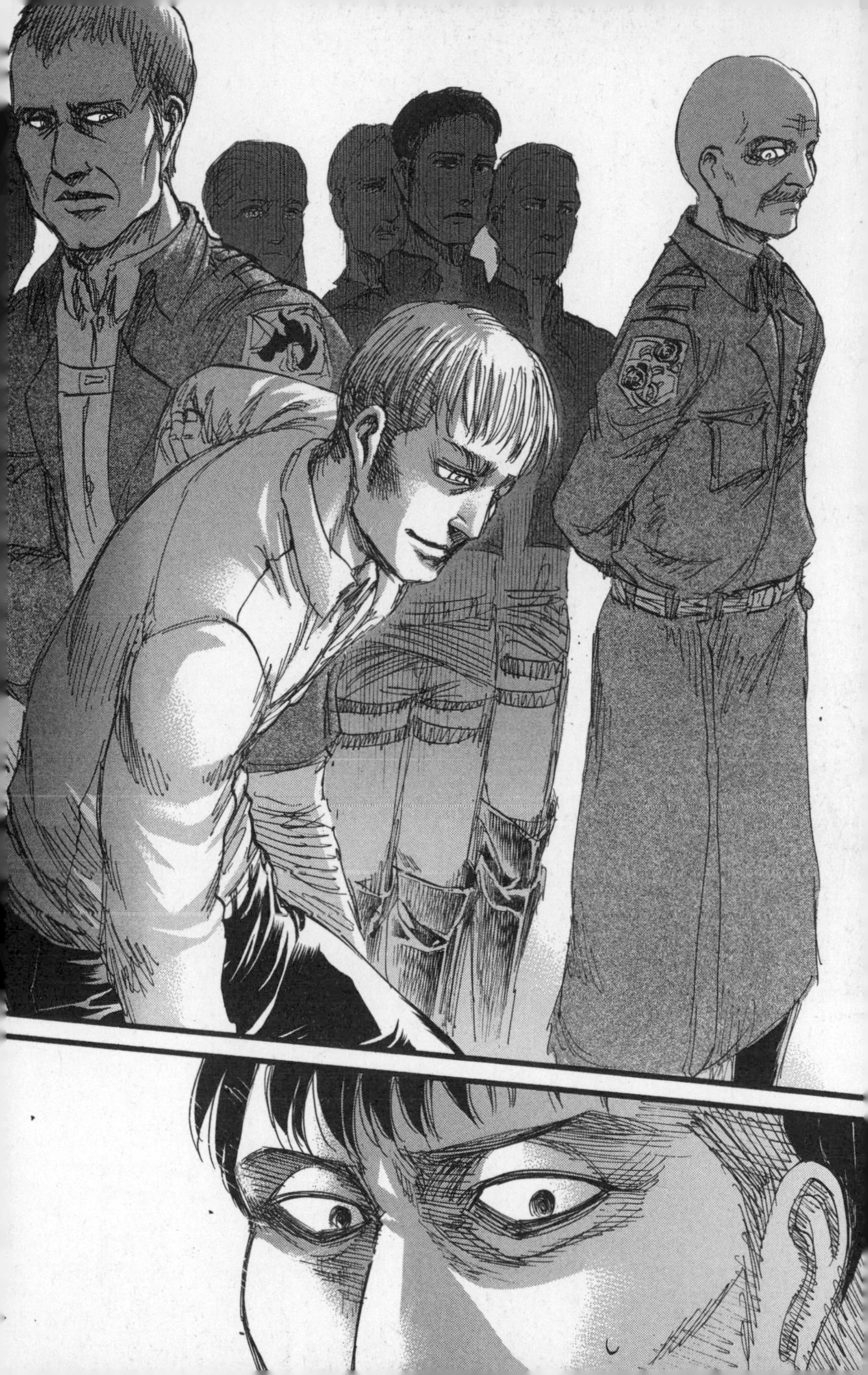

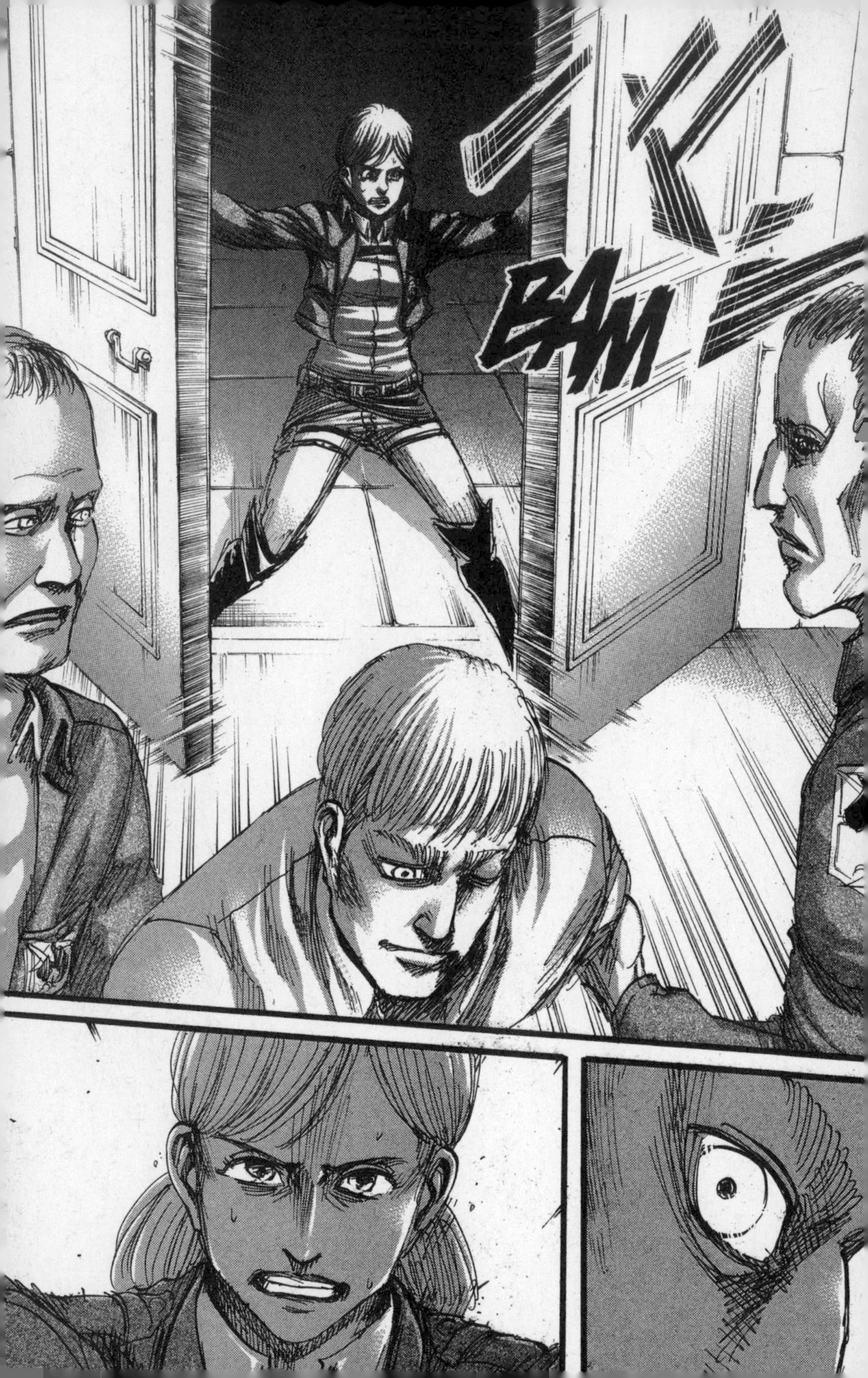
BAM

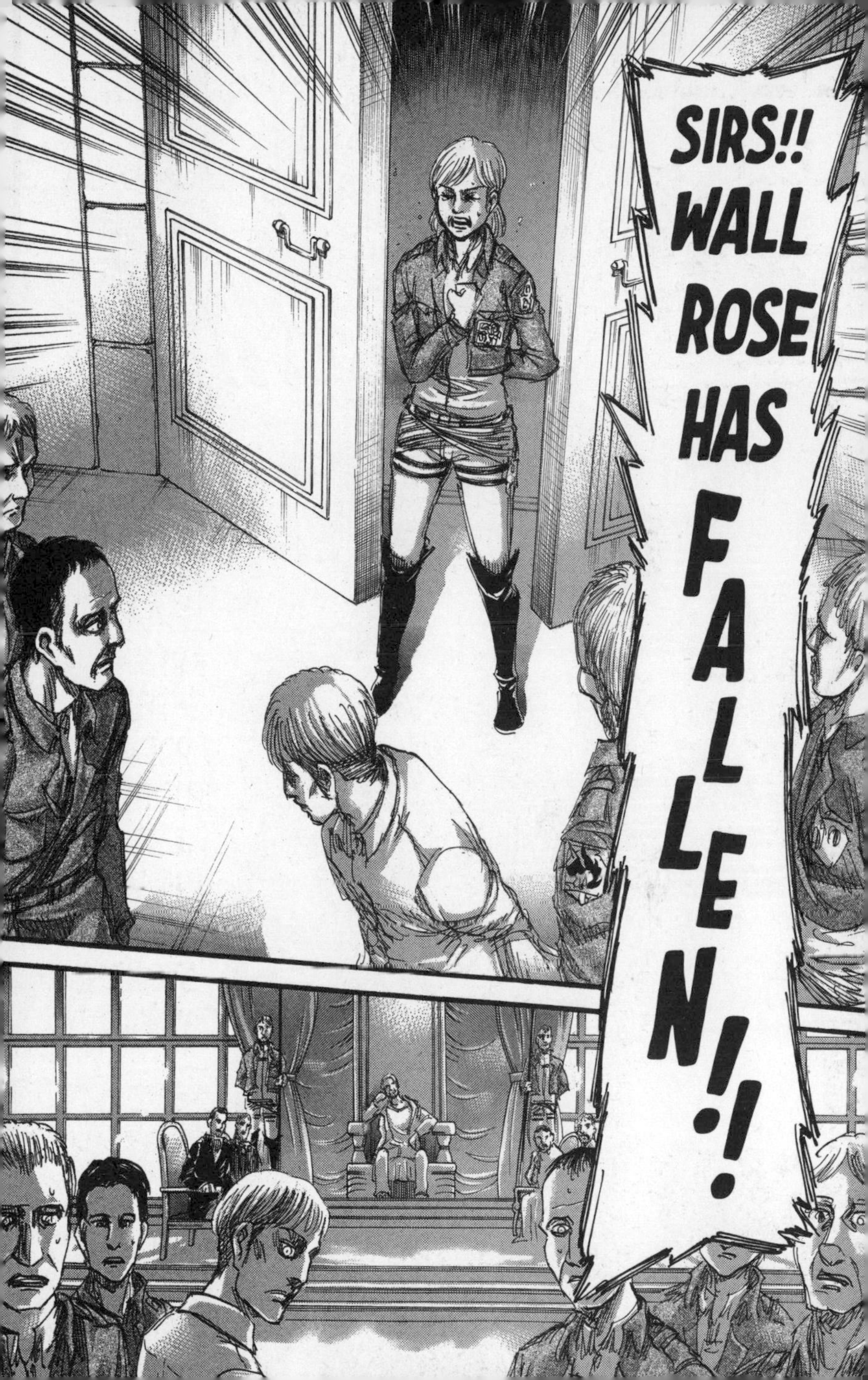
SIRS!! WALL ROSE HAS FALLEN!!

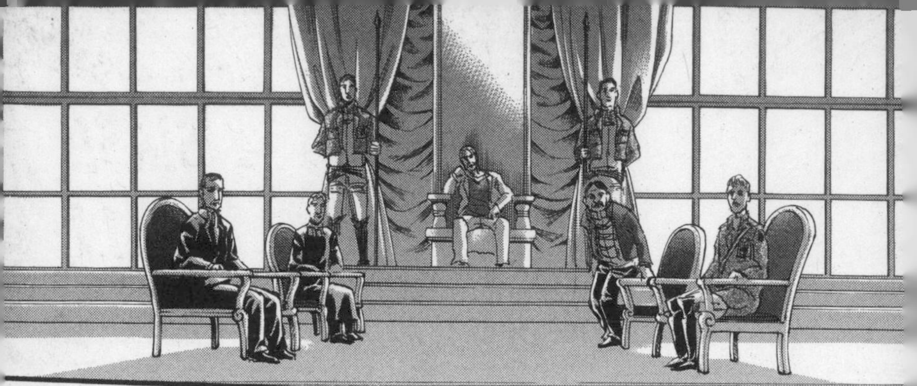

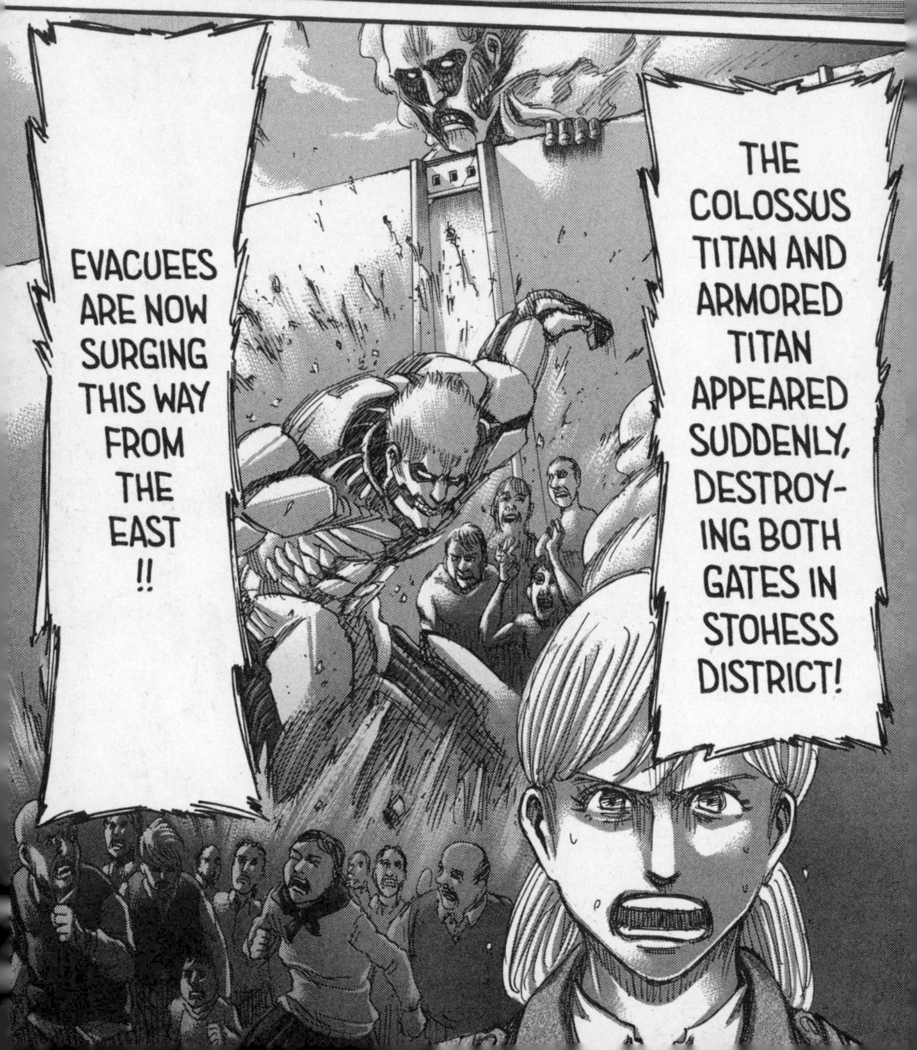
THE COLOSSUS TITAN AND ARMORED TITAN APPEARED SUDDENLY, DESTROY-ING BOTH GATES IN STOHESS DISTRICT!
EVACUEES ARE NOW SURGING THIS WAY FROM THE EAST !!

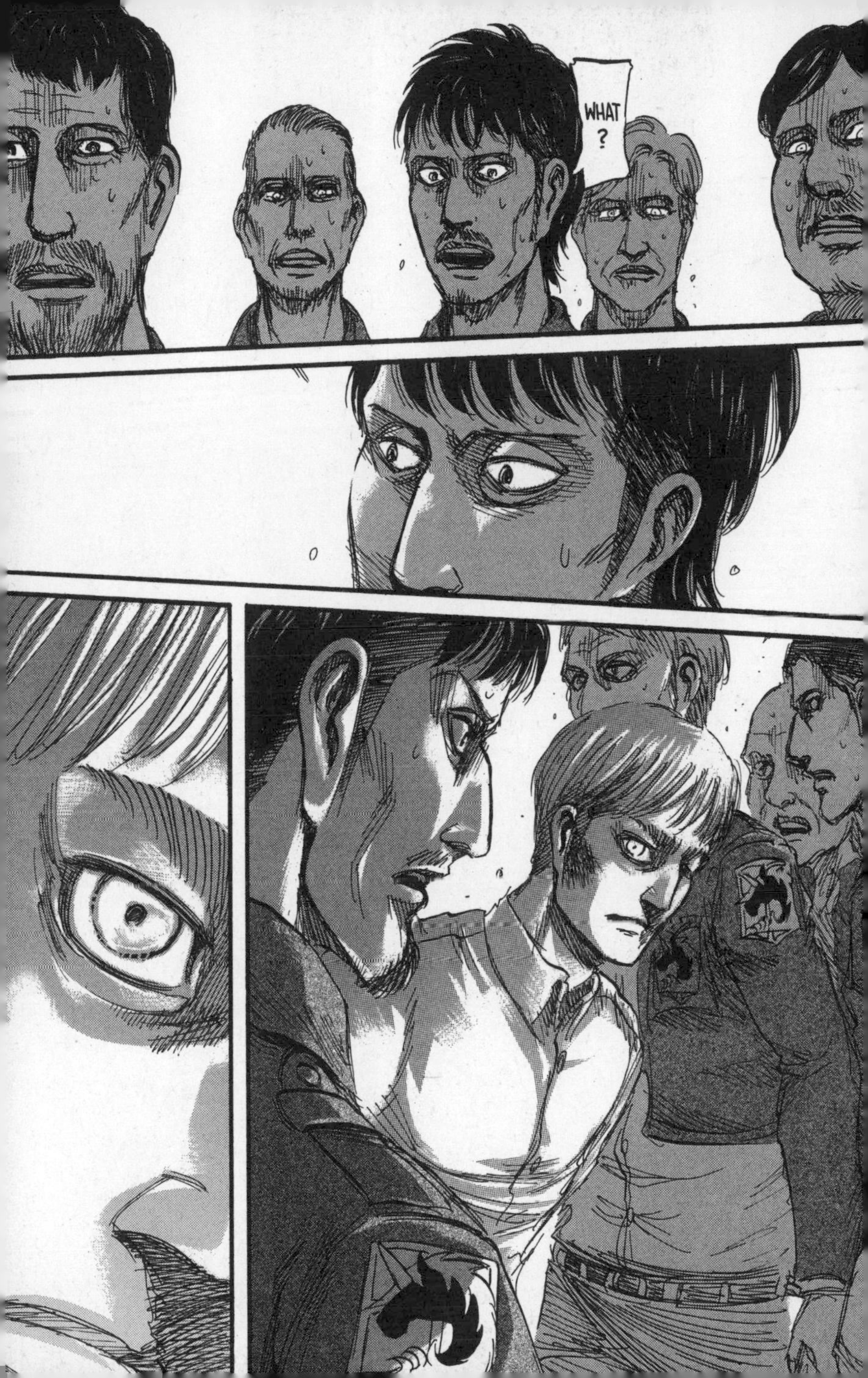
WHAT
?

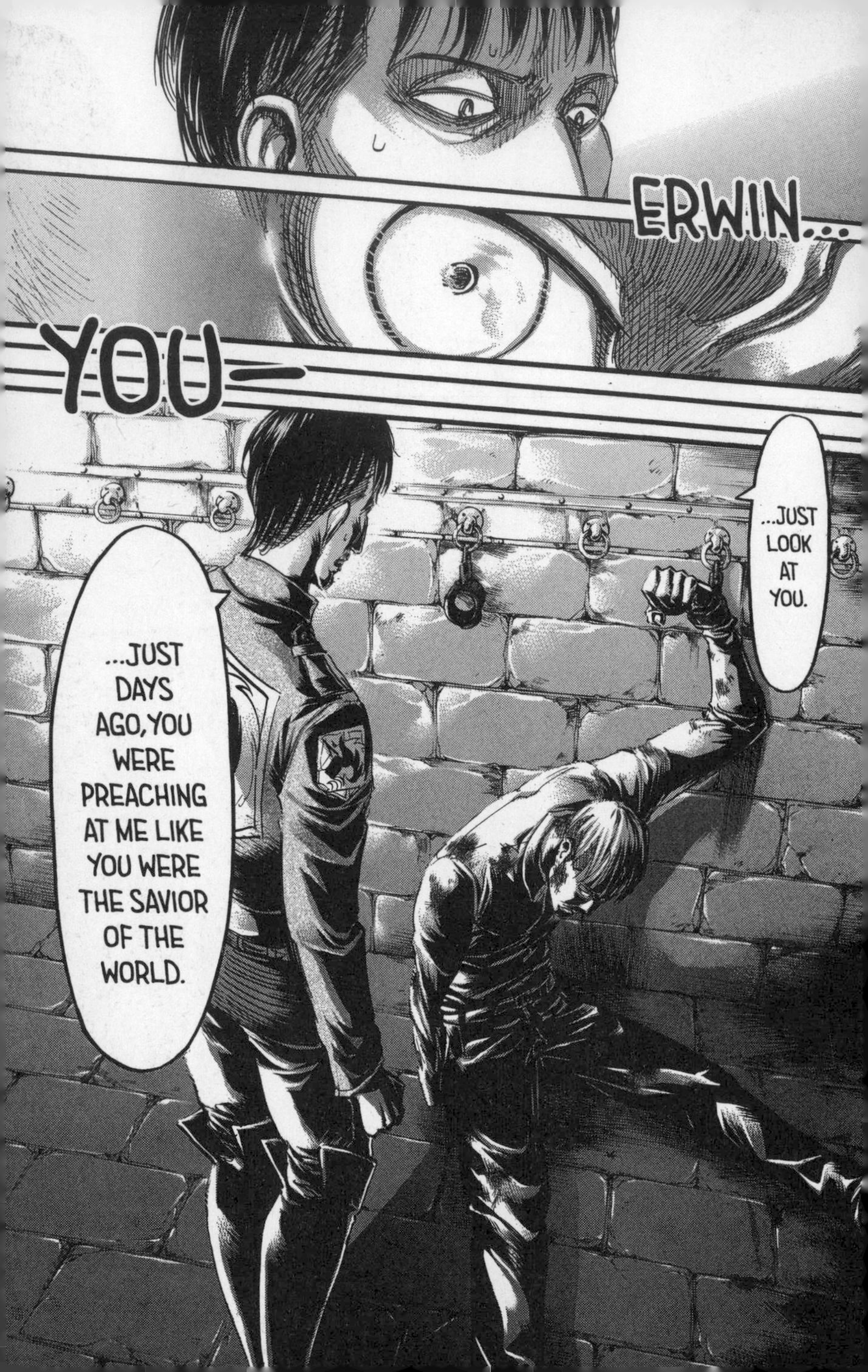
ERWIN...
YOU—
...JUST LOOK AT YOU.
...JUST DAYS AGO, YOU WERE PREACHING AT ME LIKE YOU WERE THE SAVIOR OF THE WORLD.

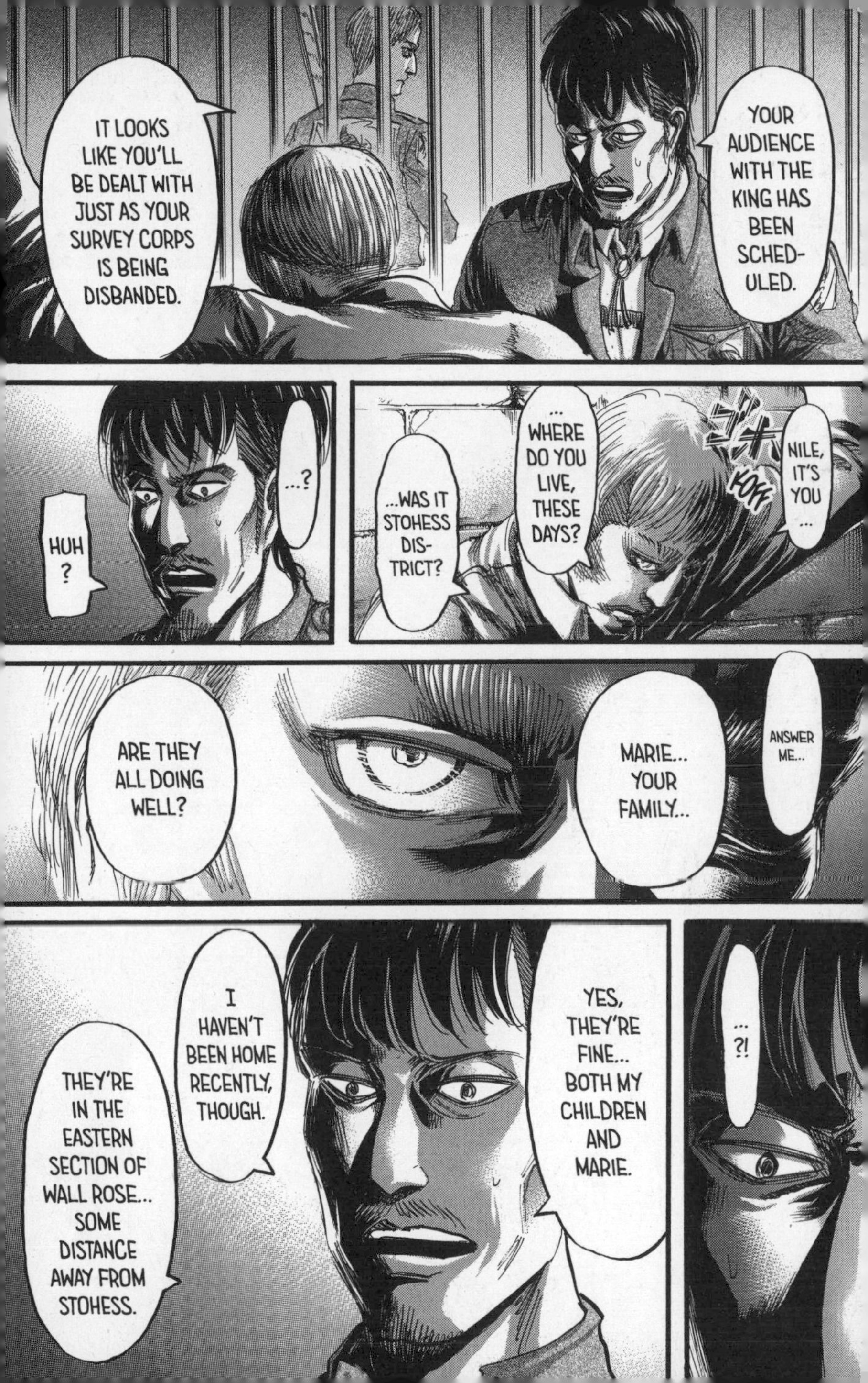
YOUR AUDIENCE WITH THE KING HAS BEEN SCHED-ULED.
IT LOOKS LIKE YOU'LL BE DEALT WITH JUST AS YOUR SURVEY CORPS IS BEING DISBANDED.
NILE, IT'S YOU ...
KOFF
... WHERE DO YOU LIVE, THESE DAYS?
...WAS IT STOHESS DIS-TRICT?
...?
HUH ?
ANSWER ME...
MARIE... YOUR FAMILY...
ARE THEY ALL DOING WELL?
... ?!
YES, THEY'RE FINE... BOTH MY CHILDREN AND MARIE.
I HAVEN'T BEEN HOME RECENTLY, THOUGH.
THEY'RE IN THE EASTERN SECTION OF WALL ROSE... SOME DISTANCE AWAY FROM STOHESS.

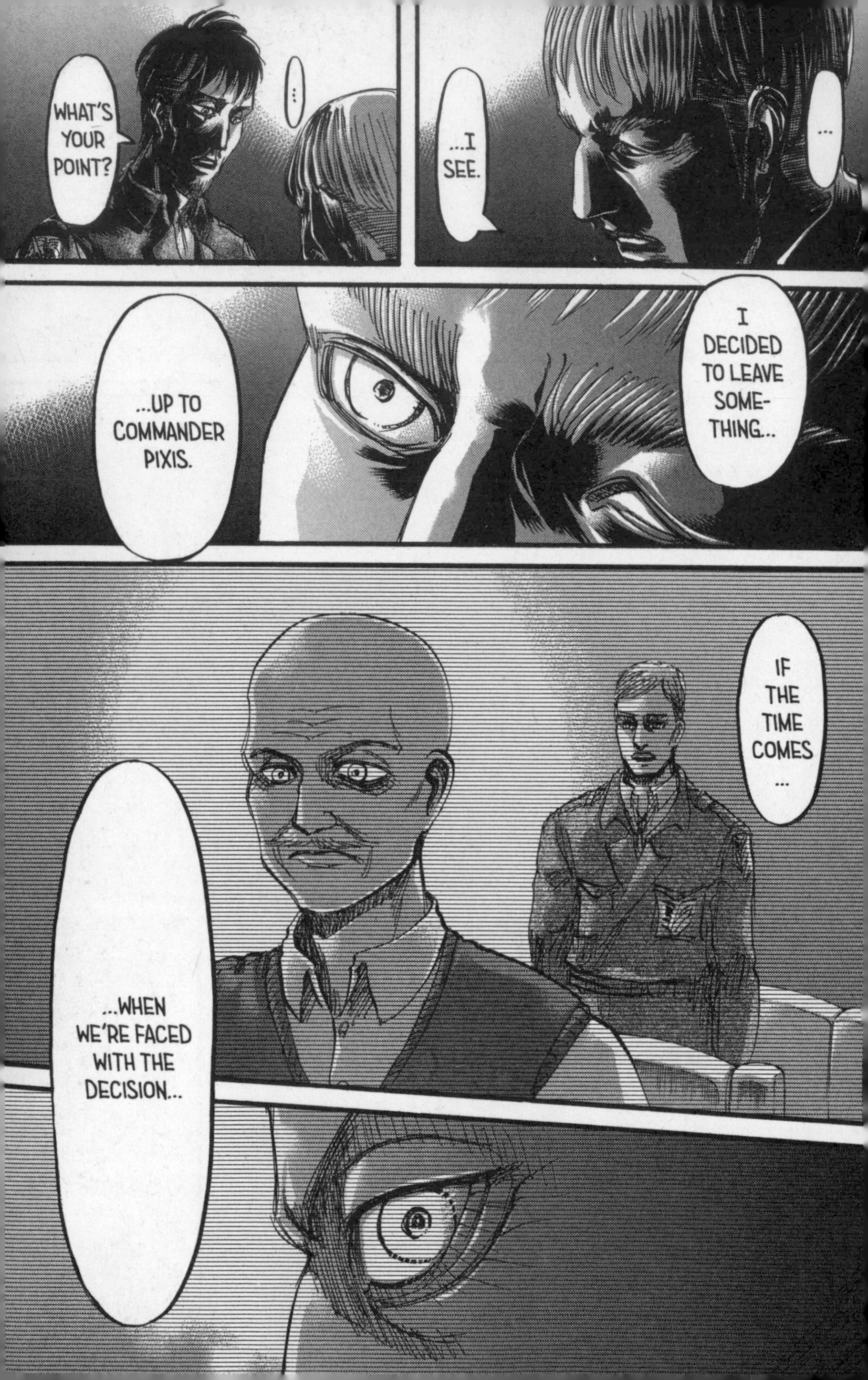
...
...I SEE.
...
WHAT'S YOUR POINT?
I DECIDED TO LEAVE SOMETHING...
...UP TO COMMANDER PIXIS.
IF THE TIME COMES ...
...WHEN WE'RE FACED WITH THE DECISION...

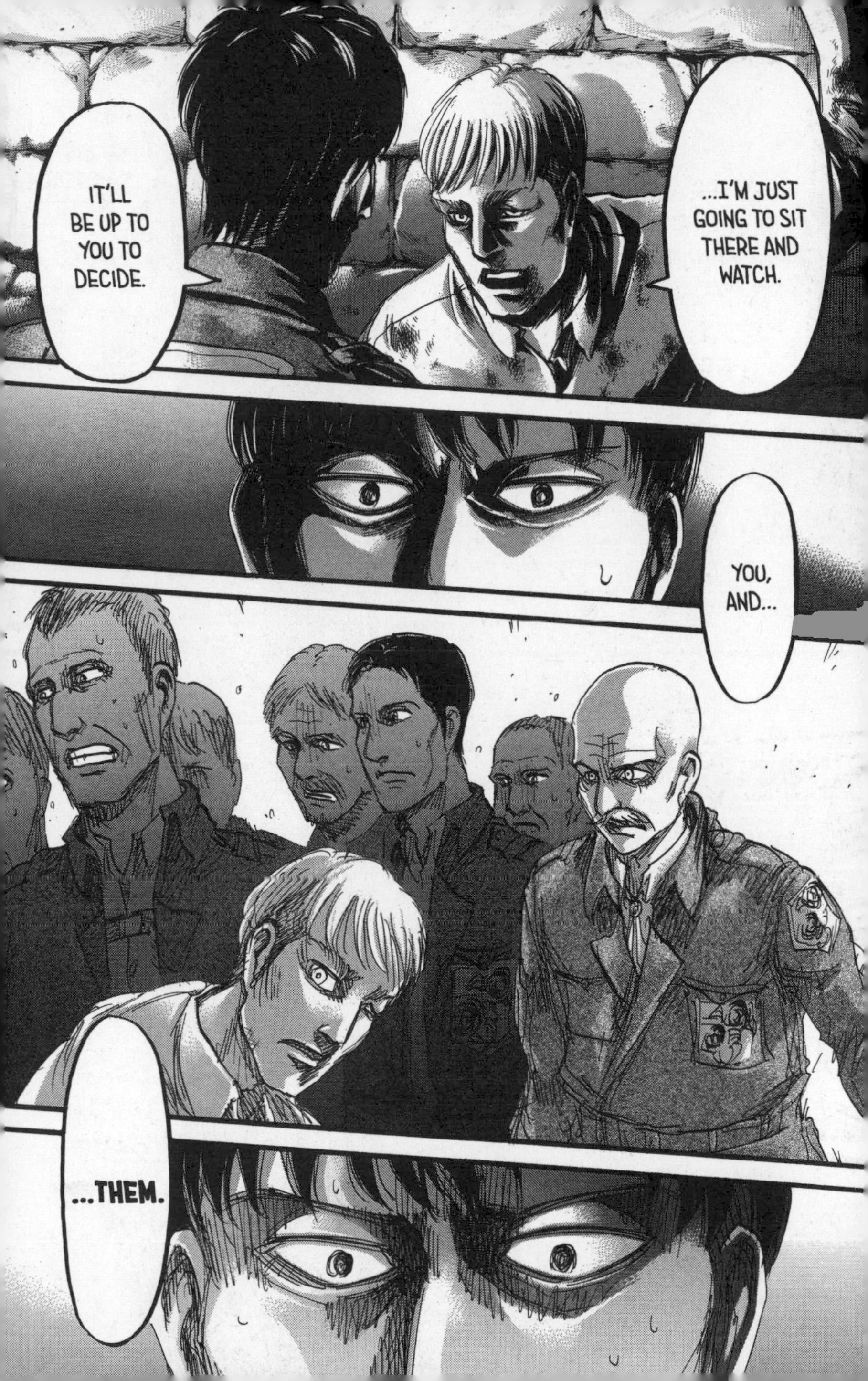
...I'M JUST GOING TO SIT THERE AND WATCH.
IT'LL BE UP TO YOU TO DECIDE.
YOU, AND...
...THEM.

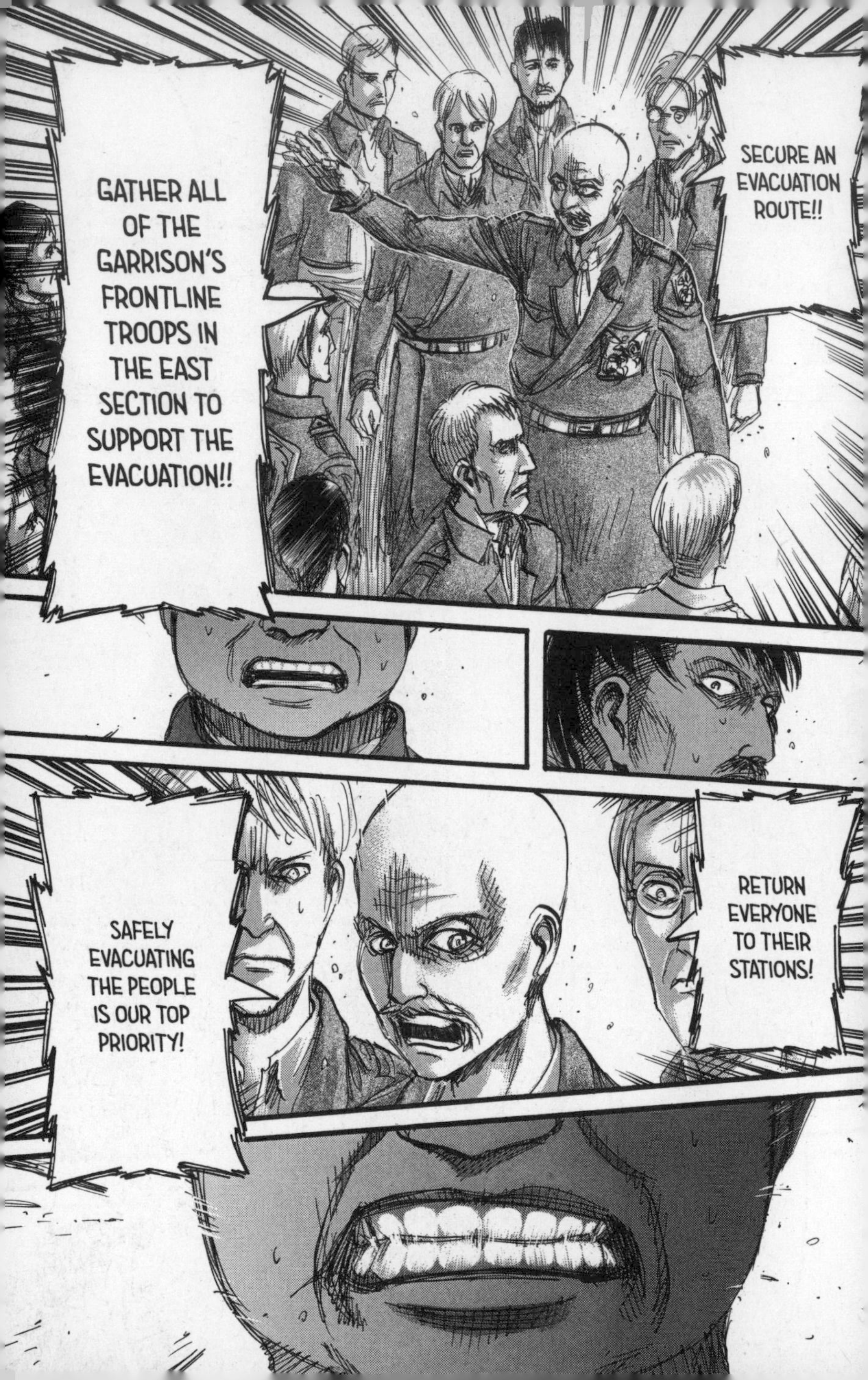
SECURE AN EVACUATION ROUTE!!
GATHER ALL OF THE GARRISON'S FRONTLINE TROOPS IN THE EAST SECTION TO SUPPORT THE EVACUATION!!
RETURN EVERYONE TO THEIR STATIONS!
SAFELY EVACUATING THE PEOPLE IS OUR TOP PRIORITY!

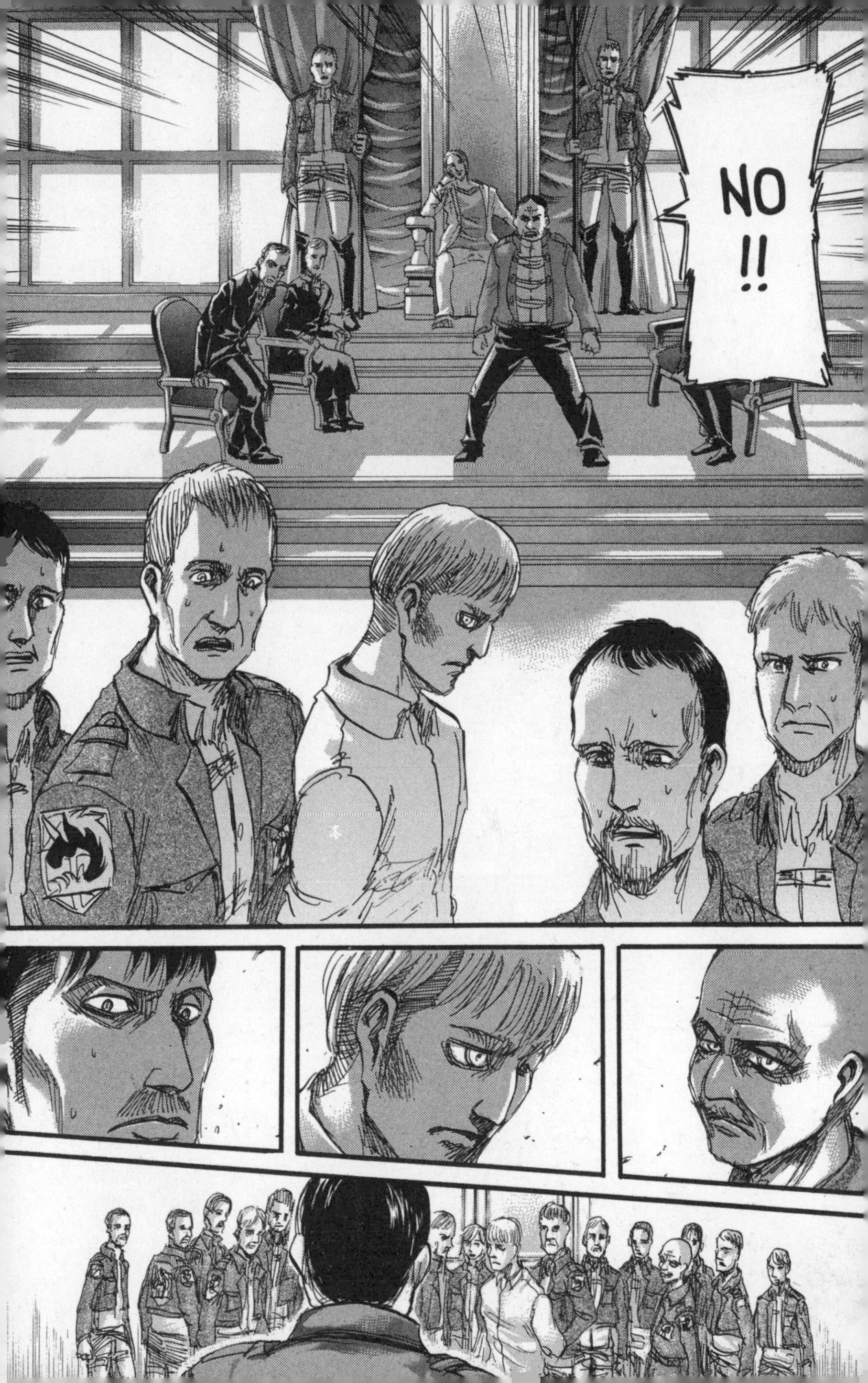
NO !!

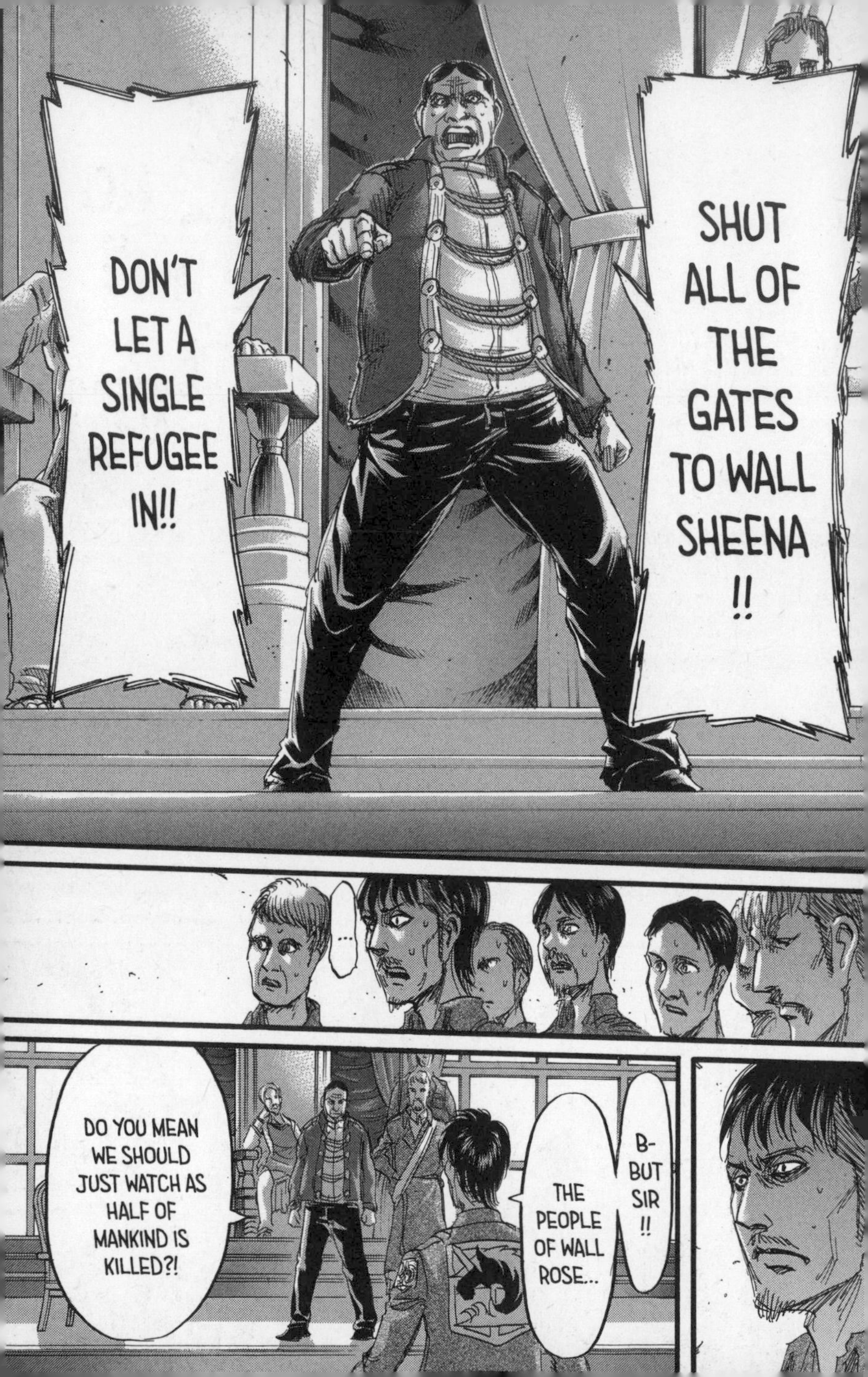
SHUT ALL OF THE GATES TO WALL SHEENA!!
DON'T LET A SINGLE REFUGEE IN!!
...
B-BUT SIR!!
THE PEOPLE OF WALL ROSE...
DO YOU MEAN WE SHOULD JUST WATCH AS HALF OF MANKIND IS KILLED?!

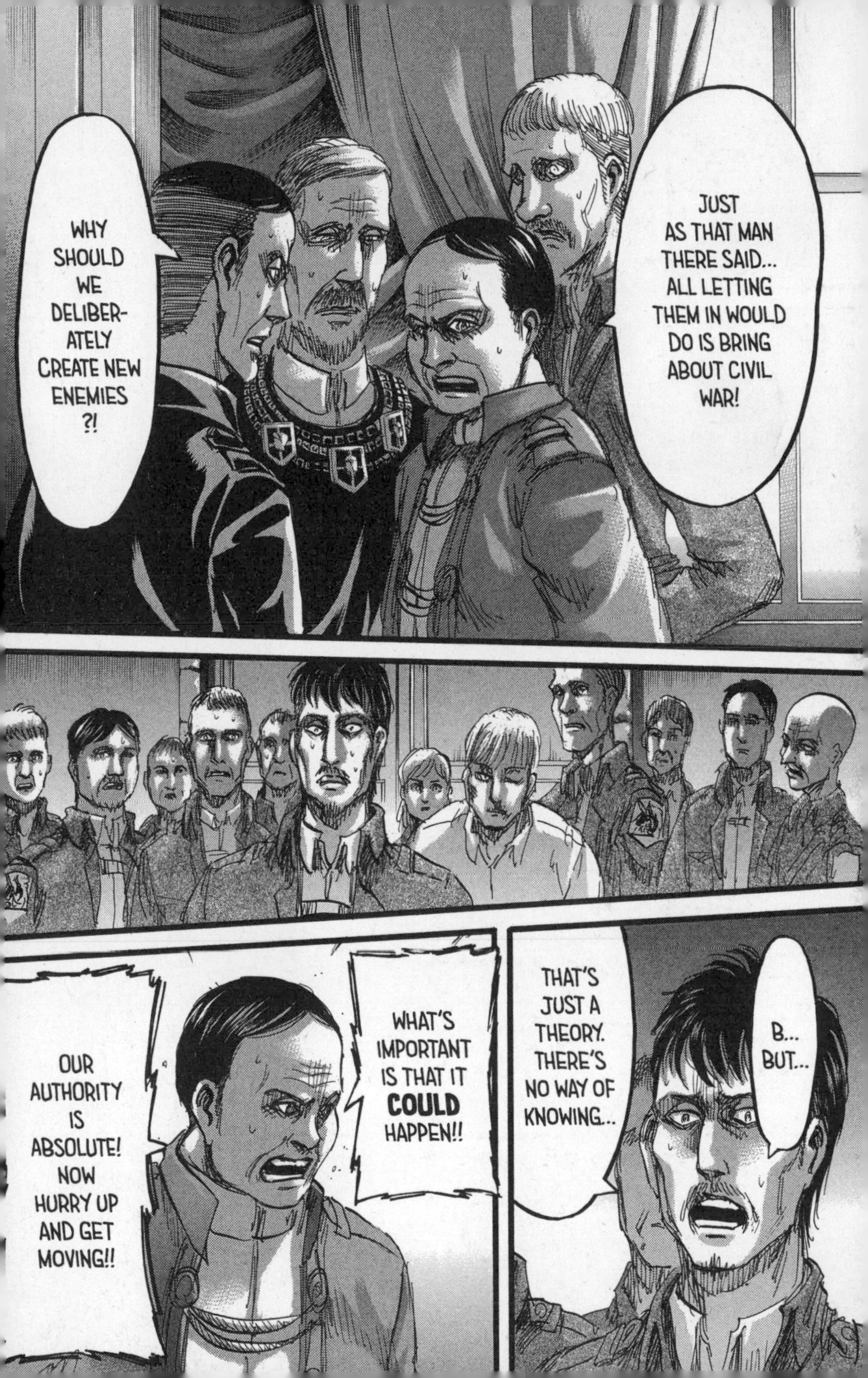
JUST AS THAT MAN THERE SAID... ALL LETTING THEM IN WOULD DO IS BRING ABOUT CIVIL WAR!
WHY SHOULD WE DELIBER-ATELY CREATE NEW ENEMIES ?!
B... BUT...
THAT'S JUST A THEORY. THERE'S NO WAY OF KNOWING...
WHAT'S IMPORTANT IS THAT IT **COULD** HAPPEN!!
OUR AUTHORITY IS ABSOLUTE! NOW HURRY UP AND GET MOVING!!

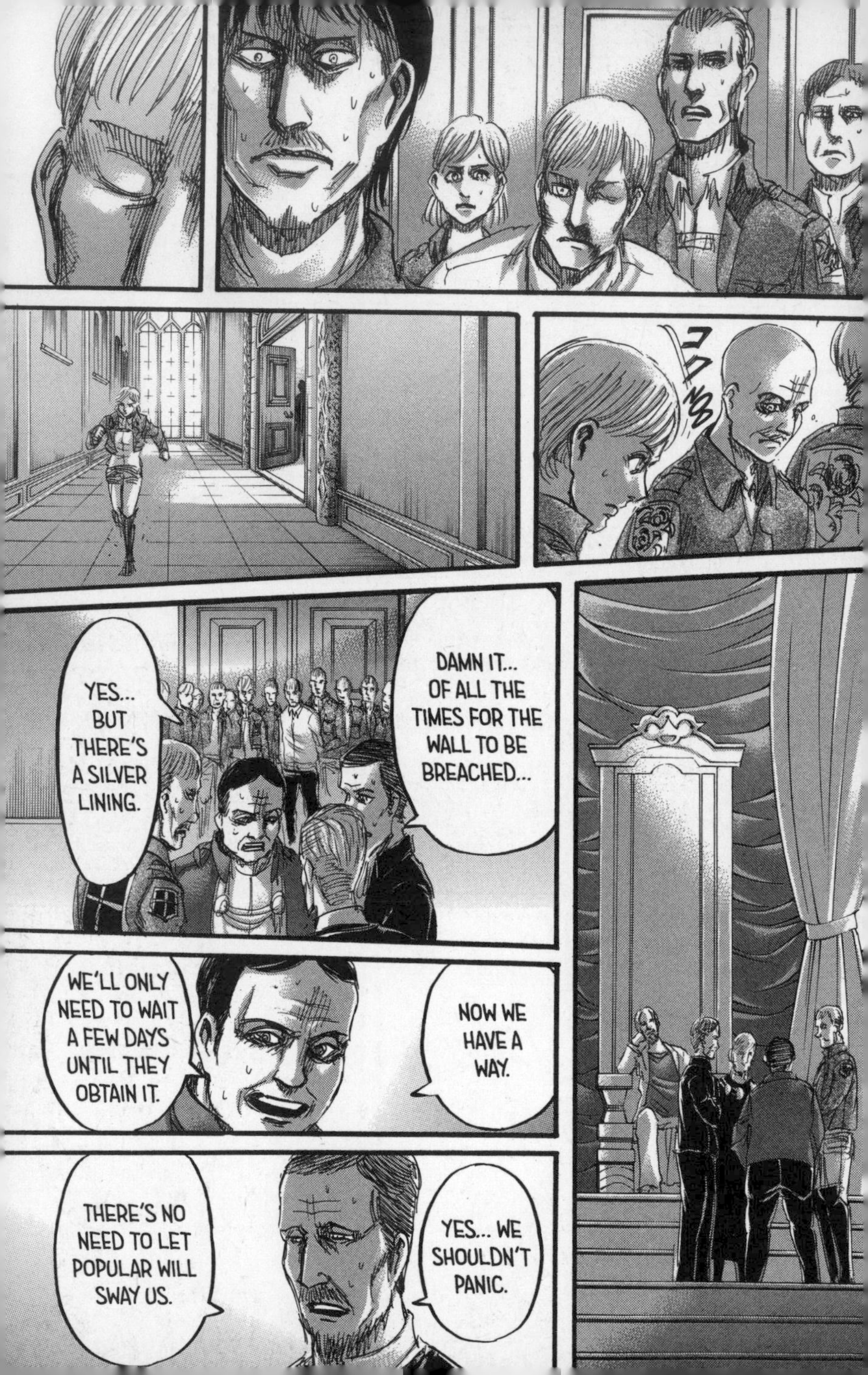
DAMN IT... OF ALL THE TIMES FOR THE WALL TO BE BREACHED...
YES... BUT THERE'S A SILVER LINING.
NOW WE HAVE A WAY.
WE'LL ONLY NEED TO WAIT A FEW DAYS UNTIL THEY OBTAIN IT.
YES... WE SHOULDN'T PANIC.
THERE'S NO NEED TO LET POPULAR WILL SWAY US.

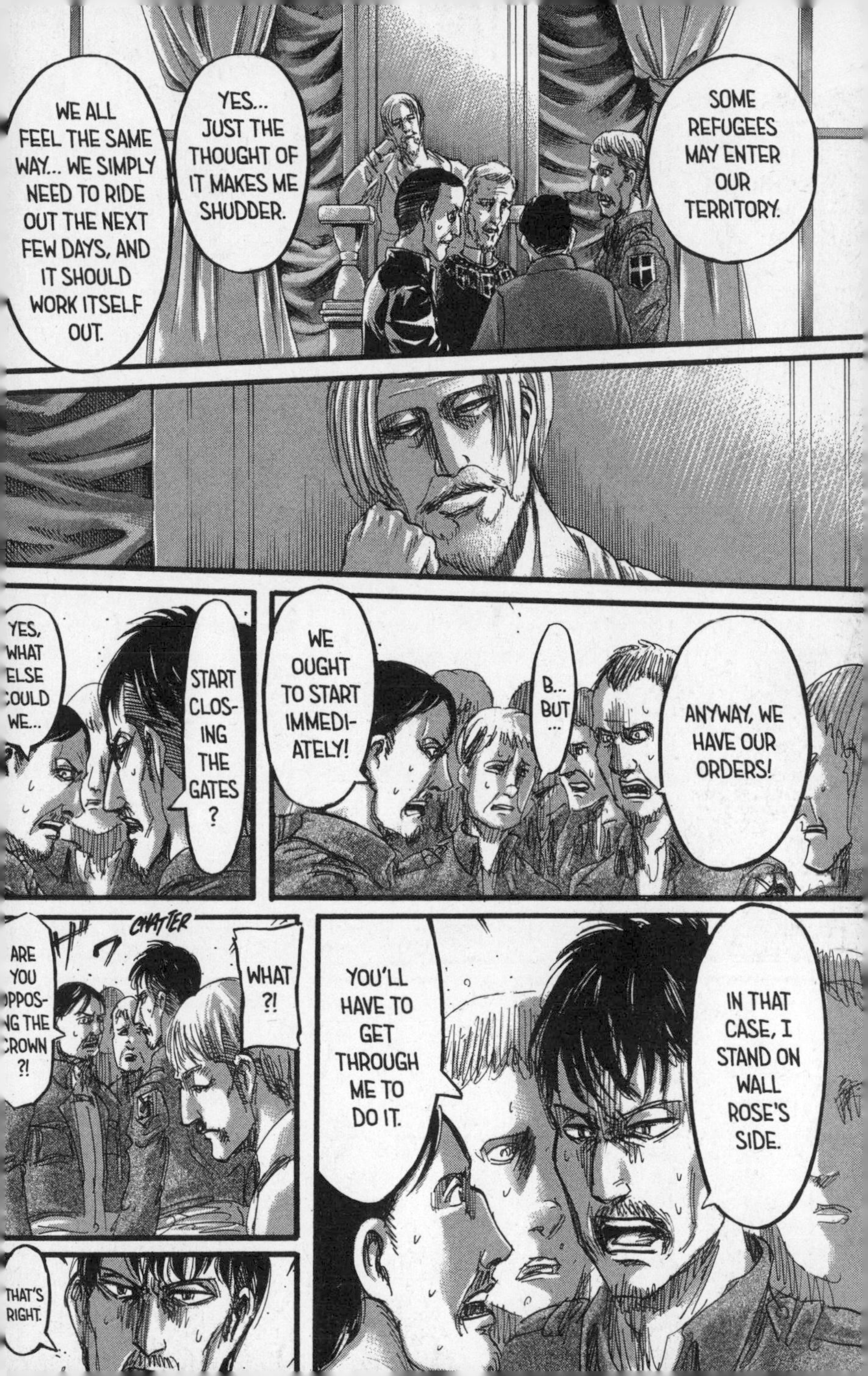
SOME REFUGEES MAY ENTER OUR TERRITORY.
YES... JUST THE THOUGHT OF IT MAKES ME SHUDDER.
WE ALL FEEL THE SAME WAY... WE SIMPLY NEED TO RIDE OUT THE NEXT FEW DAYS, AND IT SHOULD WORK ITSELF OUT.
ANYWAY, WE HAVE OUR ORDERS!
B... BUT ...
WE OUGHT TO START IMMEDIATELY!
START CLOSING THE GATES?
YES, WHAT ELSE COULD WE...
IN THAT CASE, I STAND ON WALL ROSE'S SIDE.
YOU'LL HAVE TO GET THROUGH ME TO DO IT.
WHAT ?!
CHATTER
ARE YOU OPPOSING THE CROWN ?!
THAT'S RIGHT.

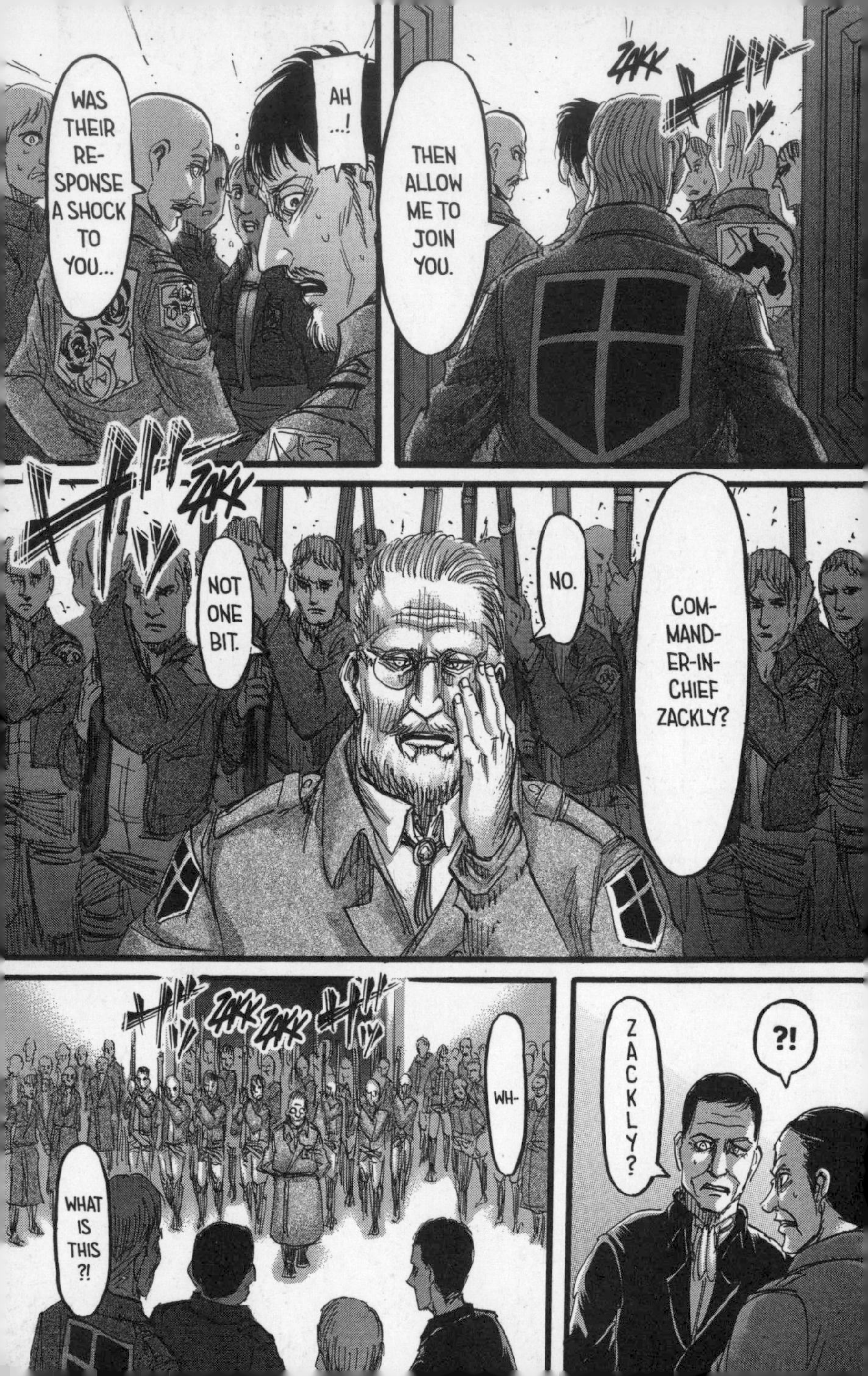
ZAKK
THEN ALLOW ME TO JOIN YOU.
AH ...!
WAS THEIR RESPONSE A SHOCK TO YOU...
COMMANDER-IN-CHIEF ZACKLY?
NO.
NOT ONE BIT.
ZAKK
?!
ZACKLY?
ZAKK ZAKK
WH-
WHAT IS THIS ?!

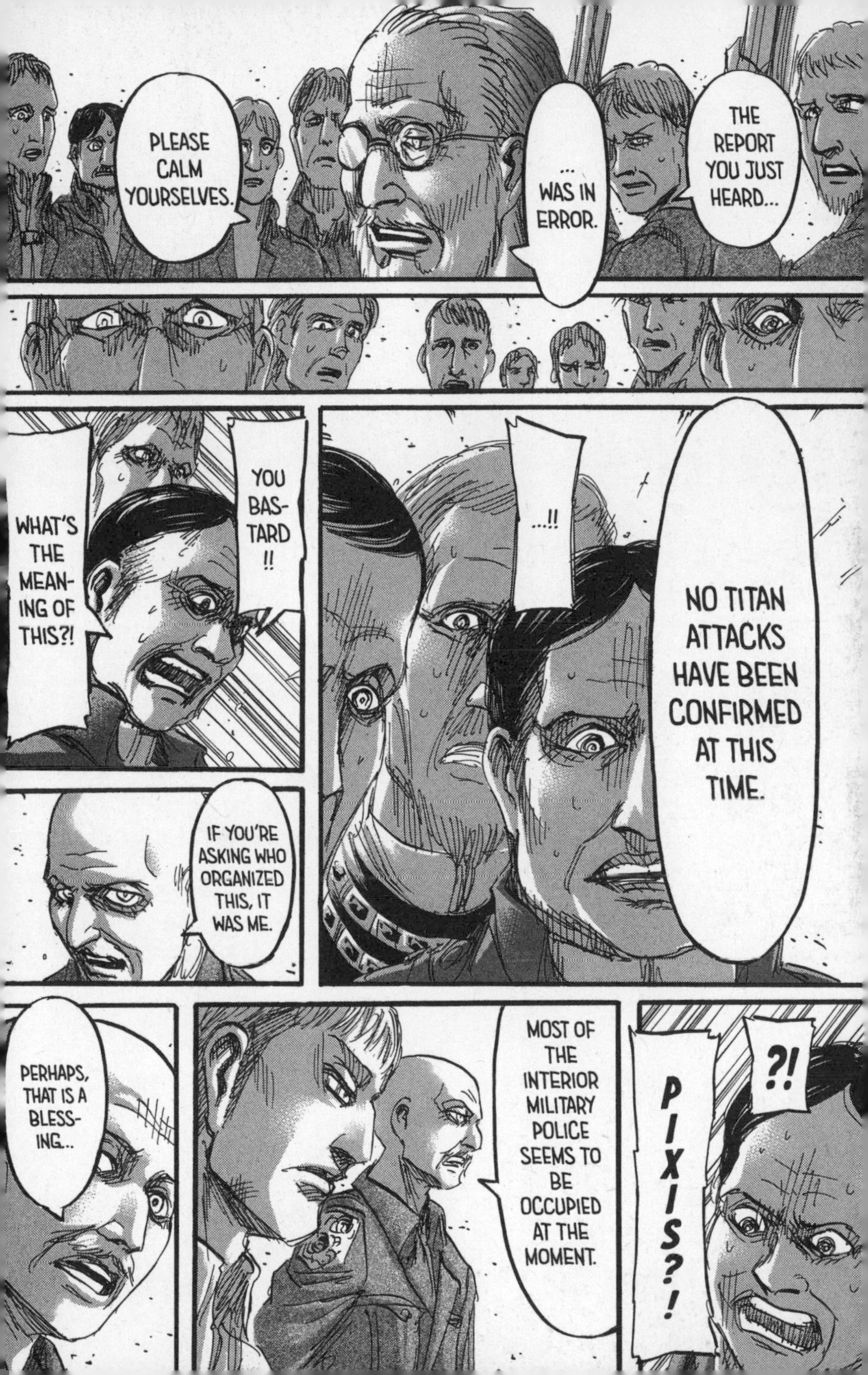
THE REPORT YOU JUST HEARD...
... WAS IN ERROR.
PLEASE CALM YOURSELVES.
NO TITAN ATTACKS HAVE BEEN CONFIRMED AT THIS TIME.
...!!
YOU BAS-TARD !!
WHAT'S THE MEAN-ING OF THIS?!
IF YOU'RE ASKING WHO ORGANIZED THIS, IT WAS ME.
?!
PIXIS?!
MOST OF THE INTERIOR MILITARY POLICE SEEMS TO BE OCCUPIED AT THE MOMENT.
PERHAPS, THAT IS A BLESS-ING...

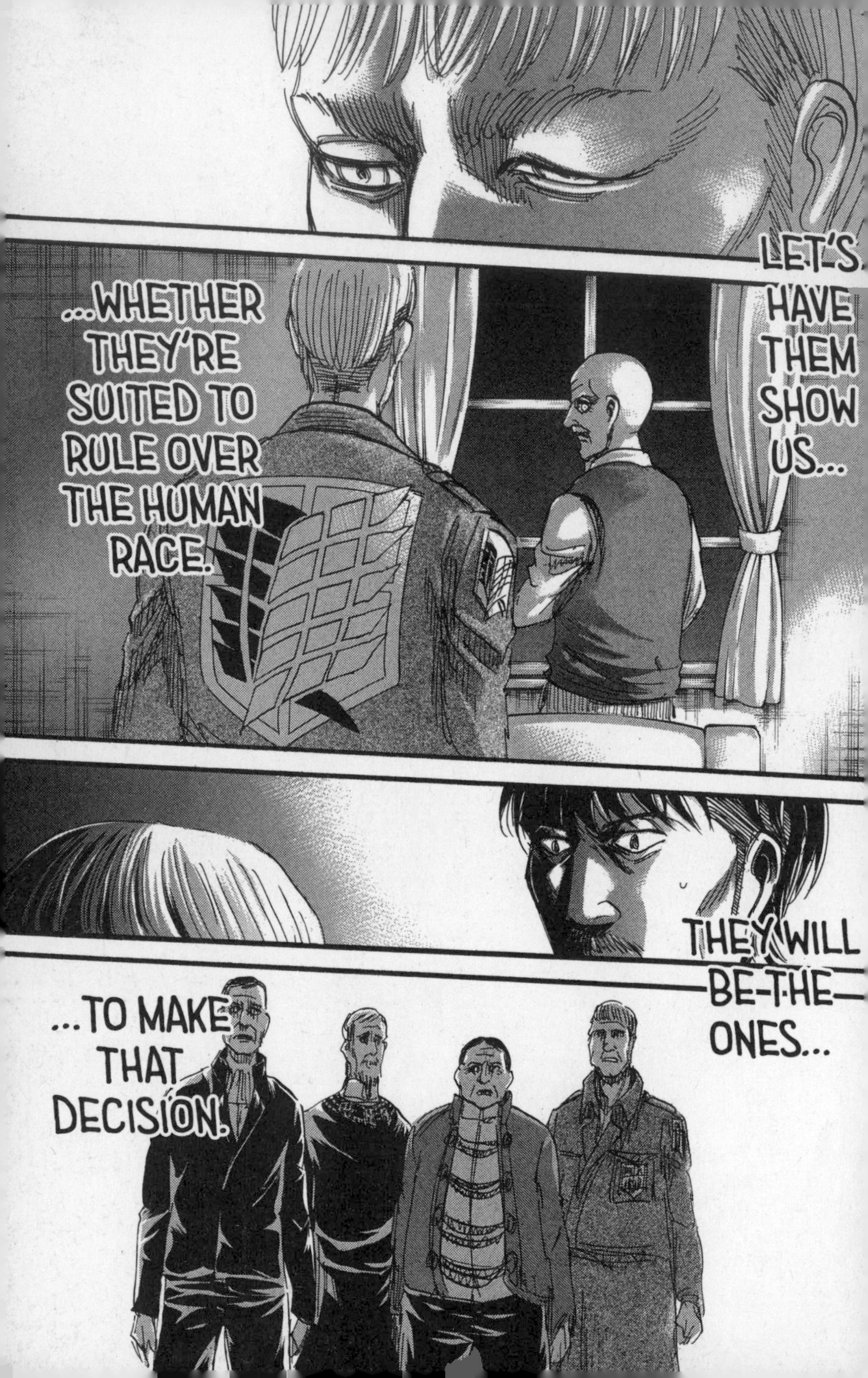
LET'S HAVE THEM SHOW US...
...WHETHER THEY'RE SUITED TO RULE OVER THE HUMAN RACE.
THEY WILL BE THE ONES...
...TO MAKE THAT DECISION.

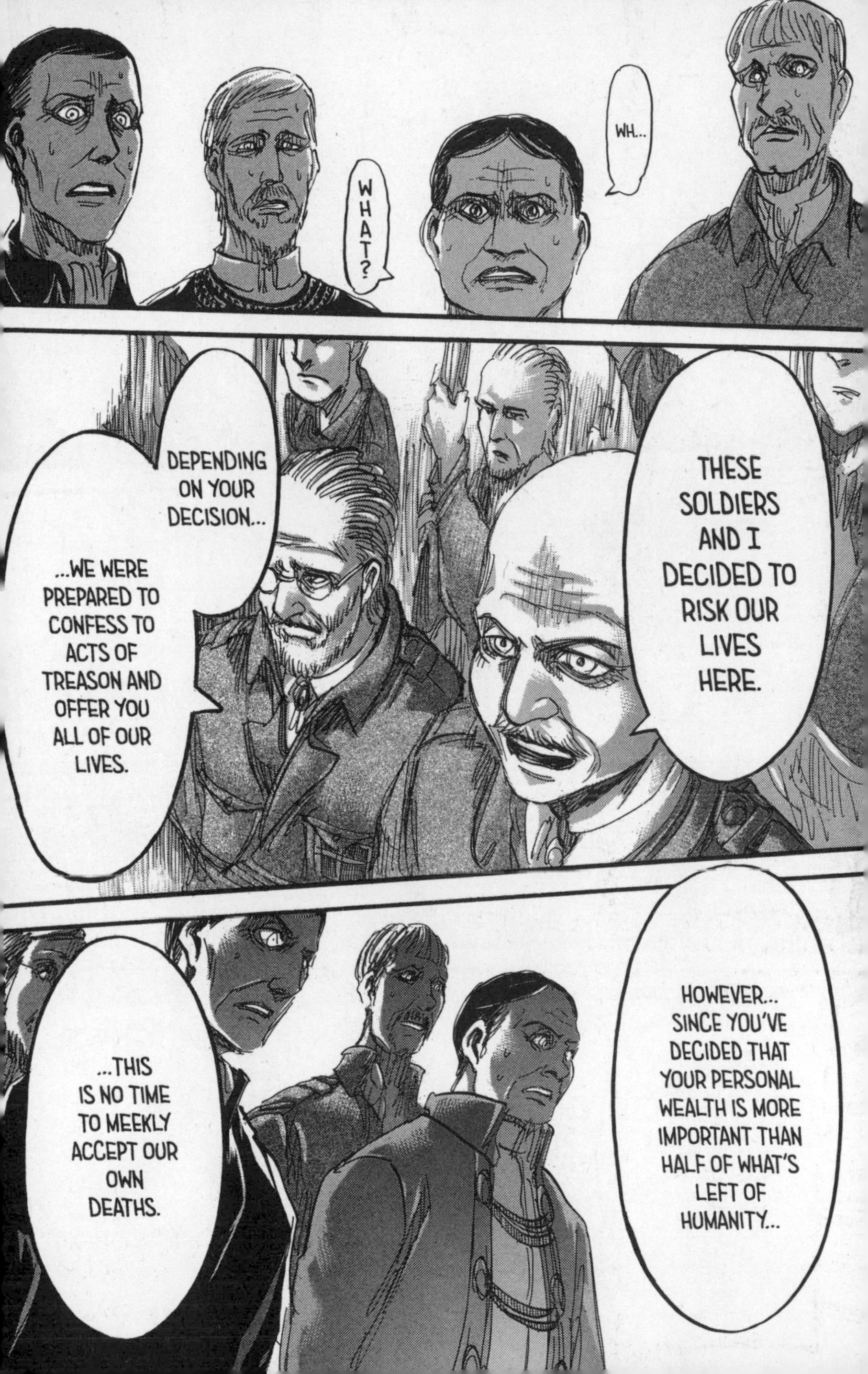
WH...
WHAT?
THESE SOLDIERS AND I DECIDED TO RISK OUR LIVES HERE.
DEPENDING ON YOUR DECISION...
...WE WERE PREPARED TO CONFESS TO ACTS OF TREASON AND OFFER YOU ALL OF OUR LIVES.
HOWEVER... SINCE YOU'VE DECIDED THAT YOUR PERSONAL WEALTH IS MORE IMPORTANT THAN HALF OF WHAT'S LEFT OF HUMANITY...
...THIS IS NO TIME TO MEEKLY ACCEPT OUR OWN DEATHS.

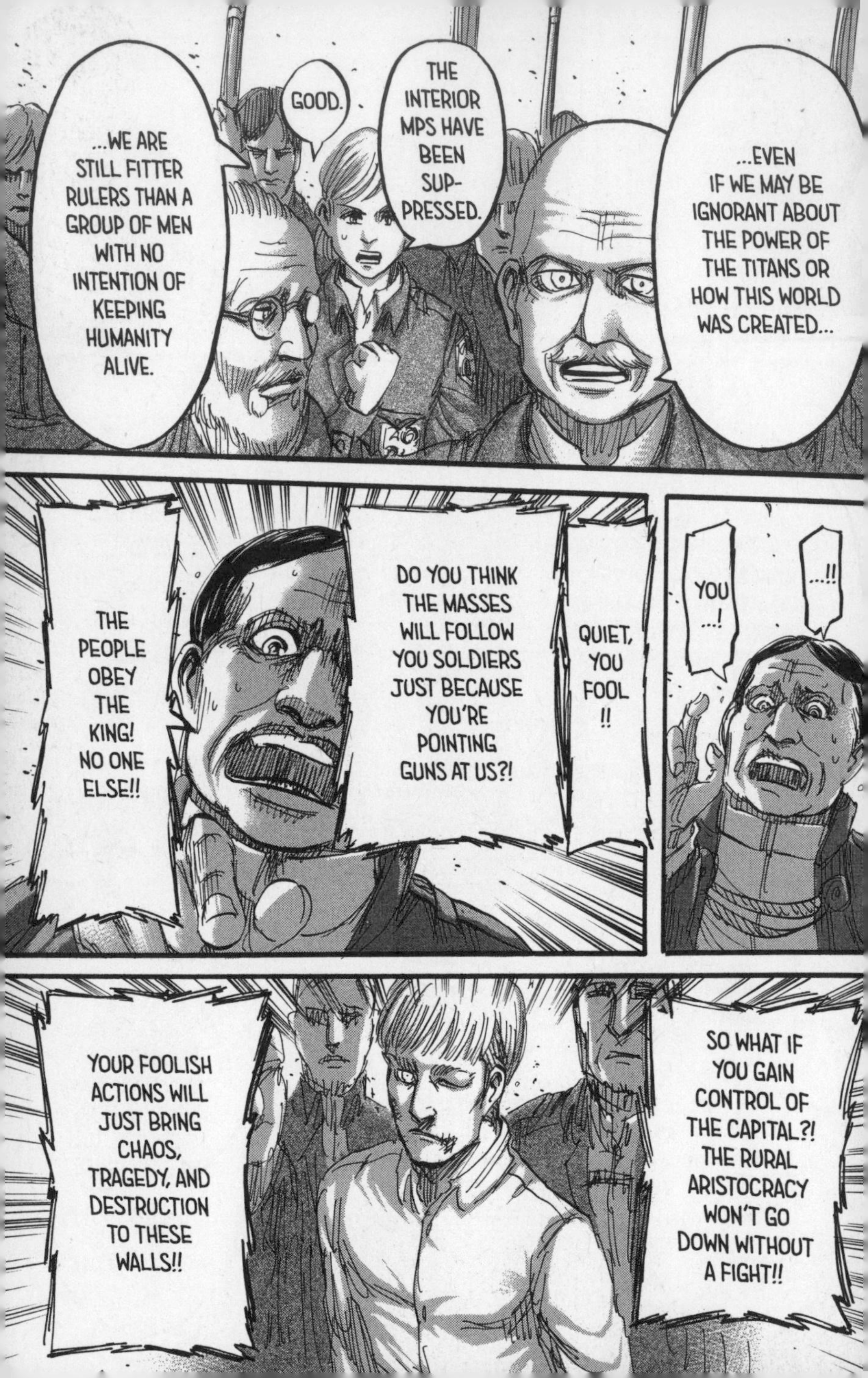
...EVEN IF WE MAY BE IGNORANT ABOUT THE POWER OF THE TITANS OR HOW THIS WORLD WAS CREATED...
THE INTERIOR MPS HAVE BEEN SUPPRESSED.
GOOD.
...WE ARE STILL FITTER RULERS THAN A GROUP OF MEN WITH NO INTENTION OF KEEPING HUMANITY ALIVE.
...!!
YOU ...!
QUIET, YOU FOOL !!
DO YOU THINK THE MASSES WILL FOLLOW YOU SOLDIERS JUST BECAUSE YOU'RE POINTING GUNS AT US?!
THE PEOPLE OBEY THE KING! NO ONE ELSE!!
SO WHAT IF YOU GAIN CONTROL OF THE CAPITAL?! THE RURAL ARISTOCRACY WON'T GO DOWN WITHOUT A FIGHT!!
YOUR FOOLISH ACTIONS WILL JUST BRING CHAOS, TRAGEDY, AND DESTRUCTION TO THESE WALLS!!

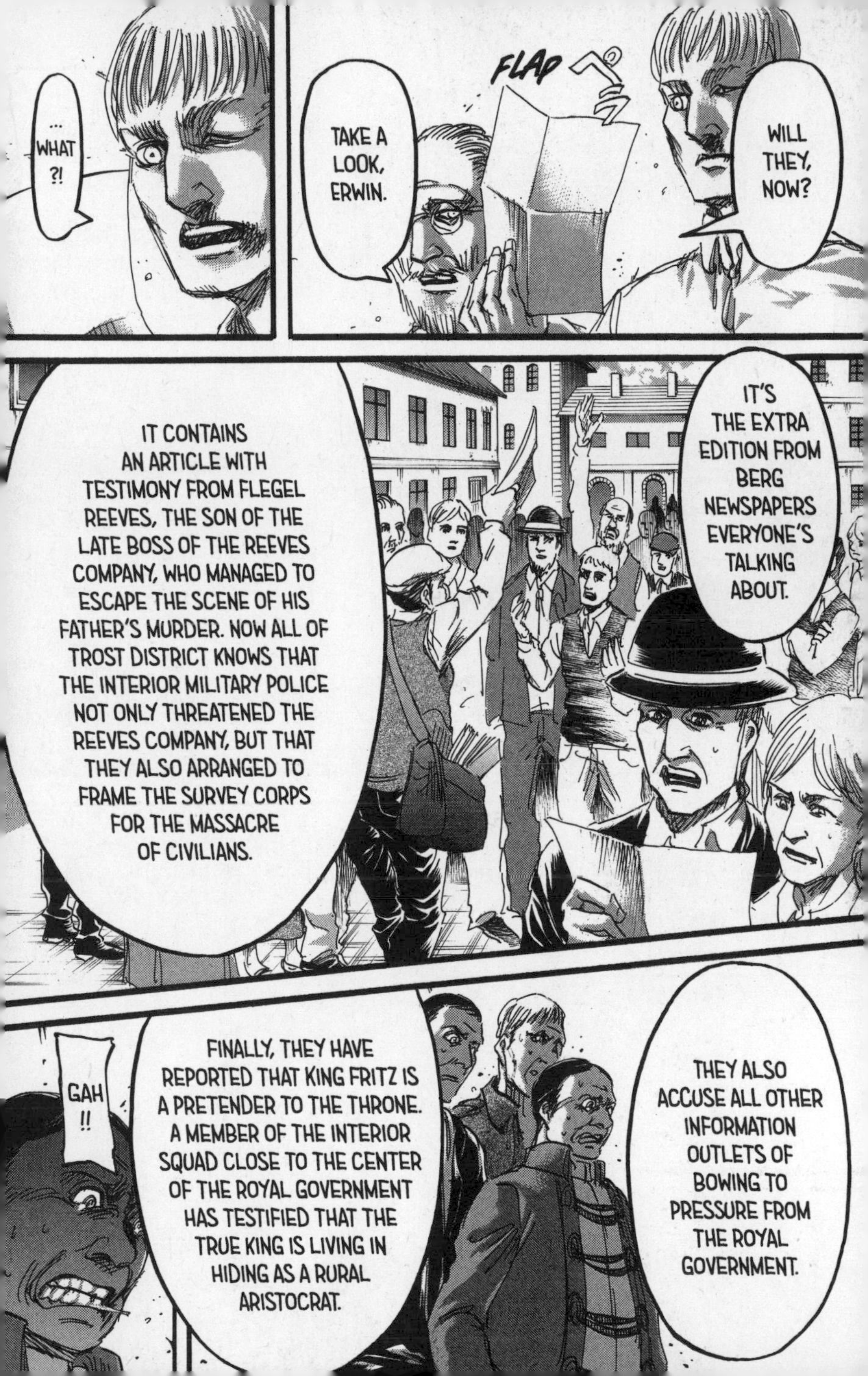
WILL THEY, NOW?
FLAP
TAKE A LOOK, ERWIN.
... WHAT ?!
IT'S THE EXTRA EDITION FROM BERG NEWSPAPERS EVERYONE'S TALKING ABOUT.
IT CONTAINS AN ARTICLE WITH TESTIMONY FROM FLEGEL REEVES, THE SON OF THE LATE BOSS OF THE REEVES COMPANY, WHO MANAGED TO ESCAPE THE SCENE OF HIS FATHER'S MURDER. NOW ALL OF TROST DISTRICT KNOWS THAT THE INTERIOR MILITARY POLICE NOT ONLY THREATENED THE REEVES COMPANY, BUT THAT THEY ALSO ARRANGED TO FRAME THE SURVEY CORPS FOR THE MASSACRE OF CIVILIANS.
THEY ALSO ACCUSE ALL OTHER INFORMATION OUTLETS OF BOWING TO PRESSURE FROM THE ROYAL GOVERNMENT.
FINALLY, THEY HAVE REPORTED THAT KING FRITZ IS A PRETENDER TO THE THRONE. A MEMBER OF THE INTERIOR SQUAD CLOSE TO THE CENTER OF THE ROYAL GOVERNMENT HAS TESTIFIED THAT THE TRUE KING IS LIVING IN HIDING AS A RURAL ARISTOCRAT.
GAH !!

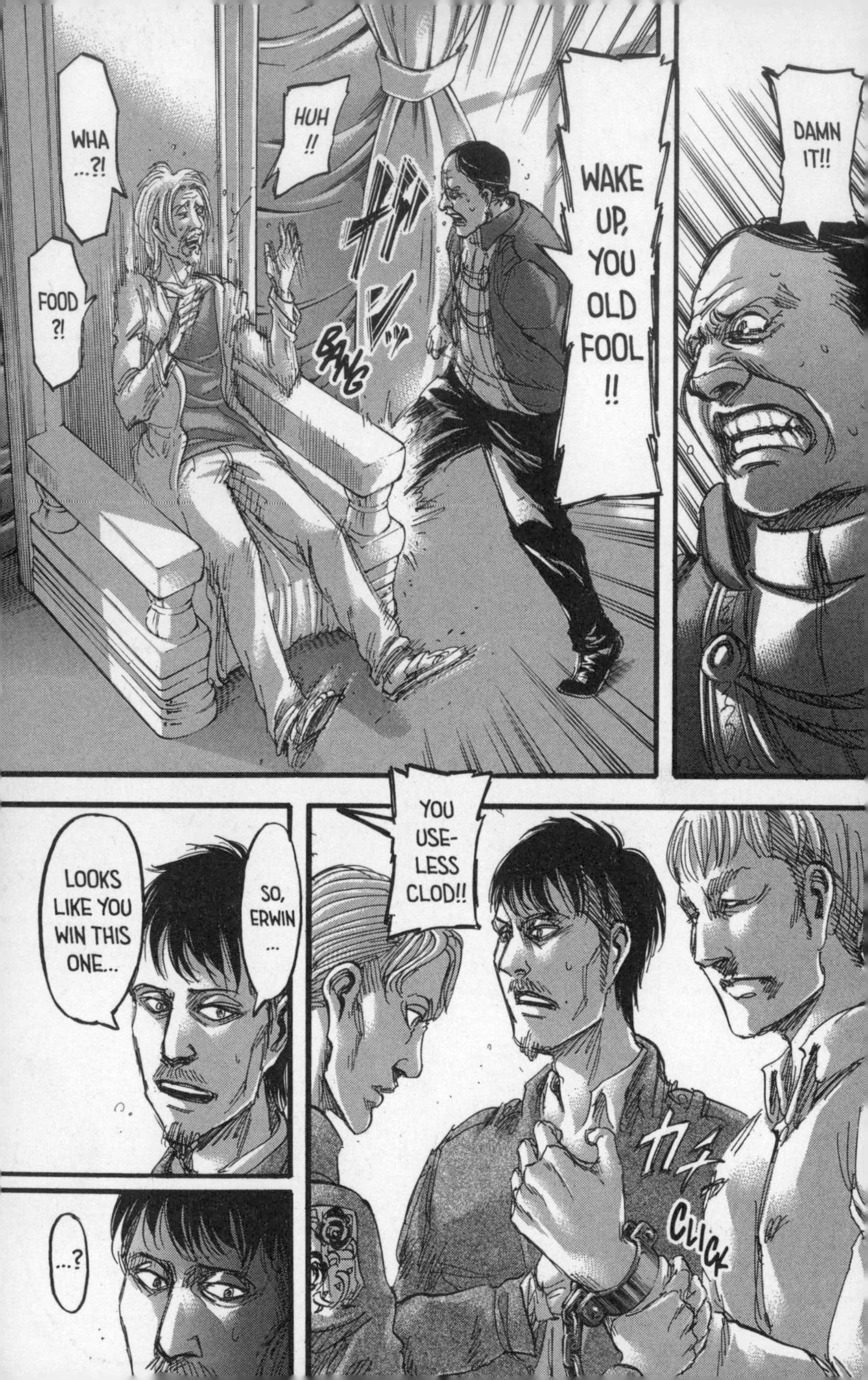
DAMN IT!!
WAKE UP, YOU OLD FOOL!!
BANG
HUH!!
WHA...?!
FOOD?!
YOU USE-LESS CLOD!!
CLICK
SO, ERWIN...
LOOKS LIKE YOU WIN THIS ONE...
...?

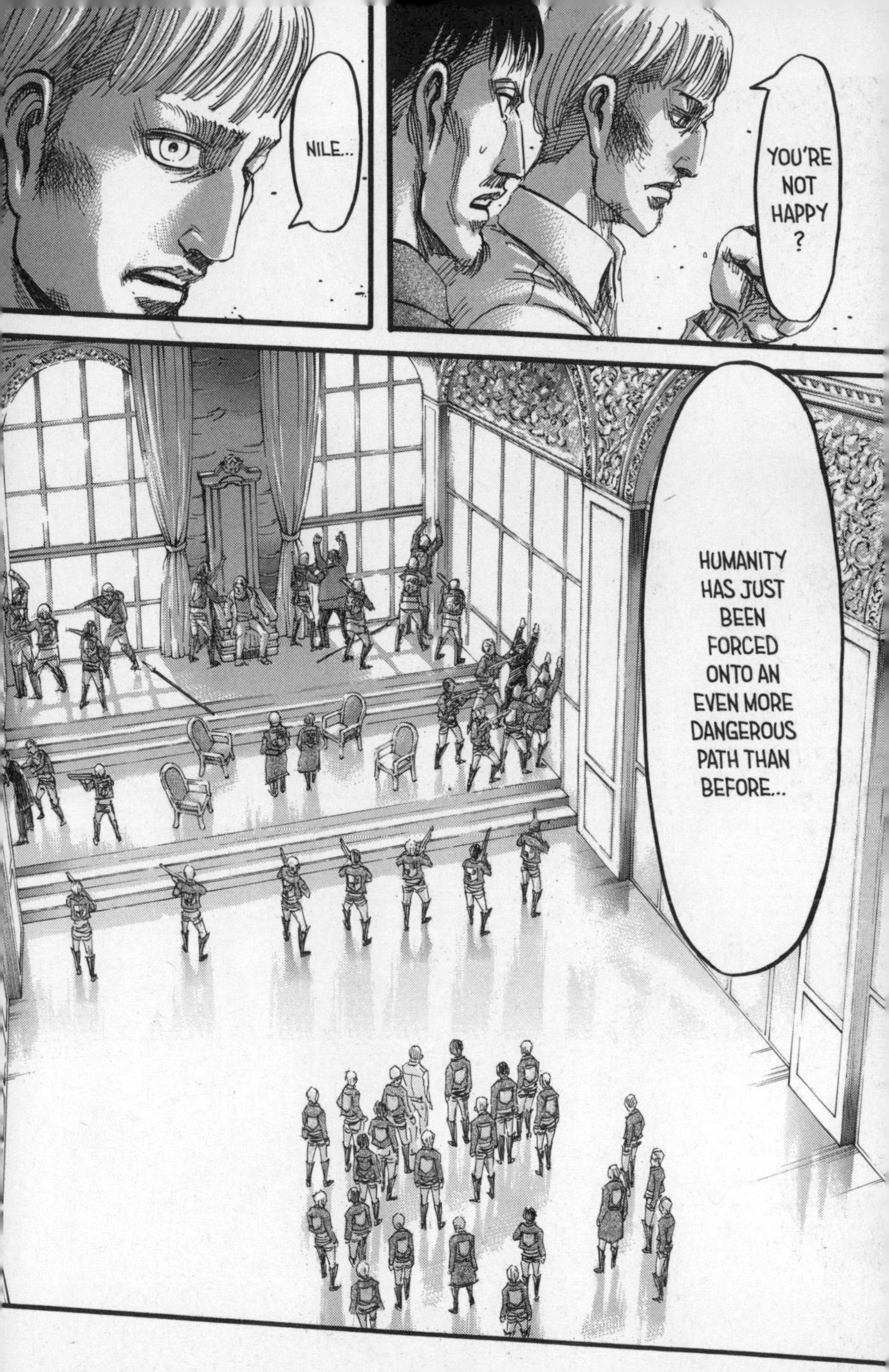
YOU'RE NOT HAPPY?
NILE...
HUMANITY HAS JUST BEEN FORCED ONTO AN EVEN MORE DANGEROUS PATH THAN BEFORE...

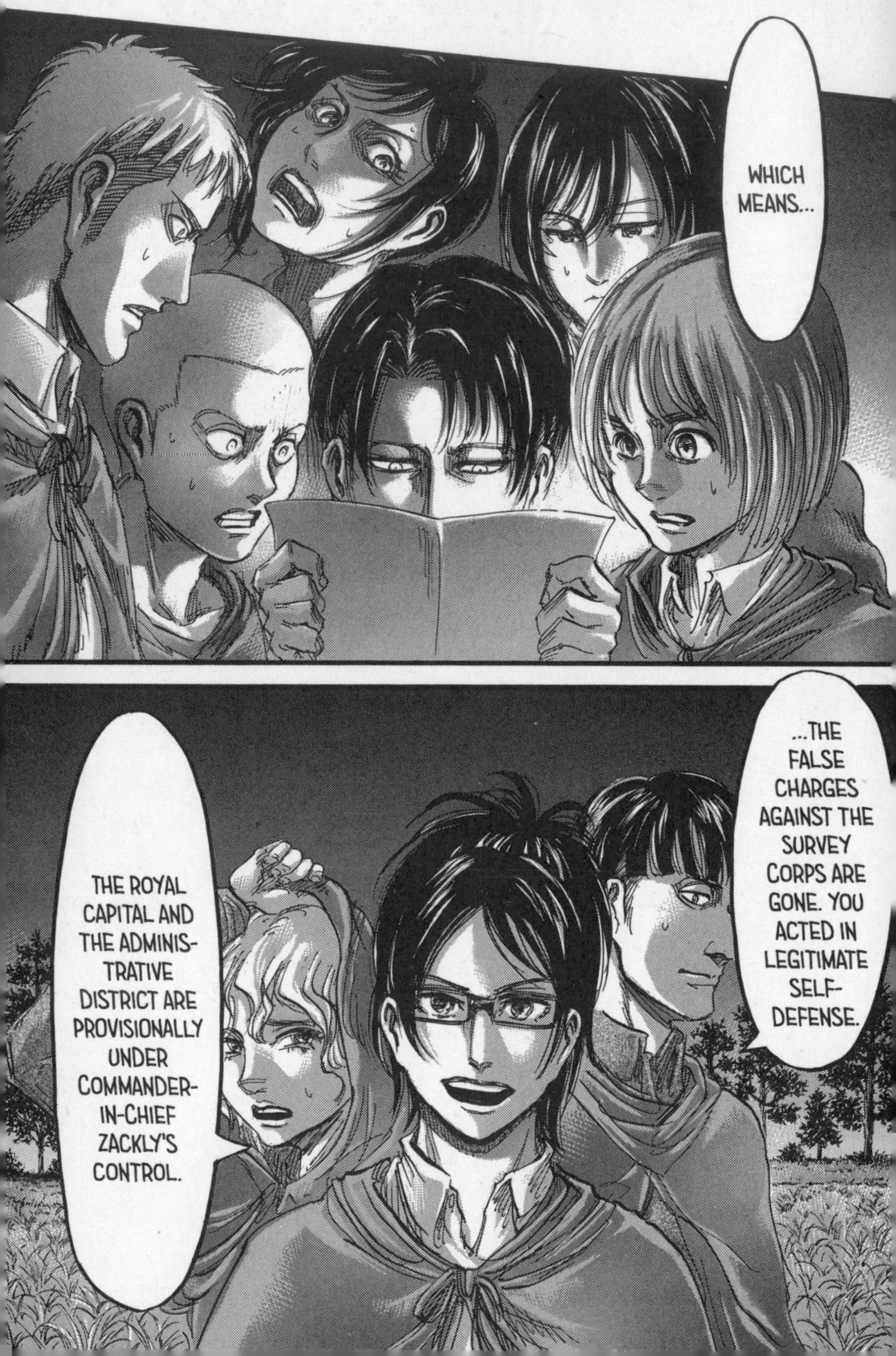
WHICH MEANS...
...THE FALSE CHARGES AGAINST THE SURVEY CORPS ARE GONE. YOU ACTED IN LEGITIMATE SELF-DEFENSE.
THE ROYAL CAPITAL AND THE ADMINISTRATIVE DISTRICT ARE PROVISIONALLY UNDER COMMANDER-IN-CHIEF ZACKLY'S CONTROL.

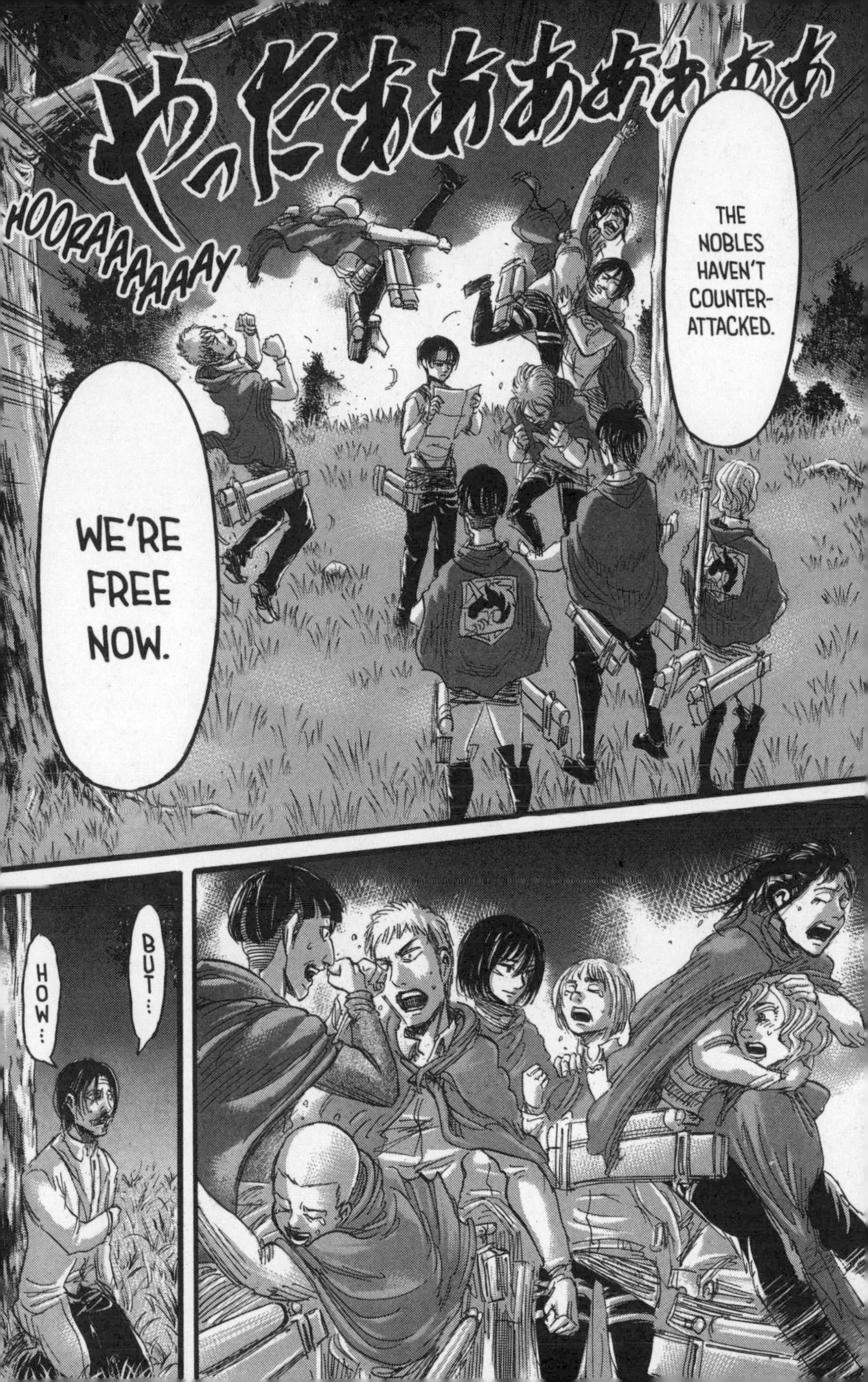
HOORAAAAAAAY
THE NOBLES HAVEN'T COUNTER-ATTACKED.
WE'RE FREE NOW.
BUT...
HOW...

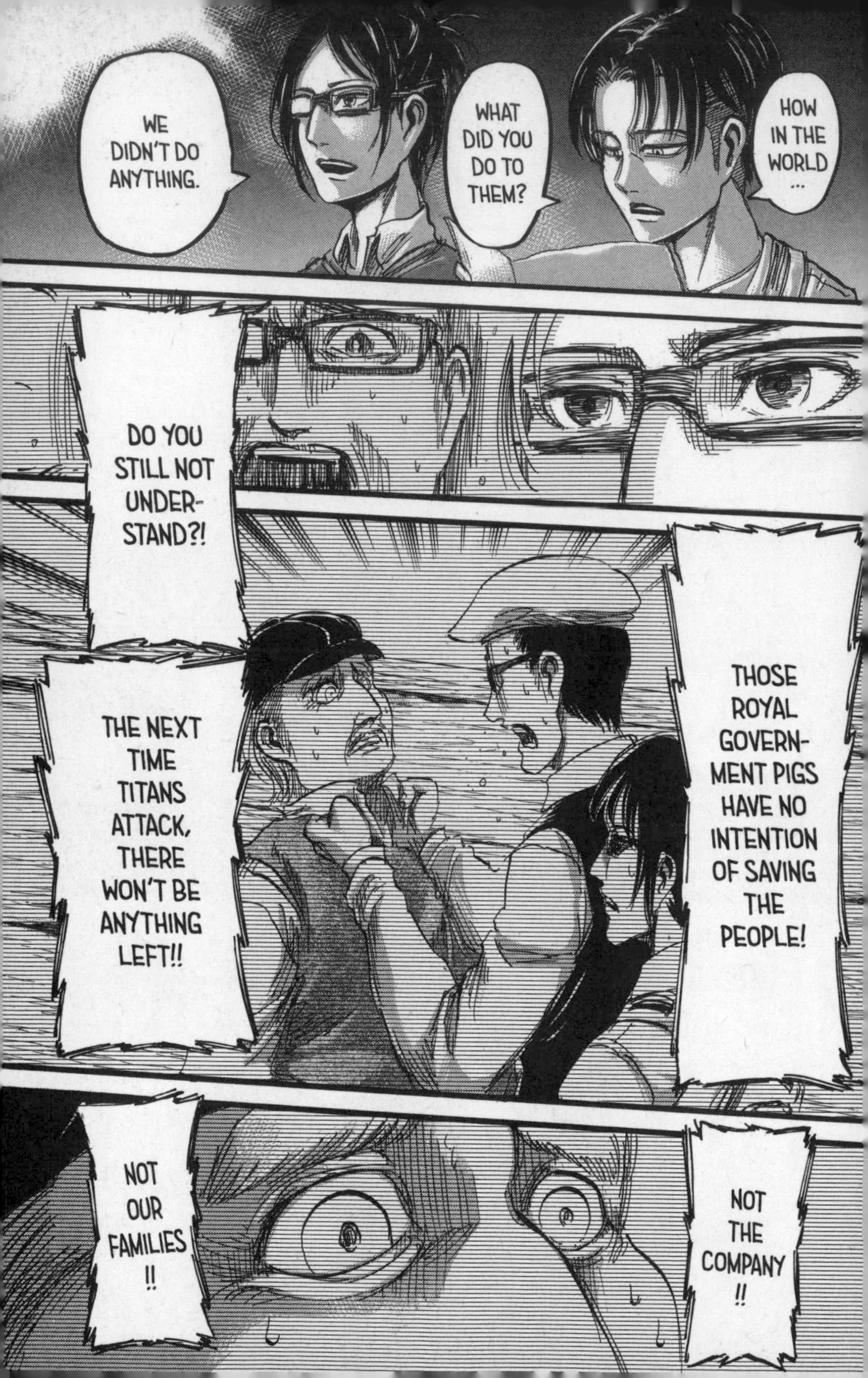
HOW IN THE WORLD ...
WHAT DID YOU DO TO THEM?
WE DIDN'T DO ANYTHING.
DO YOU STILL NOT UNDER-STAND?!
THOSE ROYAL GOVERN-MENT PIGS HAVE NO INTENTION OF SAVING THE PEOPLE!
THE NEXT TIME TITANS ATTACK, THERE WON'T BE ANYTHING LEFT!!
NOT THE COMPANY !!
NOT OUR FAMILIES !!

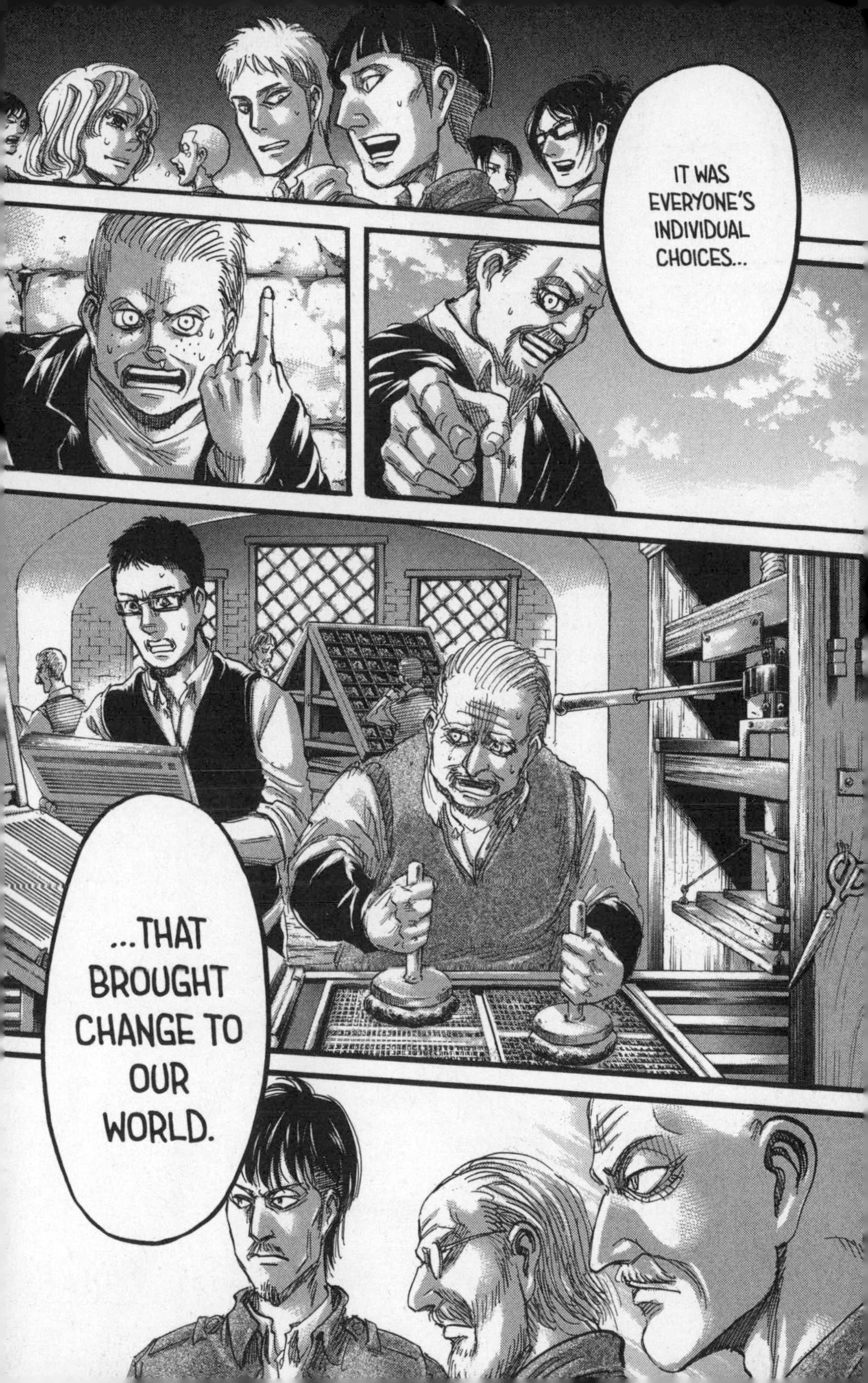
IT WAS EVERYONE'S INDIVIDUAL CHOICES...
...THAT BROUGHT CHANGE TO OUR WORLD.

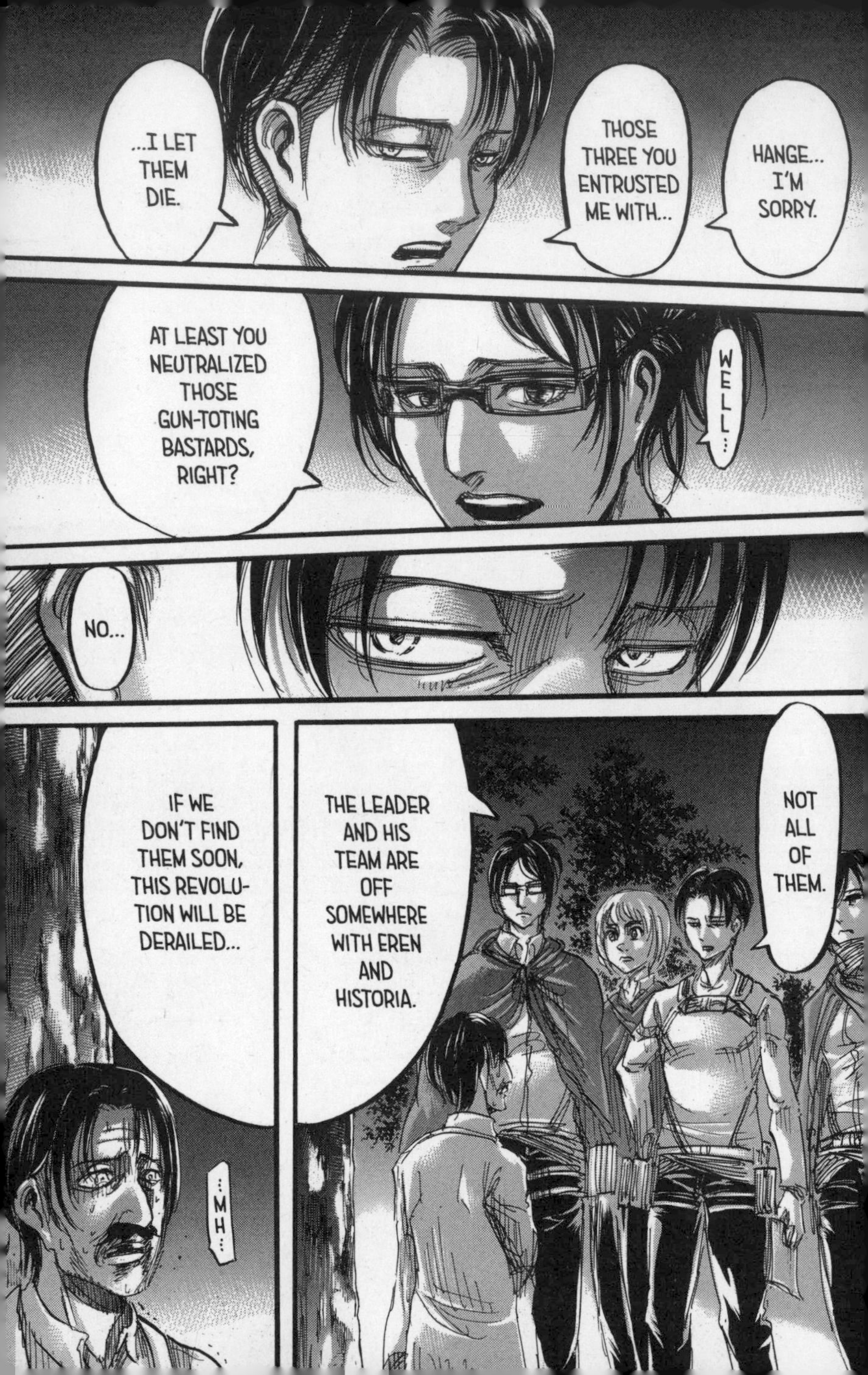
HANGE... I'M SORRY.
THOSE THREE YOU ENTRUSTED ME WITH...
...I LET THEM DIE.
WELL...
AT LEAST YOU NEUTRALIZED THOSE GUN-TOTING BASTARDS, RIGHT?
NO...
NOT ALL OF THEM.
THE LEADER AND HIS TEAM ARE OFF SOMEWHERE WITH EREN AND HISTORIA.
IF WE DON'T FIND THEM SOON, THIS REVOLUTION WILL BE DERAILED...
...MH...

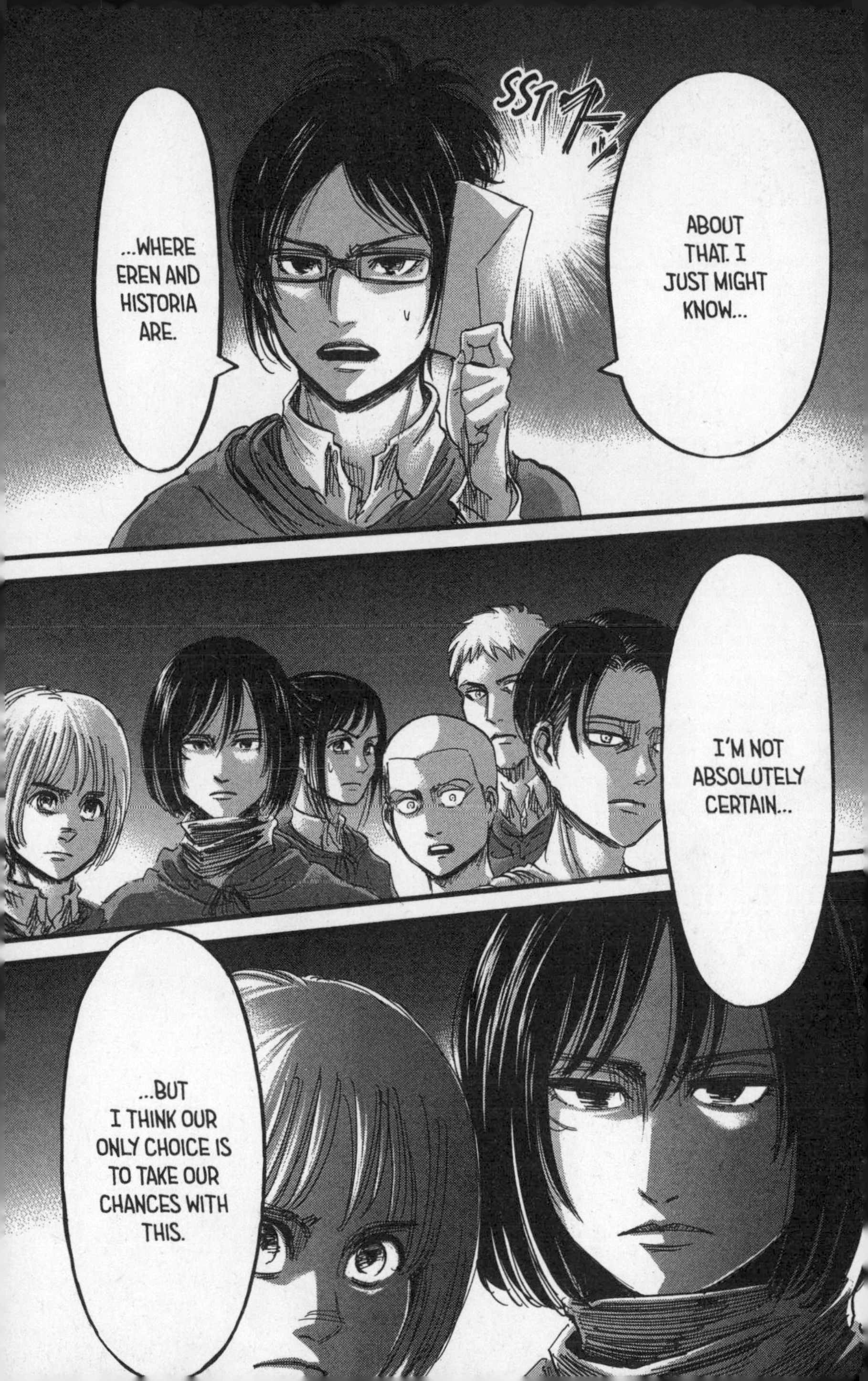
SST
ABOUT THAT. I JUST MIGHT KNOW...
...WHERE EREN AND HISTORIA ARE.
I'M NOT ABSOLUTELY CERTAIN...
...BUT I THINK OUR ONLY CHOICE IS TO TAKE OUR CHANCES WITH THIS.

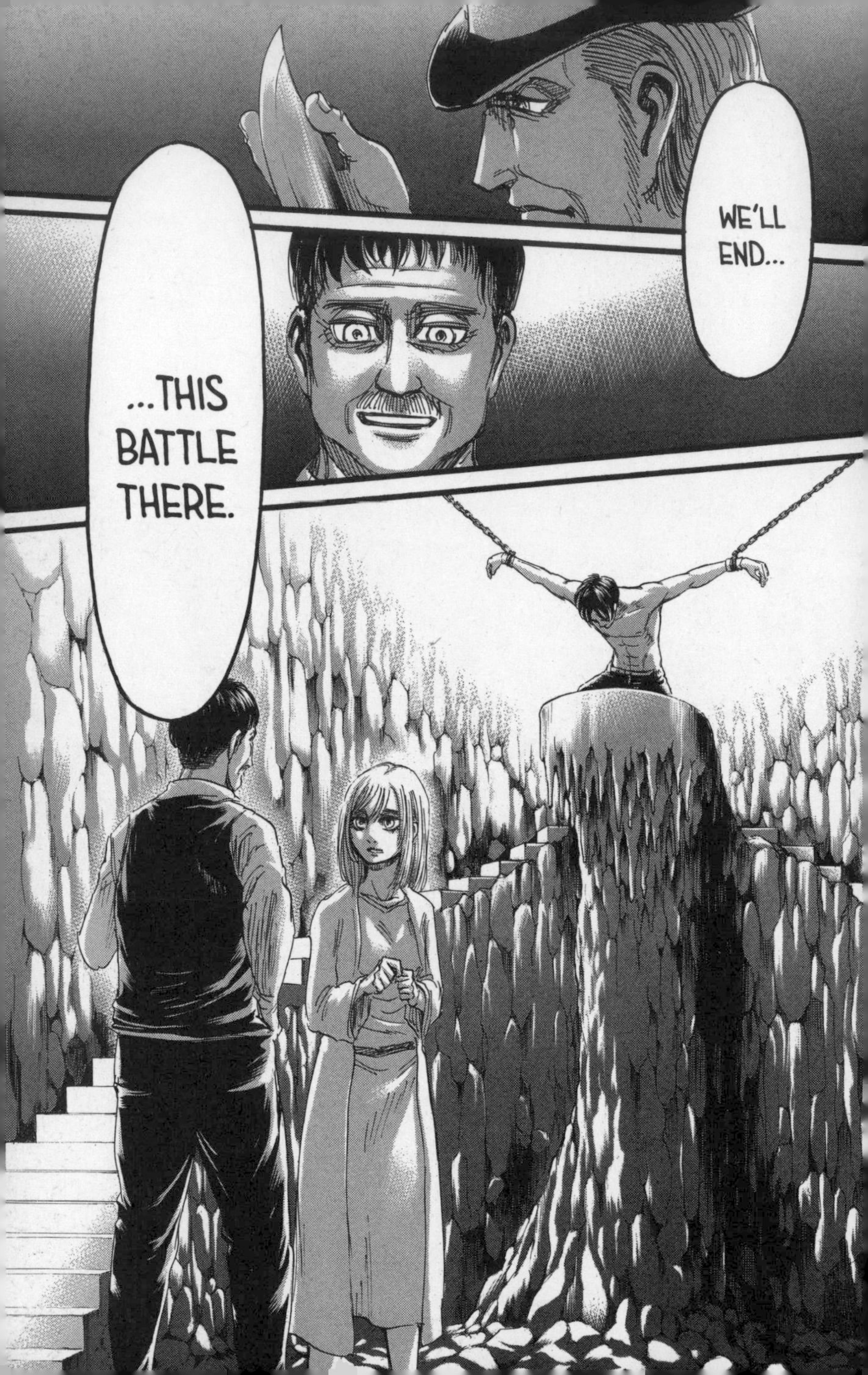
WE'LL END...
...THIS BATTLE THERE.

# ATTACK on TITAN

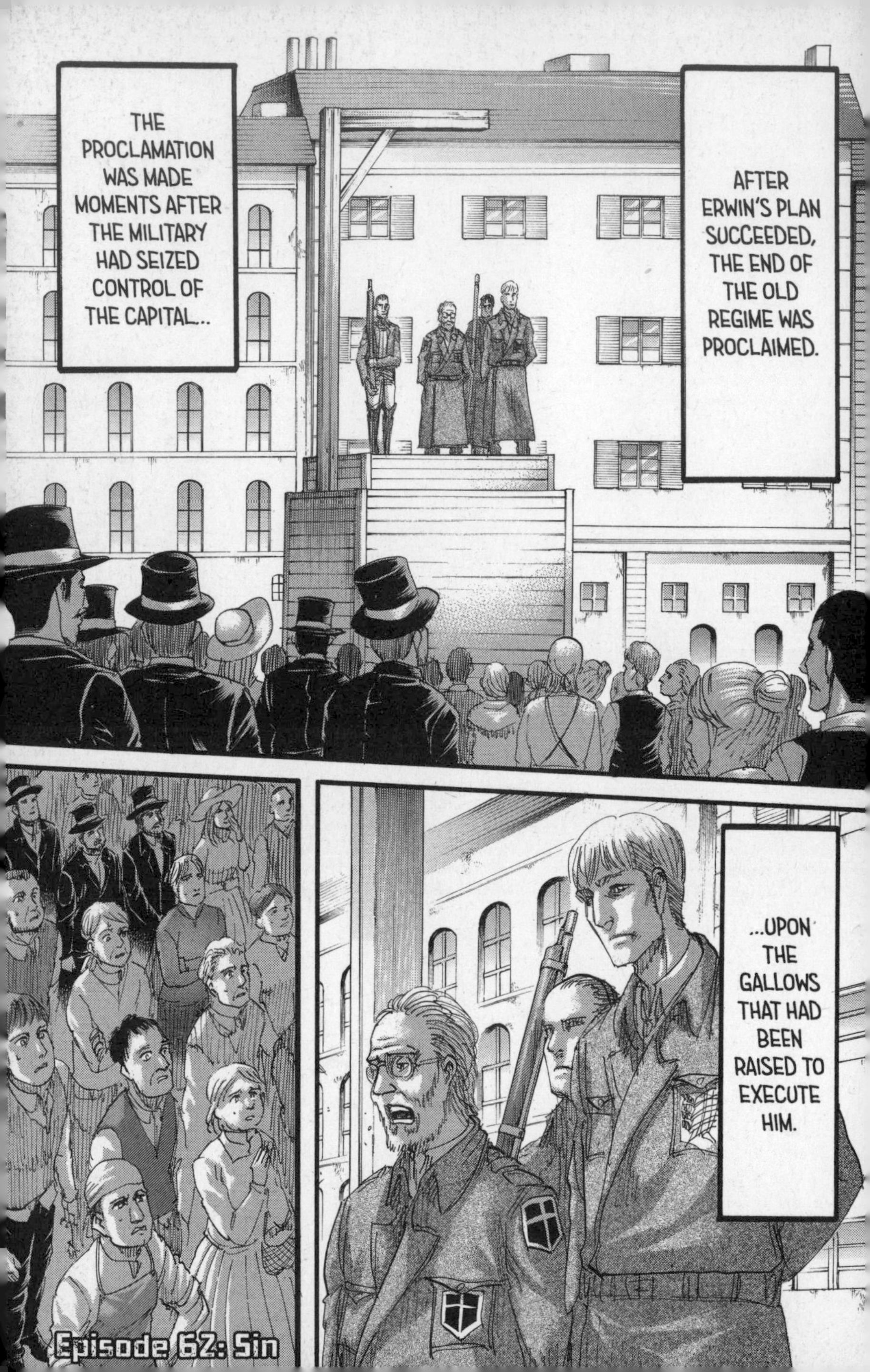
AFTER ERWIN'S PLAN SUCCEEDED, THE END OF THE OLD REGIME WAS PROCLAIMED.
THE PROCLAMATION WAS MADE MOMENTS AFTER THE MILITARY HAD SEIZED CONTROL OF THE CAPITAL...
...UPON THE GALLOWS THAT HAD BEEN RAISED TO EXECUTE HIM.
Episode 62: Sin

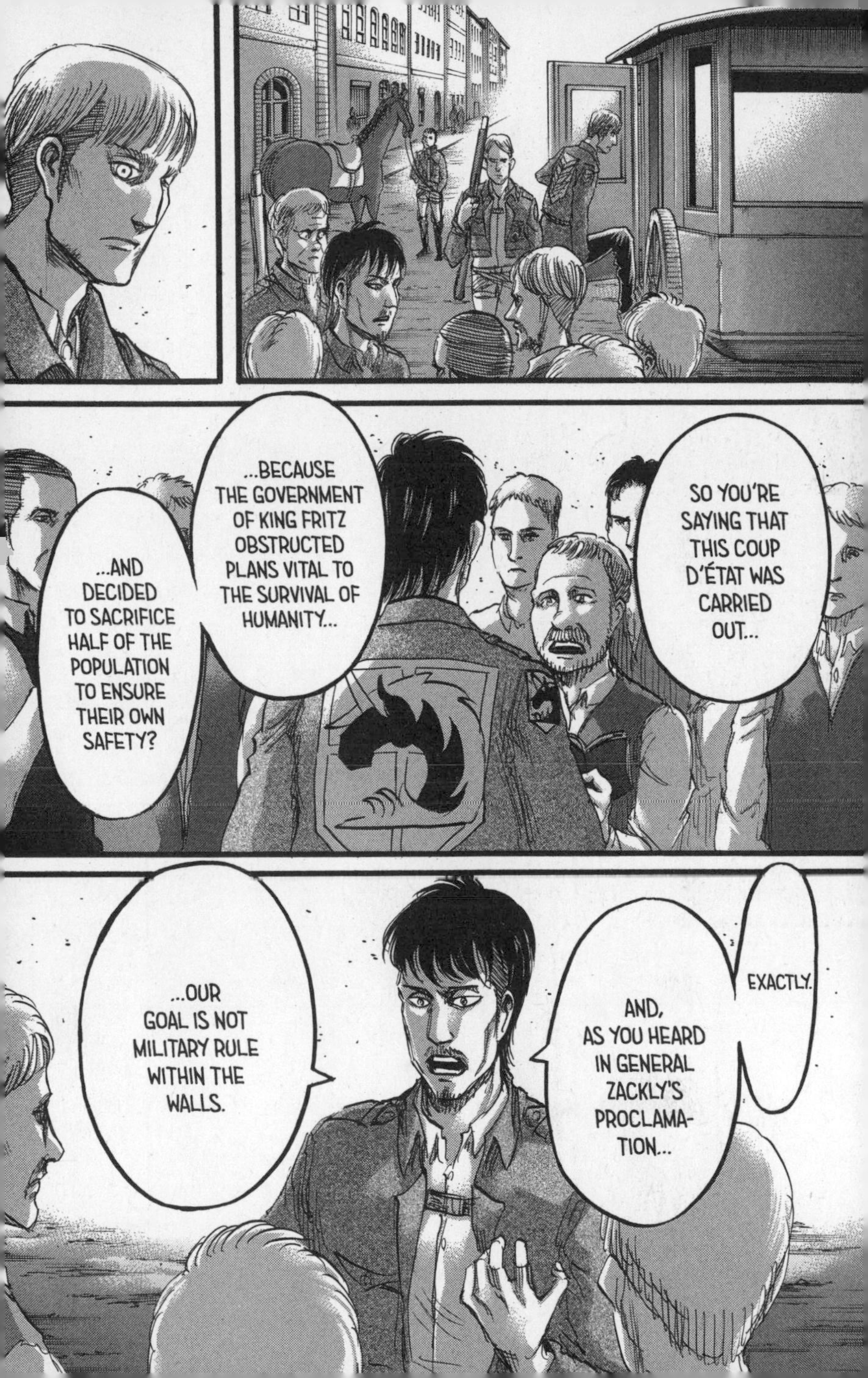
SO YOU'RE SAYING THAT THIS COUP D'ÉTAT WAS CARRIED OUT...
...BECAUSE THE GOVERNMENT OF KING FRITZ OBSTRUCTED PLANS VITAL TO THE SURVIVAL OF HUMANITY...
...AND DECIDED TO SACRIFICE HALF OF THE POPULATION TO ENSURE THEIR OWN SAFETY?
EXACTLY.
AND, AS YOU HEARD IN GENERAL ZACKLY'S PROCLAMA-TION...
...OUR GOAL IS NOT MILITARY RULE WITHIN THE WALLS.

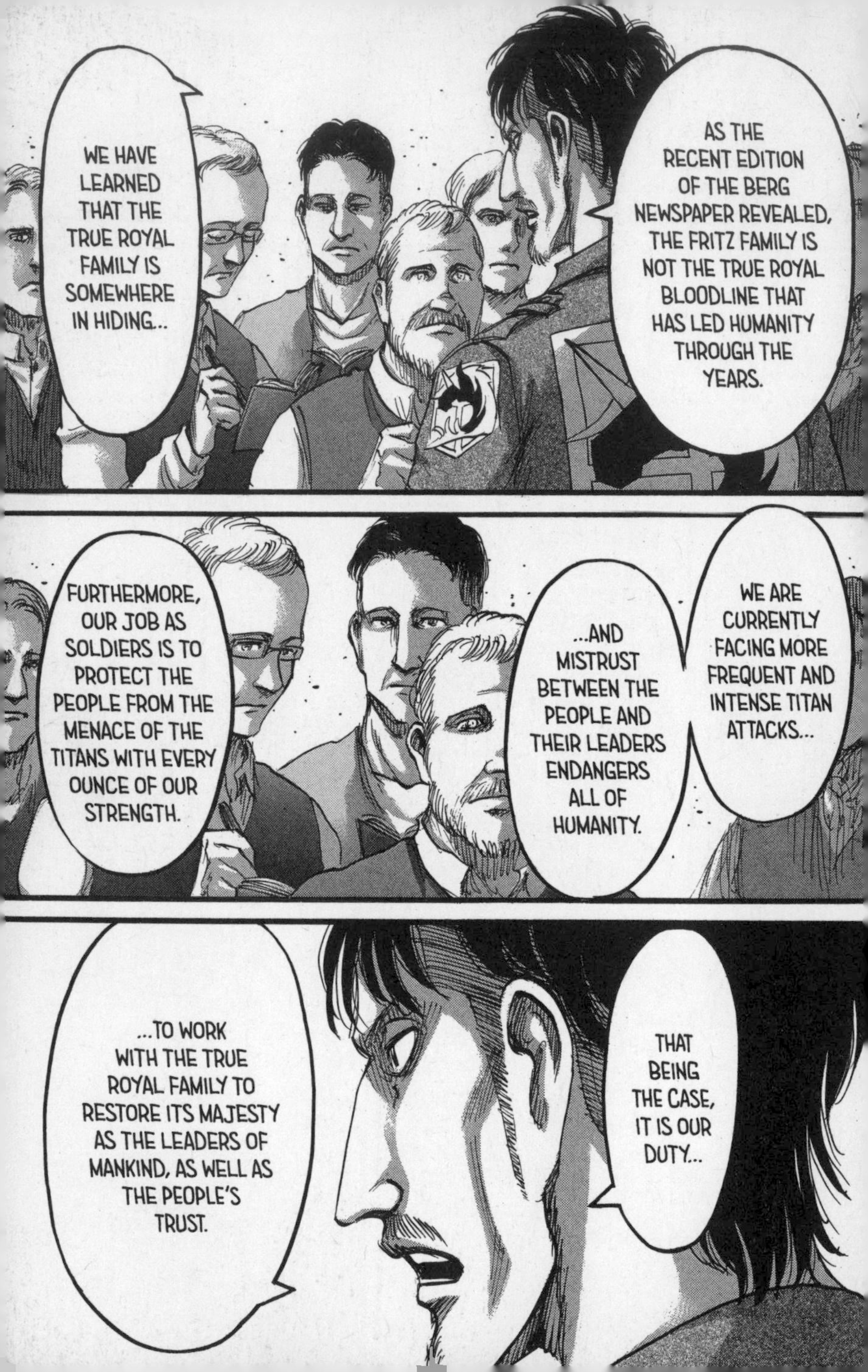
AS THE RECENT EDITION OF THE BERG NEWSPAPER REVEALED, THE FRITZ FAMILY IS NOT THE TRUE ROYAL BLOODLINE THAT HAS LED HUMANITY THROUGH THE YEARS.
WE HAVE LEARNED THAT THE TRUE ROYAL FAMILY IS SOMEWHERE IN HIDING...
WE ARE CURRENTLY FACING MORE FREQUENT AND INTENSE TITAN ATTACKS...
...AND MISTRUST BETWEEN THE PEOPLE AND THEIR LEADERS ENDANGERS ALL OF HUMANITY.
FURTHERMORE, OUR JOB AS SOLDIERS IS TO PROTECT THE PEOPLE FROM THE MENACE OF THE TITANS WITH EVERY OUNCE OF OUR STRENGTH.
THAT BEING THE CASE, IT IS OUR DUTY...
...TO WORK WITH THE TRUE ROYAL FAMILY TO RESTORE ITS MAJESTY AS THE LEADERS OF MANKIND, AS WELL AS THE PEOPLE'S TRUST.

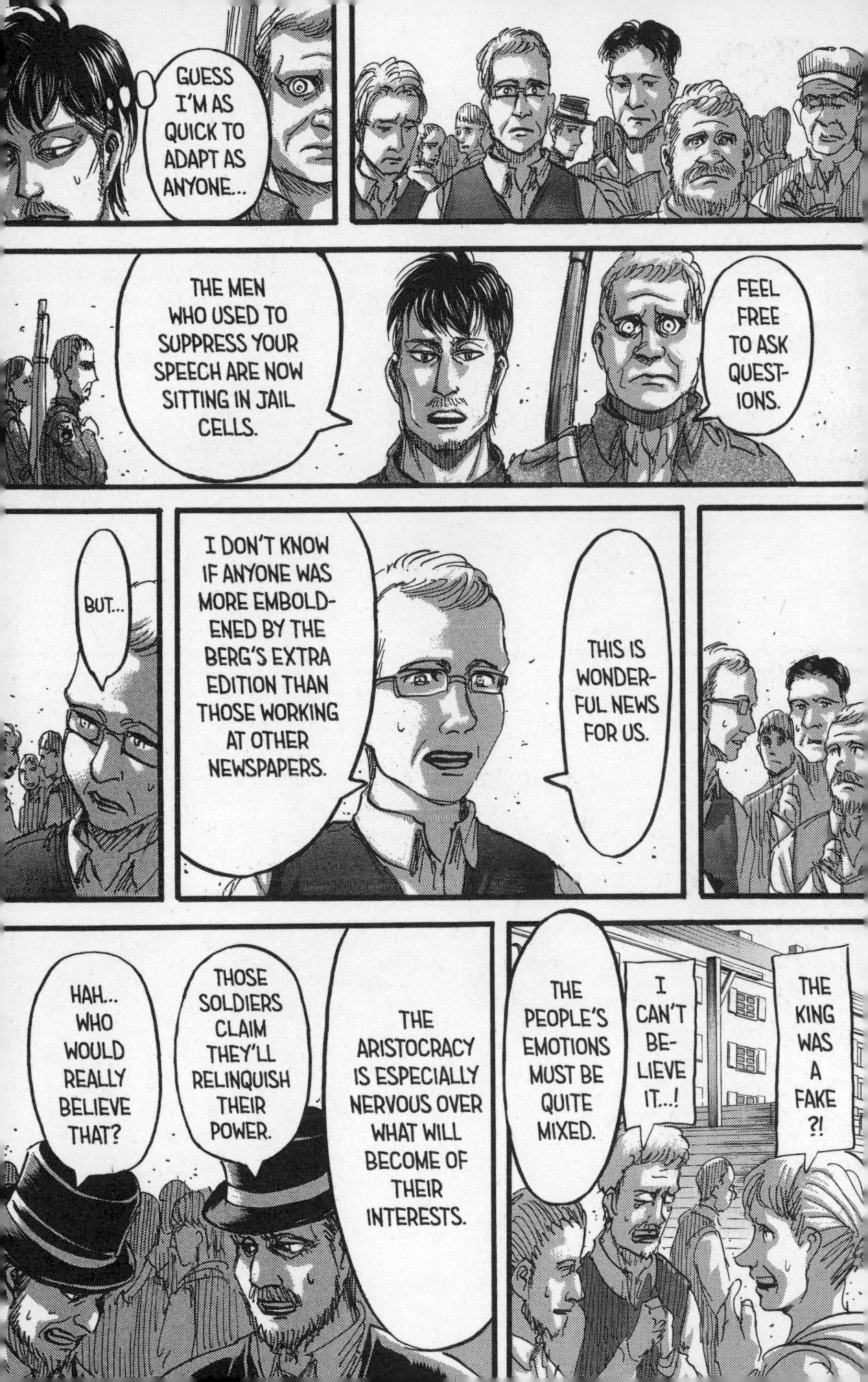
GUESS I'M AS QUICK TO ADAPT AS ANYONE...
FEEL FREE TO ASK QUESTIONS.
THE MEN WHO USED TO SUPPRESS YOUR SPEECH ARE NOW SITTING IN JAIL CELLS.
THIS IS WONDERFUL NEWS FOR US.
I DON'T KNOW IF ANYONE WAS MORE EMBOLDENED BY THE BERG'S EXTRA EDITION THAN THOSE WORKING AT OTHER NEWSPAPERS.
BUT...
THE KING WAS A FAKE?!
I CAN'T BELIEVE IT...!
THE PEOPLE'S EMOTIONS MUST BE QUITE MIXED.
THE ARISTOCRACY IS ESPECIALLY NERVOUS OVER WHAT WILL BECOME OF THEIR INTERESTS.
THOSE SOLDIERS CLAIM THEY'LL RELINQUISH THEIR POWER.
HAH... WHO WOULD REALLY BELIEVE THAT?

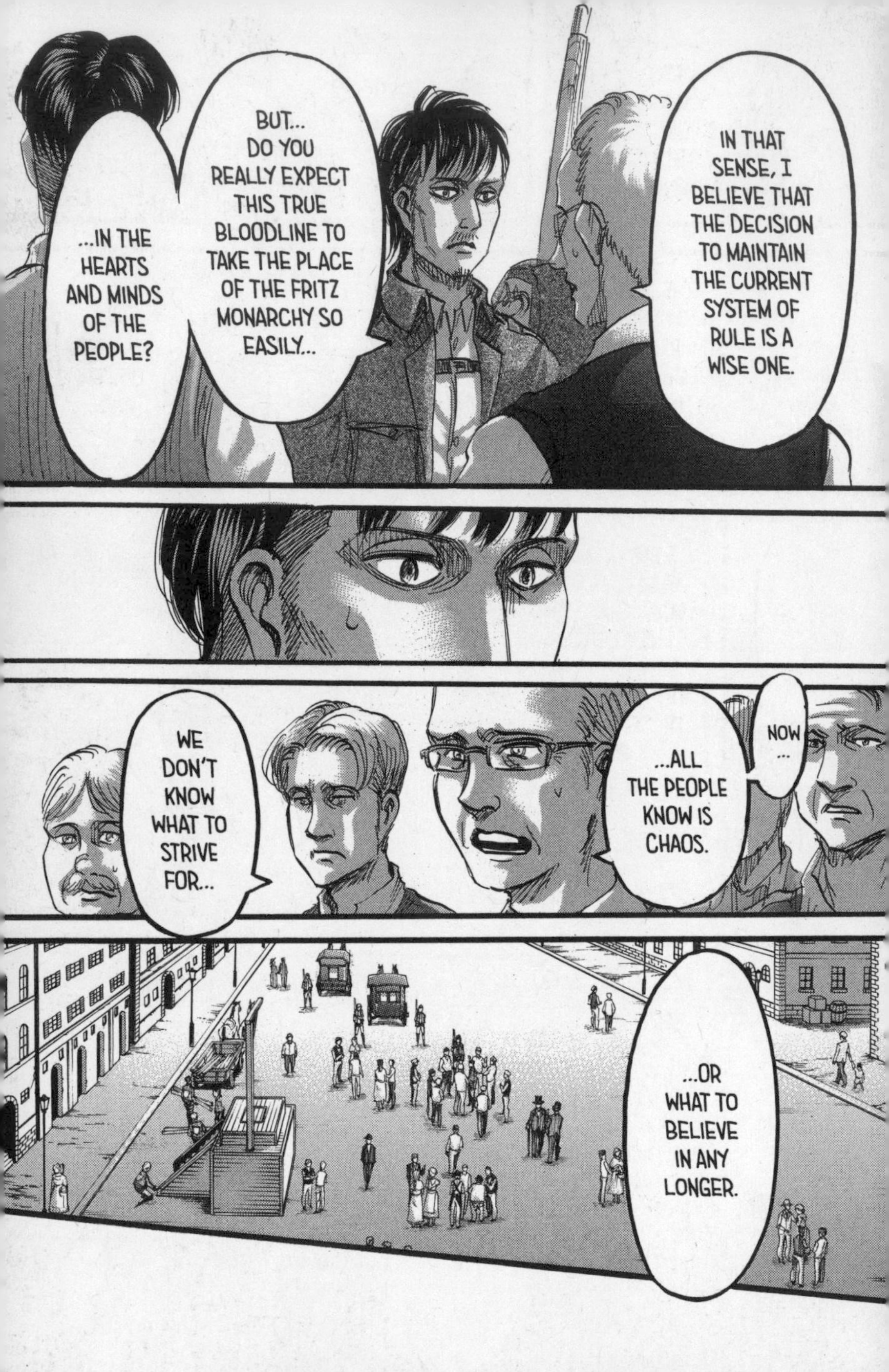
IN THAT SENSE, I BELIEVE THAT THE DECISION TO MAINTAIN THE CURRENT SYSTEM OF RULE IS A WISE ONE.
BUT... DO YOU REALLY EXPECT THIS TRUE BLOODLINE TO TAKE THE PLACE OF THE FRITZ MONARCHY SO EASILY...
...IN THE HEARTS AND MINDS OF THE PEOPLE?
NOW...
...ALL THE PEOPLE KNOW IS CHAOS.
WE DON'T KNOW WHAT TO STRIVE FOR...
...OR WHAT TO BELIEVE IN ANY LONGER.

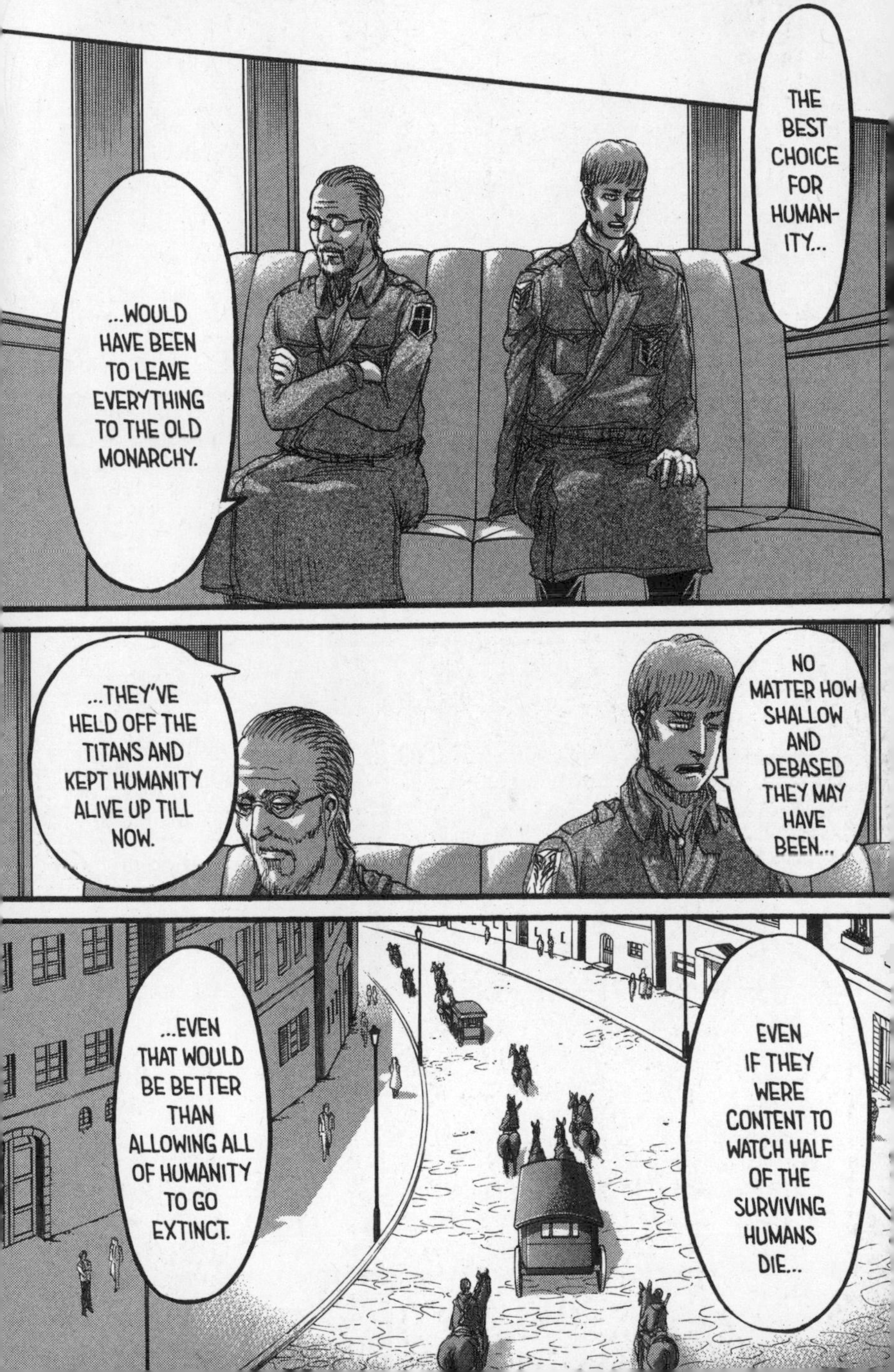
THE BEST CHOICE FOR HUMAN-ITY...
...WOULD HAVE BEEN TO LEAVE EVERYTHING TO THE OLD MONARCHY.
NO MATTER HOW SHALLOW AND DEBASED THEY MAY HAVE BEEN...
...THEY'VE HELD OFF THE TITANS AND KEPT HUMANITY ALIVE UP TILL NOW.
EVEN IF THEY WERE CONTENT TO WATCH HALF OF THE SURVIVING HUMANS DIE...
...EVEN THAT WOULD BE BETTER THAN ALLOWING ALL OF HUMANITY TO GO EXTINCT.

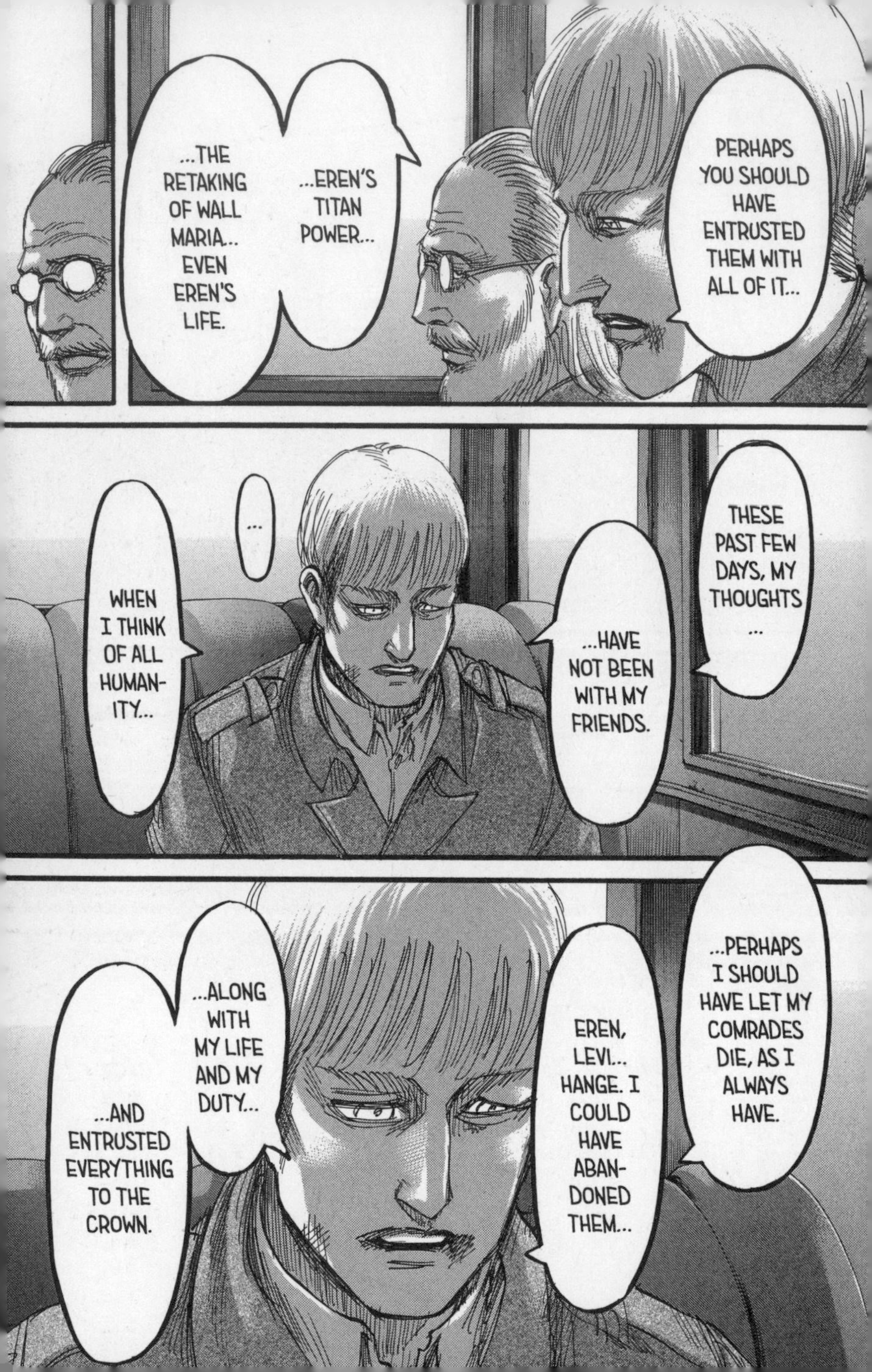
PERHAPS YOU SHOULD HAVE ENTRUSTED THEM WITH ALL OF IT...
...EREN'S TITAN POWER...
...THE RETAKING OF WALL MARIA... EVEN EREN'S LIFE.
THESE PAST FEW DAYS, MY THOUGHTS ...
...HAVE NOT BEEN WITH MY FRIENDS.
...
WHEN I THINK OF ALL HUMANITY...
...PERHAPS I SHOULD HAVE LET MY COMRADES DIE, AS I ALWAYS HAVE.
EREN, LEVI... HANGE. I COULD HAVE ABANDONED THEM...
...ALONG WITH MY LIFE AND MY DUTY...
...AND ENTRUSTED EVERYTHING TO THE CROWN.

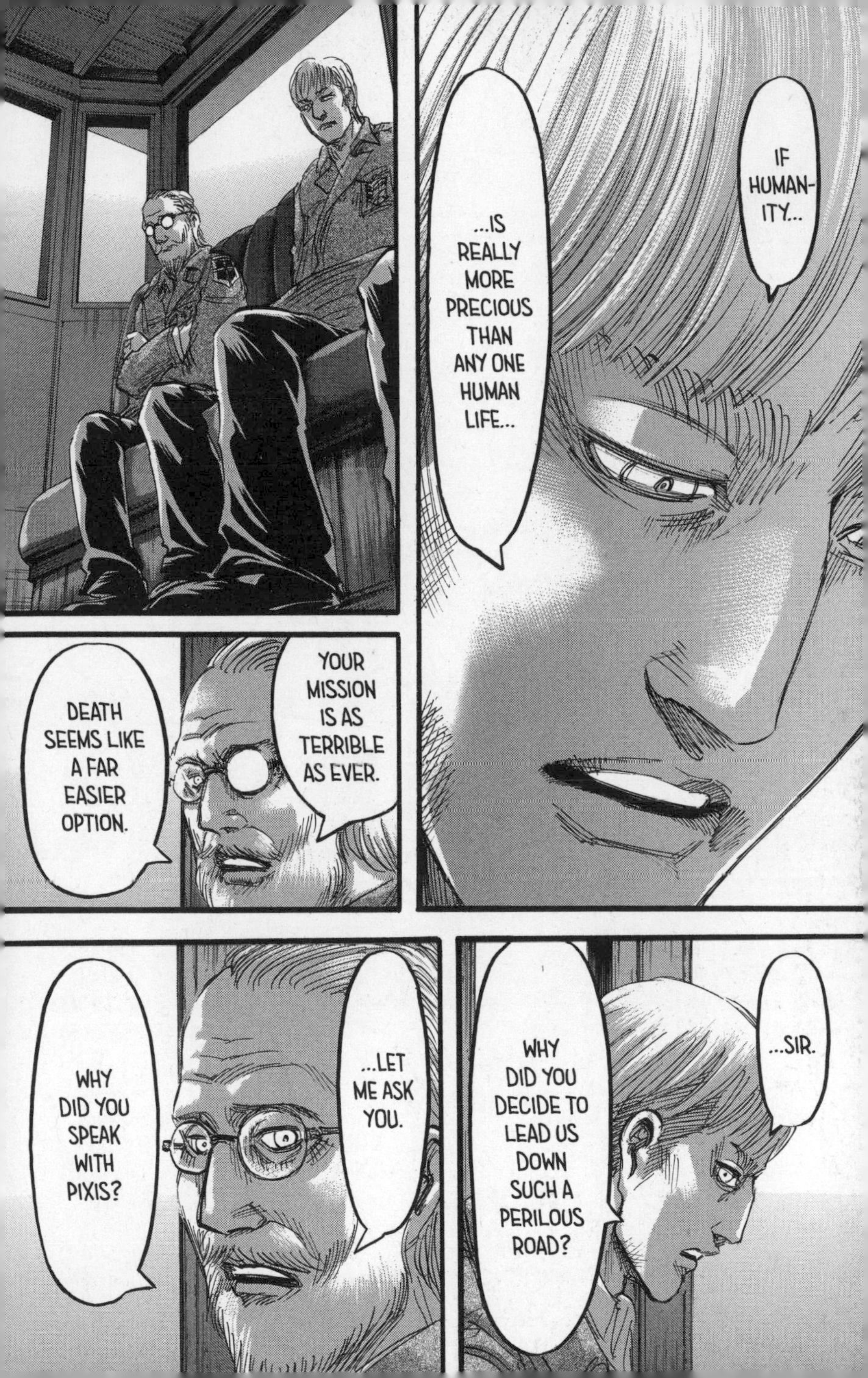

IF HUMAN-ITY...
...IS REALLY MORE PRECIOUS THAN ANY ONE HUMAN LIFE...
YOUR MISSION IS AS TERRIBLE AS EVER.
DEATH SEEMS LIKE A FAR EASIER OPTION.
...SIR.
WHY DID YOU DECIDE TO LEAD US DOWN SUCH A PERILOUS ROAD?
...LET ME ASK YOU.
WHY DID YOU SPEAK WITH PIXIS?

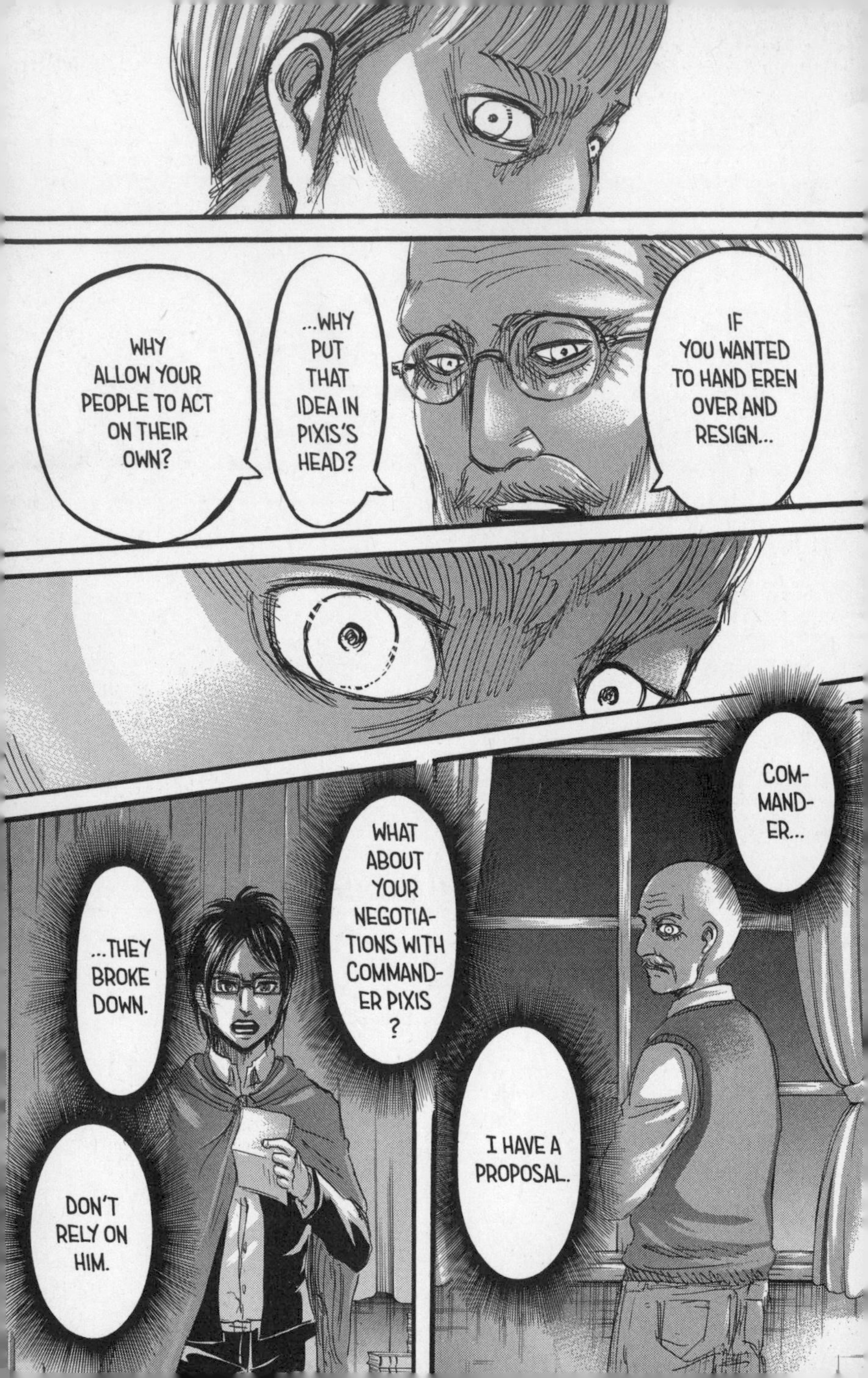
IF YOU WANTED TO HAND EREN OVER AND RESIGN...
...WHY PUT THAT IDEA IN PIXIS'S HEAD?
WHY ALLOW YOUR PEOPLE TO ACT ON THEIR OWN?
COMMANDER...
WHAT ABOUT YOUR NEGOTIATIONS WITH COMMANDER PIXIS?
...THEY BROKE DOWN.
I HAVE A PROPOSAL.
DON'T RELY ON HIM.

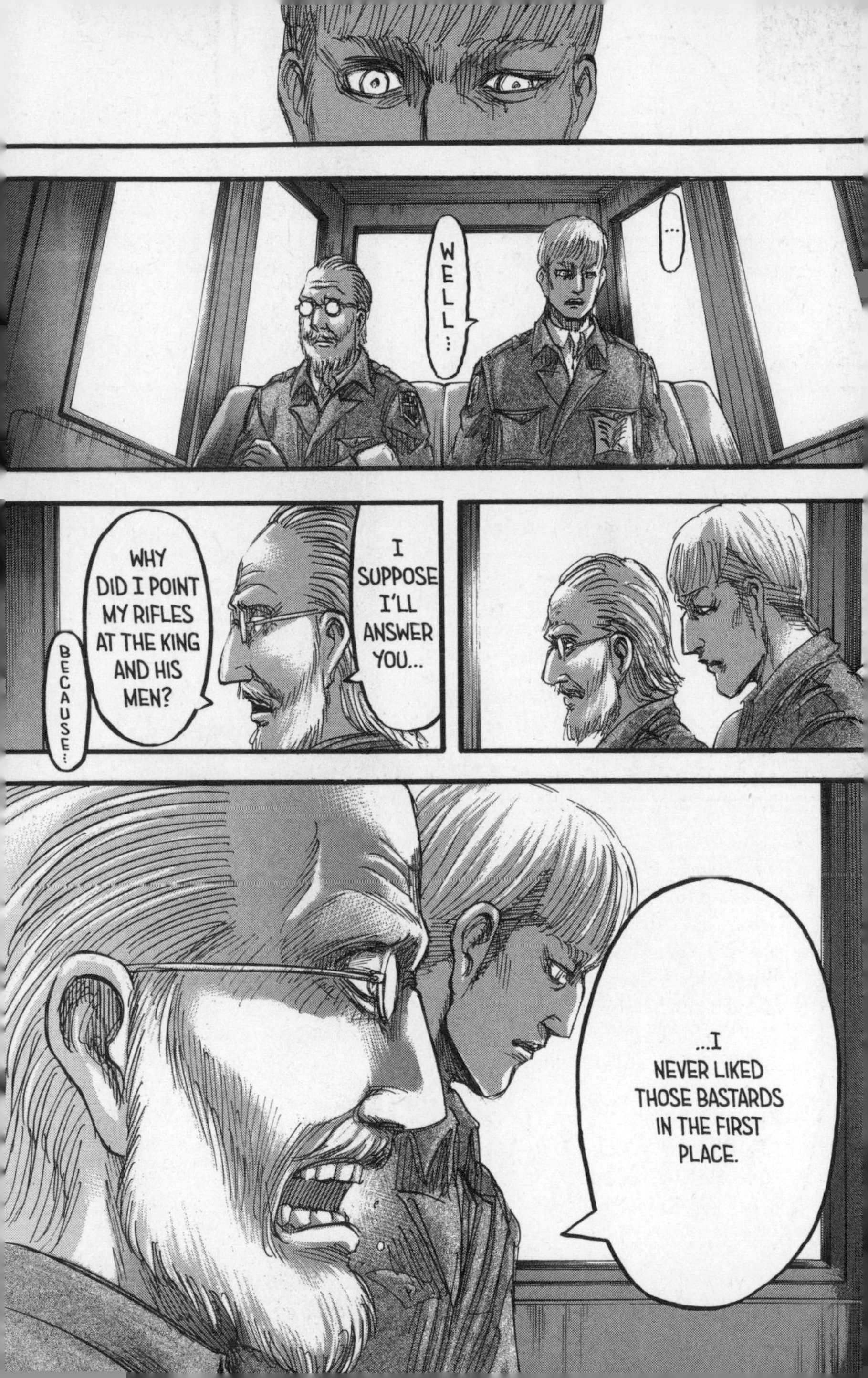
...
WELL...
I SUPPOSE I'LL ANSWER YOU...
WHY DID I POINT MY RIFLES AT THE KING AND HIS MEN?
BECAUSE...
...I NEVER LIKED THOSE BASTARDS IN THE FIRST PLACE.

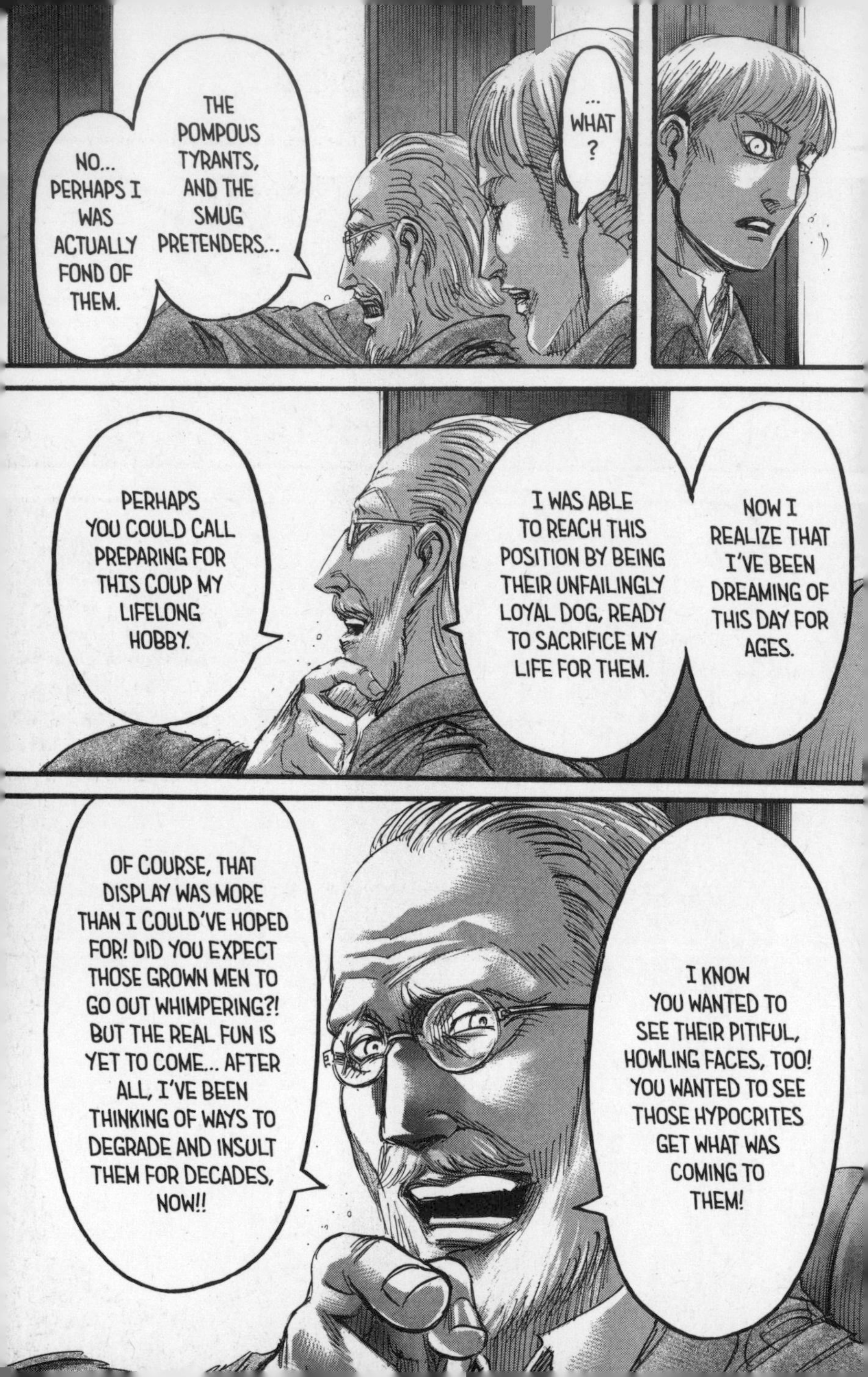
...WHAT?
THE POMPOUS TYRANTS, AND THE SMUG PRETENDERS...
NO... PERHAPS I WAS ACTUALLY FOND OF THEM.
NOW I REALIZE THAT I'VE BEEN DREAMING OF THIS DAY FOR AGES.
I WAS ABLE TO REACH THIS POSITION BY BEING THEIR UNFAILINGLY LOYAL DOG, READY TO SACRIFICE MY LIFE FOR THEM.
PERHAPS YOU COULD CALL PREPARING FOR THIS COUP MY LIFELONG HOBBY.
I KNOW YOU WANTED TO SEE THEIR PITIFUL, HOWLING FACES, TOO! YOU WANTED TO SEE THOSE HYPOCRITES GET WHAT WAS COMING TO THEM!
OF COURSE, THAT DISPLAY WAS MORE THAN I COULD'VE HOPED FOR! DID YOU EXPECT THOSE GROWN MEN TO GO OUT WHIMPERING?! BUT THE REAL FUN IS YET TO COME... AFTER ALL, I'VE BEEN THINKING OF WAYS TO DEGRADE AND INSULT THEM FOR DECADES, NOW!!

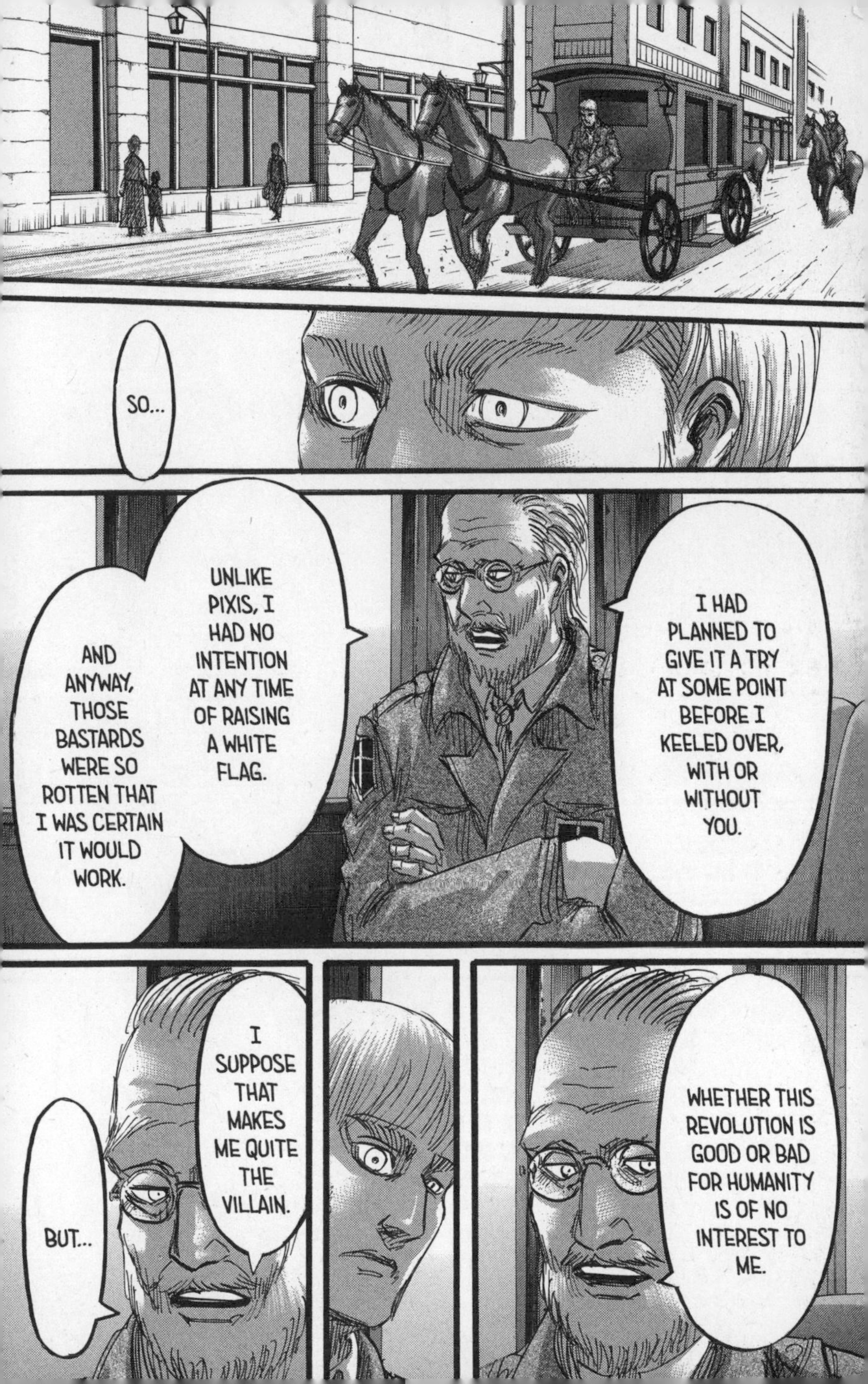
SO...
I HAD PLANNED TO GIVE IT A TRY AT SOME POINT BEFORE I KEELED OVER, WITH OR WITHOUT YOU.
UNLIKE PIXIS, I HAD NO INTENTION AT ANY TIME OF RAISING A WHITE FLAG.
AND ANYWAY, THOSE BASTARDS WERE SO ROTTEN THAT I WAS CERTAIN IT WOULD WORK.
WHETHER THIS REVOLUTION IS GOOD OR BAD FOR HUMANITY IS OF NO INTEREST TO ME.
I SUPPOSE THAT MAKES ME QUITE THE VILLAIN.
BUT...

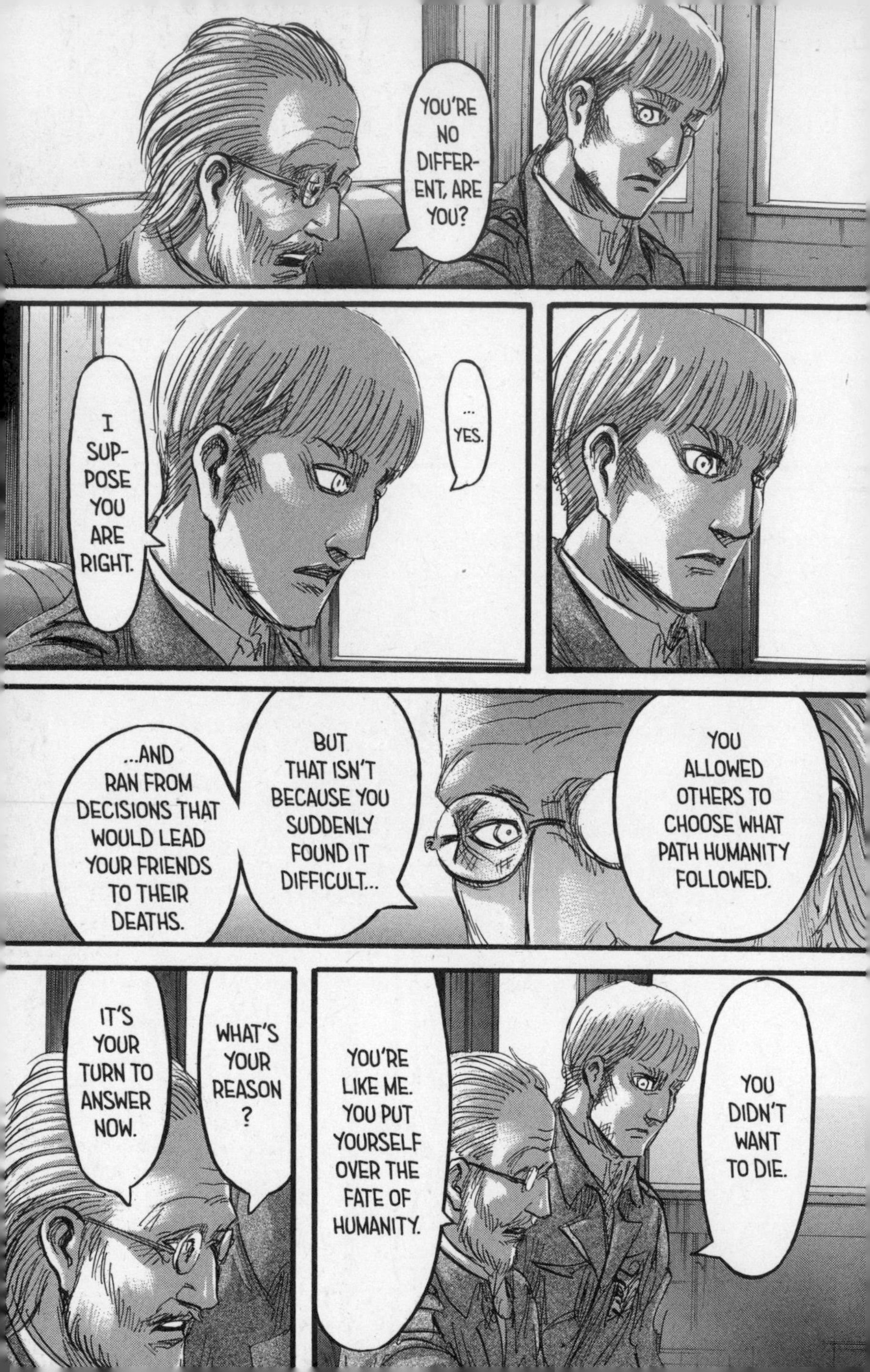
YOU'RE NO DIFFERENT, ARE YOU?
... YES.
I SUPPOSE YOU ARE RIGHT.
YOU ALLOWED OTHERS TO CHOOSE WHAT PATH HUMANITY FOLLOWED.
BUT THAT ISN'T BECAUSE YOU SUDDENLY FOUND IT DIFFICULT...
...AND RAN FROM DECISIONS THAT WOULD LEAD YOUR FRIENDS TO THEIR DEATHS.
YOU DIDN'T WANT TO DIE.
YOU'RE LIKE ME. YOU PUT YOURSELF OVER THE FATE OF HUMANITY.
WHAT'S YOUR REASON?
IT'S YOUR TURN TO ANSWER NOW.

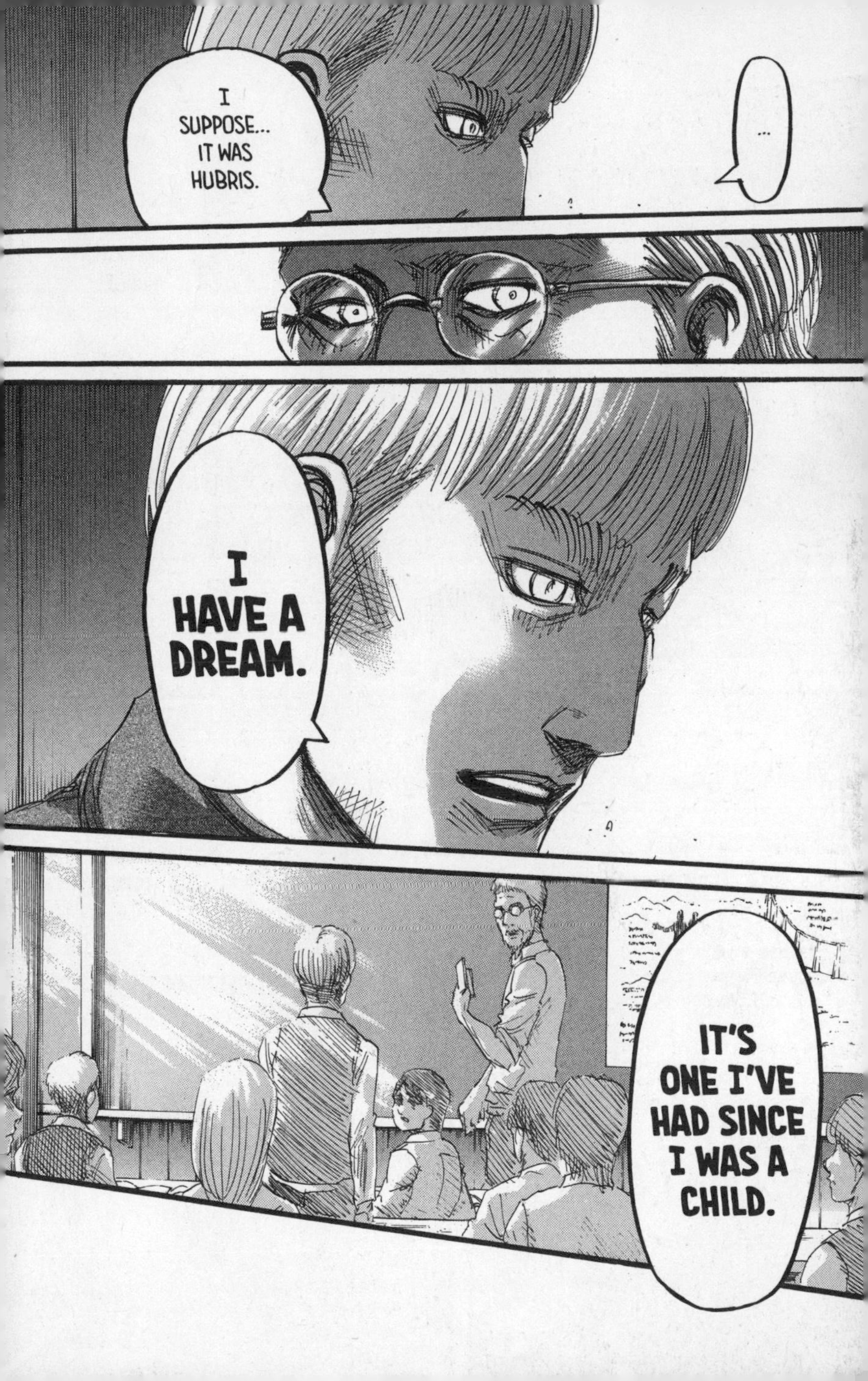
...
I SUPPOSE... IT WAS HUBRIS.
I HAVE A DREAM.
IT'S ONE I'VE HAD SINCE I WAS A CHILD.

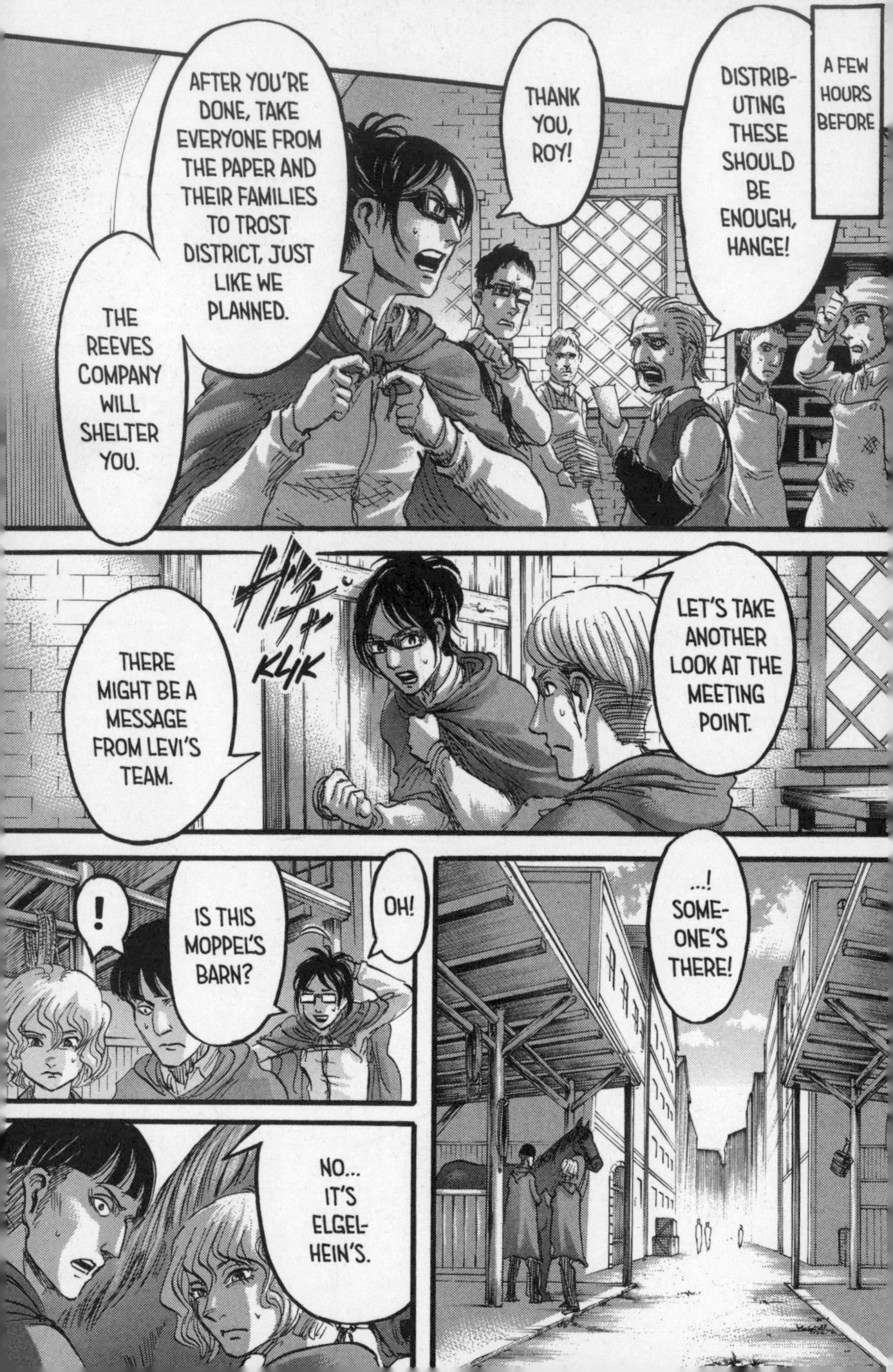
A FEW HOURS BEFORE
DISTRIBUTING THESE SHOULD BE ENOUGH, HANGE!
THANK YOU, ROY!
AFTER YOU'RE DONE, TAKE EVERYONE FROM THE PAPER AND THEIR FAMILIES TO TROST DISTRICT, JUST LIKE WE PLANNED.
THE REEVES COMPANY WILL SHELTER YOU.
LET'S TAKE ANOTHER LOOK AT THE MEETING POINT.
KLIK
THERE MIGHT BE A MESSAGE FROM LEVI'S TEAM.
...! SOMEONE'S THERE!
OH!
IS THIS MOPPEL'S BARN?
!
NO... IT'S ELGELHEIN'S.

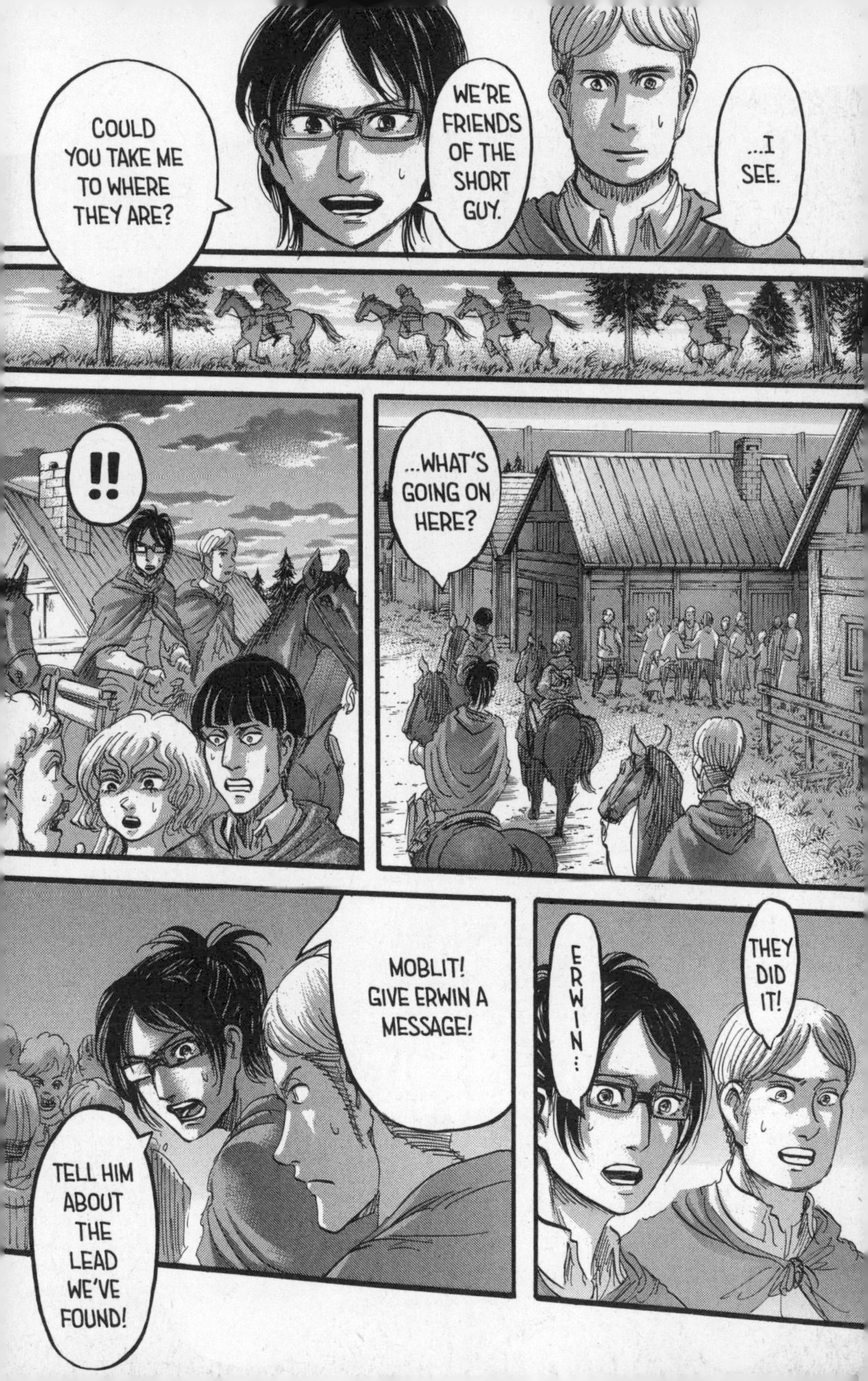
...I SEE.
WE'RE FRIENDS OF THE SHORT GUY.
COULD YOU TAKE ME TO WHERE THEY ARE?
...WHAT'S GOING ON HERE?
!!
THEY DID IT!
ERWIN...
MOBLIT! GIVE ERWIN A MESSAGE!
TELL HIM ABOUT THE LEAD WE'VE FOUND!

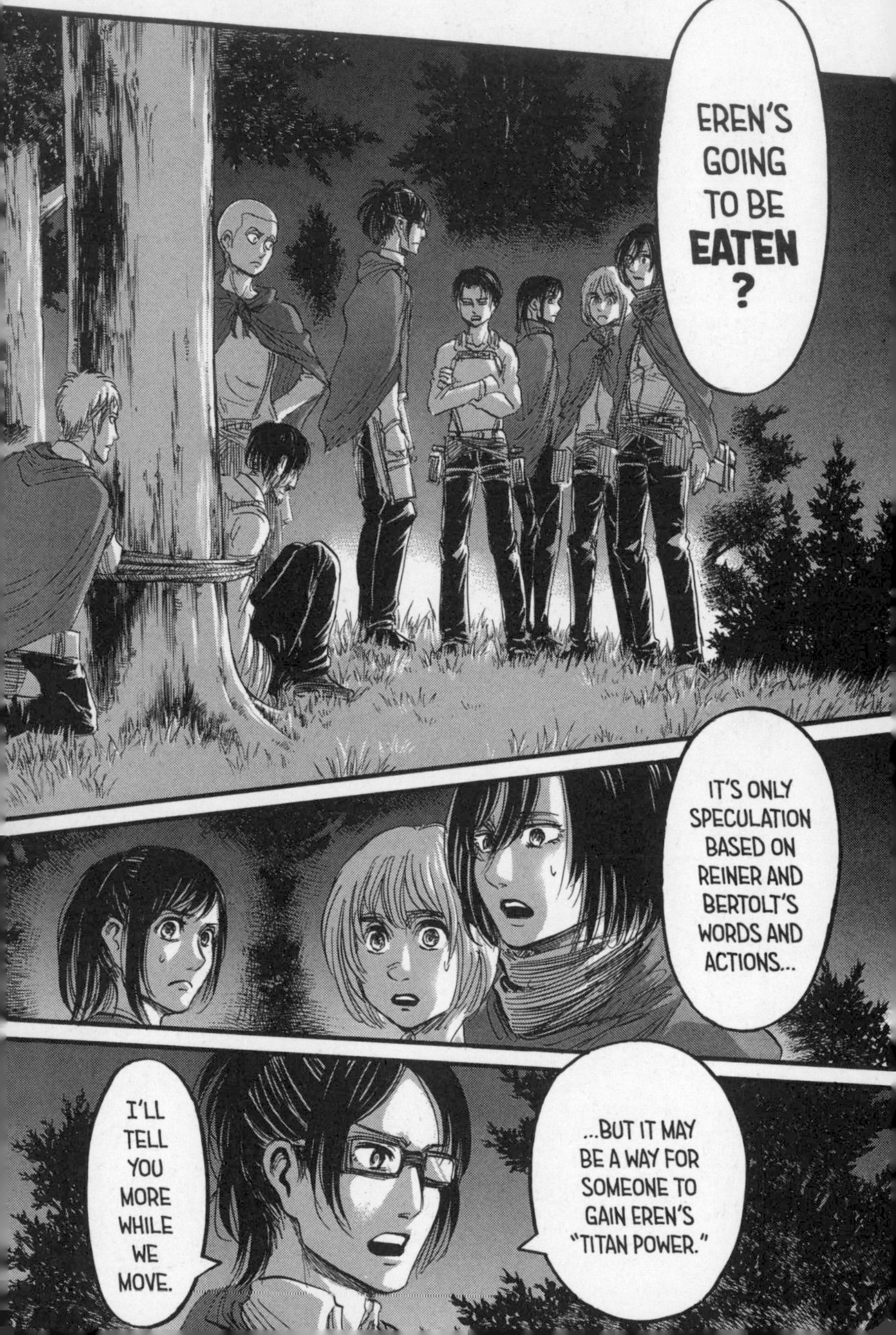
EREN'S GOING TO BE **EATEN**?
IT'S ONLY SPECULATION BASED ON REINER AND BERTOLT'S WORDS AND ACTIONS...
...BUT IT MAY BE A WAY FOR SOMEONE TO GAIN EREN'S "TITAN POWER."
I'LL TELL YOU MORE WHILE WE MOVE.

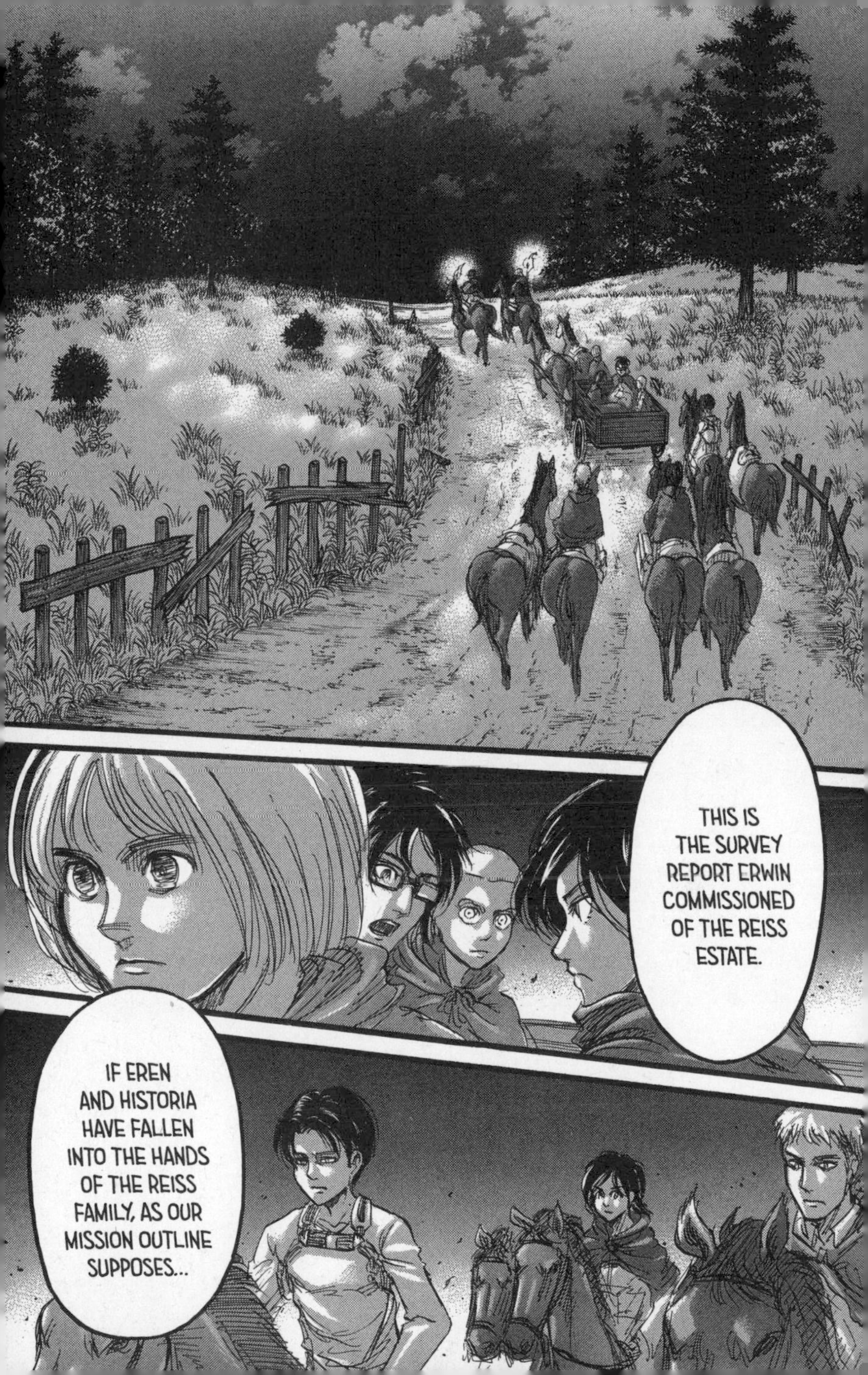
THIS IS THE SURVEY REPORT ERWIN COMMISSIONED OF THE REISS ESTATE.
IF EREN AND HISTORIA HAVE FALLEN INTO THE HANDS OF THE REISS FAMILY, AS OUR MISSION OUTLINE SUPPOSES...

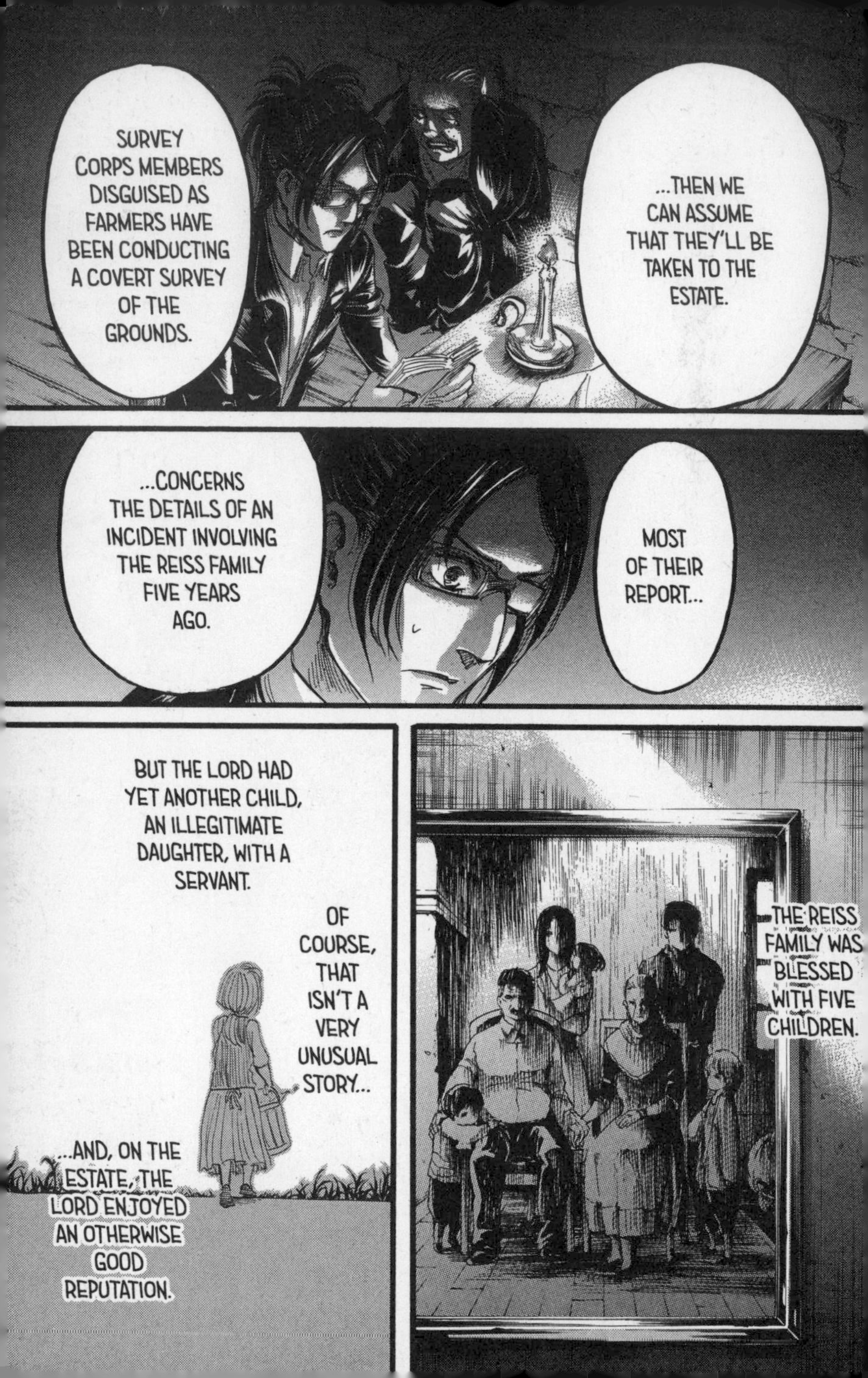
...THEN WE CAN ASSUME THAT THEY'LL BE TAKEN TO THE ESTATE.
SURVEY CORPS MEMBERS DISGUISED AS FARMERS HAVE BEEN CONDUCTING A COVERT SURVEY OF THE GROUNDS.
MOST OF THEIR REPORT...
...CONCERNS THE DETAILS OF AN INCIDENT INVOLVING THE REISS FAMILY FIVE YEARS AGO.
THE REISS FAMILY WAS BLESSED WITH FIVE CHILDREN.
BUT THE LORD HAD YET ANOTHER CHILD, AN ILLEGITIMATE DAUGHTER, WITH A SERVANT.
OF COURSE, THAT ISN'T A VERY UNUSUAL STORY...
...AND, ON THE ESTATE, THE LORD ENJOYED AN OTHERWISE GOOD REPUTATION.

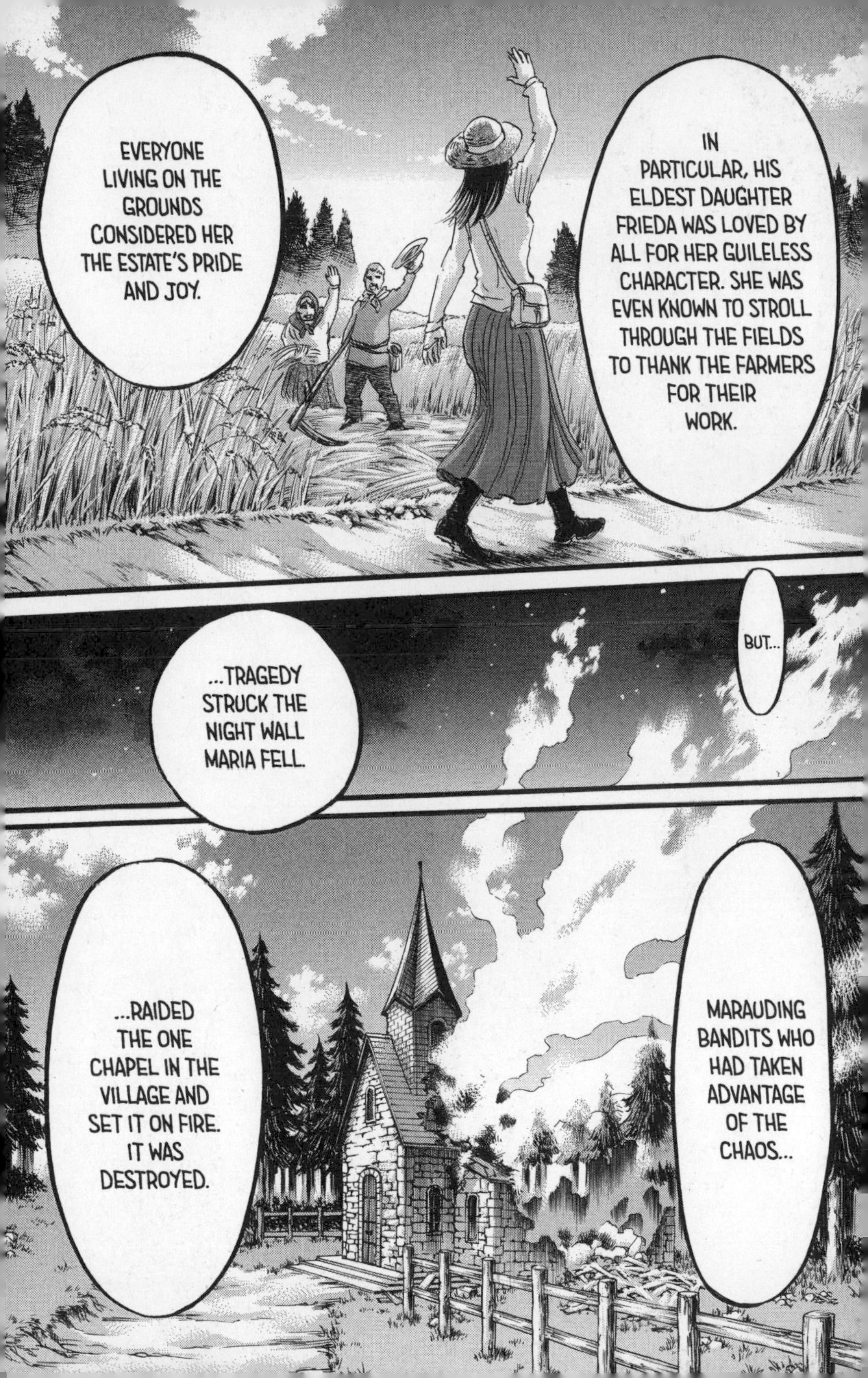
IN PARTICULAR, HIS ELDEST DAUGHTER FRIEDA WAS LOVED BY ALL FOR HER GUILELESS CHARACTER. SHE WAS EVEN KNOWN TO STROLL THROUGH THE FIELDS TO THANK THE FARMERS FOR THEIR WORK.
EVERYONE LIVING ON THE GROUNDS CONSIDERED HER THE ESTATE'S PRIDE AND JOY.
BUT...
...TRAGEDY STRUCK THE NIGHT WALL MARIA FELL.
MARAUDING BANDITS WHO HAD TAKEN ADVANTAGE OF THE CHAOS...
...RAIDED THE ONE CHAPEL IN THE VILLAGE AND SET IT ON FIRE. IT WAS DESTROYED.

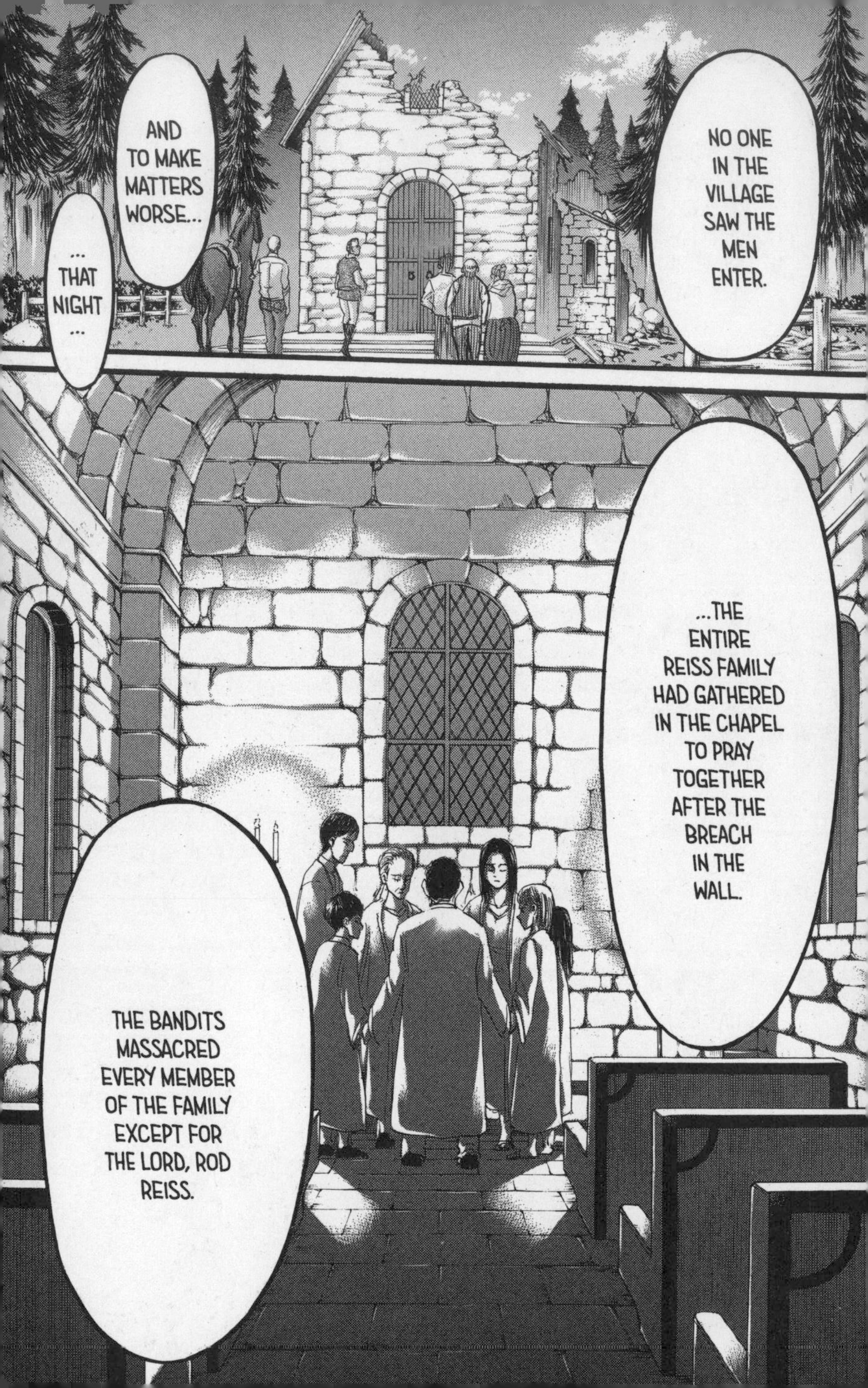
NO ONE IN THE VILLAGE SAW THE MEN ENTER.
AND TO MAKE MATTERS WORSE...
...THAT NIGHT...
...THE ENTIRE REISS FAMILY HAD GATHERED IN THE CHAPEL TO PRAY TOGETHER AFTER THE BREACH IN THE WALL.
THE BANDITS MASSACRED EVERY MEMBER OF THE FAMILY EXCEPT FOR THE LORD, ROD REISS.

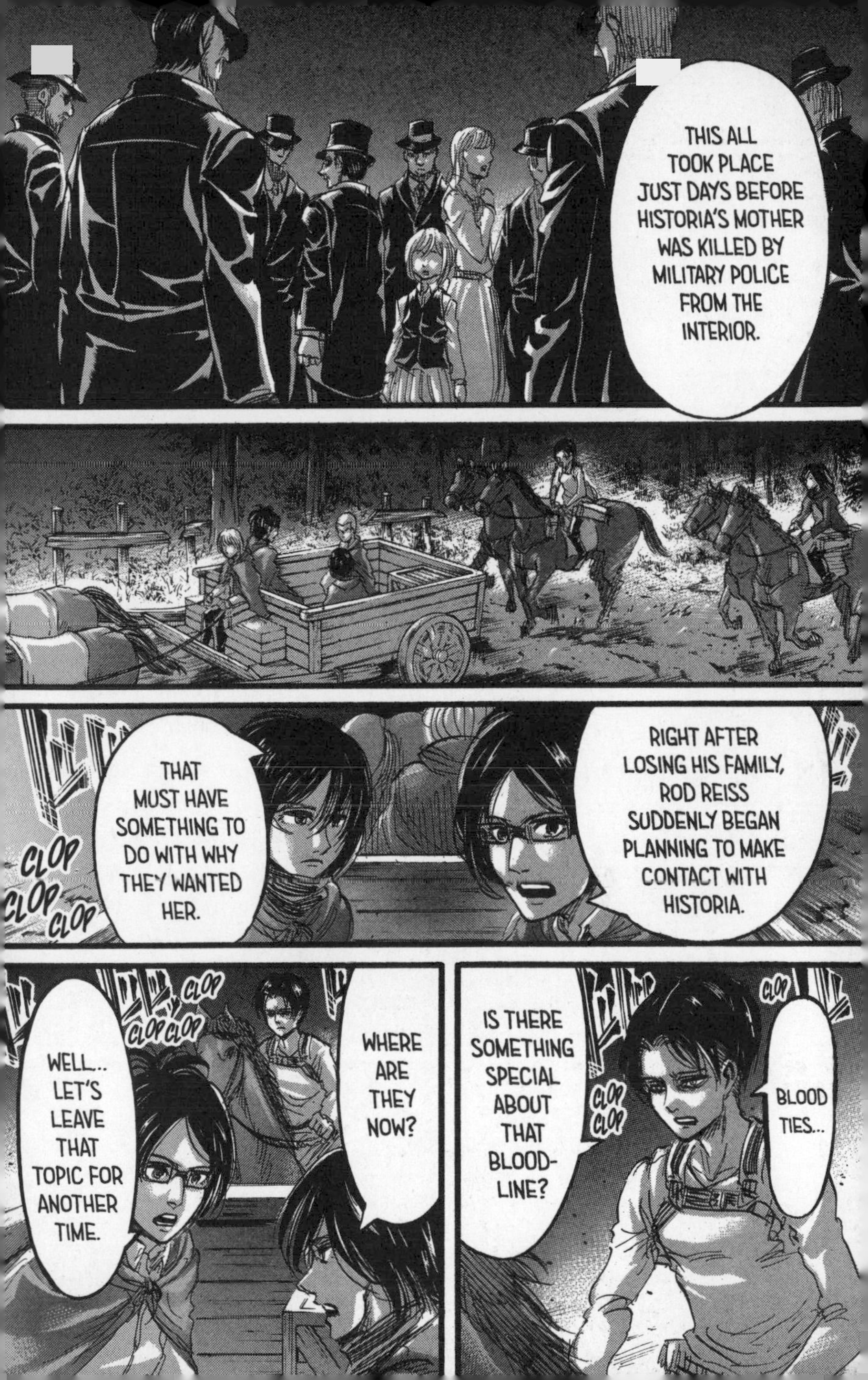
THIS ALL TOOK PLACE JUST DAYS BEFORE HISTORIA'S MOTHER WAS KILLED BY MILITARY POLICE FROM THE INTERIOR.
RIGHT AFTER LOSING HIS FAMILY, ROD REISS SUDDENLY BEGAN PLANNING TO MAKE CONTACT WITH HISTORIA.
THAT MUST HAVE SOMETHING TO DO WITH WHY THEY WANTED HER.
CLOP CLOP CLOP
CLOP
BLOOD TIES...
IS THERE SOMETHING SPECIAL ABOUT THAT BLOOD-LINE?
CLOP CLOP
WHERE ARE THEY NOW?
CLOP
CLOP CLOP
WELL... LET'S LEAVE THAT TOPIC FOR ANOTHER TIME.

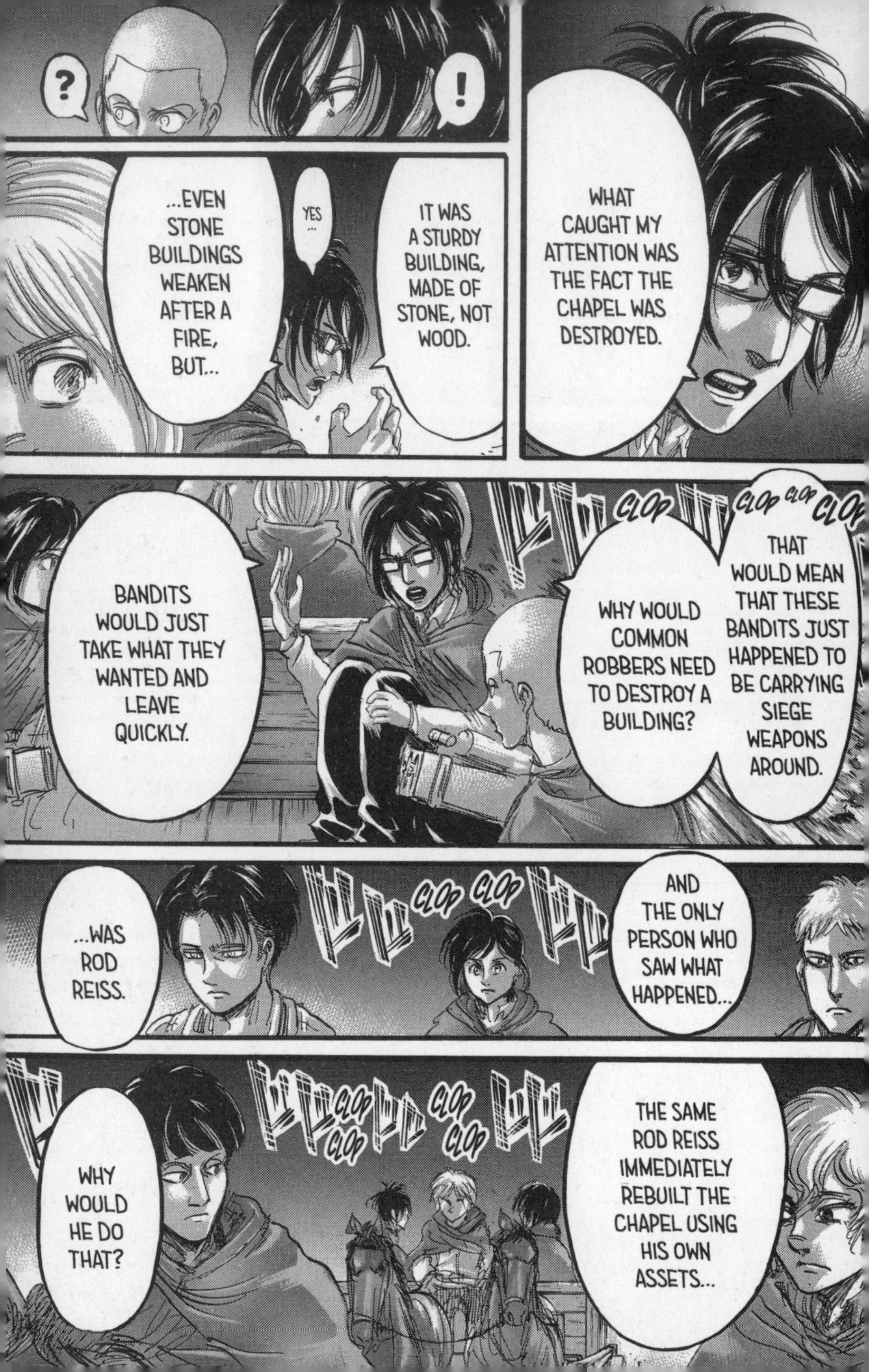
WHAT CAUGHT MY ATTENTION WAS THE FACT THE CHAPEL WAS DESTROYED.
!
?
IT WAS A STURDY BUILDING, MADE OF STONE, NOT WOOD.
YES ...
...EVEN STONE BUILDINGS WEAKEN AFTER A FIRE, BUT...
CLOP CLOP CLOP
THAT WOULD MEAN THAT THESE BANDITS JUST HAPPENED TO BE CARRYING SIEGE WEAPONS AROUND.
CLOP
WHY WOULD COMMON ROBBERS NEED TO DESTROY A BUILDING?
BANDITS WOULD JUST TAKE WHAT THEY WANTED AND LEAVE QUICKLY.
AND THE ONLY PERSON WHO SAW WHAT HAPPENED...
CLOP CLOP
...WAS ROD REISS.
THE SAME ROD REISS IMMEDIATELY REBUILT THE CHAPEL USING HIS OWN ASSETS...
CLOP CLOP
CLOP CLOP
WHY WOULD HE DO THAT?

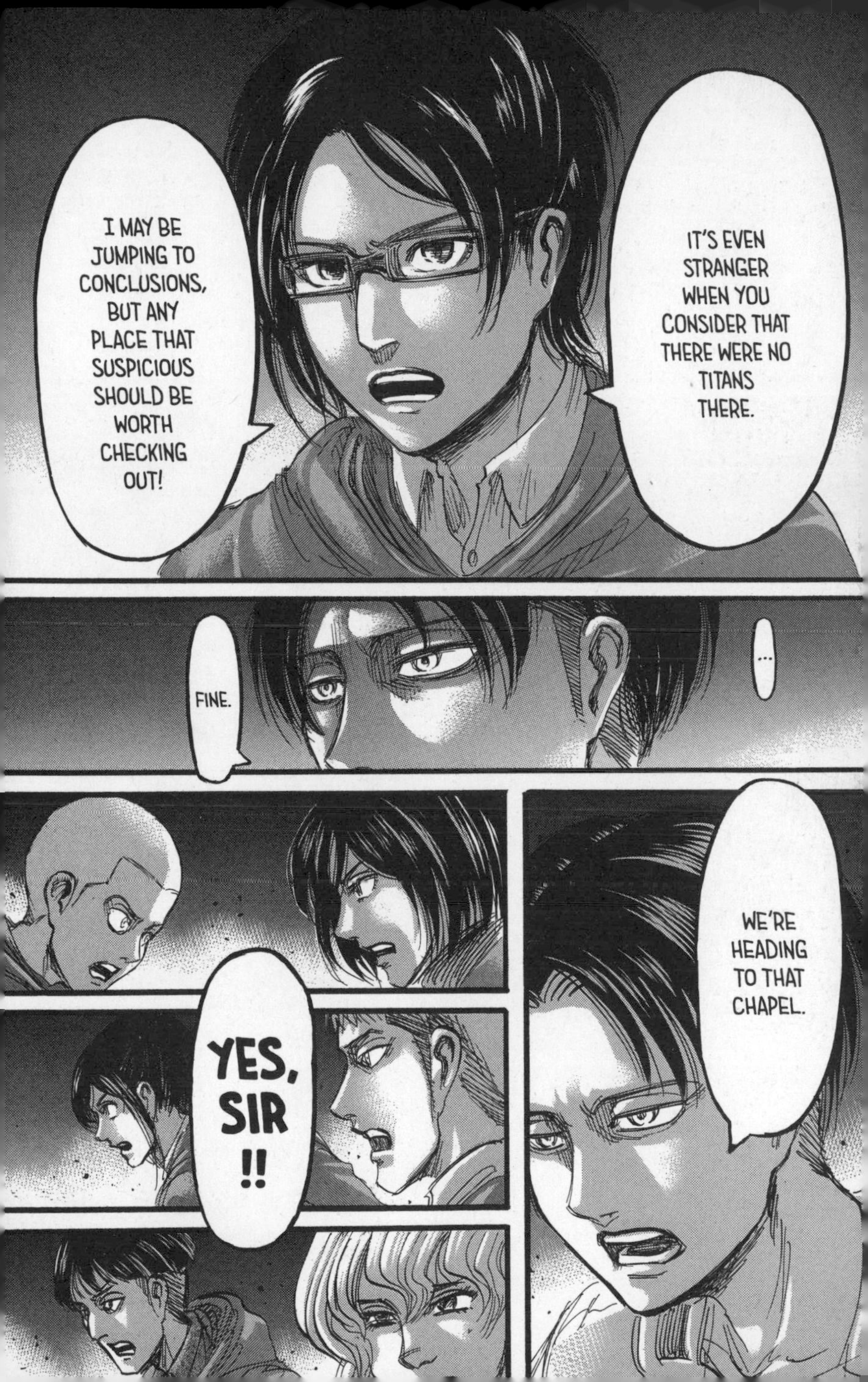
IT'S EVEN STRANGER WHEN YOU CONSIDER THAT THERE WERE NO TITANS THERE.
I MAY BE JUMPING TO CONCLUSIONS, BUT ANY PLACE THAT SUSPICIOUS SHOULD BE WORTH CHECKING OUT!
...
FINE.
WE'RE HEADING TO THAT CHAPEL.
YES, SIR!!

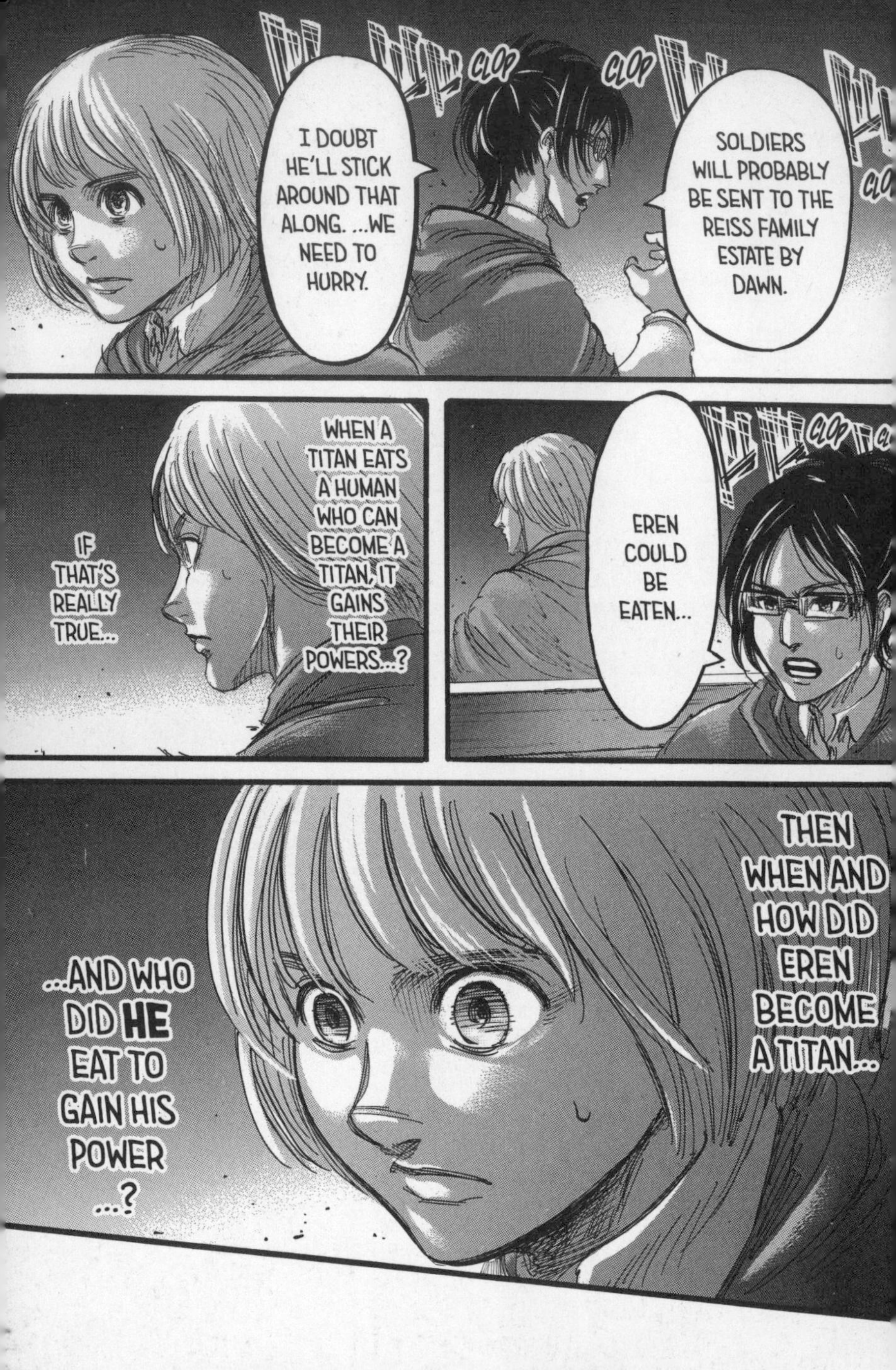
CLOP
CLOP
SOLDIERS WILL PROBABLY BE SENT TO THE REISS FAMILY ESTATE BY DAWN.
CLOP
I DOUBT HE'LL STICK AROUND THAT ALONG. ...WE NEED TO HURRY.
CLOP
EREN COULD BE EATEN...
WHEN A TITAN EATS A HUMAN WHO CAN BECOME A TITAN, IT GAINS THEIR POWERS...?
IF THAT'S REALLY TRUE...
THEN WHEN AND HOW DID EREN BECOME A TITAN...
...AND WHO DID HE EAT TO GAIN HIS POWER ...?

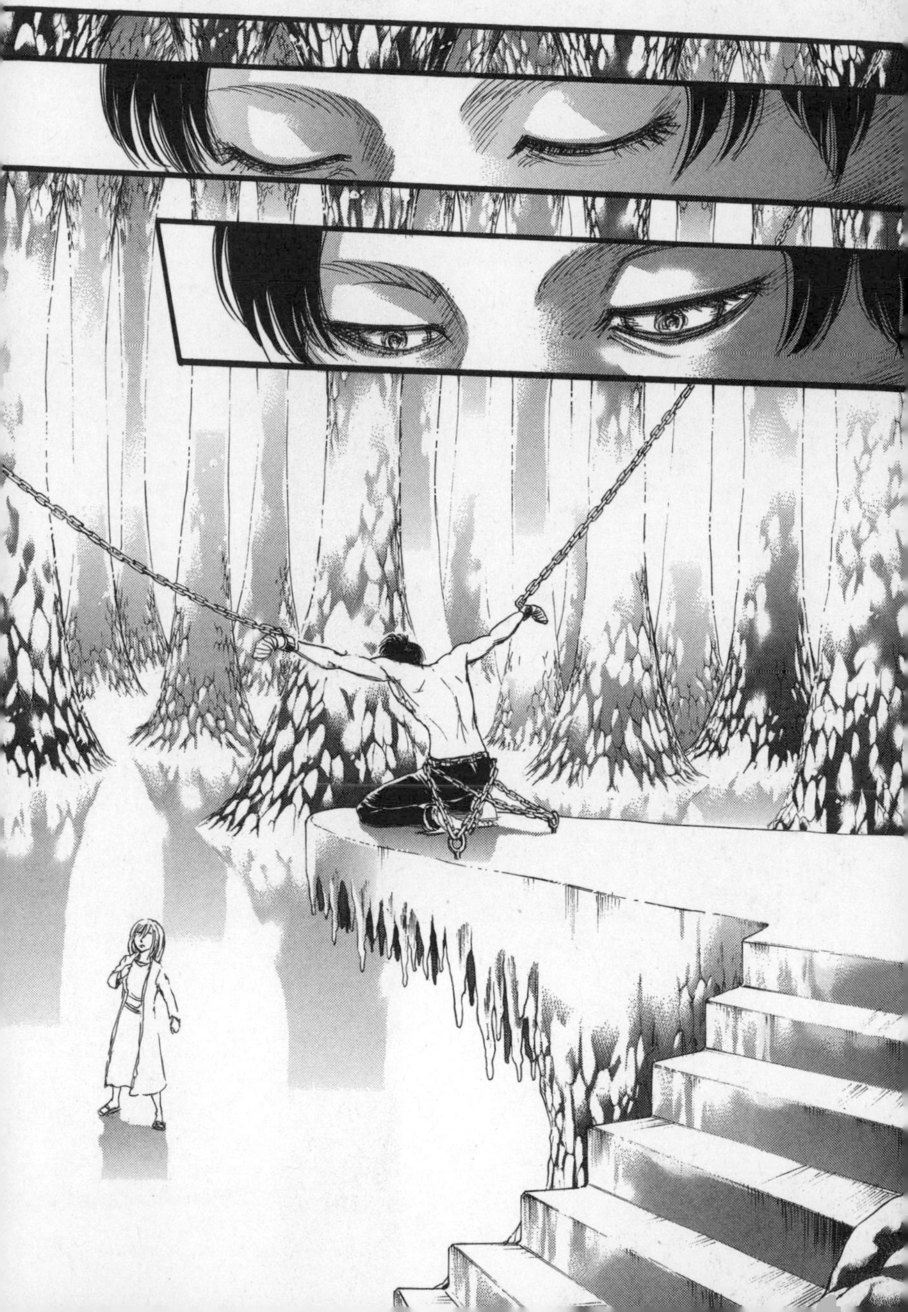

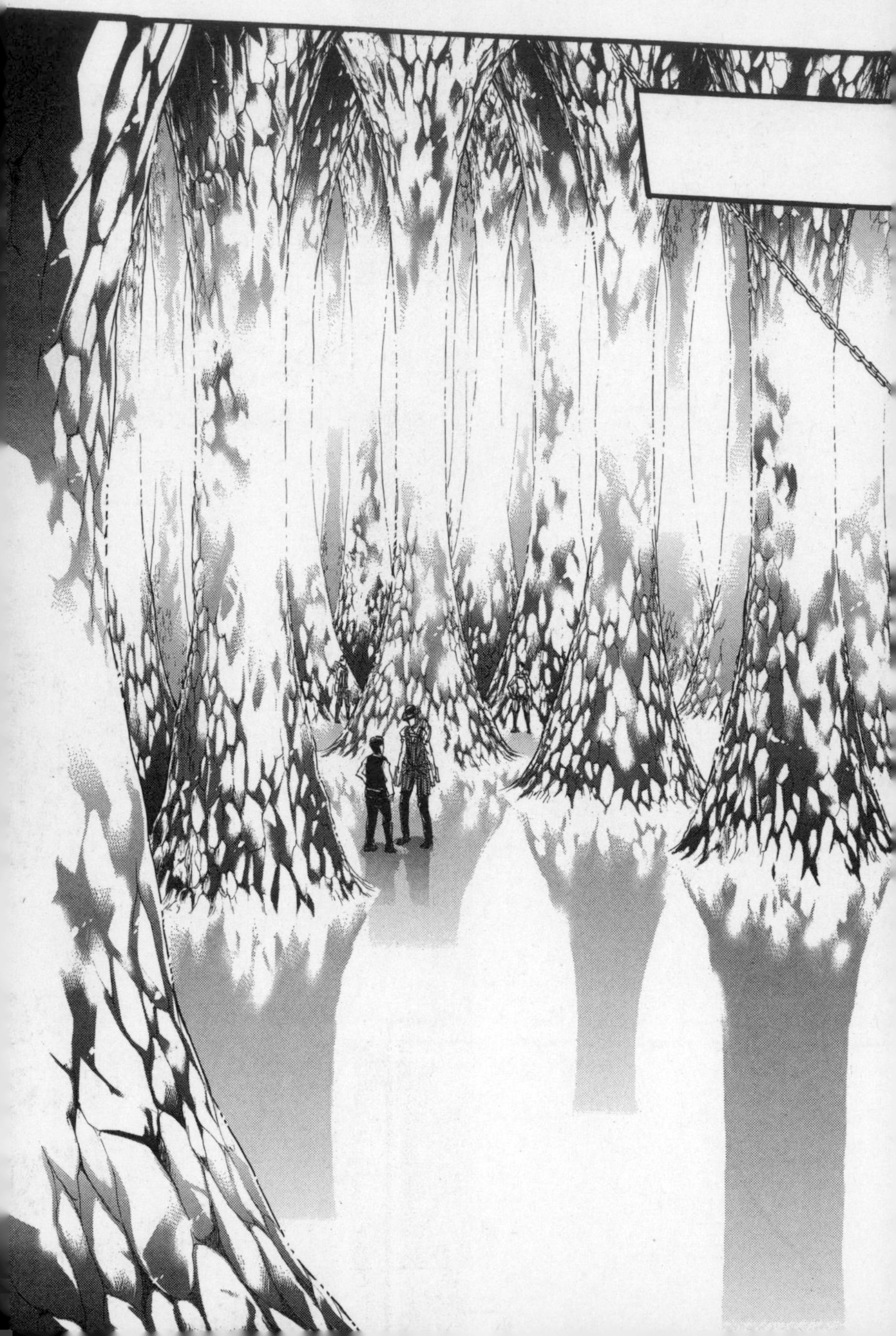

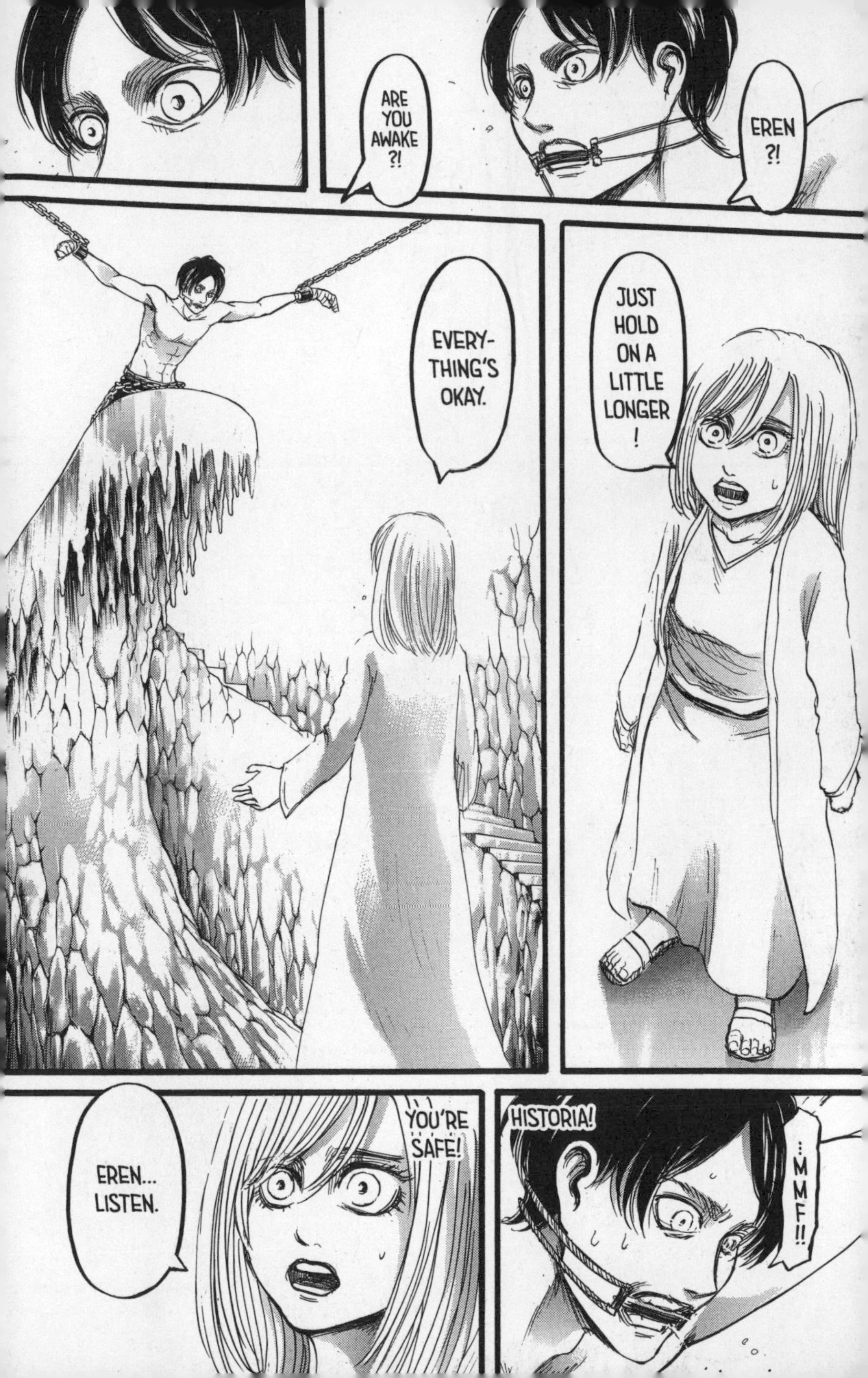
EREN ?!
ARE YOU AWAKE ?!
JUST HOLD ON A LITTLE LONGER !
EVERYTHING'S OKAY.
HISTORIA!
...MMF!!
YOU'RE SAFE!
EREN... LISTEN.

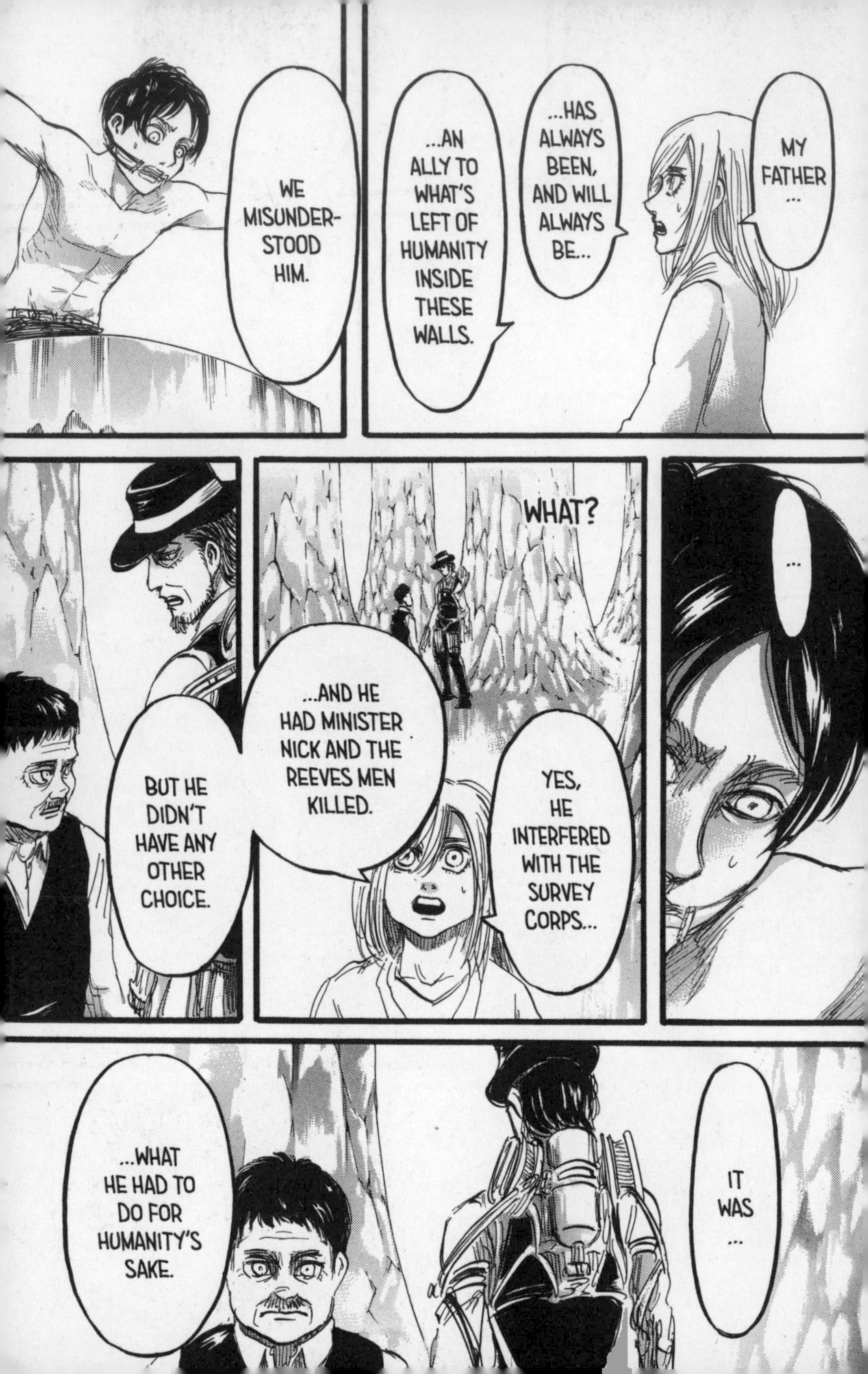
MY FATHER ...
...HAS ALWAYS BEEN, AND WILL ALWAYS BE...
...AN ALLY TO WHAT'S LEFT OF HUMANITY INSIDE THESE WALLS.
WE MISUNDER-STOOD HIM.
...
WHAT?
YES, HE INTERFERED WITH THE SURVEY CORPS...
...AND HE HAD MINISTER NICK AND THE REEVES MEN KILLED.
BUT HE DIDN'T HAVE ANY OTHER CHOICE.
IT WAS ...
...WHAT HE HAD TO DO FOR HUMANITY'S SAKE.

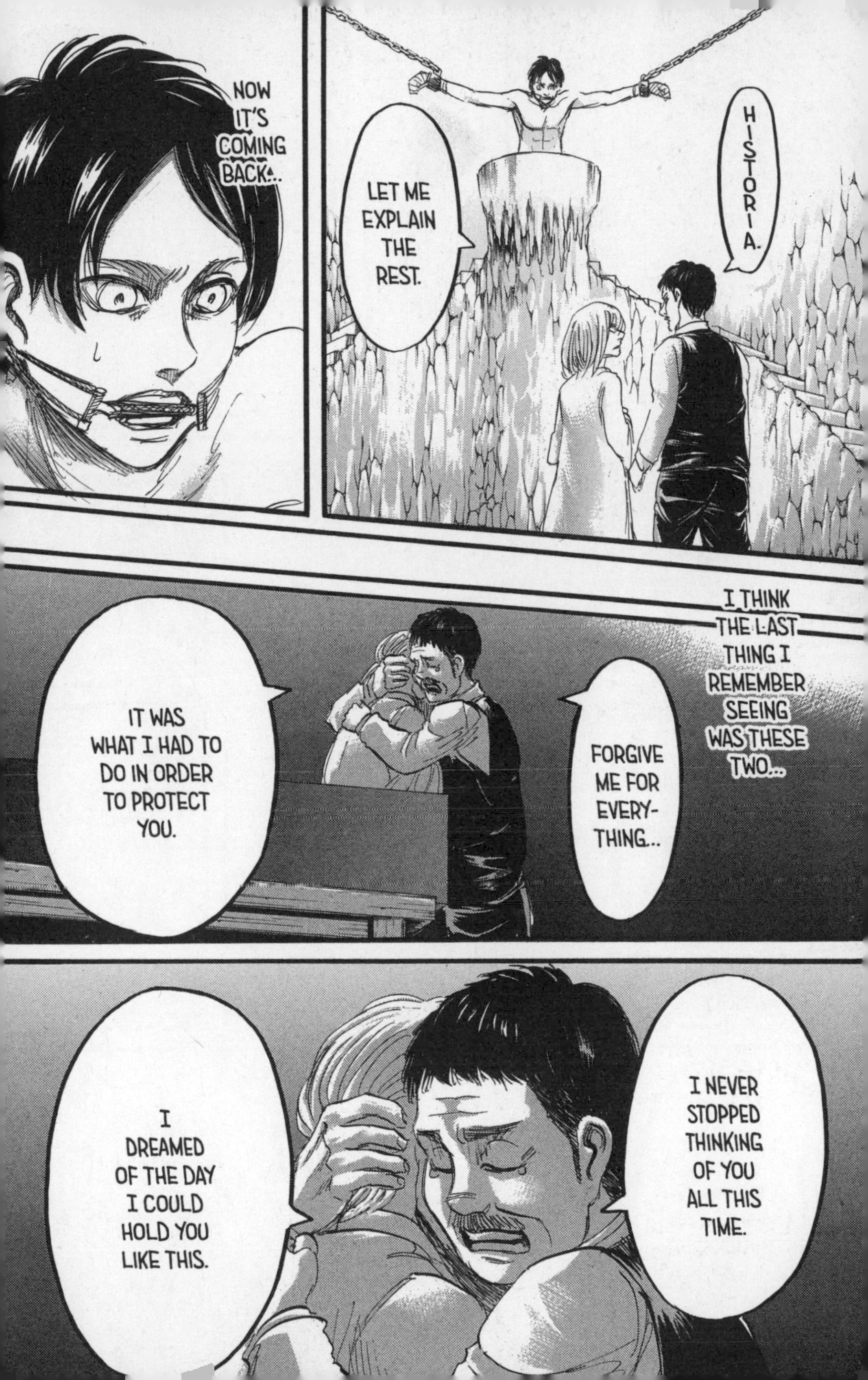
HISTORIA.
LET ME EXPLAIN THE REST.
NOW IT'S COMING BACK...
I THINK THE LAST THING I REMEMBER SEEING WAS THESE TWO...
FORGIVE ME FOR EVERY-THING...
IT WAS WHAT I HAD TO DO IN ORDER TO PROTECT YOU.
I NEVER STOPPED THINKING OF YOU ALL THIS TIME.
I DREAMED OF THE DAY I COULD HOLD YOU LIKE THIS.

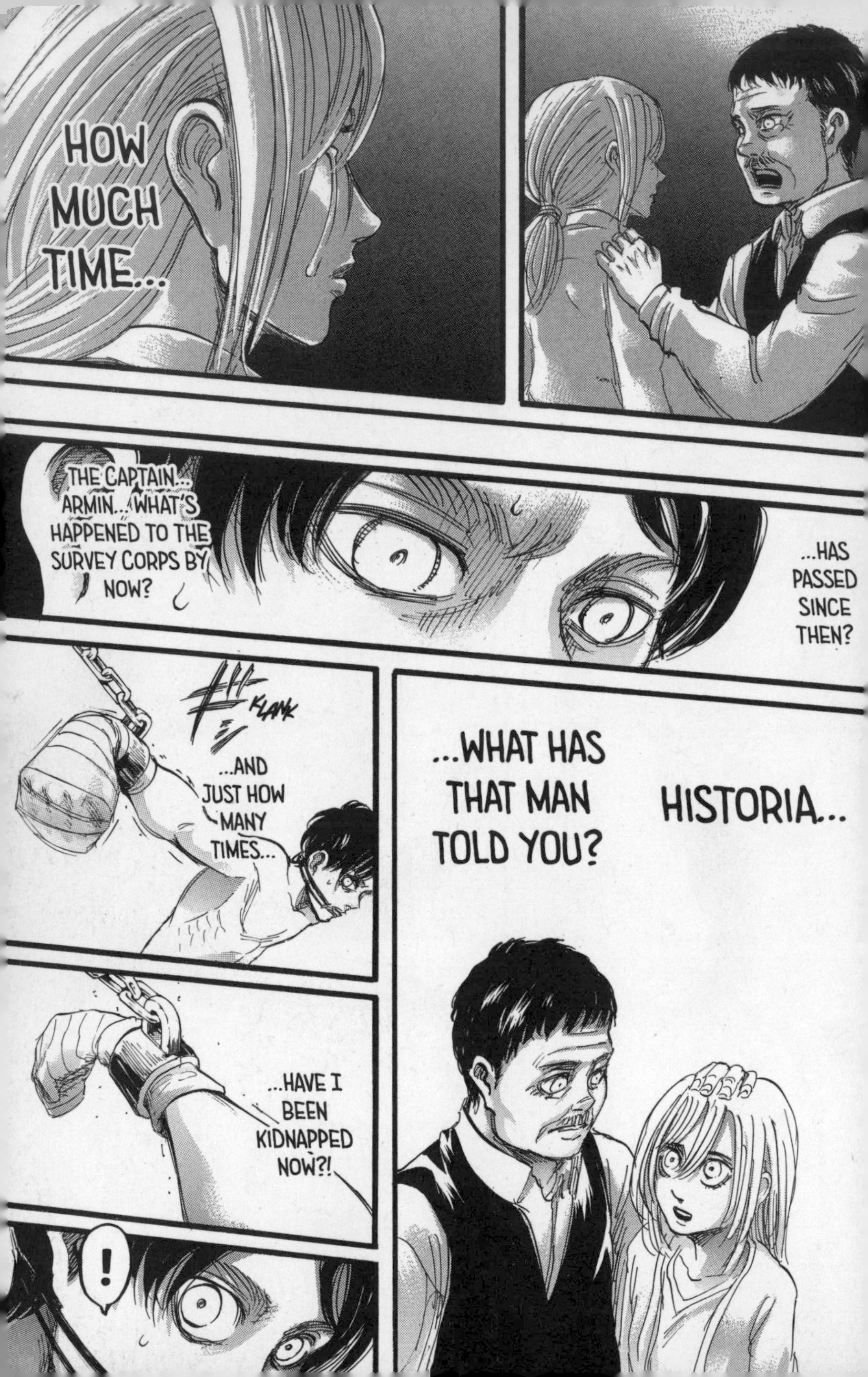
HOW MUCH TIME...
...HAS PASSED SINCE THEN?
THE CAPTAIN... ARMIN... WHAT'S HAPPENED TO THE SURVEY CORPS BY NOW?
HISTORIA...
...WHAT HAS THAT MAN TOLD YOU?
KLANK
...AND JUST HOW MANY TIMES...
...HAVE I BEEN KIDNAPPED NOW?!
!

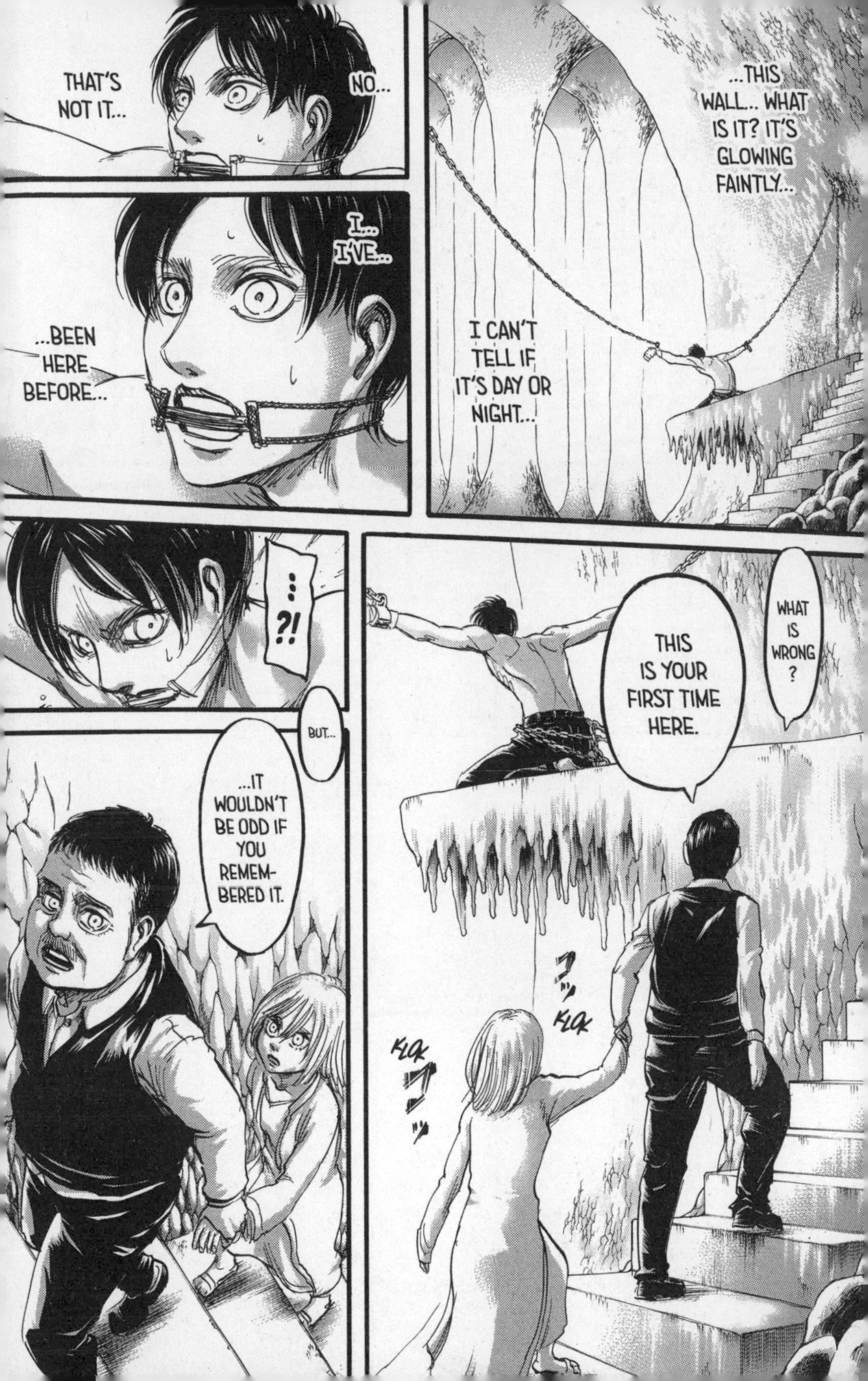
...THIS WALL... WHAT IS IT? IT'S GLOWING FAINTLY...
I CAN'T TELL IF IT'S DAY OR NIGHT...
NO...
THAT'S NOT IT...
I... I'VE...
...BEEN HERE BEFORE...
WHAT IS WRONG?
THIS IS YOUR FIRST TIME HERE.
KLOK
KLOK
...
?!
BUT...
...IT WOULDN'T BE ODD IF YOU REMEM-BERED IT.

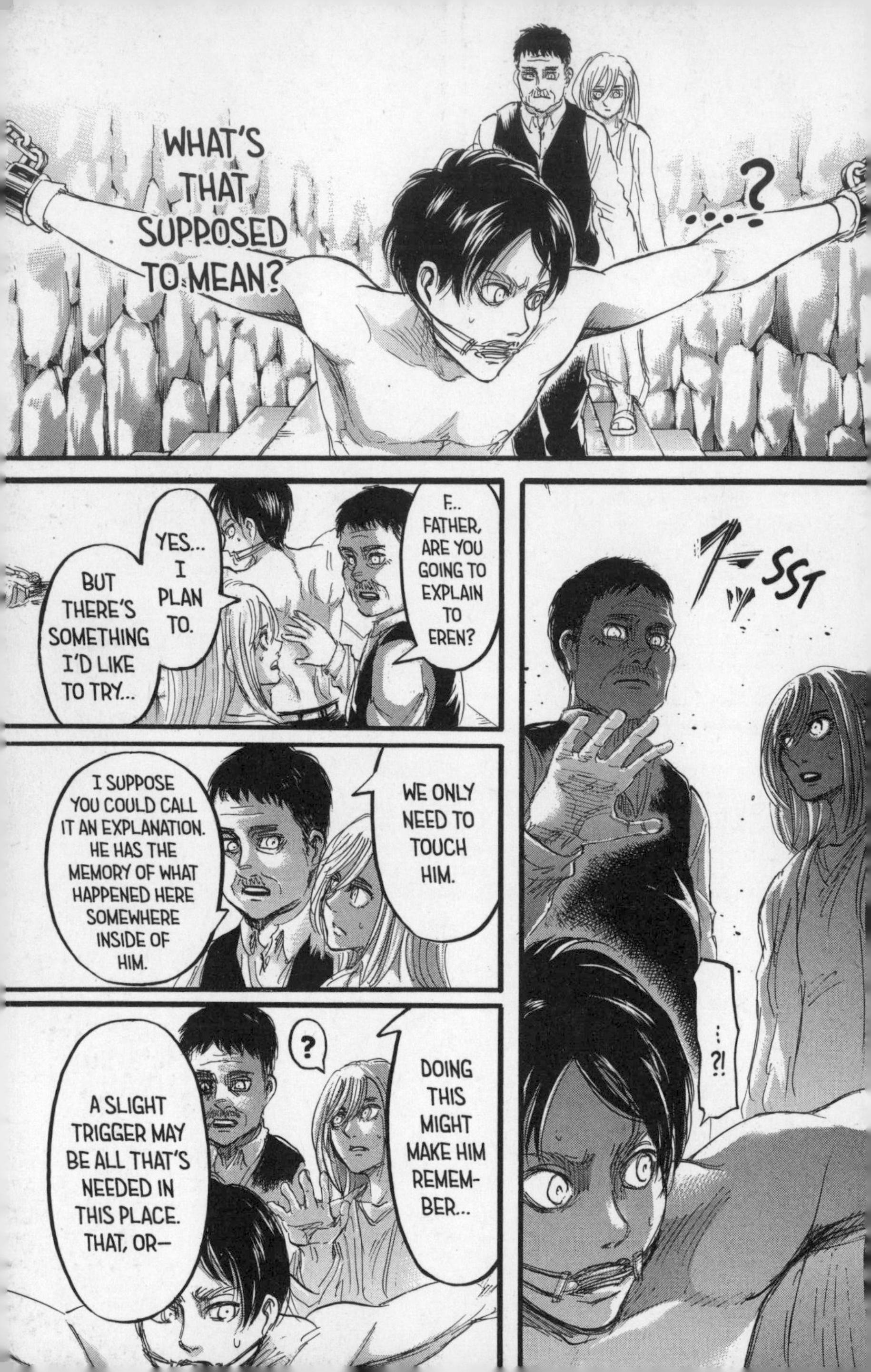
WHAT'S THAT SUPPOSED TO MEAN?
...?
SST
...?!
F.. FATHER, ARE YOU GOING TO EXPLAIN TO EREN?
YES... I PLAN TO.
BUT THERE'S SOMETHING I'D LIKE TO TRY...
WE ONLY NEED TO TOUCH HIM.
I SUPPOSE YOU COULD CALL IT AN EXPLANATION. HE HAS THE MEMORY OF WHAT HAPPENED HERE SOMEWHERE INSIDE OF HIM.
DOING THIS MIGHT MAKE HIM REMEM- BER...
?
A SLIGHT TRIGGER MAY BE ALL THAT'S NEEDED IN THIS PLACE. THAT, OR—

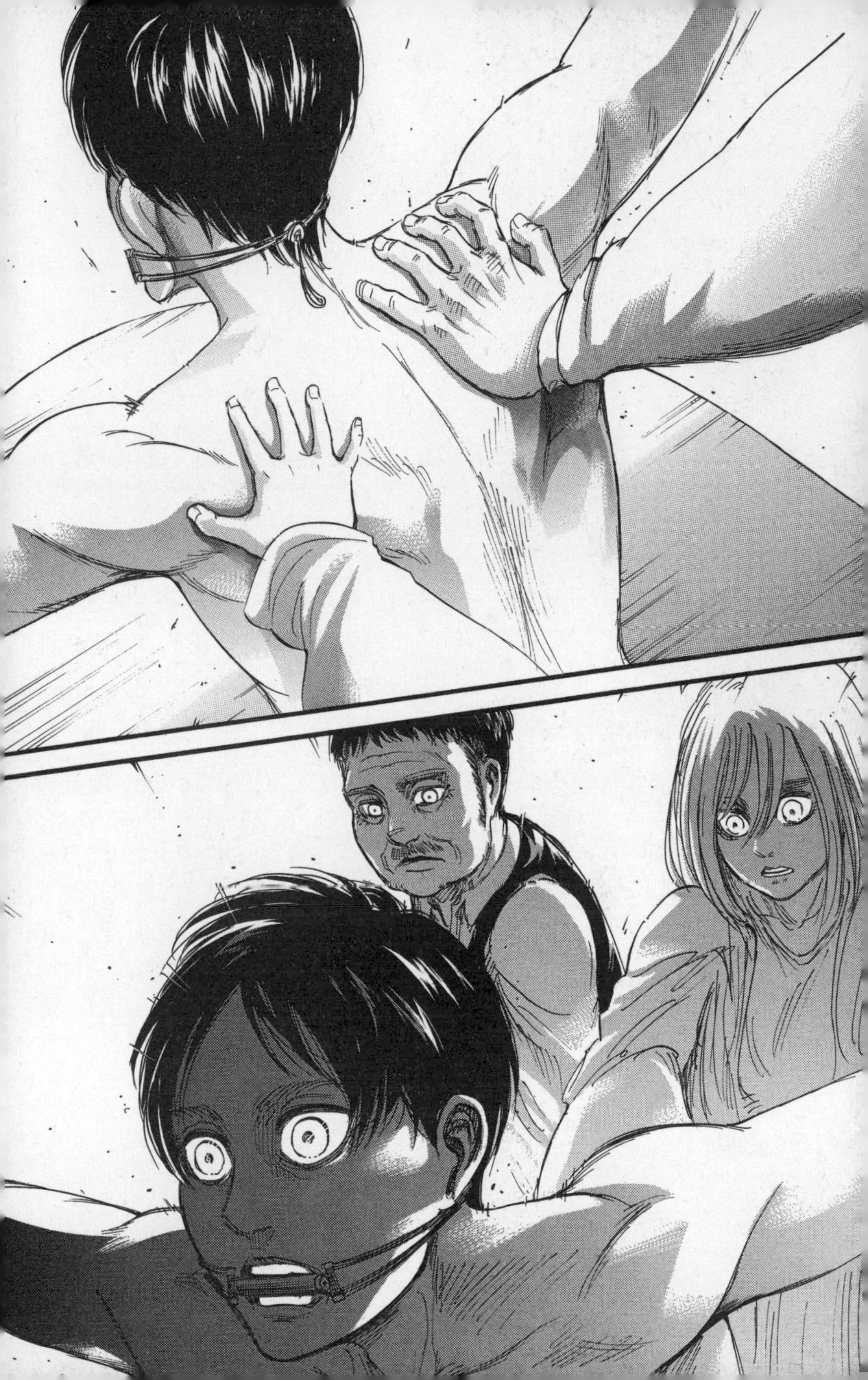

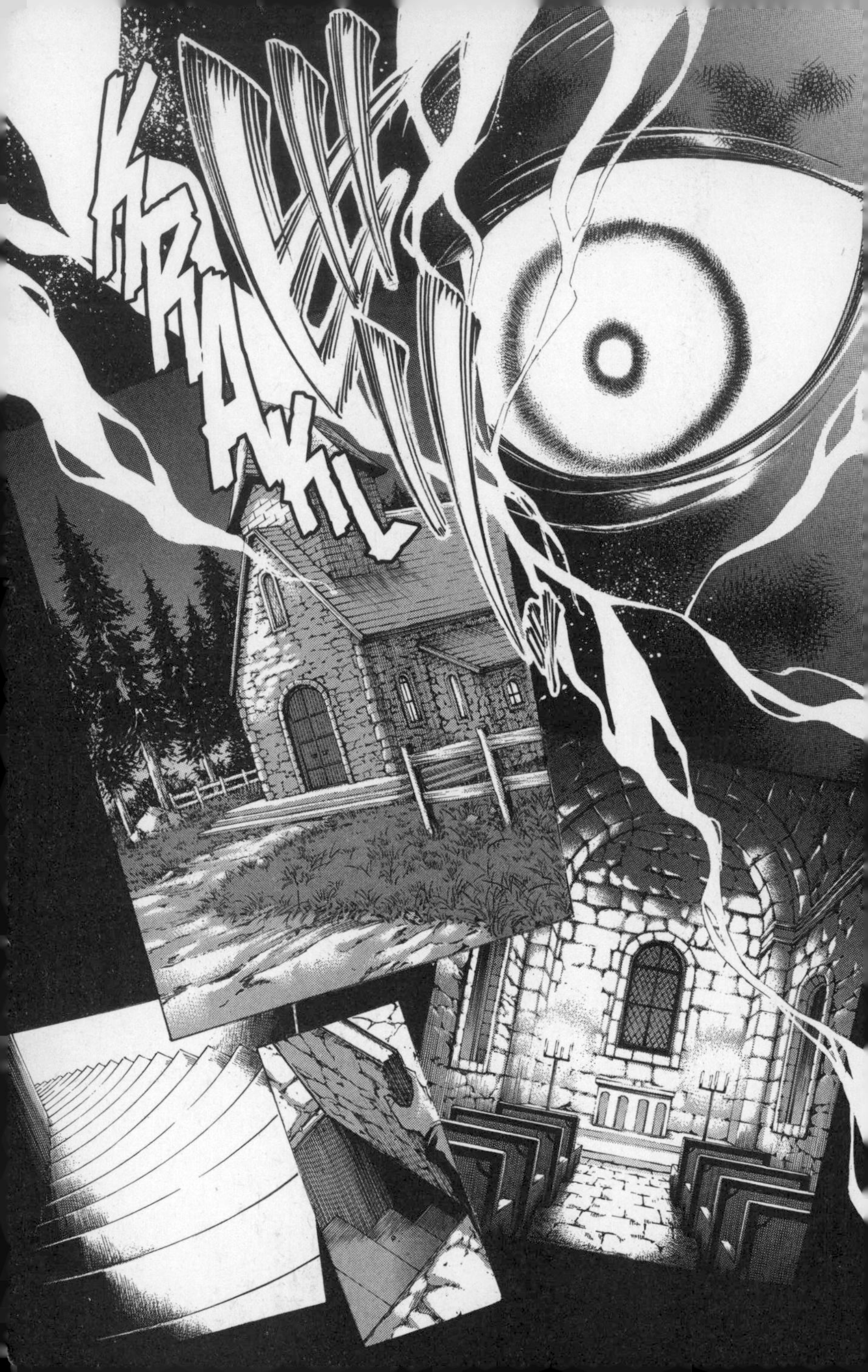
KRAKL

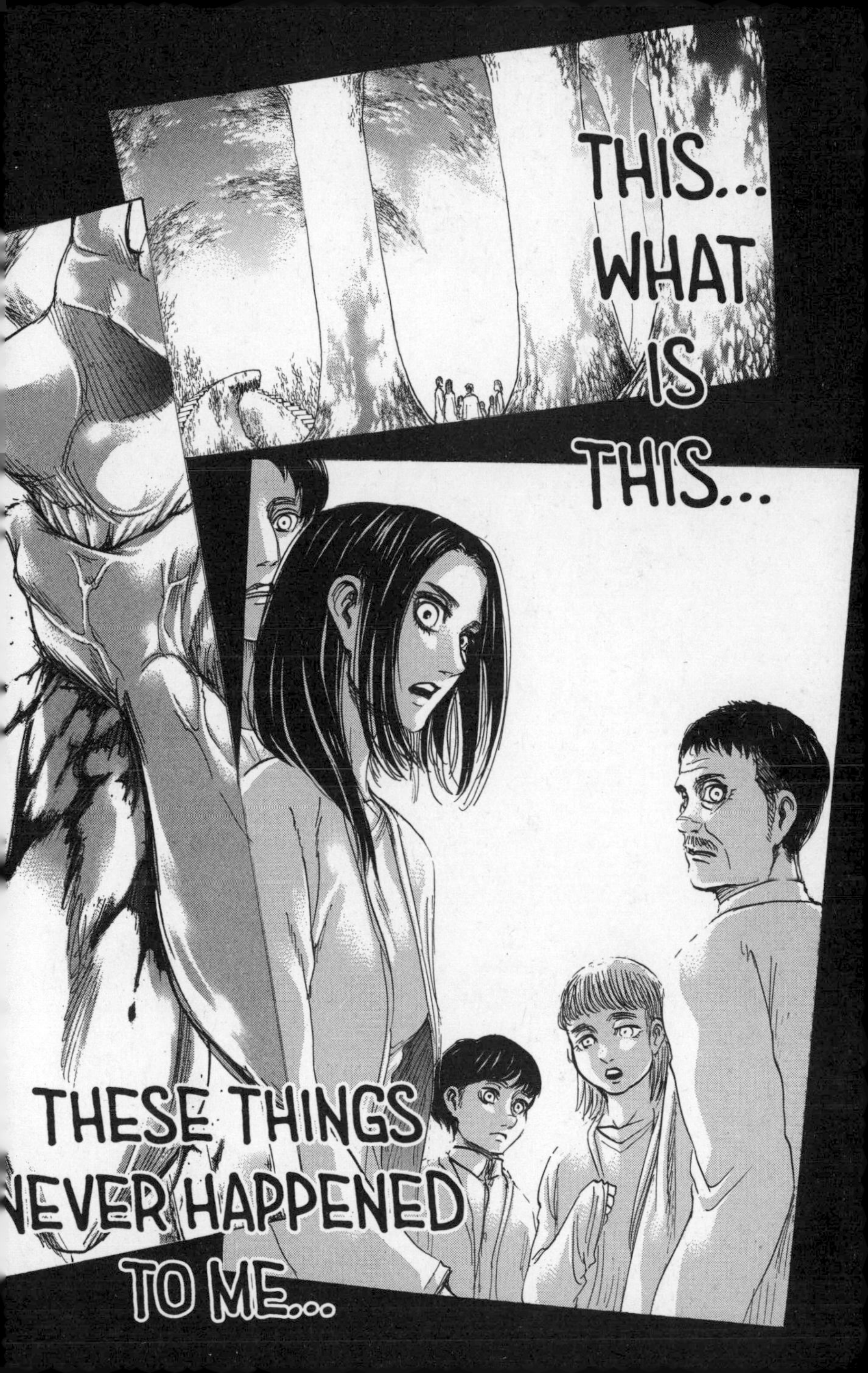
THIS... WHAT IS THIS...
THESE THINGS NEVER HAPPENED TO ME...

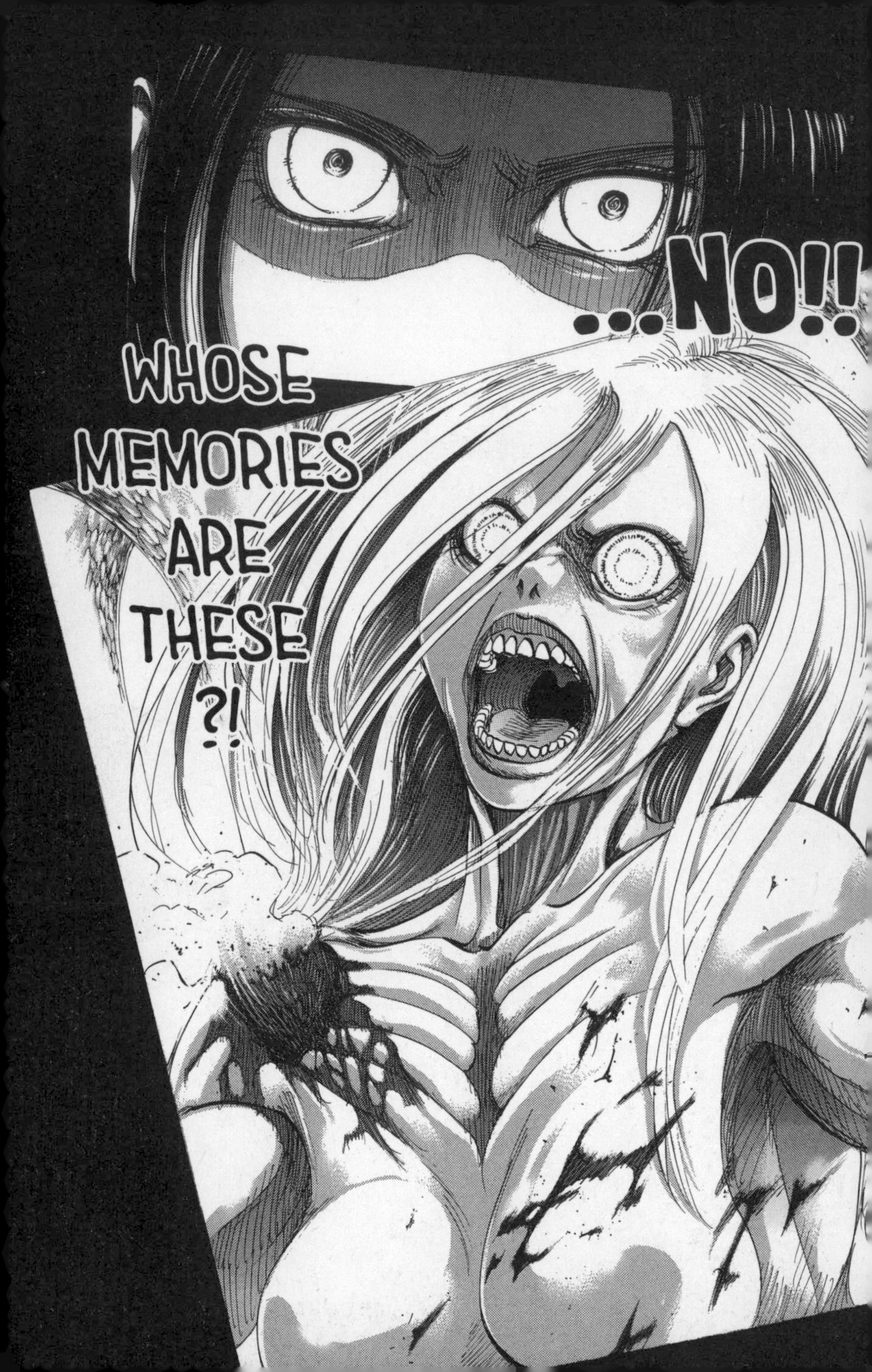
...NO!!
WHOSE MEMORIES ARE THESE?!

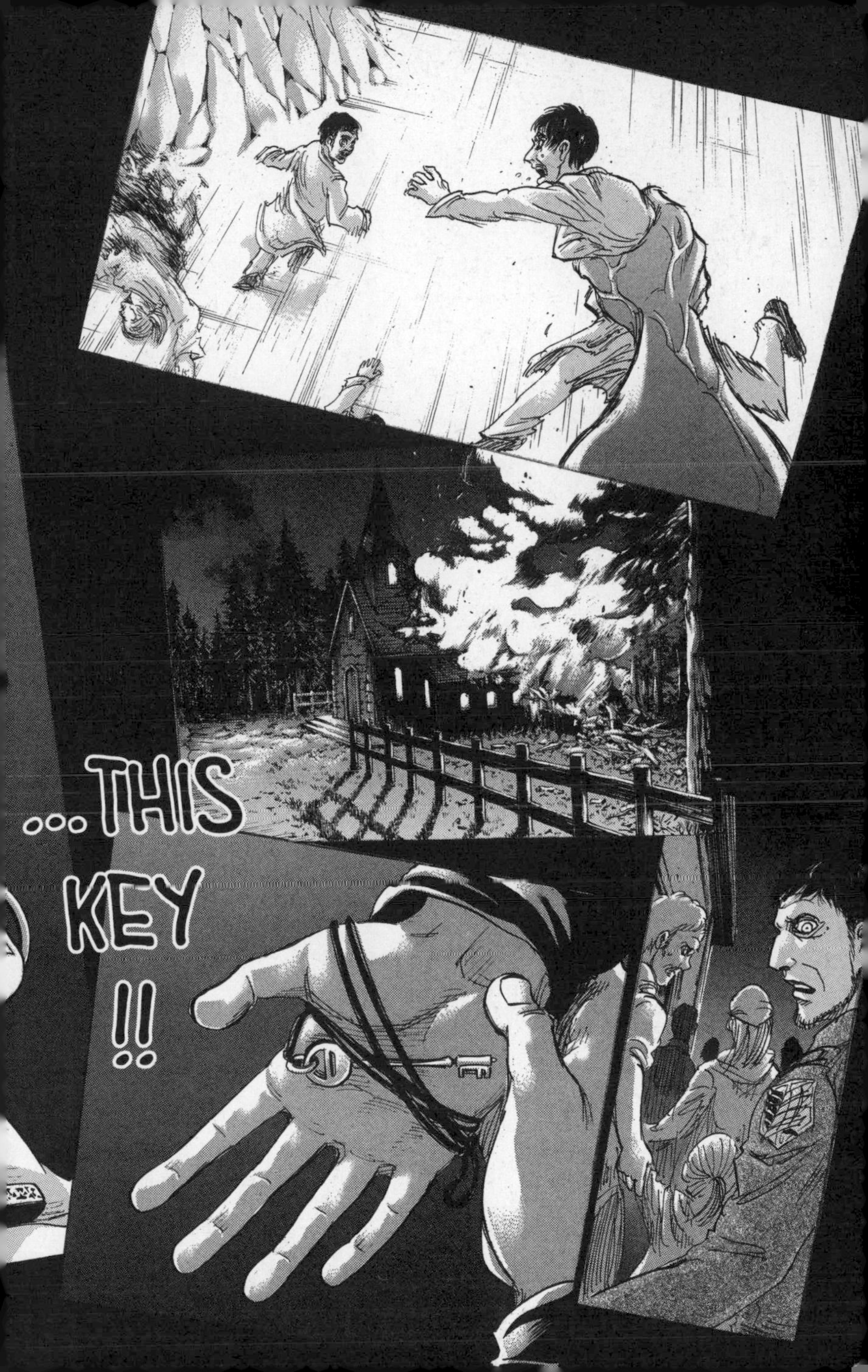
...THIS KEY !!

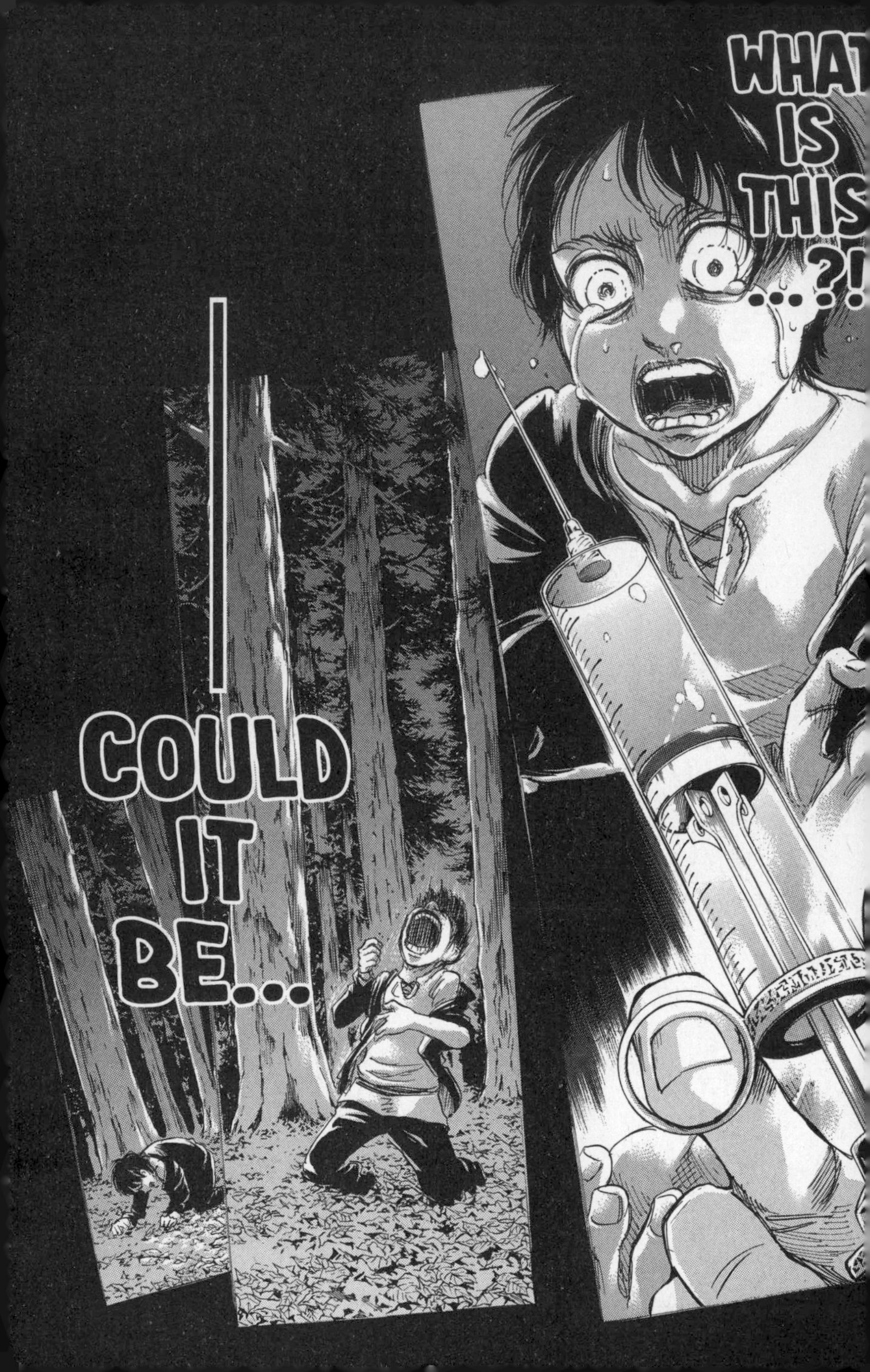

WHAT IS THIS ...?!
COULD IT BE...

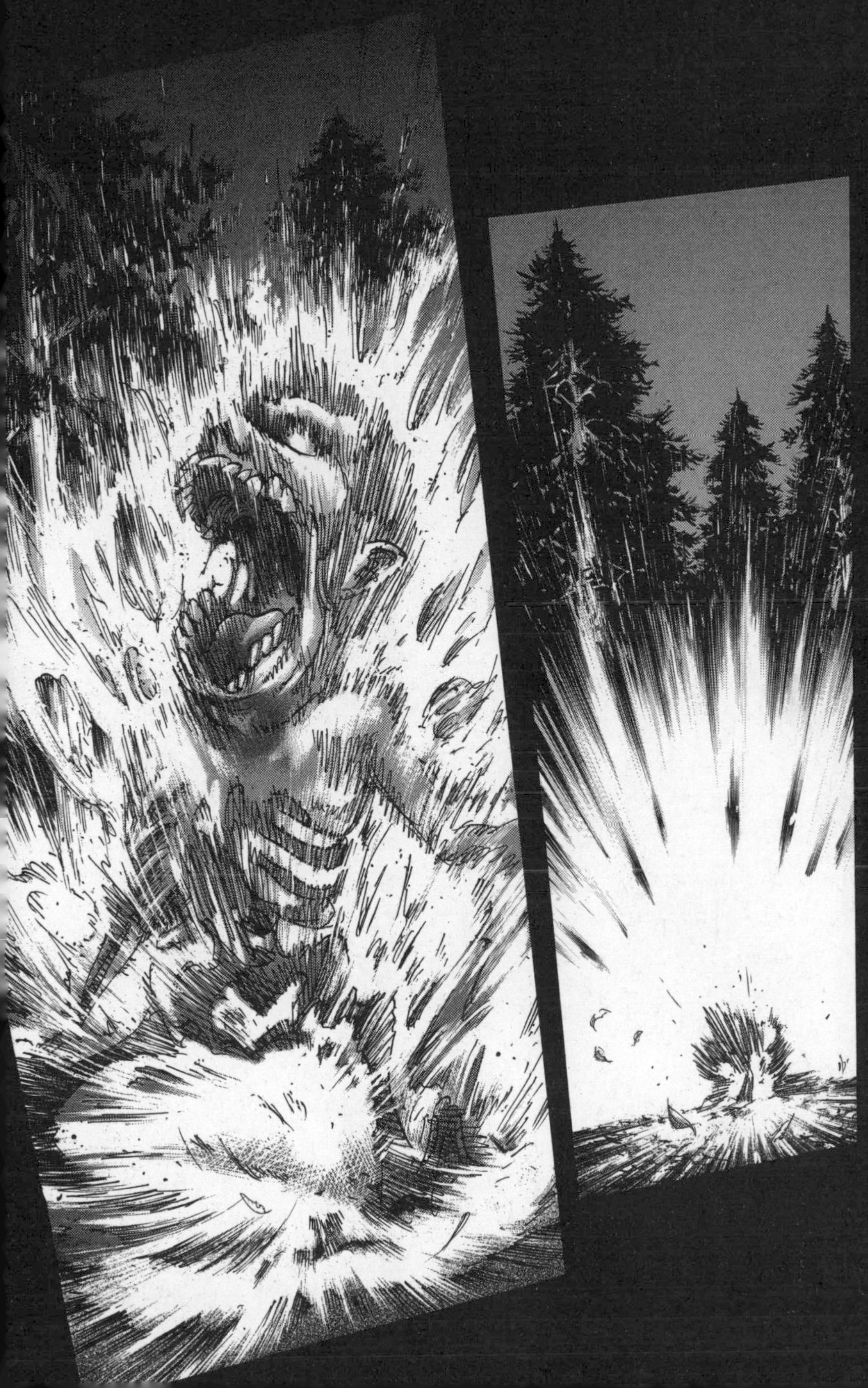

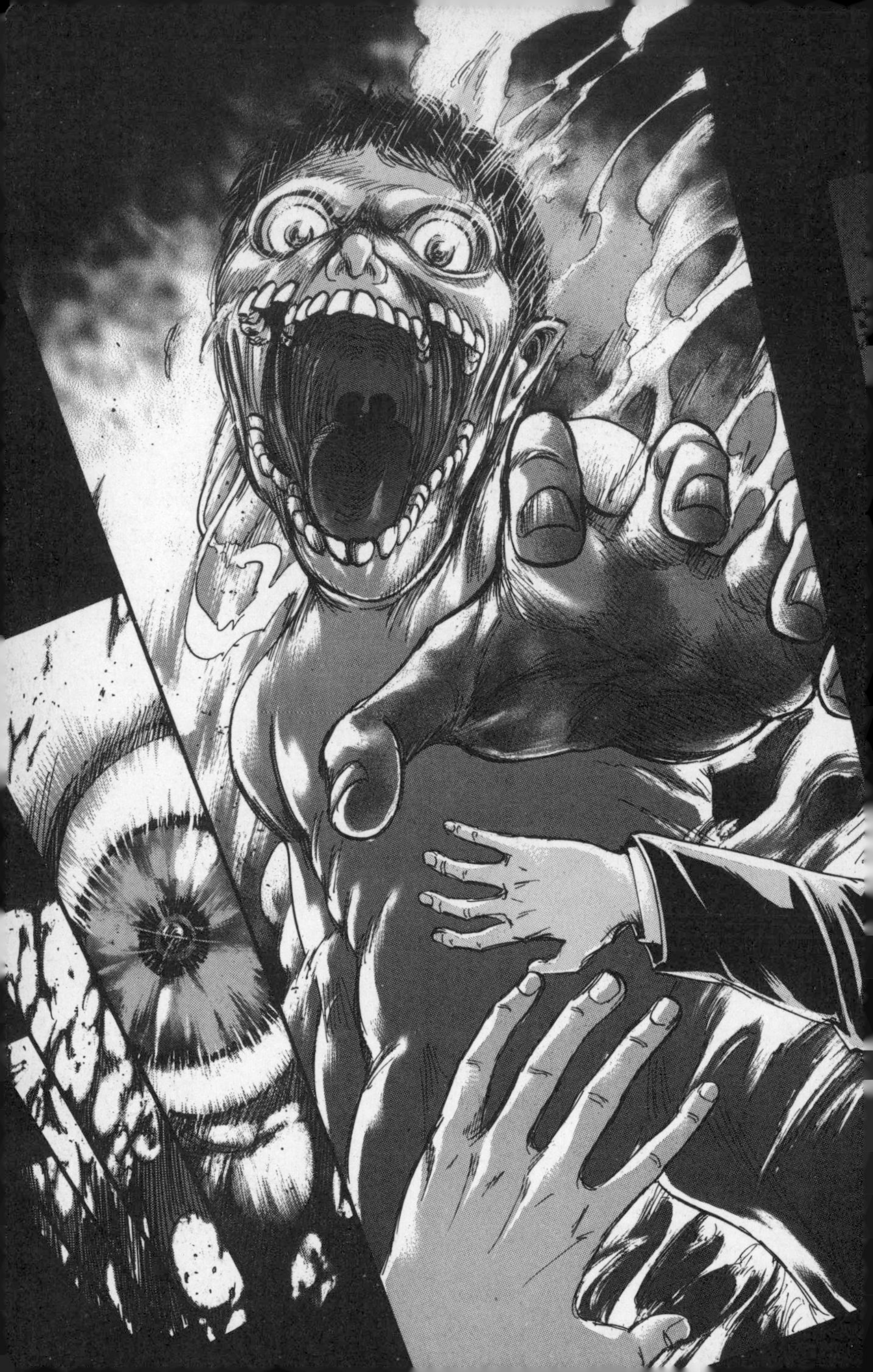

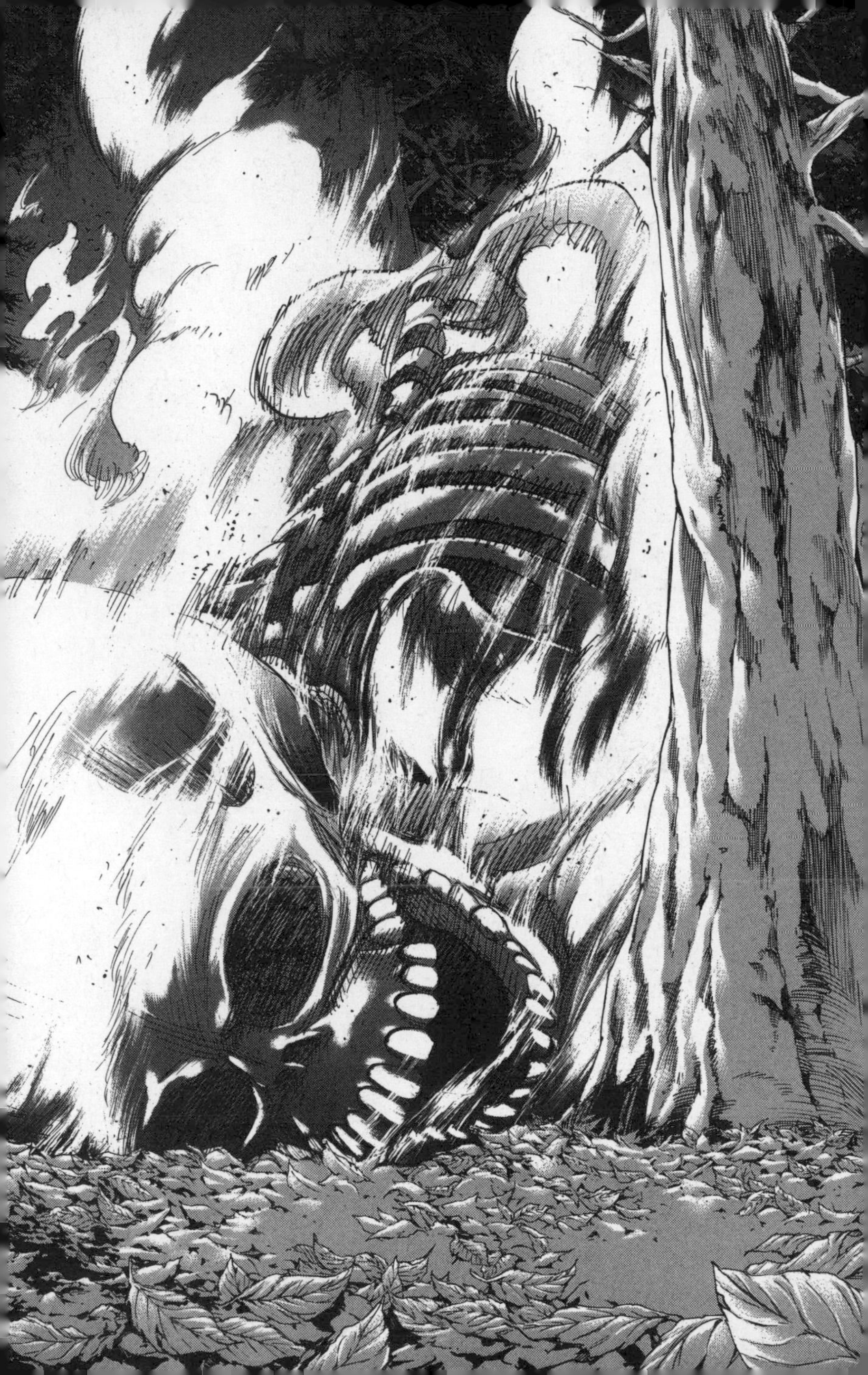

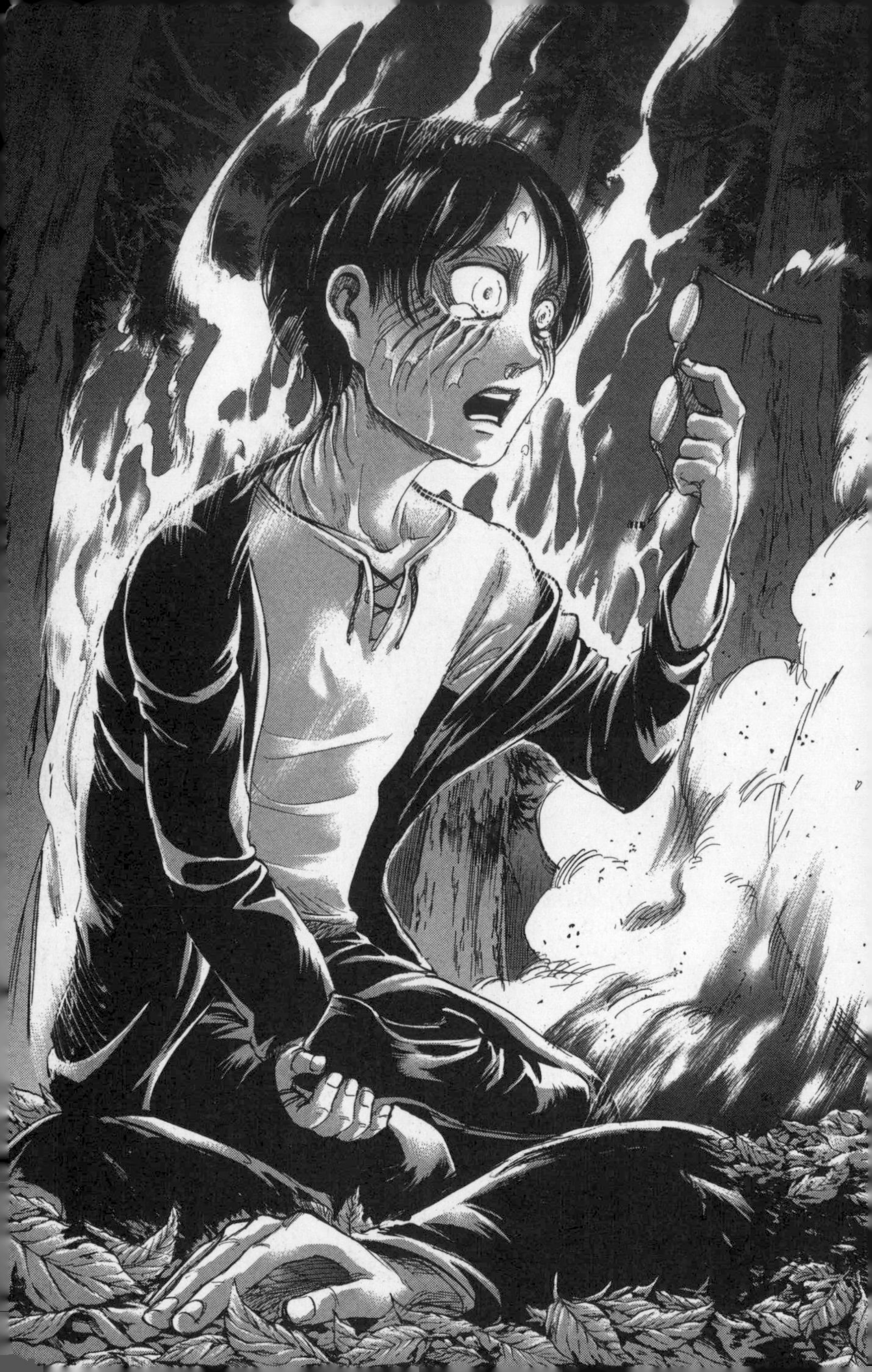

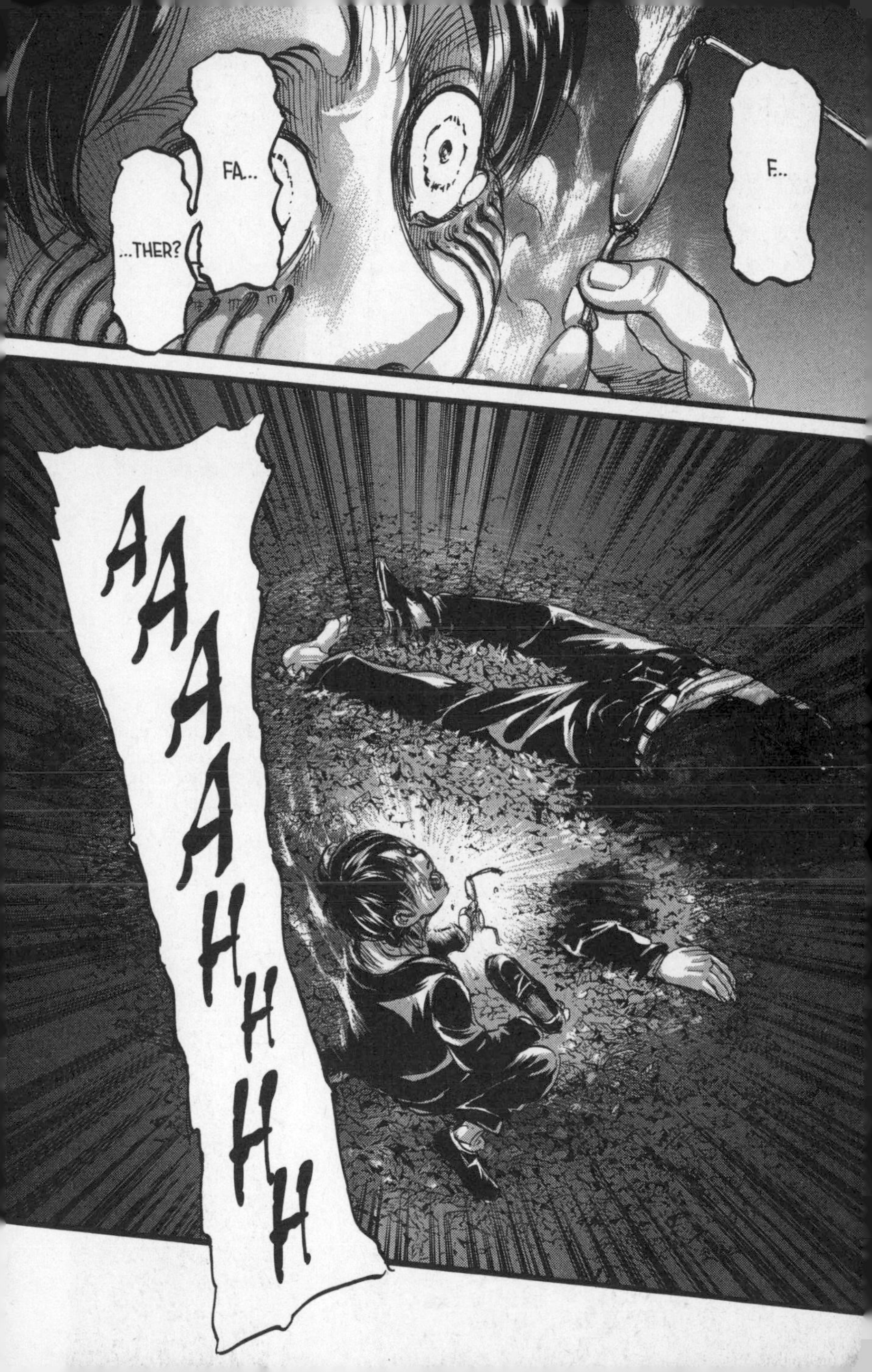
F...
FA...
...THER?
AAAAHHHH

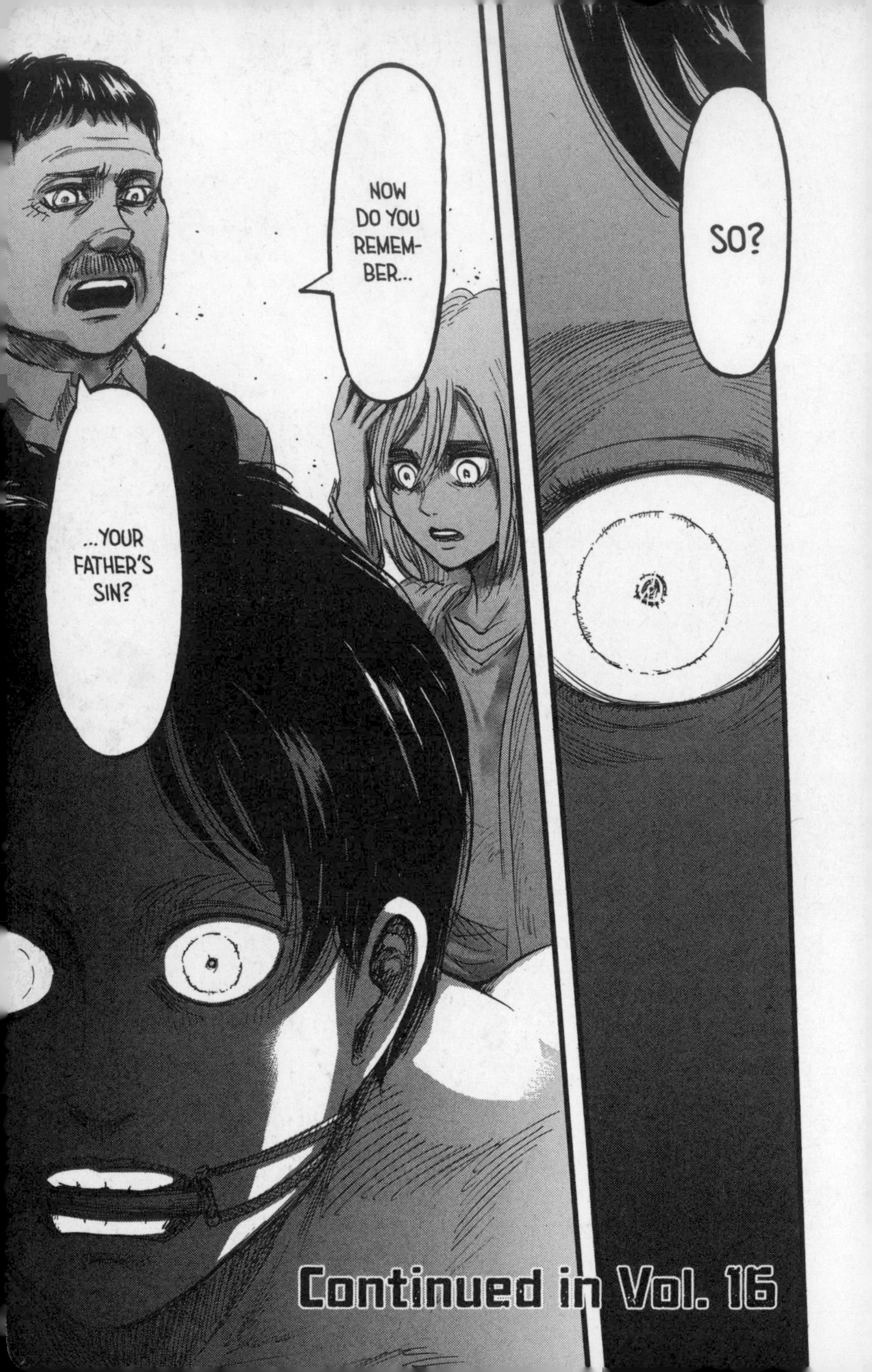
SO?
NOW DO YOU REMEMBER...
...YOUR FATHER'S SIN?
Continued in Vol. 16

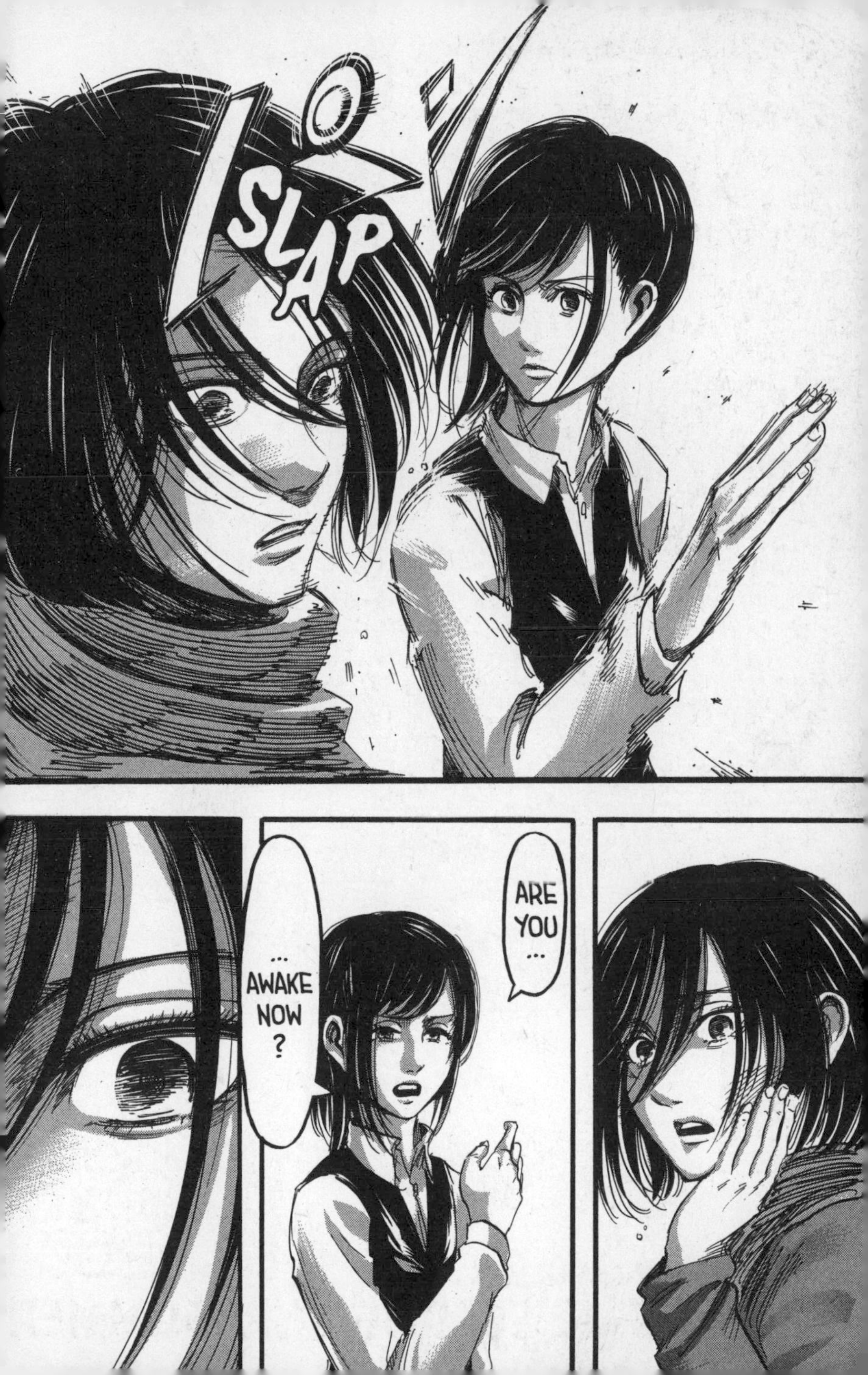
SLAP
ARE YOU ...
... AWAKE NOW ?

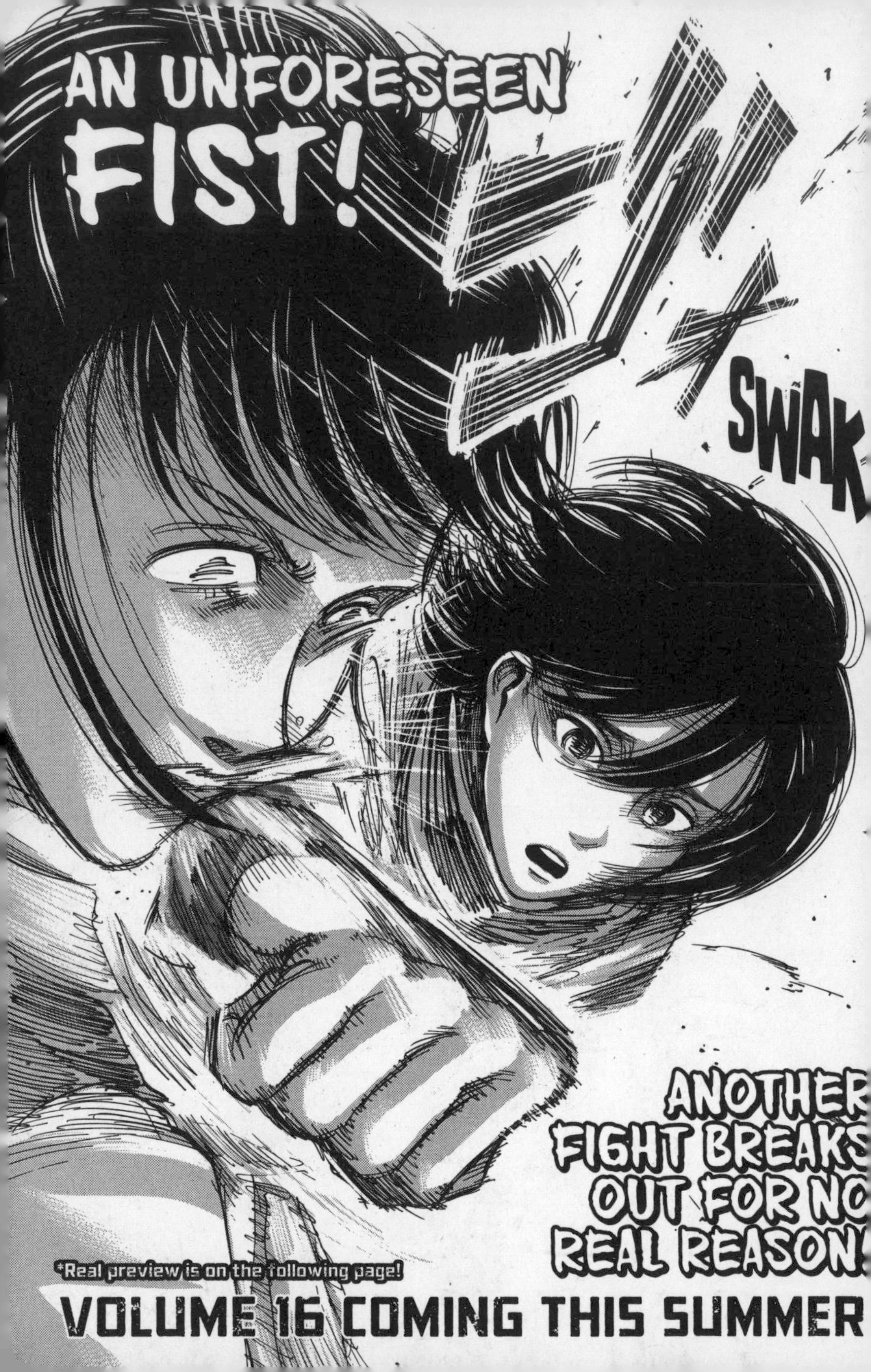
AN UNFORESEEN FIST!
SWAK
ANOTHER FIGHT BREAKS OUT FOR NO REAL REASON!
*Real preview is on the following page!
VOLUME 16 COMING THIS SUMMER

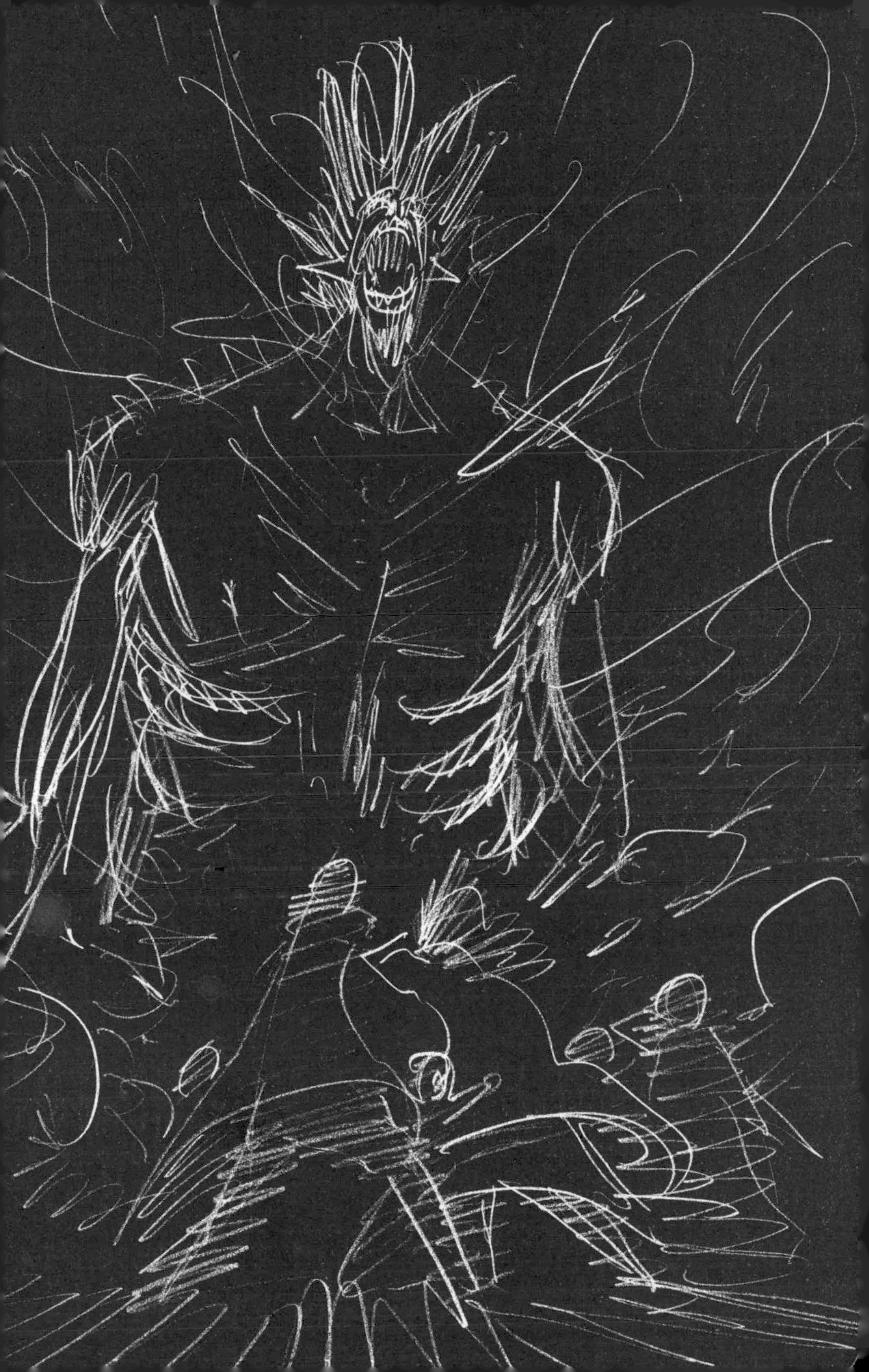

VOLUME 16 COMING THIS SUMMER!

WHAT WAS HIS FATHER'S SIN...?

WHAT WILL THE MEMORIES REVEAL ...?

*Attack on Titan* volume 15 is a work of fiction. Names, characters, places, and incidents are the products of the author's imagination or are used fictitiously. Any resemblance to actual events, locales, or persons, living or dead, is entirely coincidental.



Published in the United States by Kodansha Comics, an imprint of Kodansha USA Publishing, LLC, New York.

Publication rights for thls English edition arranged through Kodansha Ltd, Tokyo.

First published in Japan in 2014 by Kodansha Ltd., Tokyo as *Shingeki no Kyojin*, volume 15.

ISBN 978-1-61262-979-7

Original cover design by Takashi Shimoyama (Red Rooster)

Printed in the United States of America.

www.kodanshacomics.com

9 8 7 6 5 4 3 2
Translation: Ko Ransom
Lettering: Steve Wands
Editing: Ben Applegate
Kodansha Comics edition cover design by Phil Balsman